THE
BUDDHIST
DIRECTORY

Dharma in the West
is up to you Westerners now.

Be creative
in adapting the timeless essence
of the teachings
to your own culture and times.

Contribute to others,
rather than converting others.

H.H. the Dalai Lama,
quoted in *Dzogchen Foundation*,
Volume V, Spring 1996

THE
BUDDHIST
DIRECTORY

United States of America
&
Canada

BY

PETER LORIE & JULIE FOAKES

CHARLES E. TUTTLE CO., INC.
BOSTON • RUTLAND, VERMONT • TOKYO

First published in 1997 by Tuttle Publishing, an imprint of Periplus Editions (HK) Ltd., with editorial offices at 153 Milk Street, Boston, Massachusetts 02109.

Library of Congress Cataloging-in-Publication Data

The Buddhist Directory : United States of America and Canada / by Peter
Lorie and Julie Foakes
    p.   cm.
Includes index.
ISBN 0–8048–3118–1
    1. Buddhism—United States—Directories. 2. Buddhism—Canada—
Directories. I. Lorie, Peter. II. Foakes, Julie.
BQ730.B83   1997
294.3'65'02573—dc21   97–15876
                                              CIP

Distributed by

USA
Charles E. Tuttle Co., Inc.
RR 1 Box 231-5
North Clarendon, VT 05759
Tel.: (800) 526-2778
Fax.: (800) FAX-TUTL

Japan
Tuttle Shokai Ltd.
1-21-13, Seki
Tama-ku, Kawasaki-shi
Kanagawa-ken, 214
Tel.: (044) 833-0225
Fax.: (044) 822-0413

Southeast Asia
Berkeley Books Pte. Ltd.
5 Little Road #08-01
Singapore 536983
Tel.: (65) 280-3320
Fax.: (65) 280-6290

First edition
1 3 5 7 9 10 8 6 4 2   05 04 03 02 01 00   99 98 97

Cover design by Jill Winitzer
Design by Moonrunner Design, UK

Printed in the United States of America

CONTENTS

Caveat: Mention of any teacher, group or center in this book does not imply endorsement of them by the authors. This is in line with the traditions of Buddhism which has never been a centralized, authoritarian religion with a governing body dispensing or withholding approval. It is therefore up to each individual to test the ground for him/herself, guided by common sense and those indications that the Buddha himself gives in the Scriptures (e.g., the *Kalama Sutta*):

> *Believe nothing, O monks, merely because you have been told it ... or because it is traditional, or because you yourselves have imagined it. Do not believe what your teacher tells you merely out of respect for the teacher. But whatsoever, after due examination and analysis, you find to be conducive to the good, the benefit, the welfare of all beings—that doctrine believe and cling to, and take it as your guide.*

The reader is particularly referred to John Snelling's chapter on the Western Buddhist Spiritual Quest (*The Elements of Buddhism*, published by Element Books) for sound and sensible advice.

Acknowledgments: Sincere thanks to the Buddhist communities of the USA and Canada for their help in supplying information and for their friendliness, especially as most centers are staffed by voluntary help.

Inclusion in Future Editions: Buddhist organizations who would like to be in the next edition of this book should write to Peter Lorie & Julie Foakes, c/o Tuttle Publishing, 153 Milk Street, 5th Floor, Boston, MA 02109, giving your address, telephone and fax numbers.

Use of language: Some of the Buddhist terms used within this book are derived from the dead Indian languages of Pali and Sanskrit or from Tibetan. As none of these languages use a Roman alphabet, they are usually transcribed phonetically into European script. When transcribed into English, Pali and Sanskrit versions of the same terms may have slightly different spelling, but are still recognizable, e.g., Dharma (Sanskrit) and Dhamma (Pali). As Pali is the language of Theravada Buddhism and Sanskrit the language of Mahayana Buddhism, we have taken the spelling used by the center concerned. In all cases, we have not used diacritical marks or accents for words from these languages.

> *Words!*
> *The way is beyond language,*
> *for in it there is*
> *no yesterday*
> *no tomorrow*
> *no today.*
>
> Sengstan, Hsin Hsin Ming

INTRODUCTION

T HIS IS AN EXCITING TIME TO EXPLORE THE ANCIENT RELIGION OF BUDDHISM, FOR NOT only is it going through changes in the U.S., in its adjustment to Western culture, but it is also experiencing a revival in Asia, where it also faces the challenge of growing consumerism and technology.

Buddhism has, throughout its long and varied history of contraction and expansion, always been able to change and adapt. When taken to new countries, it has been able to mutate and integrate cultural elements. When Buddhists themselves felt that established practices had become stale, inaccessible, or moved away from the original spirit of the Buddha's teachings, new schools were born. Great thinkers and mystics have made their own changes, developing new lines of thought or reverting to an idea of something pure from the past. It has also survived being nearly eradicated from some countries, including India, its country of origin.

Buddhism's adaptability stems partly from its tradition of having no central authority to judge what is and what is not acceptable within an established canon. This is a religion of practice and not of dogma, where the Buddha himself taught that each person needed to discover a personal truth.

As a result, over twenty-five hundred years after the life of the Buddha, there now exists an incredible variety of traditions. These range from the colorful, ritualistic Tibetan lineage with its secret Tantric teachings through to the austere, strictly minimalist approach of Zen, with many colors and degrees in between. At one end of the scale Theravadins emphasize individual responsibility, while Nichiren schools emphasize the efficacy of faith alone. And all these schools are now found in the West.

Some Buddhist centers were set up by Asian–Americans to serve the spiritual and cultural needs of their communities and retain the language and culture of their homeland. Others have adapted enormously to the needs of Western lifestyles and attitudes, and both teachings and practices are being translated by them into English; some centers now conduct practices in English rather than in an Eastern language. An increasing number of Westerners trained by Eastern masters—either here or in the East—go on to influence the way Buddhism is taught in the West.

One of the distinctive features of Buddhism in the West is a movement toward dialogue between both Buddhist schools and other religions. Many centers offer teachings culled from a combination of traditions and lineages. Many are open to all newcomers, regardless of religious persuasion. Buddhists feel that their practices can be of use to everyone, regardless of religious or cultural background. The only school that stands apart from this is Nichiren Shoshu, which has historically avoided relations with other Buddhist groups.

Anyone approaching Buddhism in North America has an incredible range of options open to him or her, both in terms of which school to choose and how Westernized it has become. There is something for everyone and if there is a problem with this, it lies only in the danger of being overwhelmed by the number of options.

When visiting centers, readers should be aware that the physical environment between one location and another will vary considerably. This is dictated not only by the tradition involved, but also by the kind of physical space available. Buddhists practice everywhere from specially constructed and elaborate temples, through hired halls, to people's front rooms. You may find dedicated centers, communities, groups that meet in private homes on a regular basis, and venues used by several schools of Buddhism.

Although some centers have a missionary aim, Buddhism generally aims to make the Buddha's teachings available to all, but never to impose them on others. You are encouraged to investigate various schools and centers before choosing which one is best for you—if you don't like one school or center, others may be very different in style and approach.

Buddhism is an expanding religion. People in the West are opening up to spiritual alternatives, often becoming disillusioned with their own spiritual traditions, which may seem too authoritarian in an increasingly individualistic society. Buddhism is attractive in that it emphasizes the role of the individual in finding his or her own path while offering sound spiritual methods tested over many centuries and with many able teachers. There also continues to be substantial academic interest in Buddhist psychology, philosophy, science, medicine, and art. We hope our efforts in making these centers and details available help you all.

How This Book Was Compiled

About two thousand requests for information were sent out, and entries for each center have been compiled from replies to a questionnaire, brochures, and other literature received in reply. Only centers that replied or we were able to verify either directly or through an umbrella organization have been included. We have tried to be true to the spirit of each center's information as given to us, although it has had to be adapted to a relatively standard format. Entries for each center are based upon the information sent by the centers themselves and do not reflect the personal opinion of the authors. All entries are necessarily brief—contact centers directly for more information.

Useful Information on Entries for Centers

Within each state, centers are ordered alphabetically by town and then by name within each town. Length of entry depends on the information sent by the center and is no indication of relative size or importance to a particular school.

The name of the school of Buddhism practiced is in brackets after the name of the center—see section on schools for more information. Affiliations are listed under the name. Some addresses are private residences, as may be telephone numbers. Statements within quote marks are taken directly from the reply send back by the center or from its own literature.

When applicable, there is information on retreats, and this varies in content according to the tradition followed and the topic of the retreat. At some centers, there is a fairly relaxed attitude about attending session; at others, the behavior asked of you is very strict and may require you to comply fully with monastic life and behavior.

Apart from directly spiritual practices, other activities may be offered. These may be methods of self-development (physical or psychological), cultural activities, healing practices, or creative expression—for Tibetan Buddhism, this may be thangka painting; for Zen, it may be archery, calligraphy, or tea ceremonies. Some traditions have started using Western psychotherapeutic techniques. Exercises such as Tai Chi Chuan and Hatha Yoga combine physical exercise with meditative practice.

Founder/Guru   The term *Guru* usually refers to Tibetan Buddhism.

Residents   Where applicable, numbers of both lay and monastic residents are noted.

Festivals   As Buddhists use a lunar calendar, the dates for festivals vary from year to year, so the names only have been included—refer to the section on festivals for more information.

Facilities   Practice rooms rather than living quarters or kitchens are given.

Food   Although most centers offer vegetarian food, the Buddha refused to make vegetarianism compulsory. For him it was more important that the sangha, who lived by begging for their food, should eat with gratitude whatever was put in their bowls.

Fees

U.S. prices are in U.S. dollars; Canada prices are in Canadian dollars.

Most Buddhist centers are nonprofit or charity organizations entirely dependent on donations, often incorporated as such. There is a general policy of making the teachings accessible to everyone who is interested, so most will accommodate differing financial states of people wanting to attend. Generosity is a Buddhist virtue and giving (*dana*) is a central part of Buddhist practice. The way this is expressed may vary. Some make no charge for teachings, but only to cover costs; some expect participants to donate what is appropriate to their income, and some have concessionary prices for those with little or no income. Many centers offer membership for a monthly fee, which may confer privileges such as discounts or free newsletters.

Expected Behavior

This varies tremendously from place to place, ranging from the most casual to very strict adherence to set rules. There are also sometimes cultural dictates, such as the Thai custom of not showing the soles of the feet to either another person or to a Buddha image, as this would be disrespectful. The precepts are often specified—see *Appendix: Precepts* for details.

How to Get There

Travel instructions are often confined to public transport. Contact center for fuller instructions if necessary.

SCHOOLS AND AFFILIATIONS REPRESENTED   •

IN THIS DIRECTORY

A **American Zen Association:** American branch of Association Zen Internationale (AZI) (see separate entry). President is Robert Livingston, based at New Orleans Zen Temple, Louisiana.

Association Zen Internationale: A Soto Zen school. Soto Zen was brought to Europe by Taisen Deshimaru Roshi in 1967; until then, it had been known in Europe only through books. Kodo Sawaki Roshi, from whom Tasien Deshimaru received transmission, endeavored throughout his life to return Zen to its purest source—the teaching of Dogen Zenji and the practice of zazen. By 1982, when he died, Deshimaru Roshi had left a long line of books and publications as well as over a hundred meditation centers and several thousand followers. Headquarters are in Paris, France.

B **Bon:** A Tibetan school. Spiritual tradition, possibly of Zoroastrian or Kashmiri Buddhist origin and distinct from indigenous Tibetan beliefs, widespread in Tibet prior to the official introduction of Buddhism, from which it has assimilated many teachings.

Buddha's Light International Association (BLIA): Worldwide organization for Chinese Buddhism based in Taiwan (see *Major Centers in Asia*).

Buddhist Churches of America: (Jodo Shinshu) American name for the Hongpa Hongwanji. Headquarters in San Francisco.

Buddhist Society for Compassionate Wisdom: A Zen school. Formerly the Zen Lotus Society. North American Buddhist order founded by Ven. Samu Sunim in 1967. Now consists of three temples in Ann Arbor, Michigan, Toronto, Canada, and Ann Arbor, Illinois. Holds biennial precept-taking ceremony for those wanting to make a formal commitment.

C **Ch'an:** Chinese Zen (see also Zen) that developed in the sixth and seventh centuries and stressed the possibility of sudden and direct enlightenment.

Chagdud Gonpa Foundation: A Nyingma Tibetan school. Established 1983 by H.E. Chagdud Tulku Rinpoche. Headquarters are Rigdzin Ling, California; more than twenty centers in North and South America.

Chinese Buddhism: China may have received Buddhist missionaries as early as 200 BCE, and it quickly became the greatest center of Mahayana Buddhism, especially as Hinduism reasserted itself in India. Over the centuries, interaction with other Chinese religions created numerous variations (including Ch'an) which finally evolved into what is usually an eclectic mix of Buddhism, Confucianism, and Taoism. The most popular forms center on Amida Buddha's Pure Land or Lotus Heaven. Since lack of religious designation in China is confusing, when asked their religion in Hawaii, Chinese immigrants usually said they were Buddhists. Chinese Buddhist centers in the USA are usually cultural centers for Chinese Americans where Chinese languages rather than English is spoken. See also **Buddha's Light International Association** and **True Buddha School.**

Dharma Realm Buddhist Association: A Pure Land and Ch'an school. Formerly Sino-American Buddhist Association. Founded by Master Hsuan Hua 1959 in USA. Headquarters is City of Ten Thousand Buddhas, California.

Diamond Sangha: A Zen school. Founded 1959 by Anne and Robert Aitken. Headquarters was Palolo Zen Center, Hawaii, but Diamond Sangha Network now includes all affiliate sanghas as equal participants. See also **Harada–Yasutani Lineage.**

Drikung Kagyu: See **Tibetan** and **Kagyu Buddhism.**

Dzogchen: A Tibetan school which has its roots in pre-Buddhist Bon religion of Tibet. It cannot be classified as a religious or philosophical tradition or as a school or sect; it is knowledge that Masters have transmitted without being limited by religious or scholastic tradition. It is not based on intellectual understanding but on awareness of the individual's true condition. Over the centuries it has been practiced by adepts from all schools and traditions, although historically it has spread mostly in the Bon and Nyingma traditions. Can be taught, understood, and practiced in any cultural context.

Foundation for the Preservation of the Mahayana Tradition (FPMT): A Tibetan Gelug school founded in 1975 by Lama Thubten Yeshe. The majority of the FPMT centers are set up around the central activities of study and meditation, providing the means for their students to hear the teachings and meditate upon them. The FPMT seeks to integrate Buddha's teachings with the relief of physical as well as mental suffering and so runs healing centers around the world. In Bodh Gaya in India (the place of Buddha's enlightenment) a statue of Maitreya is being planned for placement in a specially created meditation grove. Two years after Lama Yeshe passed away, a Spanish child, Osel Hita Torres, was recognized as his reincarnation. He was ordained as a novice monk by the Dalai Lama at the age of three and is now studying and training as a monk and future master to prepare him to continue the work he started in his previous life. Lama Zopa Rinpoche is currently the FPMT spiritual director. The FPMT strives to follow the example and inspiration of His Holiness the Dalai Lama in his compassionate service to humanity. Office for North and South American region is at 2 Wild View Drive, Ligonier, Pennsylvania 15658, Tel: (412) 238–3863.

Friends of the Western Buddhist Order (FWBO): Founded by Venerable Sangharakshita, a London-born Buddhist monk, in 1967. Draws from all main Buddhist traditions to take what is useful for the spiritual needs of Westerners. Most centers also offer classes in various "indirect means" of development, such as Hatha Yoga, Tai Chi Chuan, karate, and massage. Either men or women may lead classes and meetings. There is only one ordination in the FWBO, the Dharmachari (for men) or Dharmacharini (for women). There are also Mitras who have formulated a special connection with the FWBO. Neither monastic nor lay in that these distinctions have more to do with lifestyle than commitment to the Three Jewels. Some members live in monastic celibacy, some in communities, and some in families. The FWBO places special emphasis on friendship as the Buddha stated that "friendship is the whole of the spiritual life." The two main meditation techniques taught initially are Mindfulness of Breathing, which enhances awareness and peace of mind, and Metta Bhavana, which develops loving-kindness. Principal center is London Buddhist Center, London, England (see *Major Centers in the UK*).

G **Gelug:** A Tibetan school. Founded by the chief disciples of Tsongkhapa (1357–1419), a Tibetan monk who wanted to restore Tibetan Buddhism to the purity of its Indian sources and stressed the importance of ethics and the monastic virtues for monks. He encouraged study and rigorous intellectual evaluation so that practitioners might have a clear understanding of the nature and aim of the Buddhist path. Its highest award for philosophical study is the title Geshe. The Gelugpas held spiritual and temporal preeminence in Tibet from the sixteenth century through to 1959. Dalai Lama was the title originally given by the Mongols to the third head of this school and has been carried by its head since. Current practices include debate in Tibetan and English, reflective meditation on the Graduated Path (Lamrim), and Tantric visualization techniques. Many Gelug centers are directed by Tibetan monk-lamas, and although they aim to preserve the purity of the tradition, many now incorporate elements of Western culture, such as psychological approaches. Laypeople within this tradition may practice to as high a level as they are able within the constraints of everyday life. Also sometimes referred to as the New Kadampa school.

H **Harada–Yasutani Lineage:** (also known as Sanbo Kyodan or Three Treasures) A Zen school established in Japan by Harada Roshi and his student Yasutani Roshi, combining Soto and Rinzai Zen elements. The majority of Zen teachers in the USA are Dharma Heirs of this lineage and include founders of the White Plum lineage (Taizan Hakuyu Maezumi), Diamond Sangha (Robert Aitken), Kanzeon Sangha (Dennis Genpo Merzel), Rochester Zen Center (Philip Kapleau), and Mountains and Rivers Order (John Daido Loori) (see separate entries).

Hongwanji: A Pure Land school. Headquarters of the True Pure Land (Jodo Shinshu), and due to a historical split there is now a Honpa Hongwanji and a Higashi Hongwanji—the Honpa having been the more progressive and adaptive to change. See *Major Centers in Asia* for head center.

Kempon Hokke Shu: A Nichiren school. See Kempon Hokke Kai, Oregon.

I **International Meditation Center (IMC):** An organization of Theravada centers worldwide. Founded in 1979 by the Sayagyi U Ba Khin Memorial Trust to provide for the instruction and practice of Theravada Buddhist meditations. Its main center is in Yangon, Myanmar (formerly Rangoon, Burma) (see *Major Centers in Asia*) and was founded by Sayagyi U Ba Khin.

International Shakyamuni Dzogchen Heart Lineage: (Tibetan–Dzogchen, Nyingma/Kagyu) Worldwide community of practitioners dedicated to the teachings and practices of Dzogchen. Represents an intuitive form of the Buddha's teachings known as the Heart Tradition understood by practitioners through direct experience of the nature of mind (Dzogchen). Founded by Padma Karma Rinpoche in 1991 in Zhejiang Province, China. Established the Center for Dzogchen Studies, Connecticut, in 1994, and Dharma Heir, Lama Pema Dzogtril, established sister center in Santa Fe, New Mexico. Also practitioners in Europe, Hong Kong, and other parts of the USA. Center in South America planned.

International Zen Institute of America (IZIA): A Rinzai Zen organization which aims to disseminate Zen Buddhist teaching and practice in Western society. Founded in 1983 by Ven. Gesshin Myoko Prabhasadharma Roshi, who is its president. Headquarters is International Zen Institute of America, California, where Ven. Prabhasadharma is resident.

Jodo Shin: Literally: The School of the Pure Land. Present school founded by Honen (1133–1212 BCE). Unlike Jodo Shinshu, it has a monastic life. See also **Pure Land.**

Jodo Shinshu: Literally: The True School of the Pure Land. Founded by the Japanese Buddhist Shinran Shonin (1173–1262 BCE), who taught that the actual recitation of the Nembutsu was not as important as the quality of faith underlying it, and that is a gift of pure grace. He saw that Buddhist life could be lived by ordinary people outside monasteries, so taught a lay tradition and himself married and had children. See also **Pure Land**.

Kagyu: A Tibetan school. Founded in the eleventh century by Gampopa. It is about practical mysticism rather than scholarship. It emphasizes meditation and has produced many successful solitary meditators. Naropa (1016–1100 BCE), after a life of scholarship, had a vision of an old crone who revealed the hard truth that the knowledge he had acquired was merely dry intellectual stuff, not the transrational knowledge of the heart. This shock drove him to the verge of suicide, but he was saved by discovery of his guru, Tilopa (988–1069 BCE), and underwent a grueling twelve-year training in Tantra. After suppression of first transmission of Buddhism to Tibet, the Tibetans collected gold and went to India to obtain scriptures. One of them, Marpa (b. 1012), studied with Naropa among other great masters. Among the teachings he received were the Six Yogas of Naropa and Mahamudra. On returning to Tibet, Marpa settled down to ordinary life as a farmer and family man. His most famous disciple and heir to the lineage was Milarepa (1052–1135), who avoided both institutions and ordination as a monk—he is the prototype of the freewheeling yogi and poet following his own spontaneous spiritual path in lonely places. His most influential disciple was Gampopa (1079–1153), author of the classic text *The Jewel Ornament of Liberation*, and from his many disciples stem the three Kagyu subschools—Druk, Drikung, and Karma. His main spiritual heir was the first Gyalwa Karmapa. Since that time, the Karmapas have reincarnated again and again to guide their tradition. The present Karmapa is the seventeenth and was discovered in Tibet in 1992.

Kanzeon Sangha: A Zen school. Basically Soto Zen, strong emphasis on zazen. International organization founded in 1984 to support work of Genpo Merzel Roshi, second successor of the late Taizan Maezumi Roshi, but also includes teachings of the Rinzai school. Kanzeon Zen Center Utah in Salt Lake City is the international headquarters. See also **Harada–Yasutani Lineage.**

Karma Kagyu: See **Tibetan Buddhism** and **Kagyu**.

Kwan Um School of Zen: Korean school of the Chogye Order founded in USA by Seung Sahn Sunim. Main center at Kwan Um School of Zen, Rhode Island.

 Mahayana: Whereas Theravada Buddhism is about individuals attaining enlightenment for themselves, Mahayana stresses the ideal of the Bodhisattva who aspires to Buddhahood solely that he might help others. All schools that are not Theravada are Mahayana.

Mountains and Rivers Order: Founded by John Daido Loori (see also **Harada-Yasutani Lineage**). Headquarters Zen Mountain Monastery, New York.

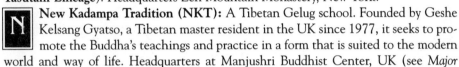 **New Kadampa Tradition (NKT):** A Tibetan Gelug school. Founded by Geshe Kelsang Gyatso, a Tibetan master resident in the UK since 1977, it seeks to promote the Buddha's teachings and practice in a form that is suited to the modern world and way of life. Headquarters at Manjushri Buddhist Center, UK (see *Major Centers in the UK* for details).

Nichiren: A Japanese tradition founded by Nichiren Shonin (1222–1282 CE), who espoused the doctrine that the Lotus Sutra represents the embodiment of the genuine teachings of the Buddha. This belief is affirmed by chanting "Namu Myoho Renge Kyo," meaning "Adoration to the Sutra of the Lotus of the Perfect Truth," and Nichiren schools believe Buddhahood can be attained through recitation of this formula. It teaches that our destiny lies in our own hands and we must take responsibility for our own lives and make the necessary positive moves to settle our problems and release our full potential. Members are therefore actively counseled, helped, and supported by the movement and are encouraged to take up a threefold practice involving faith, study, and chanting. Faith is in the power of the Gohonzon, a scroll on which Nichiren Shonin wrote "Namu Myoho Renge Kyo" in mandalic form. The original is at head temple (Minobusan Kuonji in Japan, established by Nichiren Shonin in 1274), but members obtain their own copy and chant before it twice daily. Emphasis is on the earthly Buddha realm and Buddhist sociopolitical action. They strive to engender peace within themselves and throughout the world by actively disseminating their teachings. See also **Nichiren Shu** and **Nichiren Shoshu**.

Nichiren Shoshu: Literally: True School of Nichiren. Venerates Nichiren as a Buddha and is a lay organization with no priesthood. Currently unique within Buddhism in avoiding relations with other Buddhist groups and for having a highly active policy for promoting itself. See also **Soka Gakkai International, Reiyukai,** and **Rissho Kosei-kai**. Other subschools include Nipponzan Myohoji.

Nichiren Shu: Literally: The School of the Lotus of the Sun. Unlike the Nichiren Shoshu, they have a priesthood. See also **Nichiren** and **Nichiren Shoshu**.

Nonsectarian: Tolerance is part of the Buddhist tradition. In coming to the West, there have been great moves for dialogue between both other schools of Buddhism and other religions.

Nyingma: A Tibetan school which dates back to the first transmission of Buddhism to Tibet. They are more anarchic and less inclined to monastic life, leaning more toward magic than the other newer Tibetan traditions. They also particularly venerate Padmasambhava (also known as Guru Rinpoche), a Tantric adept who transmitted

Buddhism to Tibet in the seventh century and who is also highly esteemed by other Tibetan traditions. He did not deliver all his teachings at that time, however, but hid some both geographically and in the mind for discovery later when people would be better prepared to understand them.

Order of Buddhist Contemplatives: See **Serene Reflection Meditation Tradition.**

Community of Mindful Living: Serves as a liaison between Plum Village and practioners worldwide. Founded by Thich Nhat Hanh, a Vietnamese monk based at Plum Village, France (see *Major Centers in Europe*). Main center in U.S. is Community of Mindful Living, California.

O **Ordinary Mind Zen School:** Founded by Charlotte Joko Beck and composed of her and her Dharma successors, and those formally authorized by this group. No affiliation with other Zen groups, but membership does not preclude affiliation with other groups. Each Dharma successor may apply diverse practice approaches and determine the structure of any organization developed to facilitate practice. "An important function of this school is the ongoing examination and development of effective teaching approach to ensure comprehensive practice in all aspects of living." Three centers: Zen Center San Diego and Bay Zen Center, California, and Prairie Zen Center, Illinois.

P **Pure Land:** Unlike other forms of Buddhism, which emphasize one's own efforts to attain Enlightenment, Pure Land schools emphasize the role of faith and ask Amitabha (Japanese: Amida), the Buddha of Infinite Light, to intercede spiritually on their behalf. Also known as Other-power Buddhism, because it teaches reliance on or surrender to the Power of the Buddha, rather than relying on one's own efforts. The basic sutra of Pure Land tells how Amida, while still a Bodhisattva Lokeshvararaja, vowed that he would found a "Pure Land in the West" and not become a Buddha until all living things were redeemed. "Whoever relies on my vow and calls my name will without exception be taken into my pure land." The principal practice is the recitation of the name of Amida Buddha in the Japanese form, Namu Amida Butsu, known as the Nembutsu. It was the first really democratic form of Buddhism, concentrating on a simple theology of faith, and Nembutsu practice and adherents remain firmly anchored in everyday life. It stresses humility rather than attainment, study and mediation being distrusted as leading to intellectual and spiritual arrogance. Great emphasis on good works, generating much charitable work. In Japan it is the most widespread school of Buddhism, with twelve million followers. Jodo Shin and Jodo Shinshu (see separate entries) are Japanese, but there are also Chinese and Vietnamese forms.

R **Rigpa:** A Tibetan Nyingma school. International network of centers and groups named Rigpa where the teachings of Buddha are followed under the guidance of Sogyal Rinpoche.

Rime: A Tibetan school started in the last century by Jamyang Khyentse Wangpo and Jamgon Kongtrul Rinpoche which seeks to overcome sectarianism within Tibetan Buddhism and has especially influenced the Karma Kagyu and Nyingma schools.

Rinzai Zen: A Japanese Zen school. Meditation is usually practiced sitting in straight lines facing a partner. After meditative practice to bring about calmness and concentration, there is usually koan practice. Koans are riddles used by early masters in real-life situations to enlighten their students. They are extremely active devices for throwing the student against the ultimate question of his or her own nature.

Rissho Kosei-kai: Offshoot of Nichiren Shoshu. Founded in Japan in 1938 by Nikkyo Niwano (b. 1906), who was the president until 1991. He was succeeded as president by Nichiko Niwano. Began after the founder's first encounter with the Lotus Sutra. Teachings can be summed up in two points: honoring parents and venerating ancestors, and practicing the Bodhisattva way, which means unconditional reverence for the Buddha-nature in all people. Works toward interfaith dialogue and cooperation, world peace, and charitable works. Members read aloud from the Lotus Sutra and take part in Hoza, which is "a unique form of group counseling that helps members learn how to apply the Buddha's teaching in everyday life." Headquarters in Japan (see *Major Centers in Asia*).

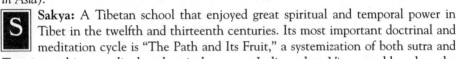

Sakya: A Tibetan school that enjoyed great spiritual and temporal power in Tibet in the twelfth and thirteenth centuries. Its most important doctrinal and meditation cycle is "The Path and Its Fruit," a systemization of both sutra and Tantric teachings credited to the ninth-century Indian adept Virupa and based on the Hevajra Tantra. By following this path it is apparently possible to gain enlightenment in a single lifetime. Present supreme head is H.H. Sakya Trizin.

Sanbo Kyodan: See **Harada-Yasutani Lineage.**

Serene Reflection Meditation Tradition: A Soto Zen school founded by Rev. Master Jiyu-Kennet. Can be followed as either a layperson or a monk. Their monastics are known as The Order of Buddhist Contemplatives, and men and women have equal status and recognition, training together in the priesthood. All ranks and both sexes are addressed as *Reverend* and are referred to as *monks* and *priests*. Main center is Shasta Abbey, California.

Shambhala International: A Nyingma and Kagyu Tibetan school. Teachings on study and practice originally from Chogyam Trungpa Rinpoche and carried on by Sakyong Mipham Rinpoche. Involves the Shambhala training program of meditation and study and the Nalanda traditions of contemplative arts, education, health, and livelihood. Classes and training include the Sacred Path of the Warrior. International headquarters Shambhala Center, Nova Scotia, Canada.

Shaolin Zen: Chinese system of Buddhism involving martial arts exercises, more usual meditation practices. Derived from system of exercises devised by Bodhidharma. Shaolin monks may also practice medicine.

Shin: An abbreviation of Jodo Shinshu—see **Jodo Shinshu** and **Pure Land.**

Soka Gakkai International: A Nichiren school. Founded 1930 in Japan by Makiguchi Tsunesabwo. Based on the teachings of Nichiren (1222–1282), who espoused that all people inherently possess the potential for Buddhahood and can manifest this potential in every aspect of life. 1960 to 1990 were the formative years of SGI-USA, in which its religious and social identity as an American organization was shaped. In 1990, the organization disengaged from clerical relations. As part of the international association of SGI, the SGI-USA subscribed in 1995 to the concerns and principles for social engagement as outlined in the Charter of SGI. President Daisaku Ideka. American headquarters in Santa Monica, California. See also **Nichiren** and **Nichiren Shoshu**.

Soto Zen: A Japanese Zen school. Founded by Dogen Zenji (1200–1253), its meditation practice (zazen or shikantaza) is usually done facing a blank wall and is not about concentration, introspection, or any kind of thinking—there should be no expectations or endeavor of any kind. The practice and realization are the same thing—just to sit is to be a Buddha, and it makes no distinction between new and advanced students.

Tendai: See **Karuna Tendai Dharma Center**, New York.

Thai Forest Tradition: A Theravada school which flourishes in the northeast of Thailand with a strong tradition of highly effective meditation and vinaya practice. Brought to the West by Ven. Ajahn Chah, a highly respected teacher from Thailand.

Theravada: The earliest form of Buddhism still surviving today. All forms of Buddhism use the Pali canon, but Theravada uses it exclusively. Has a strong monastic tradition, with monks shaving their heads and wearing traditional ochre or orange robes. They are committed to a life of poverty, mendicancy, and chastity and are bound at all times by numerous precepts and rules. The daily routine is austere and hierarchy is important. Monastics and laypeople have a special relationship, the monastery being the spiritual focus of a community. In the West, there is usually a lay association which takes care of the monks' material welfare, as the usual custom of monks making daily alms rounds with begging bowls is not feasible. There is a school of thought that maintains that real practice is possible only for the ordained sangha, but intensive lay practices have been established in the West, most notably by Mahasi Sayadaw and U Ba Khin. Thai, Sri Lankan, and Myanmar forms vary slightly due to cultural differences.

Tibetan Buddhism: The most colorful and ritualistic school of Buddhism present in the West. Seclusion of Tibet enabled Tibetans to preserve the Mahayana and Tantric Buddhism of India for over a millennium and create a uniquely rich spiritual culture. "Unfortunately in 1950, the Chinese Communists felt the need to 'liberate' these people from the thrall of Western imperialism. Despite the fact that there were virtually no Westerners—and certainly imperialists—in Tibet at the time, the Chinese went ahead . . . and became imperialists themselves, taking over the government of what had hitherto effectively been an autonomous nation, colonizing it, plundering its mineral and natural wealth, and making the Tibetans themselves virtual aliens in their own land. The Tibetans voted with their feet against this 'liberation,' and when the Chinese finally—and bloodily—completed their takeover in 1959, tens of thousands fled to exile in India. The virtual destruction of Buddhism in Tibet was completed during the Cultural Revolution (1966–76). Yet these violent and destructive events did have one positive outcome: they made the spiritual riches of Tibetan Buddhism accessible to Westerners for the first time." Quoted from John Snelling, *The Elements of Buddhism*. Several schools are currently represented in the West—see **Kagyu, Bon, Nyingma, Gelug, Rime,** and **Sakya.**

True Buddha School: Chinese Buddhist school. More than four million disciples, three hundred chapters, and twenty temples worldwide. Founder Living Buddha Lian, master of Taoism, Sutrayana, and Vajrayana. First temple—Ling Shen Ching Tze Temple, Washington.

V **Vietnamese Buddhism:** Although Buddhism first entered Korea in 372, its influence there has waxed and waned considerably, several times being subject to government control. This has led to the various schools emphasizing their similarities, uniting in 1935 to form a single organization, the Chogye sect, from which most contemporary groups derive. It is represented mostly in the U.S. by the Kwan Um School of Zen (founded by Seung Sahn Sunim) and the Order of Interbeing (founded by Thich Nhat Hanh), although there are some centers which serve the Vietnamese American community.

Vipassana: A meditation technique often taught at centers, often nondenominational, dedicated to this one practice. Although preserved in the Buddhist tradition, it contains nothing of a sectarian nature and can be accepted and applied by people of any culture or religion. Some consider it was devised by the Buddha; others that it was rediscovered by him and is much older. Five centuries after the Buddha, it had disappeared from India, but was preserved in Burma. It has now been reintroduced to India and to eighty other countries under the influence of the renowned Burmese teacher, Sayagyi U Ba Khin and his disciples, including S N Goenka. It involves opening the mind and whatever arises in the field of attention is observed. It is a form of psychotherapy in which old fears, traumas, and repressions, if merely treated to bare attention, simply pass away.

Vipassana centers in the tradition of S. N. Goenka: Although there is no headquarters, in the USA Vipassana Meditation Center, Massachussetts, is the oldest and most established of North American centers—see entry for list of others. Over thirty permanent centers in thirty-five countries worldwide. Timetable, retreat format, and meditation instructions are the same at all courses worldwide (in thirty-five languages).

W **White Plum Sangha:** A Zen school founded by Taizan Hakuyu Maezumi. See also **Harada–Yasutani Lineage.**

Won Buddhism: Started in Korea 1916 by Chungbin Pak (1891–1943), later called Sot'aesan Taejongsa. Object of faith is the Truth of Irwon, symbolized by the form of a circle representing the source and totality. In Won Buddhism, there are no external images of Buddhas, as they "offer respect to whatever work they participate in, whomever they meet, and whatever object they handle" (quoted from Won Buddhism brochure). Does not exclude other faiths or views as the symbol of Irwon points to the sameness of the enlightened mind of all Buddhas and saints. The current Head Dharma Master since 1994 is Ven. Chwasan.

Z **Zen:** Probably originated in India but came into its own in China in the sixth and seventh centuries and is now found mainly in Japan and Korea. Places great emphasis on sitting meditation. Tends not to rely on words and logical concepts for communicating the Dharma, but stresses the primary importance of the enlightenment experience more than any other school. Teaches the practice of zazen, or sitting medication, as the shortest, albeit the steepest, way to awakening. See also **Soto Zen** and **Rinzai Zen.**

Zen Lotus Society: See **Buddhist Society for Compassionate Wisdom.**

TEACHERS

This section is intended to cover teachers mentioned in this directory and is not an exhaustive list. Abbreviations: H.H. = His Holiness; H.E. = His Eminence. See the *Glossary* for meanings of titles, e.g., Tulku or Ajahn.

16th Gyalwa Karmapa see **Karmapa, H.H. the 16th**
17th Gyalwa Karmapa see **Karmapa, H.H. the 17th**

Aitken Roshi, Robert (Zen) Resident Palolo Zen Center, Hawaii. Began Buddhist practice in California in 1948 with Senzaki Nyogen Sensei and continued training in Japan and Hawaii with Nakagawa Soen Roshi, Yasutani Roshi, and Yamada Roshi. Authorized to teach by Yamada Roshi 1974 and received full transmission as Roshi 1985. Closely associated with Diamond Sangha. Author of several books. Retired 1996.

Amaro, Ajahn (Theravada–Thai Forest Tradition) Monk since 1979. Abbot of Abhayagiri Buddhist Monastery, California. Book due for publication 1996.

Anzan Hoshin, Zen Master (Zen) Dharma Heir of Yasuda Joshu Dainen, who established Hakukaze-ji, first Soto Zen Buddhist monastery in Canada. Disbanded Hakukazi-ji in 1980 and entered nine-month forest hermitage, followed by study with Tibetan masters such as H.H. Dudjom Rinpoche and Geshe Khenrab Gyatso. In 1985 established White Wind Zen Community, Canada. Resident teacher Ottawa Zen Center.

Ayang Rinpoche, Venerable (Tibetan–Drikung Kagyu) Born 1941 in Tibet. Lived in monastery ages 9–18. In 1959 left Tibet. Founded monastery in southern India. Specialist in Phowa practices and carries blessings of the three Phowa lineages— Nyingma, Drikung, and Namcho Phowa. At request of Dalai Lama, taught Phowa in Japan and frequently visits Europe and USA, where he conducts Phowas courses and teaches at his various centers.

Bardor Tulku Rinpoche (Tibetan–Karma Kagyu) Resident lama and head of monastery construction project at Karma Triyana Dharmachakra, New York. Born 1950 in East Tibet and recognized at an early age by his personal teacher, H.H. 16th Gyalwa Karmapa. Fled to Sikkim 1959 and studied all Kagyu lineage methods at Karmapa's seat in exile. Karmpa sent him to U.S. 1976.

Barrett, Deborah Teacher of Zen meditation and practice at Newport Mesa Zen Center, California. Zen monk and Roman Catholic sister. Serious meditation practitioner since early 1970s, focusing on Christian and Zen awareness methods. Certified pastoral counselor with a PhD in psychology, MA in theology, and also an attorney.

Bays, Jan Chozen, Sensei (Zen) Dharma Heir of Taizan Maezumi. Resident teacher Oregon Zen Community, Oregon.

Brodsky, Barbara (Mixed) Founder and guiding teacher of Deep Spring Center, Michigan. Practiced meditation since 1960 and taught since 1989. Roots in Buddhist (Theravadan and Dzogchen) and Quaker traditions. Deaf since 1972. Channel for the spirit, Aaron, and teachings from both her and Aaron.

Carlson Sensei, Kyogen (Zen–Soto) Abbot of Dharma Rain, Oregon. Trained as monk for five years and ordained by Roshi Jiyu-Kennett 1972 at Shasta Abbey. Remained another five years as staff member and personal assistant to Roshi Jiyu-Kennett. Married to Gyokuko Carlson Sensei 1982 when he set up the independent school, Dharma Rain, in Oregon, with his wife.

Carlson, Gyokuko Sensei (Zen–Soto) Director Dharma Rain, Oregon. Ordained 1975 by Roshi Jiyu-Kennett at Shasta Abbey. Graduated from seminary program 1980 and remained there until 1982, when she married Kyogen Carlson Sensei and set up the independent school, Dharma Rain, in Oregon, with her husband.

Chagdud Tulku Rinpoche, H.E. (Tibetan–Nyingma) Born 1930 in Tibet. Mother famous practitioner. Recognized as reincarnation of previous Chagdud Tulku aged three. Studied at Drukpa Kagyu Monastery from childhood. Three-year retreat at age eleven. Training under Jamgon Kongtrul, Jamyang Khyentse Chokyi Lodro, and many others. Root lama Khenpo Dorje. Empowerments from Dudjom Rinpoche and Dilgo Khyentse Rinpoche. Left Tibet 1959 and used medical knowledge and taught Phowa in Indian refugee camps. Requested by Americans to come to USA 1979 and lived one year in California. Oversees centers in U.S. and Canada of Chagdud Gonpa Foundation. Published several works.

Chah, Ajahn (Theravada–Thai) Meditation master of the Thai Forest tradition. Born in rural northeast Thailand. Ordained at early age. Studied basic Dhamma, discipline, and scriptures as a young monk and later practiced meditation under several masters of the Forest tradition. Lived as an ascetic for several years, then spent short time with Ajan Mun and eventually settled in a thick forest grove near his birthplace. Large monastery grew up around him (Wat Pah Pong) and from this, numerous branch temples sprang up in northeast Thailand and elsewhere. Wat Pah Nanachat set up in 1975 as special training monastery for Westerners. Visited UK and USA in late seventies. Author of several books.

Chang Sik Kim, Zen Master (Zen) Founding Master of Shim Gum Do. Korean who entered Hwa Gye Temple at age thirteen and was taught by Dae Seung Sahn Lee. After eight years' formal training, underwent one hundred-day retreat in 1965, during which the Art of Shim Gum Do (Mind Sword Path) was realized and he attained enlightenment. Came to the U.S. in 1974 and began teaching Shim Gum Do. 1978 established American Shim Gum Do Association and in 1991, the World Shim Gum Do Assoc.

Chon Toan, Ven. Thich (Vietnamese) Ordained as Buddhist monk at age seven, spent most of his youth in Tuong-Van Monastery, Vietnam. Graduated Van-Hanh University of Saigon with degree in Buddhism and Eastern philosophy. Vice-Chairperson of Buddhist Sangha Council Ministry of Ontario 1995.

Dae Gak, Zen Master (Zen–Korean–Kwan Um) American-born Dharma Heir of Zen Master Seung Sahn. Received final teaching transmission in 1994. Ordained monk and 79th Patriarch in the Korean Chogye Lineage. Founder of Furnace Mountain, Kentucky, and guiding teacher to centers in Cincinnati, Indianapolis, and Queensland, Australia. PhD in clinical psychology and practiced psychotherapy for twenty-five years.

Dalai Lama, H.H. the 14th (Gyalwa Tenzin Gyatso) (Tibetan) Spiritual and temporal head of the Tibetan people. Born 1935 in Tibet and recognized as Dalai Lama reincarnation at age two. Taken to Lhasa in 1939 and formally enthroned 1940. Began education at six years old at Sera, Drepung, and Gendun Monasteries. Awarded Lharampa Geshe degree with honors at age twenty-four. Assumed full temporal powers early at age sixteen due to Chinese threat. Held discussions in Peking in 1954 on behalf of his people, but was unsuccessful. Left Tibet 1959 and given sanctuary in India. Since then has campaigned for peaceful return of Tibet to independence. In 1963 promulgated draft democratic constitution for Tibet and has since conducted his government-in-exile in Dharamsala, India, along those lines. Worked very successfully to resettle a hundred thousand Tibetan refugees and preserve Tibetan culture. Travels worldwide teaching and lecturing and has met political and spiritual leaders, scientists, doctors, writers, and philosophers. Impresses people everywhere with his Buddhist message of peace and kindness. Author of several books. Considered one of the great Dalai Lamas along with the 5th and 13th. Won Nobel Peace Prize in 1989.

Deshimaru Roshi, Taisen (Zen–Soto) (1914–1982) Japanese who started religious training with Kodo Sawaki late in life and received Dharma transmission. Settled in France 1967 and based himself in Paris. Founded Association Zen Internationale in 1970, which expanded to centers in France, Belgium, Germany, USA, North Africa, and South America. Died in Tokyo after teaching in France for fifteen years. Author of a number of books.

Dilgo Khyentse Rinpoche, H.H. (1910–1991) (Tibetan–Nyingma) Born in Tibet. Head of the Nyingma school and one of main lineage holder of the Dzogchen Longchen Nyingthig tradition. Recognized as an incarnation while still unborn and entered monastery at eleven. Enthroned as the wisdom-mind emanation of Jamyang Khyentse Wangpo (1820–1892) by his teacher, Zhechen Gyaltsab Rinpoche, who imparted to him all the essential instructions and empowerments of the Nyingma tradition. Studied intensively with many great masters and scholars from all four lineage traditions. Practiced for years in remote caves and solitary hermitages. Whilst in Tibet spent more than twenty years in retreat. Went into exile after Chinese occupation, establishing Zhechen Tenyi Dhargye Ling Monastery in Nepal and becoming spiritual advisor to the Bhutan royal family. Built new stupa at Bodhgaya and planned construction of seven other stupas in pilgrimage places associated with life of Buddha. Traveled extensively throughout India, Southeast Asia, and the West. One of most outstanding Nyingma masters and renowned for Dzogchen practices. Author and famous for outstanding scholarship and wisdom. Important in preserving Tibetan spiritual heritage.

One of founders of Longchen Foundation in the UK.

Dudjom Dorje, Ven. Lama (Tibetan–Karma Kagyu) Holds Acharya degree in higher Buddhist studies. Resident California and teaches regularly at Karma Triyana Dharmachakra, New York, and affiliate centers.

Dudjom Rinpoche, H.H. (1904–1987) (Tibetan–Nyingma) Born into noble family in Tibet. Recognized as an incarnation of famous discoverer of many hidden teachings (Termas). Studied with many of most outstanding Lamas of his time. Only receiver of transmissions of all the existing teachings of the Nyingma tradition. Great terton (discoverer of hidden teachings) whose Termas are now widely taught and practiced. Leading exponent of Dzogchen. A master of masters. Prolific author and meticulous scholar. Founded centers in India, Nepal, and the West.

Dzogchen Ponlop Rinpoche, H.E. (Tibetan–Nyingma) (Karma Sungrab Ngedon Tenpe Gyaltsen) Born at Rumtek Monastery in Sikkim 1965. Recognized as next Dzogchen Ponlop before birth. Officially recognized by Dalai Lama at one month old. Enthroned 1968. Received most of Kagyu and Nyingma teachings and empowerments from the Karmapa, Dilgo Khyentse Rinpoche, and other great teachers. Began studies of Buddhist philosophy at fourteen. Ka Rabjampa degree 1991; Acarya degree 1991. Studied English and religion at Columbia University, New York; studied other languages also. First traveled 1980 with Karmapa and continues to travel and teach in West and Asia.

 Fletcher, Charles Tenshin, Sensei (Zen) Acting abbot and resident teacher of Zen Mountain Center, California. Born in Manchester, England; came to U.S. to live and train with Zen Master Hakuyu Taizan Maezumi Roshi. One of his twelve Dharma Successors and studied with him for sixteen years.

Foster, Nelson, Roshi (Zen) Roshi of Ring of Bone Zendo, California, and of Honolulu Diamond Sangha, Hawaii, from 1996.

 Glassman, Bernard Tetsugen Roshi (Zen–Soto) Founder and abbot of Zen Community of New York and its affiliates. Born 1939 in New York. PhD in applied mathematics. Worked in space program for fifteen years. Began studying Zen 1958 and zazen practice 1963 in Los Angeles with Sumi Roshi. Started practice with Maezumi Roshi 1968 and ordained 1970. Dharma transmission received from him 1977 and succeeds him as spiritual head of White Plum Sangha.

Goenka, S. N. (Vipassana) At Vipassana International Academy, near Bombay, India. Disciple of Vipassana meditation in the tradition of Burmese teacher, Sayagyi U Ba Khin. Indian by descent, but raised in Burma, where he met Sayagyi U Ba Khin, with whom he trained for fourteen years. Began conducting Vipassana courses in India 1969; after ten years began teaching in other countries. Founder and spiritual director of Vipassana centers around the world.

Graef, Sensei Sunyana (Zen) Began training 1969 at Rochester Zen Center (RZC) as disciple of Roshi Kapleau. Nine years on RZC staff. Ordained as priest 1986 and sanctioned as Dharma Heir 1987. Moved to Vermont 1988 and established Zen center at Shelburne. Asked to be teacher of Toronto Zen Center 1994, where she regularly visits to teach.

Gyatrul Rinpoche, Ven (Tibetan–Nyingma) Born in China near Tibetan border and recognized as tulku at age seven. Master of many traditions of Tibetan Buddhism. Fled

Tibet in 1959. Taught in India for several years and came to North America at request of H.H. the Dalai Lama and H.H. Dudjom Rinpoche. Resident teacher of Pacific Region Yeshe Nyingpo, Oregon.

Harada Roshi, Sogaku (1870–1961) (Zen) Japanese master trained in Rinzai and Soto traditions. Entered Soto Zen temple at age seven. Attained kensho and received inka from Dokutan Roshi. Taught at Komazawa University for twelve years, combining Zen teaching with academic work. Abbot of Hosshin-ji for forty years. Conducted sesshins until nearly age ninety.

Henepola Gunaratana, Bhante (Theravada) PhD. Monk since 1940s and expert in Western and Buddhist psychology. Founder of Bhavana Society, West Virginia. Author of several books.

Hsing Yun, Ven. Master (Chinese Buddhism–Buddha's Light International Association) Born 1927 in China. Started monastic training at age twelve and fully ordained 1941. In 1947 graduated from Chiao Shan Buddhist College and recognized as forty-eighth lineage holder of Lin-chi school. Concurrently, principal of primary school, editor of a magazine, and Abbot of Hua Tsang Temple. Left China 1949 to go to Taiwan, where he taught at a temple. Mid-1970s started work on Fo Kuang Shan, now largest Buddhist center in Taiwan. Feels that modernization of Buddhism inevitable. Various charitable concerns. Provided initiative for Sutric-Tantric Conferences 1986 and 1989 bringing together Tibetan Lamas of four main lineages and representatives of Mahayana and Theravada traditions. Reinstated right of women to highest ordination 1988. Organized Christian-Buddhist Conference 1989. Honorary doctor of philosopy from University of Oriental Studies, California, in recognition of contribution to Buddhism in America.

Hsuan Hua, Ven. Master (Ch'an) Also known as An Tz'u and Tu Lun. Name Hsuan Hua was bestowed on him after he received transmission of the Wei-Yang Lineage of the Chan school from Ven. Elder Master Hsu Yung. When nineteen became monk at Three Conditions Monastery in Harbin, Manchuria. On death of his mother, lived in thatched hut by her graveside for three years as an act of filial respect. During that time cultivated Chan Samadhi and studied the Buddha's teachings. In 1948 visited Hong Kong, where he built Western Bliss Garden Temple and the Buddhist Lecture Hall and renovated Tz'u Hsing Monastery on Lantau Island. Came to teach in America and the West. Established Dharma Realm Buddhist Association with branches in many locations. Abbot of Gold Mountain Monastery, California, and City of Ten Thousand Buddhas, California.

Hyunoong Sunim, Venerable (Zen–Rinzai–Korean) Born South Korea. Zen monk since age twenty, including ten years of traditional training in Zen meditation halls and six years of practice alone in remote mountain hermitage where began ten year apprenticeship under a Taoist hermit who later gave him sanction to teach. Taoist studies include breathing meditation, I-Ching, five elements, and Chinese herbs. Taught in Switzerland 1985 and in North America from 1986. Established Zen & Taoist Healing Centers (Sun-do) in Vancouver and Seattle. Resident Zen and Taoist master at Sixth Patriarch Zen Center, California, and teaches also at Dohn-O Zen Center, Washington.

Ikeda, Daisaku (Nichiren) President of Soka Gakkai International. Born 1928 in Tokyo. Came across Soka Gakkai when about nineteen "and knew instantly that this was a way of life he must follow." Became president on death of previous incumbent in 1960. Set out to raise membership to three million, which he did by 1962. Formed Soka Gakkai International in 1975 and began holding dialogues with eminent world leaders and leading intellectuals, arranging cultural exchanges, etc. UN Peace Award in 1972. Author of a number of books.

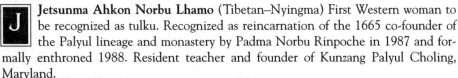 **Jetsunma Ahkon Norbu Lhamo** (Tibetan–Nyingma) First Western woman to be recognized as tulku. Recognized as reincarnation of the 1665 co-founder of the Palyul lineage and monastery by Padma Norbu Rinpoche in 1987 and formally enthroned 1988. Resident teacher and founder of Kunzang Palyul Choling, Maryland.

Jigdal Dagchen Sakya Rinpoche, H.H. (Tibetan–Sakya) Founder and principal lama of Sakya Monastery, Washington. Born 1929 in Tibet as future head of Sakya school and educated accordingly (father was last throneholder in Tibet). Long series of study and meditation retreats. After father's death, chose to give up rulership of Sakya school to study with Dzongsar Jamyang Choki Lodro and Dilgo Khyentse Rabsal Dawa among others, from which he developed nonsectarian approach. In 1959 fled to India with his wife and family and became Sakya representative to the Tibetan Religious Office in Exile. In 1960 invited to research project on Tibetan civilization at the University of Washington and resided in Seattle thereafter. Teaching extensively throughout U.S., Canada, Europe, and Asia.

Jiyu-Kennett, Rev. Master (1924–1996) (Zen–Soto) Abbess and spiritual director of Shasta Abbey and Order of Buddhist Contemplatives. Born in England and trained at Trinity College of Music, London. Ordained in Malaysia by the V.V. Seck Kim Seng, archbishop of Malacca. Received Dharma Transmission in Japan from Very Rev. Keido Chisan Koho Zenji, chief abbot of Dai Hon Zan Soji-ji, and later certified as Zen Master by him. After his death, came to U.S. to fulfill his wish for Zen Buddhism to be transmitted to the West by a Westerner and founded Shasta Abbey 1970. Has taught at University of California and Institute of Transpersonal Psychology. Founded temples and meditation groups in the U.S., Canada, and UK. Several books.

Joko Beck, Charlotte (Zen–Ordinary Mind) Trained under Hakuun Yasutani Roshi and Soen Nakagawa Roshi in 1960s. In 1983 became third Dharma Heir of Hakuyu Maezumi Roshi. Together with Dharma Heirs, established Ordinary Mind Zen School 1995. Head of San Diego Zen Center. Author of two books, *Everyday Zen* and *Nothing Special: Living Zen.*

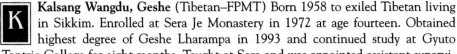 **Kalsang Wangdu, Geshe** (Tibetan–FPMT) Born 1958 to exiled Tibetan living in Sikkim. Enrolled at Sera Je Monastery in 1972 at age fourteen. Obtained highest degree of Geshe Lharampa in 1993 and continued study at Gyuto Tantric College for eight months. Taught at Sera and was appointed assistant supervisor of the study program. Time divided between Californian FPMT centers.

Kalu Rinpoche (1905–1989) (Tibetan–Kagyu) Born 1905 in Tibet to parents who were Rime students. Recognized as tulku but not ordained, wandering freely instead and educated by father. At thirteen began formal studies. Received ordination from eleventh Tai Situpa. Studied sutra and Tantra teachings, receiving empowerments from many great Lamas. At sixteen underwent three-year retreat under direction of Norbu Tondrup, from whom he received complete transmission of teachings of Karma Kagyu and Shangba Kagyu traditions. At age twenty-five went into twelve-year solitary retreat. Became director of three-year retreats at Palpung at request of Tai Situpa. Recognized by 16th Gyalwa Karmapa as incarnation of Jampgon Kontrul Lodro Thaye. Toured Tibet in 1940s and asked to leave in 1955 by Karmapa. Established two centers in Bhutan and ordained three hundred monks. Pilgrimages to in India. 1965 established headquarters in Darjeeling, India, and another three-year retreat. Invited to the West in 1971. With the blessing of the Dalai Lama and the Karmapa, founded Karma Ling in 1980. The tradition passed to his disciple Lama Denys Teundrop. Founded several centers for practice of Chenrezig Sadhana in France and USA. Principal center in North America in Vancouver. Began three-year retreats for Westerners in France at his two centers. Author of a number of books. Venerated by all lines of Tibetan Buddhism.

Kapleau, Roshi Philip (Zen) American born 1912. Court reporter International Military Tribunals at Nuremberg and Tokyo 1946–1947. Spent thirteen years undergoing Rinzai and Soto Zen training in Japan under Harada Roshi, Yasutani Roshi, and Nakagawa Soen Roshi before being ordained 1965 and given permission to teach. Came to Rochester, New York, 1966 to found Rochester Zen Center. Established centers across USA, Canada, and Europe. Author of several books. Teaching schedule at semi-retirement level and resident in Hollywood, Florida.

Karma Dorje, Lama (Tibetan–Karma Kagyu) Founder and resident teacher Karma Shenpen Kunchab (KSK) Tibetan Buddhist Center, New Mexico. "Lama Dorje was born in Sikkim, he's around sixty-three, did a three-year retreat with Kalu Rinpoche, who then sent him to the U.S. to start a center." (Supplied by KSK.)

Karma Rinchen, Lama (Tibetan–Kagyu) Born 1931 in Tibet. Entered Palpung Monastery at age eleven. At sixteen entered three-year, three-month retreat. At nineteen moved to Tsurphu Monastery, then Gelugpa Monastery. In 1959 went to India and studied under Kalu Rinpoche until 1976, when moved to Hawaii and established centers there.

Karma Tenpa Gyeltsen (Tibetan) Resident at Bodhisattva Institute, Tucson, Arizona. American monk ordained by H.H. Kalu Rinpoche in Bodhgaya, India, and remains under the guidance of Lama Lodru Rinpoche.

Karmapa, H.H. the 16th Gyalwa (Rangjung Rigpe Dorje 1923–1981) (Tibetan–Kagyu) Born in Tibet. Recognized as new incarnation early on. At age seven received ordination from Tai Situpa and Vajra Crown and Karmapa robes one year later. Enthroned by Situ Rinpoche at Palpung. Studied for four years with Beru Khyentse Rinpoche and Bo Kangkar Mahapandita. Received empowerments and transmissions from Situ Rinpoche in 1937. Intensive practice and pilgrimage 1940–1944. Full monk ordination 1945. Became master of Mahamudra in 1948. Visited Beijing with Dalai Lama in 1954. Given empowerment of a thousand-armed *Avalokiteshvara* from Dalai Lama. Started to send Lamas out of Tibet in 1957 and left himself in 1959 for Bhutan, then Sikkim, where he set up headquarters at Rumtek. World tour in 1974. Established number of centers, notably Dhagpo Ling in France 1977 and Karma Triyana Dharmachakra, New York, 1981. Died in Chicago.

Karmapa, H.H. the 17th Gyalwa (Urgyen Trinley Dorje) Born 1985 in Tibet. Enthroned 1992.

Karthar Rinpoche, Khenpo (Tibetan–Karma Kagyu) Abbot of Karma Triyana Dharmachakra, New York. Born Tibet 1925. Formal Buddhist training began age twelve. At twenty received Mahayana and Vajrayana ordinations, then devoted five years to solitary meditation retreat followed by advance studies in Buddhist philosophy, psychology, logic, and metaphysics. Abbot of Tashi Choling Monastery in Bhutan. Given title Choje Lama by Karmapa. Asked to come to the U.S. 1976 by H.H. 16th Gyalwa Karmapa to establish and guide KTD and its affiliates.

Keido Chisan Koho Zenji (1879–1968) (Zen–Soto) Born Japan and ordained 1901. Chief Abbot of Soji-ji and Kanto Plains. Received honor of *Daikyosei* (Great Teacher) from emperor. Two world tours in 1950s, during which he met Jiyu Kennett Roshi and invited her to train with him. First Founder of Shasta Abbey posthumously.

Kelsang Gyatso Rinpoche, Venerable Geshe (Tibetan–Gelug) Born 1932 in Tibet. Ordained and entered Jampa Ling Monstery 1940. Moved to Sera Monastery. Left Tibet in 1959 and undertook intensive meditation retreats in Nepal and India until 1977. Awarded Geshe degree 1972. Resident in Britain since 1977 and became naturalized British citizen. Founded New Kadampa Tradition (NKT) and spiritual director of the worldwide community of NKT centers. Author of a number of books.

Kitzes, Jeff (Zen–Kwan Um School) Practiced Zen from 1975. Given teaching authority by Zen Master Seung Sahn 1992 after practicing with him from 1979. Licensed psychotherapist specializing in integration of Zen and Western psychology. Abbot and guiding teacher of Empty Gate Zen Center, California.

Kjolhede, Sensei (Zen) Spiritual director of Rochester Zen Center, New York. Born 1948 in Michigan. BA in psychology. Ordained 1976 and completed twelve years of koan training under Roshi Philip Kapleau before starting to teach in 1983. Formally installed as Philip Kapleau's Dharma Heir 1986.

Kogan Seiju Mammoser (Zen–Rinzai) founder and Abbot Albuquerque Zen Center, New Mexico. Began study with Joshu Roshi in 1974, ordained monk 1978, and ordained as Osho (zen priest) in 1982.

Konchog Gyaltsen, Khenpo (Tibetan–Drikung Kagyu) Born Tibet 1946. Studied in India until 1976 and awarded Acharya degree. Three-year, three-month retreat under guidance of Kyunga Rinpoche and awarded Khenpo of all Drikung Kagyu monasteries. Taught Buddhist philosophy and meditation to Easterners and Westerners in Ladakh 1981–1982. Began teaching at Tibetan Meditation Center, Washington, DC, in 1982. Travels worldwide teaching. Established three centers in Chile and several in USA. Several books published.

Kornfield, Jack (Vipassana) PhD. Trained as Buddhist monk in monasteries of Thailand, India, and Burma. Founder of Insight Meditation Society, Massachusetts, and Spirit Rock Meditation Center, California, and taught internationally from 1974. Husband and father. Author of several books.

L **Langlois Roshi, Rev. Kongo** (Richard Langlois) (Zen–Soto) Born in Chicago. Worked professionally as jazz musician. Served in army 1954–1956 and after enrolled in American Conservatory of Music and studied piano until 1962. Became increasingly interested in Eastern philosophy. From 1956 studied under masters of meditation and yoga. Began study with Matsuoka Roshi 1960 and ordained Soto Zen priest 1967. Abbot of Zen Buddhist Temple of Chicago from 1970. Roshi degree bestowed 1974. In 1987 presented with inka from Rinzai Primate. From 1966 studied with Professor Huo Chi-Kwang, founder of the Chinese Cultural Academy and master of calligraphy, painting, poetry, and boxing; scholar of Chinese literature, history, and philosophy. Director/head instructor of Chinese Cultural Academy.

Lian-Shen, Living Buddha see Lu, Grand Master Sheng-yen.

Lobsang Tharchin, Khen Rinpoche Geshe (Tibetan–Gelug) Entered monastery in Tibet as a young boy. Awarded Hlarampa Geshe (highest rank Doctor of Philosophy) from Sera Me Monastic University; one of the last Hlarampa Geshes educated in Tibet. Graduated from Gyume Tantric College of Lhasa and was its administrator. Permanent director and an abbot emeritus of Sera Me Monastic College and founder of the Mahayana Sutra and Tantra Centers of New Jersey, New York, and Washington, DC, Connecticut, and Asian Classic Institute. Spiritual director of Asian Classics Institute, New York. Resident in New Jersey. Translated and written a number of books.

Loori, John Daido Roshi (Zen–Soto/Rinzai) Background as scientist, arts, naturalist, and Zen priest. Dharma Heir of Hakuyu Taizan Maezumi. Spiritual leader and abbot of Zen Mountain Monastery, New York. Founder and director of Mountains and Rivers Order. Author of several books.

Lu, Grand Master Sheng-yen (Living Buddha Lian-Shen) Prominent in Southeast Asia. Born in 1945 in Taiwan. Settled in United States in 1982 to promote Buddhist teachings in the West. Originally a Christian, a profound mystical experience at the age of twenty-six led to him to study Taoism, Sutrayana, and Tantric Buddhism. After intense training and practice over fourteen years, he became an enlightened master. Revered as a Living Buddha by his disciples. Author of over a hundred and ten books in Chinese, many of which are being translated into English.

Maezumi, Hakuyu Taizan, Roshi (1931–1995) (Zen–Rinzai–White Plum Sangha) Born in Japan. Ordained Zen monk at eleven. Degrees in Oriental literature and philosophy from Komazawa University. Dharma transmission from two major lines of Rinzai Zen. Holds credentials as training master. Went to Los Angeles in 1956 as priest of Zenshuji Temple. Founded Zen Center of Los Angeles in 1967 and Kuroda Institute for Transcultural Studies in 1976. Founding influence behind Zen Arts Center, New York. Author of a number of books.

Mahasi Sayadaw, H.H. (U Sobhana Mahathera 1904–1982) (Theravada–Myanmar) Began studying in monastery at age six. Became Samanera at twelve and Bhikkhu at twenty. Studied with U Narada and after intensive meditation course worked as teacher of Buddhist scriptures. Passed government-sponsored Pali and scholastic exams with distinction. Asked to give meditation instruction in Rangoon in 1949 by prime minister and another member of Buddha Sasananuggaha Association, where he held intensive training courses; an estimated forty-five thousand received instruction in Rangoon, and six hundred thousand across the nation. Many ancillary centers set up in Myanmar and also spread abroad to Thailand, Bangladesh, India, Sri Lanka, Europe, South Africa, Australia, and the USA. Author of several books.

Moore, Robert (Zen–Kwan Um School) Given teaching authority by Zen Master Seung Sahn 1986. Teaches in West Coast Kwan Um centers. Founder of New Haven Zen Center.

Namkhai Norbu, Chogyal (Tibetan–Dzogchen) Born in Tibet, recognized as great Dzogchen master at age two. Educated in traditional way, receiving instruction and transmissions from many of the most famous teachers in Tibet. Later received initiation into and transmission of the essential teachings of Dzogchen from Chang Chub Dorje, his root master. Lived with his family in Italy from 1960. Recently retired as professor of oriental philosophy at the University of Naples. Director of several projects to aid Tibetan people. Leader of Dzogchen Community. Fluent in several languages, including Chinese, Mongolian, Italian, and English.

Namse Rinpoche, Ven. Choje Lama (Tibetan–Karma Kagyu) Born 1930 in Tibet. Became monk at fifteen. Studied and did retreats until Chinese invasion in 1959. Served as meditation master in Sonada, India, at monastery of his teacher, Kalu Rinpoche. At age thirty-seven received important empowerments and instructions from 16th Gyalwa Karmapa and in 1974 was sent to Europe, where teaches regularly. Resident teacher at Karma Kagyu Center of Toronto, Canada.

Nechung Tulku, Ven. Rinpoche (Tibetan–Nyingma) Identified as reincarnation at early age and entered Nechung Monastery at age five. Following exile from Tibet went to India until he went to Hawaii in 1975 and became teacher of Nechung Dorje Drayang Ling. Now deceased.

Ngawang Kaldan, Geshe (Tibetan) Born Tibetan. Studied for fifteen years in Drepung University and received Geshe Lharampa degree from H.H. Dalai Lama. Escaped Tibet 1959 and emigrated to Canada 1974, where he taught meditation and Tibetan language at Grant MacEwan College, Edmonton. Taught Tibetan and Buddhism at University of Toronto in late 1980s. Helped establish several centers and shares teaching responsibilities for a number of centers across Canada with Zasep Tulku Rinpoche. Spiritual director of Gaden Samten Ling, Edmonton.

Nichiren Shonin (1222–1282) (Nichiren) Japanese founder of Nichiren schools. Sent to monastery to study at age eleven and ordained at fifteen. From early age wondered why there were so many schools of Buddhism when the Buddha expounded only one. After considerable study of all the schools, he concluded that the Lotus Sutra represented the perfect culmination of the teaching of the Buddha. In 1253, started preaching at a time when Japan was in turmoil due both to political factions and natural disasters and the people in a state of panic amid famine and plague. Wrote *Rissho Ankoku Ron* (*Treatise on Spreading Peace Throughout the Country by Establishing Righteousness*), in which he attributed the disasters to the foolishness of the government and the degeneracy of the people, who were superstitious and had "misguided religious beliefs." He suggested they convert to his faith. Despite persecution, his missionary zeal continued and he wrote several more works. Buried at Mount Minobu.

Nikkyo Niwano, Rev. (Rissho Kosei-kai) Born 1906 in Japan. Founded Rissho Kosei-kai 1938 with Myoko Naganuma. Honorary president of World Conference on Religion and Peace and International Association for Religious Freedom. Succeeded by Rev. Nichiko Niwano.

 Ogui, Rev. Koshin Ogui (Jodo Shinshu and Zen) Eighteenth-generation priest of Jodo Shinshu, with extensive training in Zen practices also. Came to U.S.

1962. Zen training in Japan and with Suzuki Roshi of San Francisco Zen Center. Colleague of Eido Shimano Roshi. Studied world religions at Yale Divinity School. Resident minister of Los Angeles Buddhist Temple, Oxford and Santa Barbara Buddhist Temples, and San Francisco Buddhist Temple. Trustee of the Council of the Parliament of World Religions. Member of a task force for a Chicago interreligous metropolitan initiative.

Ohtani, H.E. Lord Patriarch Kosho (Pure Land) Chief Abbot Emeritus of Nishi Hongwanji, Kyoto.

Ole Nydahl, Lama (Tibetan–Karma Kagyu) Born and educated in Denmark. After studying philosophy in Copenhagen, studied meditation practice from 1968 with H.H. Gyalwa Karmapa and other teachers in Tibet, Nepal, and India. With his wife, he was his the Karmapa's first Western student. Authorized to teach Dharma. Has worked as a meditation teacher round the world and founded many centers worldwide in the name of the Karmapa. Fluent in several Western languages. Travels the world year-round.

P **Packer, Toni** (Nontraditional, nonsectarian) Resident at Springwater Center, New York, half the year. Also runs retreats in California and Europe. Born Germany. Student of Roshi Philip Kapleau at the Rochester Zen Center, became teacher, and eventually asked to take charge of the center. Became disillusioned with traditional, hierarchical framework and inspired by the writings of Krishnamurti, left to found the Genesee Valley Zen Center with friends. Zen forms eventually dropped and name changed to Springwater Center. Several books, videos, and audiotapes available of her talks.

Padma Karma Rinpoche (Tibetan–Dzogchen, Nyingma/Kagyu) Born 1952 and raised in the Virgin Islands. Lifetime of diverse spiritual exploration involving Episcopalian and Catholic faiths, Transcendental Meditation, Taoism, and Buddhism. Involved with Tibetan Buddhism from 1985 while in mainland China working as an educator. Acknowledged as Rinpoche by Tulku Padma Dorje Rinpoche, with full authorization to teach under the auspices of the Nyingma and Kagyu schools. Founded Shakyamuni Dzogchen Heart Lineage in 1991 in Zhejiang Province, China. Established the Center of Dzogchen Studies in New Haven, Connecticut, in 1994. His Dharma Heir Lama Padma Dzogtril established a sister center in Santa Fe, New Mexico.

Padma Norbu (Penor) Rinpoche, H.H. The Third Drubwang see **Penor Rinpoche.**

Palden Sherab Rinpoche, Ven. Khenchen (Tibetan–Nyingma) Tibetan. Trained in monasteries from age six. Fled to India 1960. Founding member and in charge of Nyingmapa Department at Central Institute of Higher Studies at Varanasi for over fifteen years. Many honors for scholarship for H.H. Dudjom Rinpoche and other Tibetan leaders. Author of several works and Tibetan-language books. Dzogchen master. Abbot and spiritual guide of Padmasambhava Buddhist Centers worldwide, together with brother, Ven. Khenpo Tsewang Dongyal Rinpoche.

Pema Dzogtril, Lama (Tibetan–Dzogchen, Nyingma/Kagyu) Dharma Heir of Padma Karma Rinpoche. Teacher in International Shakyamuni Dzogchen Heart Lineage.

Penor Rinpoche, H.H. The Third Drubwang, Padma Norbu (Tibetan–Nyingma) Supreme head of the Nyingma school. Born 1932 in eastern Tibet. Recognized as a young child as the incarnation of a famous teacher. At five, taken to Palyul Monastery and installed as eleventh throne holder. Escaped from Tibet in 1960 holding many lineages which otherwise would have disappeared. Rebuilt his monastery in south India. Bestows empowerments and gives spontaneous teachings. One of main goals to establish series of centers for study and practice in the U.S.

Prabhasadharma, Ven. Gesshin Myoko (Zen–Rinzai) Zen Master and Bhikshuni trained in Japanese and Vietnamese Rinzai Zen tradition. Entered Zen training in 1967 in Los Angeles under Japanese Zen Master, the Most Ven. Joshu Kyozan Denkyo-Shitsu Roshi. In 1973 and 1974 trained in Zen monastery in Kyoto, Japan. In 1985 received "Dharma Mind Seal Transmission of a Great Master" from the Most Ven. Dr. Thich Man Giac and became the forty-fifth Generational Heir in the Vinitaruci lineage of Vietnamese Rinzai Zen. Dedicated to deeper understanding between world religions and the strengthening of the position of women in religious traditions. Founding member of American Buddhist Congress. Founder and president of International Zen Institute of America. Author of several books and publications.

R **Reichenbach Roshi, Seijaku Stephen** (Zen–Soto) Abbot and spiritual director of Jizo-An Monastery, New Jersey, and founder of The Zen Society. Teacher and student of contemplative practices, Eastern and Western mysticism and Zen studies since early 1970s. Acclaimed Roshi by his sangha 1993. Regular guest speaker on Zen Buddhism and Chado at various academic and religious organizations.

Roach, Michael, Geshe Lobsang Chuzin (Tibetan) Fully ordained American monk. First American to earn Geshe degree, which he received from Sera Me Monastery after twenty-two years of study there and in the U.S. Taught Buddhism from 1991. Scholar of Sanskrit, Tibetan, and Russian and has translated and published numerous works. Founder of the Asian Classics Input Project and director of the Asian Classics Institute. Resides in New Jersey with his teacher, Khen Rinpoche, Geshe Lobsang Tarchen. Director of a large diamond firm and active in the restoration of Sera Me Monastery.

S **Sakya Trizin, H.H.** (Tibetan–Sakya) Born in Tibet in 1945 of royal family descent. Head of the Sakya tradition since age seven upon the death of his father. Has received intensive training in the study and practices of the Sakya tradition. Seven-month retreat while still a child. In 1959 at age fourteen left Tibet and went to India and received instruction on the Rime collections, the Collection of Tantras, and the Lamdre. Holds the three main Sakya lineages of Sakya, Tsar, and Ngor. Also holds complete teachings of both the Iron Bridge and Great Perfection lineages of Nyingma. Has founded numerous monasteries throughout India and east Asia. Seat in exile is at Rajpur, India. Since 1974 has made several world tours, teaching in Europe, USA, and Southeast Asia. Fluent in English.

Sakyong Mipham Rinpoche (Tibetan–Nyingma and Kagyu) Eldest son of Chogyam Trungpa Rinpoche. Born in India in 1962 and moved to Scotland to be with his father at the age of eight. Joined his father in the USA in 1972 after a two-year separation in which he continued his Western education and started extensive training in Buddhadharma and Shambhala arts. Empowered as the Sawang (Earth Lord) and heir to Shambhala lineage in 1979 and continued training under close guidance from father, gradually taking on responsibilities and starting to teach. After death of Chogyam Trungpa in 1987, he returned to Asia to train with H.H. Dilgo Khyentse Rinpoche, who asked him to return to the West and lead the Shambhala International community in 1990. Recognized as a tulku by H.H. Pema Norbu Rinpoche, head of the

Nyingma lineage. Enthroned as Sakyong Mipham Rinpoche 1995.

Samu Sunim, Ven. (Zen–Korean–Chogye) Born South Korea 1941 and entered the Chogye Order 1958. Dharma Successor to Zen Master Solbong Sunim (1890–1969). Came to USA 1967. President of the Buddhist Society for Compassionate Wisdom and founding teacher and Zen master of the society's three temples in Toronto, Ann Arbor, Michigan, and Chicago and of sangha in Mexico City. On the International Advisory Board of the Council for a Parliament of the World's Religions.

Sangharakshita (D. P. E. Lingwood) (Friends of the Western Buddhist Order) Founder of the Friends of the Western Buddhist Order (FWBO). English Buddhist monk born 1925 in London who spent twenty years in India, practicing, studying, teaching, and writing. Ordained as Theravadin monk in 1949 after living as a wandering ascetic and meeting many spiritual teachers. When Dr. B. R. Ambedkar died a few weeks after founding a movement for mass conversion to Buddhism of ex-"Untouchables" to remove them from the terrible stigma imposed on them by the caste system, Sangharakshita stepped into the breach. Following the Chinese invasion of Tibet, he met many eminent Lamas who had fled to India. Received Bodhisattva precepts from the Ven. Dhardo Rinpoche and Vajrayana initiations from others, including Jamyang Khyentse Rinpoche, Dilgo Khyentse Rimpoche, and Dudjom Rinpoche. Returned to the UK in 1964 and established the FWBO in 1967. Author of many books.

Sasaki Roshi, Joshu (Kyozan Joshu Roshi) (Zen–Rinzai) Born 1907 in Japan; entered Zen training at fourteen. Came to USA 1962 and taught in Los Angeles area. Established Cimarron Zen Center, California, Mount Baldy Zen Center, California, and Jemez Bodhi Mandala, New Mexico in 1970s (umbrella organization, Rinzai-ji). Resident Mount Baldy, California.

Sayagyi U Ba Khin (Theravada–Myanmar) Founder of the International Meditation Center (IMC) in Yangon, Myanmar (formerly Rangoon, Burma), and it is after him that Sayagyi U Ba Khin Tradition of Theravada Buddhist meditation is named. Lived in Myanmar from 1899 to 1971 and taught meditation from 1941 until his death. Established the IMC Yangon in 1952 with the construction of a Dhamma Yaung Chi Ceti (Light of the Dhamma Pagoda). At the same time as being an eminent meditation teacher, was Accountant General of Myanmar from 1948 to 1953 and subsequently held a number of senior posts in government. Learned meditation from a lay teacher, Saya U Thetgyi, who, in turn, studied under the well-known and much-respected Myanmar monk, Ven. Ledi Sayadaw.

Seung Sahn, Zen Master (Dae Soen Sa Nim) (Zen–Kwan Um School of Zen) First Korean Zen master to teach in the West. After World War II, disillusioned with politics and academic study, did a hundred-day retreat and received Dharma transmission from Zen Master Ko Bong. Worked to reorganize Korean Buddhism and spent several years in Japan, founding temples and teaching Zen. Came to U.S. 1972 and formed Providence Zen Center, Rhode Island, now head temple of Kwan Um School of Zen, with over thirty-six Zen centers worldwide. Has published several books. Recognized for his efforts to connect Zen practice with Christian contemplative prayer.

Shaneman, Jhampa (Tibetan) One of first Western monks in Tibetan tradition. From 1970 lived in India learning Tibetan language and studying Buddhism within all four

Tibetan sects. Entered traditional three-year retreat 1980 and on completion returned to Canada. Lives at Thubten Choling, British Columbia, Canada and translates for visiting Lamas.

Shelton, Patricia (Zen) Studied with several great Eastern masters, including Koan practice with Soeng Sahn Soen Sa Nim in Korean Zen tradition from 1976; Kalu Rinpoche and Trungpa Rinpoche, whom she sponsored to the U.S. Director and spiritual teacher of Clear Light Society, Massachussetts, which services the terminally ill and their families.

Sheng-Yen, Ven. Ch'an Master Dr. (Ch'an) Born in China. Monk at age thirteen and received training in both Lin-chi (Rinzai) and Ts'ao-tung (Soto) schools. Studied under monastic system until Communist takeover and moved to Taiwan to continue study and practice. Six years of solitary retreat in mountains, then went to Tokyo for advanced Buddhist study. Dharma Heir of Master Tung-chu and Master Ling-yuan and second-generation descendant of Master Hsu-yun, patriarch of modern Ch'an. Doctorate in Buddhist literature. Abbot of two monasteries in Taiwan and founded Ch'an Meditation Center, New York, 1978, where he is resident teacher. Travels twice yearly between New York and Taiwan.

Shimano Roshi, Eido Tai (Zen–Rinzai) Founder, teacher, and abbot of New York Shobo-ji, and International Dai Bosatsu Zendo Kongo-ji, New York. Encountered Americans who went to Japan during 1960s to study at Ryutaku-ji, Rinzai Zen Monastery, near Mount Fuji. Sent by abbot, Soen Nakagawa, to bring the Dharma to the U.S. Studied at University of Hawaii 1960, began teaching Zen in New York 1965. Attendant monk and translator for Yasutani Roshi for several years. 1968 established New York Zendo Shobo-ji. 1972 Dharma Heir of Soen Nakagawa Roshi. Author of several books.

Shinran Shonin (b. 1173) (Pure Land–Jodo Shinshu) Japanese founder of Jodo Shinshu. Born near Kyoto and orphaned early in life. Became a monk on Mount Hiei, the greatest center of Buddhist learning at the time and studied learning, discipline, and meditation. After more than twenty years, he was still very much aware of his imperfections and inability to attain what he so desperately sought. In desperation, he left the monastery and soon after met Honen Shonin, who was the founder of Jodo Shu and whom he acknowledged as his teacher. He married and had children and referred to himself as neither monk or layman.

Sogyal Rinpoche (Tibetan–Nyingma–Rigpa) Born in Tibet in the early 1950s. Raised mostly at Dzongsar Monastery in the care of renowned lama Jamyang Khyentse Chokyi Lodro, who recognized him as the reincarnation of Terton Sogyal, a discoverer of many hidden texts and a Dzogchen master. Studied poetry, drama, logic, and various Buddhist texts from private tutors. Taken to Sikkim in 1954 due to growing Chinese occupation. Following the death of his root lama, he continued his studies with Dudjom Rinpoche and Dilgo Khyentse Rinpoche and also began to study English in 1959. University in Delhi studying Indian philosophy and took up scholarship to Cambridge University in England to study comparative religion. Served as translator and aide to Dudjom Rinpoche, the inspiration for his work in the West, for a number of years. Established number of teaching centers in Europe and North America, the Rigpa Fellowship, who practice under his guidance. Spends most of his time traveling and teaching around the world, specializing in presenting Tibetan views on death and dying and Dzogchen. Author of several books.

Sopa, Geshe Lhundrup (Tibetan–Gelug) Born Tibet 1923. Entered monastery age nine. Moved to Sera Je 1941 to study and teach. Fled Tibet 1959 to Bengal. Awarded Lharampa Geshe degree 1962, and moved to the U.S. in 1963. Professor of Tibetan Buddhist Studies at University of Wisconsin from late 1960s and has also taught in Europe. Founder and resident teacher at The Deer Park, Wisconsin. Author of several books.

Sot'aesan Taejongsa (Chungbin Pak) (1891–1943) Founder of Won Buddhism. Born in Korea. "Accomplished the great awakening" after twenty years' searching. Wrote doctrine and institutional system of Won Buddhism and established its headquarters in Iri City.

Surya Das, Lama (Tibetan–Dzogchen) American-born lama. Studied and practiced with great teachers of major Tibetan schools (including Kalu Rinpoche, Dudjom Rinpoche, Dilgo Khyentse Rinpoche, and the Dalai Lama) from early 1970s. Has completed two traditional three-year retreats. Dharma Heir of Khenpo Nyoshul Khen Rinpoche. Author, poet, and translator particularly interested in effective transmission of Buddhism into Western forms. Founder and spiritual director of Dzogchen Foundation; headquarters in Massachussetts.

Suzuki Roshi, Shunryu (1904–1971) (Zen–Soto) Born in Japan and began Zen training at early age. Zen master in 1930s with responsibility for many temples and monastery. Led pacifist group in World War II. Settled in San Francisco area 1959 and formally established San Francisco Zen Center 1962.

Tai Situpa Rinpoche, H.E. Twelfth (Pema Dongak Nyingshe Wangpo) (Tibetan–Kagyu) Born in Tibet 1954. Identified by the 16th Karmapa as reincarnation of Situ Tulku. When six, left for Bhutan due to Chinese occupation, then on to Sikkim. Joined Rumtek Monastery. Received full range of empowerments from 16th Karmapa and undertook rigorous program of study. Trained in arts associated with Tibetan Buddhism. Assumed full traditional responsibility 1975. Early 1980s founded Sherab Ling Monastery in north India and established his headquarters there. Since 1980 has toured extensively in West and visited Tibet 1984. Founded Maitreya Institute in USA in 1984—now has branches in USA and France. Organizes and participates in international conferences. One of regents heading the Karma Kagyu tradition until the new Karmapa is instated. Author of a few books.

Tarrant Roshi, John (Zen) Born Australia 1949. Degree in human sciences and English literature. Moved to Hawaii to study with Robert Aitken Roshi, started teaching 1983 and was authorized to teach independently 1988. Founder/resident teacher California Diamond Sangha, California. Published poet.

Tashi Namgyal, Geshe Lama (Tibetan–Sakya) Born 1992 in Tibet. Entered Sakya Monastery at age eight and full monk's vows at twenty-one. Geshe degree at twenty-five years. Taught at Sakya Monastery and appointed abbot of Jashong Monastery and its convent. Fled to India after imprisonment by Chinese occupation army 1960. Acarya degree in Benares. Founded Sakya Thubten Kunga Choling, British Columbia, Canada, 1974 and Tashi Choling, Arkansas, 1988 among others. Teacher at centers throughout USA and Canada; resident Sakya Thubten Kunga Choling (Victoria

Buddhist Dharma Society), British Columbia, Canada. Author of several books.

Tenzin Wangyal Rinpoche (Tibetan–Bon) Practiced Dzogchen from thirteen years old with masters from Bon and Buddhist schools. Graduated eleven-year course of traditional studies 1986 at Bonpo Monastic Center, India. Appointed by H.H. Dalai Lama to be representative of Bon school to government-in-exile. Invited to Italy 1988 by Chogyal Namkhai Norbu Rinpoche. Rockefeller Fellow at Rice Univerity, Houston, 1991–1992. President and resident lama of Ligmincha Institute, Virginia, which he founded 1992. Only qualified teacher in West of Bon and travels extensively in Europe and Americas. Several books and articles in Tibetan and English.

Thibaut, Master Kosen (Zen) Born France 1950 and became Deshimaru's disciple and monk ordination 1971; studied with him fifteen years. Taught Zen from 1982. Received the shiho from Master Niwa Zenji, highest authority of Zen in Japan 1984. Head and Master of a European Sangha.

Thich Nhat Hanh (Vietnamese) Born Vietnam in 1926. Became a monk at sixteen. During the Vietnam War, left monastery and was actively engaged in helping war victims and publicly advocating peace. In 1966, toured U.S. at the invitation of the Fellowship of Reconciliation "to describe the aspirations and the agony of the voiceless masses of the Vietnamese people." As a result, threatened with arrest in Vietnam and unable to return. Served as the chairman of the Vietnamese Buddhist Peace Delegation during the war in 1967 was nominated for Nobel Peace Prize by Martin Luther King, Jr. Student at Columbia University in the USA, but recalled to Vietnam to help with an attempt at an alternative to the corruption of Saigon and the Communism of Hanoi. Established Van Hahn University and the School of Youth for Social Service, which went out to help the peasantry in war-torn rural areas. Coined the term *Engaged Buddhism*. Author of over sixty books. In exile at Plum Village in France. Poet and peace activist.

Thien Nghi, Ven. Thich (Vietnamese) Born 1933 Vietnam. Became novice monk 1940. Professor of many monasteries in Saigon 1965–1967. Left for Taiwan 1968 to study and returned to Vietnam 1973. Moved to Montreal, Canada 1980. President of Union of Vietnamese Buddhist Churches in Canada, president of Chanh Phap Buddhist Society, abbot of Tam Bao Temple and Monastery.

Thien-An, Ven. Dr. Thich (1926–1980) (Zen–Vietnamese) Trained in Lin-chi (Rinzai) tradition but adopted ecumenical approach. Came to U.S. 1966 and lectured at U.C.L.A. Founder International Buddhist Meditation Center and College of Oriental Studies, California. Active in helping Vietnamese refugees to U.S. after fall of Saigon.

Thrangu Rinpoche, Ven. Khenchen (Tibetan–Kagyu) Born 1933 in Tibet. Recognized as reincarnation of Thrangu tulku at age five. Thrangu Monastery ages seven to sixteen. Full ordination at age twenty-three from Karmapa. On Chinese military takeover left for Sikkim. Awarded Rabjam degree age thirty-five. Named *Kenpo* (teacher) at all Kagyu monasteries and became abbot of Rumtek Monastery and the Nalanda Institute for Higher Buddhist Studies. Personal teacher of the four principal Karma Kagyu tulkus: Shamar Rinpoche, Situ Rinpoche, Jamgon Kongtrul Rinpoche, and Gyaltsab Rinpoche. Traveled extensively; abbot of Gampo Abbey, Nova Scotia, Canada, and Thrangu House in the U.K. Founded Thrangu Tashi Choling Monastery and building of nunnery and college in Nepal. Published several works and in project to publish collection of all Tibetan texts necessary to undertake retreats in Karma Kagyu lineage. **Trungpa Rinpoche, Chogyam** (1939–1987) (Tibetan–Kagyu) Born in Tibet and recognized as the eleventh throneholder of the Trungpa lineage at the age of eighteen months. Left Tibet in 1959 after Chinese invasion and came to England to study at Oxford University. Co-founded Samye Ling in 1968 in Scotland. In 1969 relinquished monastic vows and married. Moved to U.S. and founded Karme Choling Buddhist Meditation and Study Center in Vermont and Vajradhatu, an international Tibetan Buddhist association. 1974 established the Nalanda Foundation for nonsectarian education which includes Shambhala Training, a secular meditation program, and the Naropa Institute, an arts college. Author of many books.

Tsewang Dongyal Rinpoche, Ven. Khenpo (Tibetan–Nyingma) Tibetan. Enthroned by Dudjom Rinpoche 1978. Holder of complete transmissions and initiations of the kama and terma lineages of the Nyingma school. Recognized expert in ancient Tantric literature. Published historian and poet. Abbot and spiritual guide of Padmasambhava Buddhist Centers worldwide, together with brother, Ven. Khenchen Palden Sherab Rinpoche, for whom he often translates.

Tsulga, Ven. Geshe (Tibetan–Gelug–FPMT) Born in Tibet 1939 and became a novice monk at age seven. Geshe studies at Sera Je Monastery from age seventeen. Fled Tibet 1959 after the Tibetan uprising against Chinese occupation. After a decade in refugee camp in northeast India, went to help rebuild Sera Je Monastery in exile in south India. Graduated Geshe Lharampa with highest honors in 1988, then studied for one year at Gyume Tantric College and returned to teach at Sera Je Monastery. Invited to America by FPMT in 1992 and divides teaching time between Kadampa Center, North Carolina, Milarepa Center, Vermont, and Kurukulla Center, Massachussetts.

Tsultrim Gyamtso Rinpoche, Khenpo (Tibetan–Karma Kagyu) Born Tibet 1934. Trained under a yogin in Tibet in teens. Lam Rim Yeshe Nyingpo at age twenty from H.H. Dilgo Khyentse Rinpoche. Practiced Chod in charnel grounds. Received Mahamudra. Khenpo degree from Karmapa. Geshe Lharampa degree from H.H. Dalai Lama. Studied Gelug and Kagyu lineages and extensive Sakya teachings. In depth study of Tibetan texts and trained many Westerners to translate mainly in English. Established Marpa Translator's Institute in Nepal 1985 and has students in retreat. With Thrangu Rinpoche trained new generation of Karma Kagyu Khenpos. Well known in Kagyu centers in the U.S., Far East, and Europe. Author of several books.

W **Weitsman Roshi, Sojun Mel** (Zen–Soto) Born 1929 in Los Angeles. Broad life experience, including art study and painting, house painting, boat painter, cab driver, and music instructor. Married with son. Began practice at San Francisco Zen Center, California, in 1964 and ordained by Suzuki Roshi 1969 as resident priest at Berkeley Zendo, California. Received Dharma transmission in Japan 1984 and officially installed as abbot of Berkeley Zen Center, California, 1985. Also co-abbot at San Francisco Zen Center and Tassajara, California.

Y **Yasutani Roshi, Hakuun** (1885–1973) (Zen–Soto) Born in Japan. Sent to live in temple at age five and became novice at large Soto temple age thirteen; later Soto seminary and teacher training school. Married at thirty and had five children. Remained nominally a priest but worked as schoolteacher for about ten years. At forty trained with Sogaku Harada Roshi, resigned principalship of school, and became temple priest. Received inka from Harada Roshi at fifty-eight and appointed Dharma Heir. Led sesshins in Japan. Traveled annually to the USA 1962–1969. Extended stay in U.S. at age eighty.

Yeshe, Lama Thubten (1935–1985) (Tibetan–Gelug) Tibetan exiled from Tibet, went to live in India. Met first Western students 1965, and by 1971 had settled at Kopen, near Kathmandu, in Nepal. Due to demand began teaching with his disciple, Lama Thubten Zopa Rinpoche, to increasing numbers of travelers, who in turn started groups and centers in their own countries. In 1975, Lama Yeshe named this fledgling network the Foundation for the Preservation of the Mahayana Tradition. Author of several books. Since his passing away, Lama Zopa Rinpoche is the spiritual director of the foundation. Lama Yeshe's reincarnation, a Spanish child named Osel Hita Torres, is now studying and training to prepare him to continue the work he started in his previous life.

Zasep Tulku (Tibetan) Recognized as reincarnation of previous abbot of Zuru Gompa in Tibet and installed age five. Studied at Ser Je from age ten. Left Tibet and took full ordination in India. Studied with Geshe Ngawang Wangyal among others. Acarya degree 1975. Studied Hinayana in Thailand for eighteen months. Established centers in Canada, where he regularly teaches.

Zopa Rinpoche, Lama Thubten (Tibetan–Gelug) disciple of Lama Thubten Yeshe and succeeded him as spiritual director of the Foundation for the Preservation of the Mahayana Tradition after his death. Born 1946 in Nepal. Recognized at age four as reincarnation. Studied in Tibet until 1959, when he went to India and came under tutelage of Lama Yeshe. Tours extensively teaching at the foundation's sixty-odd centers worldwide.

MAIN BUDDHIST FESTIVALS

General

All Buddhist traditions celebrate Buddha's Birth, Buddha's Attainment of Enlightenment (Bodhi Day), and Buddha's death (Parinirvana). Some traditions mark all three on the same day of the year (Wesak or Buddha Day). Also celebrated is Preaching of Buddha's First Sermon in Benares, India (called variously Asala, Dharma Day, Dhammachakra, or Turning of the Wheel of Dharma Day). Other celebrations vary according to the major figures (Bodhisattvas or founders) in a particular tradition and national/ethnic influences, and these are shown in the listings below.

Dates for celebrations may also vary from tradition to tradition and from year to year due to the use of a lunar calendar.

Celebration of festivals at different centers varies as to how public or private they are, some being open to the public and others involving religious ceremonies suitable only for experienced practitioners. Others have a program of events, some of which are suitable for beginners, others for only more experienced practitioners. Some centers don't celebrate the festivals of their tradition, and some celebrate many. At some centers, festivals may be a cultural event for a particular Asian-origin community.

Tibetan Buddhism

Chokhor Duchen	Buddha's First Sermon, June/July
Dalai Lama's Birthday	6 July
Lha Bab Duchen	Ascent into the Tushita Heaven, October
Losar	New Year Festival, 4 days followed by a long religious ceremony, February
Ngacho Chemo	Je Tsongkhapa Day, November
Padmasambhava Day	In honor of the founder of Buddhism in Tibet
Saga Dawa	Buddha Day, May

Japanese Buddhism

Hana Matsuri	Buddha's Birth, 8 April

Higan	Spring equinox marking time of change and remembrance of dead, around 21 March
Nehan	Buddha's Enlightenment, 15 February
Obon	Also called Hungry Ghosts Festival, 4 days beginning 13 July
Rohatsu	Buddha's Enlightenment
Setsubon	Driving out evil spirits, early February
Shubun no hi	Autumn equinox marking time of change and remembrance of dead, around 20 September

JAPANESE ZEN
As for Japanese festivals plus:

Bodhidharma Day	October
Daito Zenji	22 November
Dogen Zenji	28 August
Keizan Zenji	15 August
Rinzai Zenji	10 January

NICHIREN

Buddha Nirvana Day	
Nichiren Shonin's Birthday	16 February
Buddha's Birthday	8 April
Proclamation of the establishment of a new order	28 April
NS's Exile to Izu Peninsula	12 May
Matsubagayatsu Persecution	27 August
Tatsunokuchi Persecution	12 September
Sado Exile	10 October
Oeshiki (NS's death)	13 October
Komatsubara Persecution	11 November

PURE LAND
Main Buddhist festivals plus:

Shinran Shonin's Birthday	21 May
Ho Om Ko	Shinran Shonin's Death, varies according to Head Temple followed

Theravadan Buddhism

Rains Retreats follow the Buddha's custom of monks and nuns going into retreat for about 3 months during the rainy season. Dates vary according to when the rainy season is in various countries.

Kathina Day (October/November) marks the end of Rains Retreat with the laity presenting monks with cloth for making into robes on the same day.

Uposatha Days are observed weekly at full, new, and quarter moons; full and new moons being the most important. On these days religious activities are more intense. The way they are observed varies considerably among the different traditions.

MYANMAR
Asalha	Buddha's first sermon/ start of Rains Retreat, July
Kathina	November
New Year	April
Thitingyut	End of Rains Retreat, October
Wesak	Buddha's Birth, Enlightenment and Death Day, May/June

THAILAND
End of Rains Retreat	October
Kathina	November
Loykrathong	Festival of Lights, November
Magha Puja	All Saints Day, February
Songkrang	New Year, April
Vassa	Rains retreat, July–October
Visakha Puja	Buddha's Enlightenment, May
Wan Atthami	Buddha's Cremation, May/June

SRI LANKA
Poya	Five full moon days of special importance named after the lunar months in which they occur. They are Duruthu, Navam, Wesak, Poson, and Esala.
Duruthu	Sanghamitta's arrival in Sri Lanka (female counterpart of Poson), December.
Esala/Asalha	Buddha's first sermon, July
Kathina	September
New Year	April
Poson	Establishment of Buddhism in Sri Lanka, June/July
Wesak	Buddha's Birth, Enlightenment and Death Day, May/June

Western Buddhism

Sangha Day	Expression of the spiritual community of all Buddhists, November

BUDDHIST CENTERS IN THE UNITED STATES OF AMERICA

ALABAMA

Montgomery Dhamma Society (Vipassana)
528 Seminole Place
Montgomery, AL 36117
Tel: (334) 277–6987
E-mail: jiml@mont.mindspring.com
Web site: http://www.mindspring.com/~jiml/home.htm

A small community meeting in the homes of members. Started 1996.

Vipassana meditation once a week and, once each month, all-day meditation. Introductory Vipassana classes. Newcomers welcome.

ALASKA

Anchorage Zen Community (Zen–Soto)
2401 Susitna Drive
Anchorage, AK 99517
Tel: (907) 566–0143

Community of about twenty-five people with no fixed premises as yet. Meet once a week for a sitting and service. Regular precepts discussion group and monthly mindfulness day. All activities are suitable for newcomers.

Organize three sesshins per year at a rural retreat center. Three-, five-, or seven-day retreats are offered by a visiting priest.

Publish newsletter four times a year.

Teachers   Ron Dokai Georgeson and Jan Chozen Bays visit
Opening Times   See above

Residents	None
Festivals	None
Facilities	None
Accommodation	None
Food	None
Booking	Contact center
Fees	Contact center
Expected Behavior	Contact center
How to Get There	Contact center

Juneau Dharma Study Group (Tibetan–Kagyu/Nyingma)
Affiliation: Shambhala International
Susan Chapman, Coordinator
P O Box 22146
Juneau, AK 99802-2146
Tel: (907) 780–6299
E-mail: chapman@alaska.net

See International headquarters, **Shambhala Center,** Halifax, Nova Scotia, Canada.

ARIZONA

Lhundrub Ling (Tibetan–Nyingma)
P O Box 23558
Flagstaff, AZ 86002
Tel: (520) 773–1145

Contact center for details.

Jodo Shu Dharma Center (Pure Land)
Affiliation: Jodo Shu Betsuin in Los Angeles
229 East Palo Verde Street
Gilbert, AZ 85296
Tel: (602) 545–7684

Meet in a private home in suburb of Phoenix. Small family atmosphere. Started in 1992.

Community of around ten who meet for 11:00 am Sunday service and study. Chanting 6:30 pm first Wednesday each month. Otsutome service and Nembutsu chanting are suitable for newcomers.

Founder/Guru	Contact center
Teachers	Terrence Joko Lewis resident, and Bishop Satoru Ryosho Kawai visits
Opening Times	See schedule above
Residents	1 lay person
Festivals	Hana Matsuri, Rohatsu, Honen's Memorial Day, Gyoki-e
Facilities	Dojo
Accommodation	None
Food	None
Booking	Not applicable
Fees	Not applicable
Expected Behavior	No smoking, dress respectfully, 5 precepts
How to Get There	East of Phoenix on Route 60, Gilbert Road exit, south on Gilbert Rd. Cross Elliot Road, Palo Verde St. is first left off Elliot.

Zen Center of Paradise Valley (Zen)
4801 E Moonlight Way
Paradise Valley, AZ 85253
Tel: (602) 951–3482

Contact center for details.

Haku-un-ji Tempe Zen Center (Zen–Rinzai)
1448 East Cedar Street
Tempe, AZ 85281
Tel: (602) 894–6353
E-mail: twwx80a@prodigy.com

Residential Zen center with approximately forty members in a quiet residential area of Phoenix. Founded 1994.

Sittings Mondays, Wednesdays, and Thursdays 7:00 pm; Sundays 8:30 am, including meditation, chanting, and oryoki. Thursday evening discussion on Buddhist texts. Monthly one-day sittings; two-day sittings quarterly.

Founder/Guru	Kyozan Joshu Roshi (Sasaki)
Teachers	Resident: Sokai Geoffrey Barratt, others visit
Opening Times	See sitting times above
Residents	1 monk and 2 laity
Festivals	None
Facilities	Zendo and library

Accommodation	None
Food	Vegetarian
Booking	None
Fees	$25 one-day sitting including board and lodging; $3 individual visit (donation only)
Expected Behavior	No smoking, 5 precepts
How to Get There	Phone for accurate directions

Karma Thegsum Choling (Tibetan–Karma Kagyu)
Affiliation: Karma Triyana Dharmachakra, New York
605 W Broadway
Tempe, AZ 85282
Tel: (602) 829–1479 (Bill Glover) or (602) 839–4152 (Ruth McFarland)
Fax: (602) 829–9402
E-mail: kumara@goodnet.com

Meet in Tempe, Prescott, and Sedona. Started over forty years ago, KTC affiliate since 1981. "The main purpose of the center is to encourage the practice of meditation, to apply the principle of mindful awareness to everyday life, to develop intuition, and to provide a teaching center for Tibetan Buddhist Lamas, interfaith teachers, and Erma Pounds, our resident teacher. The only requirement for attendance is a belief in the possibility of universal peace between all races and faiths."

Tempe: Meditation practice followed by study group 7:00 pm Mondays and Thursdays. Chenrezig practice 7:00 pm Tuesdays. Seminar in the mountains one weekend per month.

Prescott: Meeting with Erma Pounds 7:00 pm first Friday of the month; Chenrezig practice 7:00 pm second and fourth Tuesday of the month.

Sedona: Meeting with Erma Pounds 7:00 pm second Friday of the month.

Founder/Guru	Erma Pounds
Teachers	Erma Pounds, and others visit
Opening Times	See session times above
Residents	None
Festivals	None
Facilities	Small center in Tempe
Accommodation	None
Food	None
Booking	Contact center
Fees	By donation
Expected Behavior	No drugs, alcohol, pets, heavy perfumes, or unkind ways. Please attend with an open mind and share in a compassionate atmosphere.
How to get there	Contact center—due to move in 1997

Bodhisattva Institute (Tibetan–Karma Kagyu)
Affiliation: Kalu Rinpoche Center
714 North Desert Avenue
Tucson, AZ 85711
Tel: (520) 325–2272
Fax: (520) 326–1678
E-mail: tenpa@azstarnet.com

Three-bedroom house with plans to construct a large temple monastic complex for laity and monastics offering full programs and retreats. Current shrine room holds twenty-five people. Larger gatherings are held elsewhere. Founded in 1994.

Four daily meditations open to all—Tara puja 6:00 am, Chenrezig puja 7:00–7:30 am, Mahakala puja 7:00 pm. About fifty to a hundred participants weekly. Sunday service 10:00 am. Classes held quarterly in meditation, Buddhism, volunteering, thangka painting, yoga, and Tai Chi. Monthly one-day retreats. Teachings and empowerments from visiting teachers.

Small Dharma store. Publish monthly bulletin and quarterly newsletter.

Founder/Guru	H.E. Kalu Rinpoche
Teachers	Lama Tenpa Gyeltsen resident; many visiting teachers including guru
Opening Times	During pujas and classes
Residents	3 monks/nuns and 2 lay people
Festivals	Losar and Saga Dawa
Facilities	Shrine room, library, peace garden
Accommodation	Planned
Food	None
Booking	Contact center
Fees	$10–25 per class
Expected Behavior	Contact center
How to get there	4 miles from I-10 East on Speedway to Columbus south, then 3rd St. East to Desert Ave.

Tucson Dharma Study Group (Tibetan–Kagyu/Nyingma)
Affiliation: Shambhala International
Douglas Pittman, Coordinator
P O Box 77026
Tucson, AZ 85703
Tel: (602) 323–8379
E-mail: edw1028@aol.com

See International headquarters, **Shambhala Center,** Halifax, Nova Scotia, Canada.

Zen Desert Sangha (Zen)
Affiliation: Diamond Sangha
P O Box 44122
Tucson, AZ 85733-4122
Tel: (520) 620–6347 or (520) 327–8460
E-mail: zds@azstarnet.com

Private urban residence in Mexican/Southwest style. For lay practitioners. Active membership of around sixty; twelve to twenty-five attend each service. Founded 1982 "to fulfill the spirit of a truly democratic sangha that is open to all. We place a special emphasis on sangha."

Sitting schedule: Mondays and Thursdays 7:30–8:30 pm; Wednesdays 7:30–9:00 pm with short service, tea, and Dharma reading; Saturdays 9:00–10:30 am with full service and tea after; first Saturday of month business meeting open to all. Zazenkai second Saturday of month, 7:00 am–noon. Weekly Dharma reading and monthly minyan, zazenkai, and full moon ceremonies. Orientation for beginners. Three retreats/year with Pat Hawk, Roshi, usually spring, summer, and fall.

Founder/Guru	Contact center
Teachers	Pat Hawk, Roshi, visits
Opening Times	See sitting schedule
Residents	None
Festivals	None
Facilities	Zendo and library
Accommodation	During retreats, sleeping on grounds or in zendo
Food	Vegetarian during retreats
Booking	Retreats announced 3 months in advance
Fees	4 day retreats $100; 7 day retreats $150
Expected Behavior	Behavior as befits a Buddhist study center, including no smoking
How to get there	Available only when first contacted by phone

Wat Promgunaram of Arizona (Theravada)
17212 West Maryland Ave
Waddell, AZ 85355
Tel: (602) 935–2276
Fax: (602) 935–1174

Contact center for details.

ARKANSAS

Devachan Temple (All traditions)
5 Dickey Street
Eureka Springs, AR 72632
Tel: (501) 253–7028

Victorian retreat house with converted garage for shrine/meditation hall in Ozark Mountains surrounded by hiking trails, rolling hills, and beaver lake/dam. Established 1980 by American nun with monastic experience in Japan, Sri Lanka, and Taiwan. At time of writing, she was looking for assistant resident to take over while she is on trips to Asia.

Individual retreats only, any time, for any length of time. Retreats may include instruction in Dhamma, counseling as requested. Retreats aim to encourage individual practice, but beginners who are ready to commit to Buddhism are very welcome.

Founder/Guru	Bhikkhuni Miao Kwang Sudharma
Teachers	Bhikkhuni Miao Kwang Sudharma
Opening Times	Not applicable
Residents	Teacher
Festivals	Not applicable
Facilities	Dharma house which accommodates 5, shrine room, and meditation hall
Accommodation	$35/day; $125/week; $425/month
Food	Self-catering in Dharma house, local vegetarian cafes, only vegetarian food allowed
Booking	No deposit, just call
Fees	No fees, Miao gives as much time as needed by pilgrims
Expected Behavior	No smoking, 5 precepts
How to get there	Closest airports Drake Field—Fayetteville, Arkansas, or Springfield, Missouri. From there, 1- or 3-hour drive, respectively. Car rentals available. Call when you arrive.

Morning Star Zen Center (Zen)
Affiliation: Kwan Um School of Zen
1599 Halsell Road
Fayetteville, AR 72701
Tel: (501) 521–6925
E-mail: bt24761@uafsysa.uark.edu and jrjack@comp.uark.edu

Started 1986. Strong connection with **Kansas Zen Center.**

Weekly meditation practice 11:00 am–noon Sundays. Traditional Korean retreats, called Yong Maeng Jong Jin, of the Kwan Um School offered about once a year in the local area. Classes on retreat customs and practices. Kwan Um School publishes *Primary Point*.

Founder/Guru	Zen Master Seung Sah Soen Sa
Teachers	Contact center
Opening Times	Contact center
Residents	Jim Jackson and Barbara Taylor are lay residents
Festivals	Contact center
Facilities	Small meditation room and use dojos on other premises
Accommodation	During retreats
Food	Vegetarian during retreats
Booking	Contact center
Fees	Contact center
Expected Behavior	Contact center
How to get there	Contact center

Zen Center of Hot Springs (Zen–Soto and Rinzai)
Nonaffiliated with the Diamond Sangha, Honolulu, or Tofukuji Monastery, Kyoto, Japan
207 Ledgerock Road
Hot Springs National Park, AR 71913
Tel: (501) 767–6096

Center in developmental stage—five-bedroom house on the lake in great need of repair. "Twenty years ago, I returned to Hot Springs after studying at the University of Hawaii at Manoa and practicing Zen with Robert Aitken, Roshi of the Diamond sangha. I began to build a practice in Arkansas with the objective of having a center available for international visitors."

Stress management/Hatha Yoga weekly includes zazen exercises. Keido Fukushima, abbot of Tofukuji Monastery, Kyoto, Japan, visits Arkansas annually and has lectured at Hot Springs twice, attended by 250 in 1996. Howard Lee Kilby (founder/owner) lectures on Zen Buddhism at various churches on invitation.

All the happiness there is in this world comes from thinking of others;
all the suffering in this world comes from thinking only of oneself.

Shantideva, quoted in leaflet from The Dzogchen Foundation, Massachussetts

CALIFORNIA

Community of Mindful Living (CML) (Zen–Vietnamese)
Affiliation: Community of Mindful Living
Street: 850 Talbot Street
Albany, CA 94706
Mailing: P O Box 7355
Berkeley, CA 94707
Tel: (510) 527–3751
Fax: (510) 525–7129
E-mail: parapress@aol.com
Web site: http://www.parallax.org

Offices and meeting hall in former Nazarene church with small courtyard and garden. Resource for people around the world who are interested in mindfulness practice, also serving as clearinghouse for retreat schedules of other Dharma teachers ordained by Thich Nhat Hanh around the world. Formed 1983; Parallax Press begun 1985; CML incorporated 1990. "From our office in California, nine staff members and a number of volunteers work together on a variety of projects, including organizing and conducting mindfulness retreats; publishing and distributing books, tapes, and a newsletter on mindful living; establishing a rural, residential retreat center; and developing conducting programs for the greater community, including veterans of war and those who are in real need in Vietnam and elsewhere. CML does extensive work to organize Thich Nhat Hanh's biannual North American visits. In addition, CML's Dharma teachers lead retreats throughout the U.S. and sometimes abroad."
   Meet Tuesday evenings for sitting and walking meditation followed by Dharma talk. Evenings of music, movement, and group discussions. Monthly five precepts recitation ceremony. Full moon outdoor walking meditation in local park. One-day or weekend mindfulness retreats several times a year.
   Published nearly a hundred books and tapes through **Parallax Press** on socially engaged Buddhism. Contact this center for catalog. Also publish *Mindfulness Bell*, journal of Order of Interbeing, three times a year.

Founder/Guru	Thich Nhat Hanh
Teachers	Resident: Arnold Kotler, Wendy Johnson, Therese Fitzgerald
Opening Times	Contact center
Residents	None
Festivals	Contact center
Facilities	See above
Accommodation	During retreats only
Food	Vegetarian at retreats only included in price

Booking	Contact center
Fees	Tuesday evening program free of charge—donations accepted; days and weekends of Mindfulness vary according to expenses
Expected Behavior	5 precepts during events
How to Get There	Off Solano Ave., near San Pablo Ave.

Santa Cruz Shambhala Study Group (Tibetan–Kagyu/Nyingma)
Affiliation: Shambhala International
Michael Rogers
520 Townsend Drive
Aptos, CA 95003
Tel: (408) 685–9212

See International headquarters, **Shambhala Center**, Halifax, Nova Scotia, Canada.

American Buddhist Seminary (Theravada)
2717 Haste Street
Berkeley, CA 94704
Tel: (510) 845–4843
Fax: (510) 644–9739
E-mail: abs@slip.net
Web site: http://www.slip.net/~abs

Aim to tutor monks, nuns, and laypeople as social workers so that they are able to meet the spiritual, cultural, and social needs of Southeast Asian Americans. Established and looking for suitable location 1996. "There exists a serious social crisis in the Southeast Asian Buddhist communities of North America. A crisis which is due to a combination of economic hardship, lack of education, language barriers, and cultural differences…. For centuries the culture of Southeast Asians has been intricately interwoven with the spiritual beliefs of their predominant religion—Buddhism…. The mission of the ABS is to enhance the spiritual well-being of the nation through its focus on the Buddhist communities of North America. Our immediate attention is on the most disadvantaged in these communities—to help these individuals transform from their current condition of hopelessness to hopefulness—with an emphasis on the youth of these communities."

Comprehensive training program, "Asian Communities Services Certification," with a hands-on, practical curriculum designed to create graduates who are field-effective immediately in delivery of spiritual, cultural, and social services to Asian communities. Two-year program with over seventy percent focusing on mentorship and counseling. Students recruited from ethnic groups they will serve. On completion of the program, graduates will be placed in social services organizations throughout the country.

Berkeley Higashi Honganji (Jodo Shinshu)
Affiliation: Higashi Honganji Buddhist Temple, California
1520 Oregon Street
Berkeley, CA 94703
Tel: (510) 843–6933
Fax: (510) 849–9027

Branch temple of **Higashi Honganji Buddhist Temple,** California (see separate entry).

Berkeley Shambhala Center (Tibetan–Kagyu/Nyingma)
Affiliation: Shambhala International
2288 Fulton Street
Berkeley, CA 94704
Tel: (510) 841–6475
E-mail: jgrun@sirius.com

See International headquarters, **Shambhala Center,** Halifax, Nova Scotia, Canada.

Berkeley Zen Center (Zen–Soto)
1931 Russell Street
Berkeley, CA 94703
Tel: (510) 845–2403

Three Berkeley wood-frame houses and a meditation hall in an urban setting. Zendo interior has Japanese joinery construction. Small residential community with over a hundred members, mostly from the local area. "Great support in integrating this monastic tradition into one's life in the world." Established 1967 and moved to present location 1979.

Classes on sutras, commentaries, introduction to Buddhism, etc. all once a week in four- to six-week blocks. Ongoing discussion groups, zazen instruction once a week. Monthly and weekend sesshins, zazen sessions daily (except Sundays).

Monthly newsletter.

Founder/Guru	Shunryu Suzuki Roshi
Teachers	Resident Abbot: Sojun Mel Weitsman Roshi
Opening Times	5:40 am Monday–Friday, 6:00 am Saturday
Residents	1 monk, 8 laity
Festivals	Contact center
Facilities	Zendo and library
Accommodation	None
Food	Vegetarian during sesshins
Booking	2 weeks in advance, prepayment preferred

Fees	Classes $5; sesshins $25 per day members, $30 non-members
Expected Behavior	No smoking, 5 precepts
How to Get There	Off Interstate 80, 2 blocks from BART and buses.

California Buddhist Vihara Society (Theravada)
2717 Haste Street
Berkeley, CA 94704
Tel: (510) 845–4843
Fax: (510) 644–9739
E-mail: abs@slip.net

Started by group of Sri Lankan Buddhists in Bay Area.

Vipassana meditation classes at **American Buddhist Seminary** in Sacramento, CA (see separate entry) Tel: (510) 452–3351—newcomers taught separately. Academic courses through the **Institute of Buddhist Studies** (see separate entry). Four trained monks available for services. **Dhamma Dana** (book) series established to present Buddhism in simple English (over twenty titles). Send out free books on request and supply books to prisoners.

Empty Gate Zen Center (Zen)
Affiliation: Kwan Um School of Zen
2200 Parker Street
Berkeley, CA 94704
Tel: (510) 845–8565
E-mail: egzc@emptygatezen.com
Web site: http://www.emptygatezen.com

One-story building near University of California. "Our community is friendly and informal, and very open to helping anyone willing to practice. The emphasis is very much geared toward practice in everyday life." Founded 1977; new building purchased 1996.

Zen practice, discussion, and teaching several mornings and evenings per week. Special weekly programs on Wednesdays 7:00 pm and Saturdays 7:00 pm. Introduction to Zen Monday evenings. Wednesdays night program specially designed for people new to the practice. Abbot offers private interviews and kong-an practice most Saturday mornings. One-day retreats or three-day retreats offered alternate months. Three-month retreats occasionally.

Founder/Guru	Zen Master Seung Sahn
Teachers	Jeffrey Kitzes, Ji Do Peop Sa Nim; other teachers from Kwan Um School of Zen visit

Opening Times	Contact center
Residents	None
Festivals	Buddha's Enlightenment Day
Facilities	Dharma room, library/lounge
Accommodation	For retreats. For other accommodations, contact center
Food	Saturday morning vegetarian breakfast by donation. Some ceremonies
Booking	As early as possible
Fees	Free with exception of retreats, which are $40/day ($30/day for members); one-day retreats $30 ($20 members).
Expected Behavior	Willingness to follow forms during formal Zen practice
How to Get There	South of University of California at Berkeley campus. 2200 Parker is south of Dwight Way and east of Shattuck Ave.

Institute for World Religions (Pure Land and Ch'an)
Affiliation: Dharma Realm Buddhist Association
2304 McKinley Avenue
Berkeley, CA 94703
Tel: (510) 848–3440
Fax: (510) 548–4551
E-mail: paramita@sirius.com

Renovated Nazarene church housing a monastic community, educational institute, and center for community Dharma activities. Four hundred participants a week. Established 1994. Ven. Abbot Master Hsuan Hua said, "The purpose of the Institute is to study religions in harmony with other faiths. We do not oppose anyone's religion, nor do we reject anyone's religion. Rather, we investigate the truths of religion together with other creeds and schools. The capacity of our minds should expand to propagate the limitless and boundless spirit of the City of Ten Thousand Buddhas…. The format can combine a meditation period every morning and evening, followed by a forum for the discussion of religion in the evenings. In the classes when there are more Catholics present, you can learn about Catholicism, when there are more Jews, you can learn Judaism, or Islam, or Confucianism, etc. Invite well-known religious spokespersons to give their presentations. We are the hosts and the facilitators, but not the ones who teach there. Investigate other religions with a wholehearted, open spirit of cooperation."

Full daily monastic schedule, including morning and evening recitation and noon meal offering. Weekly bilingual sutra lectures and meditation classes in English and Mandarin. Recent activities included: meditation hours twice daily open to public; Jewish–Buddhist–Christian trialogue; weekly Ch'an meditation instruction; guest lectures from Theravada monks and nuns; interfaith dialogue with a Franciscan priest and

Theravadan monks; conversations between Buddhist monks and Catholic priests; weekly gatherings of the Movement for Jewish Renewal; science and spirituality seminars with physicists from UC Berkeley; discussions by Ahimsa; Buddhist women's practice seminars; Vipassana meditation group; Vietnamese Buddhist community programs. In 1996, there were plans to expand its MA degree programs to Berkeley and to develop a strong academic program of Buddhist studies with the University of California, the Graduate Theological Union, and the Institute of Buddhist Studies.

Monthly journal of Buddhist Studies, *Vajra Bodhi Sea*. Mahayana sutras and shastras published by Dharma Realm Buddhist University. Buddhist Text Translation Society publications in English, Chinese, Spanish, Polish, and Vietnamese.

Founder/Guru	Ven. Master Hsuan Hua
Teachers	Resident: Rev. Heng Sure
Opening Times	Daily
Residents	2 monks and 3 laymen
Festivals	Contact center
Facilities	Buddha hall, lecture hall, and library
Accommodation	None.

Institute of Buddhist Studies (All traditions, specializes in Contemporary Shin)
1900 Addison Street
Berkeley, CA 94704
Tel: (510) 849–2383
Fax: (510) 849–2158

Seminary and graduate school of fifteen to twenty-five students. Offers an accredited Master of Arts degree in Buddhist Studies which is jointly administered with the Graduate Theological Union. Specializes in Contemporary Shin Buddhist Studies; three-year program including the study of Shinran Shonin's writings and preparation in classical and modern Japanese. Students wishing to specialize in other areas of Buddhism also encouraged to apply to take the Master of Arts as a two-year program. Location in Berkeley gives students access to greatest concentration of Buddhist studies resources in the country, including facilities at Universities of California, Berkeley and Stanford Universities.

Graduate Theological Union and University of California students may take graduate academic courses for credit and without fees. Other degree students pay $3,550 per semester. Special students enrolled for academic credit but not a degree course pay $887.50 per three-unit course. Auditor's fee $200 per course. $20 registration per student.

Classes offered 1996–97: Issues in the Shin Tradition; Buddhist Ethics; History of Buddhism; Teaching of the Seven Patriarchs; Tibetan Buddhism; Early Buddhist Texts; Shin Buddhist Services and Ceremonies; Religious Pluralism in the United States; Chinese Buddhist Philosophy; Zen Buddhism; Japanese Religion; Methods in the Study of Religion; Theravada Buddhism; Tibetan Contemplative Traditions; *Kyogyoshinsho;* Mahayana Texts and Ryukoku.

Publish *Pacific World* annually.

Numata Center for Buddhist Translation & Research (Nonsectarian)
2620 Warring Street
Berkeley, CA 94704
Tel: (510) 843–4128
Fax: (510) 845–3409
E-mail: Numata@slip.net
Web site: http://www.slip.net~numata

Publisher of Buddhist texts and religious booksellers. Established 1984 by a Japanese Buddhist philanthropist, Rev. Dr. Yehan Numata, founder of Mitutoyo Corporation and Bukkyo Dendo Kyokai (Society for the Promotion of Buddhism). Center's primary mission is the translation and publication of the Taisho edition of the Chinese Buddhist canon in English and its distribution, of which ten volumes have been published so far. Books available on a subscription basis as well as retail sales through bookstores. Near the California Berkeley campus, opposite the Clark Kerr dormitories. Cross street, Derby.

Nyingma Institute (Tibetan–Nyingma)
1815 Highland Place
Berkeley, CA 94709
Tel: (510) 843–6812
Fax: (510) 486–1679
E-mail: nyingma-institute@nyingma.org

Large building decorated Tibetan-style. Five-ton prayer wheel in a pagoda in serene meditation garden ideal for relaxation and contemplation, goldleafed stupa, and many other sacred art objects. Over two hundred visitors a week. Founded 1973. "The Nyingma Institute has pioneered ways of communicating the Tibetan Buddhist tradition to the Western world for twenty-three years. Our student body ranges from dedicated Buddhists to 'just curious.' It is a mix of international students of all ages."

Daily meditation for residents and retreatants. Tibetan chanting on Sundays open to public. Full range of classes and programs geared to Western understanding. Weekly classes in traditional Buddhist studies, meditation, Buddhist psychology, Tibetan language, Kum Nye relaxation, and skillful means (using teachings to make work a source of satisfaction and inner growth). Monthly full moon chanting. Longchenpa prayers. Weekly and monthly retreats throughout the year. Eighteen-month Nyingma Education Program yearly. Five-month Mandala Practices Program once a year. Three-month Kum Nye Intensive quarterly. Training in skillful means once a year. Four-month

Human Development Training Program once a year. Two-month Integration Retreat once a year. Week-long Time, Space and Knowledge retreats once a year. Nyingma Lineage Retreat once a year. Four-week Buddhist Studies Meditation and Kum Nye retreats. Offers students the opportunity to work on sacred art projects and on Tibetan text preservation.

Bookstore. With Dharma Publishing, sponsor the Yeshe De Project, which has published over one million pages of Tibetan sacred literature and six hundred art prints—all donated back to the Tibetan people in Asia. Also associated with Tibetan Aid Project, Dharma Press, and Odiyan Retreat Center.

Quarterly newsletter, *Nyingma Gateway*.

Founder/Guru	Tarthang Tulku
Teachers	Resident: Ralph McFall, Sylvia Gretchen, June Rosenberg, Barr Rosenberg, Arnaud Maitland, Zara Wallace, Jack Petranker, Leslie Bradburn
Opening Times	Open daily all year round
Residents	25–40 laity
Festivals	World Peace Day, Buddha's Birthday, Longchenpa Parinirvana
Facilities	Meditation garden with prayer wheel and stupa, meditation room, shrine room, classrooms
Accommodation	Contact center
Food	Vegetarian included in retreat and workshop prices
Booking	2 months in advance, 10% deposit for long retreats; 1 week in advance, 10% deposit for short retreats
Fees	$400/week for retreats; $6,000 for 4-month retreat; $3,000 for 2-month retreat—including full board and instruction. $75 for Saturday workshop. $150 for 10 evening classes
Expected Behavior	No drugs or alcohol. Students are expected to follow rules of Buddhist community
How to Get There	From Hwy. I-80 take University exit, turn left on Oxford, right on Hearst, left on Highland Place. 1 block north of UC Berkeley campus.

A student came to Zen Master Dae Gak.
"What is Zen?" the student asked.
"Katz!" shouted Dae Gak Sunim.
"What is it that hears this?"

quoted in a flyer of the Dae Mun Community, Ohio, affiliate of Furnace Mountain

Rigpa San Francisco Bay Area Center (Tibetan–Nyingma)
Affiliation: Rigpa Fellowship
816 Bancroft Way
Berkeley, CA 94710
Tel: (510) 644–1858
Fax: (510) 644–9517

See **Rigpa National Office,** California, for details.

Sixth Patriarch Zen Center (Zen–Rinzai)
Affiliation: Dohn-O Zen & Taoist Center, Washington
2584 Martin Luther King Jr. Way
Berkeley, CA 94704
Tel: (510) 486 1762

Branch of **Dohn-O Zen & Taoist Center,** Washington (see separate entry for details).

Taungpulu Kaba-Aye Dhamma Center (Theravada)
18335 Big Basin Way
Boulder Creek, CA 95006
Tel: (408) 338–4050

Contact center for details.

Vajrapani Institute (Tibetan–Gelug)
Affiliation: Foundation for the Preservation of the Mahayana Tradition
P O Box 2130
Boulder Creek, CA 95006
Tel: (408) 338–6654
Fax: (408) 338–3666
E-mail: 76764.2256@compuserve.com

Set in mountainous woodland in central California. The center shares a boundary with Castle Rock State Park. Was the site of Lama Thubten Yeshe's cremation in 1984, and the "enlightenment stupa" dedicated to his life is a central attraction. Two meditation halls full of traditional Tibetan-style artwork and six cabins set up for solitary retreat. Group formed in 1975 by Lama Yeshe's students and Lama Zopa Rinpoche. Retreat center started in 1978. Buildings built by the residents and volunteers. A hundred-member local area community with twelve people running the retreat facility. Californian FPMT centers have a resident Geshe who shares his time between them—see **Vajrapani, Land of Medicine Buddha,** and **Tse Chen Ling Center** (see separate entries).

"Those who manage to find us and can make it up the gravel road find themselves transported to a Dharma realm in the redwoods. Visitors usually remember fondly the outdoor meditation space around the stupa and the main hall full of Buddhist art.... For the long-term members and residents, the fact that we have had the highest lamas in our lineage teaching here is very important and the cohesiveness of our community is one that that continues to draw people."

Emphasizes courses on Buddhist topics from the tradition of the great master Je Tsongkhapa. Offer courses and workshops on Buddhist meditation and philosophy, individual and group retreat facilities, and the facility is also available for rental by appropriate groups. Optional morning prayers and meditation. Evening pujas throughout the month according to the lunar calendar. Residential courses led by qualified Tibetan and Western teachers most weekends. Sponsors an ongoing evening class in the town of Boulder Creek. Conducts a summer residential work-study program with classes and workshops throughout the week. Two to three guided Tantric retreats a year. Schedule of events available on request. Members receive two newsletters per year plus the FPMT publication, *Mandala* magazine.

Founder/Guru	Founder: Lama Thubten Yeshe; Guru: Lama Thubten Zopa Rinpoche
Teachers	Resident: Geshe Kalsang Wangdu; Translator: Ven. Michael Lobsang Yeshe and visiting Gelugpa lamas, including Dalai Lama
Opening Times	Reception 1:00–6:00 pm
Residents	1 nun, 1 monk, 2 monk-teachers, 12 lay people
Festivals	Saga Dawa
Facilities	Teaching hall, reading area, bookstore, kitchen, dining room, outside picnic tables, small meditation hall, dormitory, stupa, and cabins for solitary retreat
Accommodation	Cabins $39/night, dorm $25/night both including food
Food	Vegetarian $15/day for 3 meals
Booking	Suggest 2 weeks' advance reservation for cabins. Deposit required
Fees	Weekend courses are around $100 total
Expected Behavior	5 precepts, no smoking in or around buildings, silence in cabin area and at certain times in the main building
How to Get There	San Jose nearest airport. From Santa Cruz to Boulder Creek, the #25 Metro bus twice an hour. From Boulder Creek need to get a ride the eight miles to the retreat center. By car, off Highway 9 midway between San Jose and Santa Cruz. At the Coast Gasoline/Mountain store 3 miles north of Boulder Creek, turn east into Pool Drive. At the stop sign, turn left onto Kings Creek Rd. Drive for 5 miles, the last 2 being gravel road.

Administrative Headquarters of Dharma Realm Buddhist Association (Pure Land
    and Ch'an)
Affiliation: Dharma Realm Buddhist Association
1825 Magnolia Avenue
Burlingame, CA 94010

Contact center for details.

International Translation Institute (Pure Land, Ch'an, Teaching, Vinaya, and
    Secret)
Affiliation: Dharma Realm Buddhist Association
1777 Murchison Drive
Burlingame, CA 94010
Tel: (415) 692–5912
Fax: (415) 692–5056

Founded by the Dharma Realm Buddhist Association in 1959. Its main task is the
translation of the main Buddhist scriptures from classical Chinese and Sanskrit into the
world's major languages. Over two hundred volumes published mostly in English and
Chinese. Also publishes monthly Buddhist journal, *Vajra Bodhi Sea*.

Tassajara Zen Mountain Center (Zen–Soto)
39171 Tassajara Road
Carmel Valley, CA 93924
Tel & Fax: contact the **San Francisco Zen Center**

One of three practice locations—see also **San Francisco Zen Center** and **Green Gulch
Farm**.
    Secluded resort deep in the Los Padres National Forest near Monterey, opened in
1967 as the first Buddhist monastery outside Asia. Numerous buildings at hot springs in
Ventana Wilderness near Big Sur area. Offers traditional fall and winter practice periods
and is open each summer to guests who want to enjoy the natural hot spring baths and
the quiet and beauty of the mountains. The summer guests season includes a variety of
programs, workshops, and retreats and the chance to join residents in meditation and
other activities. Summer guest accommodation includes individual redwood cabins,
Japanese-style tatami cabins, and stone and pine rooms. Guest cabins and pathways are lit
by kerosene lamps.
    Subjects for retreats and workshops include such titles as Wild Zen, Tassajara
History Legends & Lore, Sensory Awareness, Japanese Archery, Cultivating the
Tassajara Wilderness, Zen & Yoga, Improvisation & Zen–Action Theater, Buddhism
and Christianity, Buddhism and Judaism.

Founder/Guru	Shunryu Suzuki Roshi
Teachers	3 resident abbots: Mel Weitsman, Norman Fischer, and Blanche Hartman. Senior resident teacher: Reb Anderson. Other priests and lay teachers lecture and assist in the teaching
Opening Times	Contact center
Residents	About 50—little distinction between priest and lay—all are monks
Festivals	None
Facilities	Contact center
Accommodation	See above
Food	3 family-style vegetarian meals (including eggs and dairy) per day included in room rates
Booking	Varies on availability—deposit required
Fees	$15 per day as guest student and on up as full guest
Expected Behavior	16 Bodhisattva precepts (Mahayana)
How to Get There	Very remote location 14 miles up a dirt road which is quite steep and rugged. Discuss travel plans with center beforehand, as not all cars can safely navigate the route or take the shuttle from Jamesburg.

Higashi Honganji Temple (Jodo Shinshu)
Affiliation: Higashi Honganji Buddhist Temple, Japan
254 Victoria Avenue
Costa Mesa, CA 92627
Tel: (714) 722–1202
Fax: (714) 722–1670

Contact center for more details.

Newport Mesa Zen Center (Zen–Soto)
711 West 17th Street, A-8
Costa Mesa, CA 92663
Tel: (714) 631–5389
Fax: (714) 631–8891

Storefront center two miles from Newport Beach pier. Around sixty visitors a week. Founded 1994 to provide a Zen center in Orange County. Originally sponsored by Zen Home Stitchery on the same premises.

Beginning Instruction twice a week on Sundays. Introduction to Zen Meditation every two months and Zazen five days a week. Christian Zen program twice a week. Zazenkai every month—all-day sitting, work practice, oryoki (lunch), service, talk.

Sesshins periodically. **Zen Home Stitchery** manufactures meditation cushion, clothes, and supplies.

Founder/Guru	Deborah Barrett and Carol Mudd
Teachers	Deborah Barrett
Opening Times	See program
Residents	None
Festivals	None
Facilities	Zendo, interview room, office, library
Accommodation	None
Food	Vegetarian—oryoki
Booking	1 week in advance for zazenkai
Fees	Contact center
Expected Behavior	Contact center
How to Get There	Either: Pacific Coast Highway to Newport Blvd., left on West 17th—3 blocks; or I-55 to Newport Blvd., right on West 17th, 3 blocks.

Higashi Honganji Temple (Jodo Shinshu)
Affiliation: Higashi Honganji Buddhist Temple, California
1210 N Glendora Avenue
Covina, CA 91724
Tel: (818) 339–6326
Fax: (818) 331–0003

Branch temple of **Higashi Honganji Buddhist Temple,** California (see separate entry).

Reverend Ryobo Fujiwara (Nichiren Shu)
Affiliate: Nichiren Propagation Center
11232 Ryandale Drive
Culver City, CA 90230
Tel: (310) 398–9827

See **Nichiren Propagation Center,** Oregon.

> *When one attains the release called the Beautiful, at such a time he knows in truth what Beauty is.*
>
> Samyuta and Digha Nikaya

Medicine Buddha's Healing Center (Tibetan–Gelug)
Affiliation: Foundation for the Preservation of the Mahayana Tradition
10471 Westacres Drive
Cupertino, CA 95014
Tel: (408) 255–7178
Fax: (408) 257–6155

Contact center for details.

Davis Shambhala Center (Tibetan–Kagyu/Nyingma)
Affiliation: Shambhala International
129 "E" Street, Suite D-2
Davis, CA 95616
Tel: (916) 758–1440
E-mail: wfell@aol.com

Shrine room that accommodates thirty comfortably, multiple interview rooms, kitchen, and library. Twenty-five members and forty visitors per week. Founded 1979.

Sitting meditation (Shamatha–Vipashyana) every Sunday 9:00 am and Thursday evenings 7:30 pm for one hour. Longer sitting periods the first Sunday of every month. Classes Thursday evening at 7:30 pm on the Buddhadharma or the Shambhala teachings. Monthly newsletter and calendar.

Founder/Guru	Chogyam Trungpa Rinpoche
Teachers	Contact center
Opening Times	Sundays 9:00 am, Thursdays 7:30 pm
Residents	Nonresidential
Festivals	Not applicable
Facilities	2 shrine rooms, library, and very small bookstore
Accommodation	None
Food	None
Booking	Contact center
Fees	Voluntary donations
Expected Behavior	Contact center
How to Get There	Downtown Davis between 1st and 2nd on "E" Street in Orange Court.

Three Treasures Zen Community (Zen–Soto)
PO Box 754
Del Mar, CA 92014
Tel: (619) 481–9776 or (619) 724–9541
E-mail: jikyo@aol.com or JMGage@aol.com

Web site: planned

Has several different locations; all strive to foster the transmission of traditional Zen Buddhism to both lay and monastic students in a Western context. "The community stresses the importance of people from a variety of backgrounds coming together to practice, believing that we can learn from all traditions and that the evolution of Zen in America will encourage this approach. Additionally, art, communication skills, sacred dance, and social concerns are avenues used to develop and enrich one's practice and to help students actualize their understanding in their day-to-day lives."

Zen instruction and practice Monday through Thursday and Sundays. All-day retreats monthly and three- to seven-day sesshins throughout the year. Newsletter bimonthly.

Waken Ray Tseng Temple (True Buddha School)
11657 Lower Azusa Road
El Monte, CA 91732
Tel: (818) 455–0077
Fax: (818) 455–0556
E-mail: ahou@aol.com
Web site: http://www.tbsn.org

Largest Vajrayana temple in Greater Los Angeles area. Tibetan-style monastery with around 100 visitors/practitioners a week. Completed 1996.

Beginners meditation classes Saturdays at 8:00 pm. Classes from four preliminary practices to Mahamudra. Fire puja Sunday morning.

True Buddha Newsletter twice a month.

Founder/Guru	Grand Master Lu Sheng-Yen
Teachers	Resident: Master Allen Hou
Opening Times	12 noon to 8:00 pm
Residents	5 monastics and 5 laity
Festivals	Contact center
Facilities	Shrine room, library, gompa, study room, restaurants, main altar, Dharmapala altar, fire puja altar
Accommodation	Arrange outside motel or hotel
Food	Wholefood—free
Booking	1 week in advance recommended
Fees	Offering as wished
Expected Behavior	5 precepts, no smoking
How to Get There	10 Freeway off Peck Road north, hit Lower Azusa, turn right.

Hoko Temple Zen Center (Zen–Rinzai)
Affiliation: Rinzai-ji, Los Angeles, California
1217 Linda Lane
Fullerton, CA 92831
Tel: (714) 526–1704
E-mail: margren@aol.com

Contact center for details.

Garberville Dharma Center (Tibetan–Nyingma; Zen–Japanese; Vipassana)
434 Maple Lane
Garberville, CA 95542
Tel: (707) 923–3891
E-mail: radiantheart@asis.com

Meditation hall (twenty seats) centrally located to service a rural area of northwest California with a quiet space in the center of town for study and practice. Used by several different groups from different traditions—all Buddhists welcome to practice here. Started 1977.

Offers classes in various meditation techniques. When Tibetan lamas, Zen teachers, or Theravadin teachers are in the area, they offer teachings in their particular traditions.

Timothy Clark, who runs this center, also runs **Radiant Heart,** a prayer flag and Dharma banner business. Contact at: P O Box 1272, Redway, CA 95560, Tel for questions and information: (707) 923–3891, Tel & Fax for orders: (800) 853–2010, E-mail: radiantheart@asis.com, on-line catalog: http://www.asis.com/~radiantheart.

Founder/Guru	Contact center
Teachers	Various—see above
Opening Times	As per program
Residents	None
Festivals	Contact center
Facilities	Meditation hall
Accommodation	None
Food	None
Booking	Not necessary
Fees	Only for some yoga classes and workshops
Expected Behavior	No smoking, no shoes, general respect for the space
How to Get There	220 miles north of San Francisco on Highway 101. 434 Maple Lane is right off the main street, half a block east.

Gardena Honpoji Betsuin (Nichiren Shu)

Affiliate: Nichiren Propagation Center
15725 Raymond Avenue
Gardena, CA 90247
Tel: (213) 321–9405
Fax: (310) 329–3710

Resident priest—Rev. Kanshu Ikuta. See **Nichiren Propagation Center,** Oregon.

> *We enter a discipline like Zen practice so that we can learn to live in a sane way.... It is down-to-earth and very practical.... It is about our daily life.... It is something we do for a lifetime.*
>
> Charlotte Joko Beck quoted in Bay Zen Center, California, brochure

Hsi Lai Temple/International Buddhist Progress Society (Chinese)
Affiliation: Buddha's Light International Association
3456 South Glenmark Drive
Hacienda Heights, CA 91745
Tel: (818) 961–9697
Fax: (818) 369–1944

Chinese palatial-style buildings built around a residential area. Largest Buddhist monastery in the West, covering fifteen acres and receiving two thousand visitors a week. Based on traditional architecture of ancient Chinese monasteries but equipped with modern facilities. Grounds include shrines, theme gardens, and a museum. Construction began 1986 and completed 1988. Extension of Fo Kuang Shan Monastery in Taiwan.

Meditation class Saturday evenings. Buddhist classes with Buddhist studies in Chinese, Cantonese, and English on Sunday mornings. Women's class with Buddhist studies also Sunday mornings. Meditation course with theory and practice of meditation Saturday evenings. Retreats: five-precept and Bodhisattva-precept each once a year; eight-precept three times a year; short-term monastic retreats once a year. *Buddha's Light Newsletter* once a month.

Founder/Guru	Ven. Master Hsing Yun
Teachers	Contact center
Opening Times	Contact center
Residents	Around 5 nuns, 5 monks, and 15 laity
Festivals	Buddha's Birthday, Sangha's Day, etc.
Facilities	As above and Bodhisattva hall, main Buddha hall,

auditorium, international conference room, meditation room, 2 meeting rooms, 15 classrooms, and library

Accommodation	For 100 people, donation welcome
Food	Vegetarian
Booking	Not necessary
Fees	Donations welcome
Expected Behavior	No smoking, decent dress, no food or beverages
How to Get There	Freeway 60E to Hacienda Blvd. exit, turn left, right onto Hacienda Blvd. and the temple is on the left-hand side.

T'hondup Ling (Tibetan–Nyingma)
Affiliation: Chagdud Gonpa Foundation
2503 W 117th Street
Hawthorne, CA 90250
Tel: (213) 754–0466

Teacher is Lama Chodak Gyatso. Contact center for details.

Los Angeles Buddhist Vihara (Theravada)
1147 North Beechwood Drive
Hollywood, CA 90038
Tel: (213) 464–9698

Contact center for details.

Karma Mahasiddha Ling (Tibetan–Karma Kagyu/Rime)
P O Box 1441
Idyllwild, CA 92549
Tel: (909) 659–3401
E-mail: buddhafull@aol.com

Tibetan-style gompa which holds up to seventy-five people at 6,200 feet above sea level, surrounded by thousands of acres of pine forest in the San Jacinto Mountains of southern California. Core members have been practicing for twenty-five–thirty years and have been working with Tibetan teachers and their followers in Nepal and India since then.

Thrangu Rinpoche travels worldwide and is here for two or three weeks a year when the center hosts a ten-day meditation retreat with him at Big Bear Lake, California. The course was designed for Americans who couldn't get to Nepal. Usually around a hundred people attend.

Classes in basic meditation (Shinay) instruction and diety sadhanas (visualizations). Also Chenrezig and Guru Rinpoche sadhanas, Vipassana, and Ngondro. Weekly public sitting practice on Sunday mornings from 10:00–11:30 am.

Founder/Guru	V. Ven. Thrangu Rinpoche
Teachers	As founder
Opening Times	Always open
Residents	Around 60 members
Festivals	According to Tibetan calendar
Facilities	Large shrine/meditation room
Accommodation	Hotels nearby
Food	Emphasis on what is healthy
Booking	Contact center
Fees	Around $400 for 10-day meditation retreat
Expected Behavior	Contact center
How to Get There	Call for details.

Chagdud Gonpa Rigdzin Ling (Tibetan–Nyingma)
Headquarters: Chagdud Gonpa Foundation
P O Box 279
Junction City, CA 96048
Tel: (916) 623–2714
Fax: (916) 623–6709
E-mail: chagdud@snowcrest.net
Web site: http://www.snowcrest.net/chagdud

Two hundred and sixty-eight acres of land adjacent Trinity River and Alps on outskirts of small town. Main building is Tibetan-style with a large shrine room, commercial kitchen, and guest rooms. Campground and staff housing. Meditation park in progress 1996, with stupas, prayer wheel house, and large Guru Rinpoche statue with fountain. Library of Tibetan texts and English translations. "Principal resident of Chagdud Rinpoche in North America and headquarters of the Chagdud Gonpa Foundation and Padma Publishing. Its facilities are being developed for group and individual retreats. A teaching program is planned to offer instructions on Vajrayana Buddhism and meditation. Other projects include the Mahakaruna Foundation, a charitable organization that raises funds to help Tibetan refugees in India and Nepal, and the Tibetan library, which purchases and preserves Tibetan texts and propagates Vajrayana Buddhist arts." Established 1983, land acquired 1987.

Group practice twice daily. Several practices monthly according to phases of moon. Ongoing teachings from resident and visiting lamas on wide range of Vajrayana meditation topics. Annual retreat include seven-day Red Vajrasattva drubchen, seven-day Essence of Siddhi drubchen, seven-day Vajrakilaya drubchen, seven-day Ngondro retreat, and six-week Dzogchen retreat (latter restricted, rest suitable for newcomers). Individual retreats possible.

Biannual newsletter, *Windhorse*. **Padma Publishing** translates and prints practice texts and commentaries from Tibetan texts and books based on oral teachings of H.E. Chagdud Tulku Rinpoche. **Tibetan Treasures** sells Dharma-related gifts and supplies and Padma Publishing books: Tibetan Treasures, P O Box 279, Junction City, CA 96048.

Founder/Guru	H.E. Chagdud Tulku Rinpoche founder and head lama
Teachers	Resident: Lama Padma Drimed Norbu; many visiting lamas
Opening Times	Office hours 8:00 am–5:00 pm Monday–Friday; 8:00 am–noon Saturdays; visits may be scheduled for almost any time
Residents	30 lay practitioners
Festivals	Losar, annual Guru Rinpoche Day lama dancing
Facilities	See above
Accommodation	Private rooms in main temple, campground, and dormitory-style rooms
Food	Vegetarian or meat; $2 breakfast, $5 lunch, $3 dinner
Booking	For events, 50% deposit 2 weeks in advance
Fees	1 week events $350–450
Expected Behavior	No smoking or illegal drugs
How to Get There	Call for directions.

Blessings, Prosperity and Longevity Monastery (Pure Land and Ch'an)
Affiliation: Dharma Realm Buddhist Association
4140 Long Beach Boulevard
Long Beach, CA 90807-5400
Tel & Fax: (310) 595–4966
E-mail: drbabpl@pacbell.net

Three-story office building on main thoroughfare. Southern California Administration Center for Dharma Realm Buddhist Association. Established 1996 and at time of writing still in planning stages. "An oasis of calm within a large industrial city."

All Dharma Realm Buddhist Association branch monasteries are open to the public and have morning, afternoon, and evening ceremonies and sutra lectures every day as well as their own special programs. All activities are led by fully ordained monks or nuns.

Founder/Guru	Ven. Master Hsuan Hua
Facilities	Buddha shrine, offices, small reference and lending library, conference rooms, reception rooms, meditation hall, book distribution area, classrooms, and lecture areas

     Food Vegetarian only, including no onions, garlic, etc.
   Expected Behavior No smoking, 5 precepts, proper attire.

Khemara Buddhikaram (Cambodian Buddhist Temple) (Theravada)
2100 West Willow Street
Long Beach, CA 90810
Tel: (310) 595–0566
Fax: (310) 426–4870

Cambodian (Khmer) spoken. Contact Ven. Kong Chhean, PhD, for more information.

Long Beach Monastery (Pure Land, Ch'an, and Mahayana)
Affiliation: Dharma Realm Buddhist Association
3361 East Ocean Boulevard
Long Beach, CA 90803
Tel: (310) 438–8902

All Dharma Realm Buddhist Association branch monasteries are open to the public and have morning, afternoon, and evening ceremonies and sutra lectures every day as well as their own special programs. All activities are led by fully ordained monks or nuns.

California Buddhist University (Shaolin Zen)
3165 Minnesota Street
Los Angeles, CA 90031
Tel: (213) 628–3449

Associated with **Shaolin Buddhist Meditation Center, Kewanee Mountain Zen Center,** and **California Buddhist University's Zen Garden** (see separate entries). Started 1988 by Dr. Jefferson Chan.

 Offers courses leading to Doctor of Buddhist Culture, master's degree and bachelor's degree in Buddhist studies. Doctoral, master's, and bachelor's degree programs in business administration, Chinese culture, and psychology. Home study program. *The Shaolin Monastery* published quarterly.

 Associated bookstore with books on China, especially Chinese culture and Chinese Zen, specially built in Chinese style in Chinatown: **Student's Bookstore,** 933¹/₄ Chung King Road, Los Angeles, CA 90012, Tel: (213) 628–3449.

    Founder/Guru Dr. Chia-Ho Chan
     Teachers Contact center
   Opening Times Contact center
    Residents None

Festivals	Contact center
Facilities	Shrine room, dojo, library, study room, and meditation room
Accommodation	None
Food	None
Booking	Contact center
Fees	Classes $100 for 3 months
Expected Behavior	No smoking, alcohol, or dancing
How to Get There	Map for all 3 centers available from the Student's Bookstore.

California Buddhist University's Zen Garden (Shaolin Zen)
1947 Lansdowne Avenue
Los Angeles, CA 90032

Connected to **California Buddhist University** (see separate entry).

Dharma Zen Center (Zen–Korean)
1025 South Cloverdale Avenue
Los Angeles, CA 90019
Tel: (213) 934–0330
Fax: (213) 933–3072
E-mail: 76467.705@compuserve.com

Contact center for details.

> *So here we have the whole practice of the Buddha: refrain from evil and do good, live simply, purify the mind. That is, be watchful of our mind and body in all postures; know yourself.*
>
> Ven. Ajahn Chah

Diamond Way Buddhist Center (Tibetan–Kagyu)
432 S Curson Avenue, #2B
Los Angeles, CA 90036
Tel: (213) 931–1903
Fax: (213) 931–0909
E-mail: Gefreiter1@aol.com

Originally established by Lama Ole Nydahl for H.H. 16th Karmapa Rigpe Dorje. Now dedicated to H.H. 17th Karmapa Thaye Dorje. Weekly meditations (Thursdays 8:00 pm) as well as individual consultations.

Gay Zen Group (Zen)
Affiliation: International Buddhist Meditation Center, Los Angeles, California
P O Box 29750
Los Angeles, CA 90029
Tel: (213) 461–5042

Japanese-style zendo oriented to gay men. Founded 1986. Classes in meditation theory and practice, courses and retreats offered through International Buddhist Meditation Center. Meetings are held at 928 South New Hampshire Boulevard, Los Angeles.

Founder/Guru	See International Buddhist Meditation Center
Teachers	See International Buddhist Meditation Center
Opening Times	Contact center
Residents	None
Festivals	Contact center
Facilities	See International Buddhist Meditation Center
Accommodation	None
Food	None
Booking	Contact center
Fees	See International Buddhist Meditation Center
Expected Behavior	No smoking
How to Get There	One block west of Vermont Avenue.

Gold Wheel Monastery (Pure Land and Ch'an)
Affiliation: Dharma Realm Buddhist Association
235 N Avenue 58
Los Angeles, CA 90042
Tel: (213) 258–6668

All Dharma Realm Buddhist Association branch monasteries are open to the public and have morning, afternoon, and evening ceremonies and sutra lectures every day as well as their own special programs. All activities are led by fully ordained monks or nuns.

Higashi Honganji Buddhist Temple (Jodo Shinshu)
505 East Third Street
Los Angeles, CA 90013

Tel: (213) 626–4200
Fax: (213) 626–6850
E-mail: aw858@lafn.org (head minister Rev. N. Ito)

Twenty-year-old building with classical Japanese temple architecture. Most distinguishing feature is sharply sloping roof modeled after Todaiji temple in Japan, with nearly 40,000 roof tiles imported from Japan. Four hundred families formally in sangha. Building houses main Hondo and preschool/kindergarten, primarily for working parents. "Traditional Japanese Buddhism, but with an American flavor. Shin Buddhism offered is traditionally nonmonastic, geared for the lay person."

First Buddhist temple in southern California. Established 1904 as Los Angeles Buddhist Association to serve spiritual needs of Japanese immigrant population in area. Helped to popularize Buddhism to general public through religious gatherings and classes. Served to help acculturation of base membership by offering English language courses and day care programs for working parents. All activities ceased during World War II when all people of Japanese ancestry were interned and priests of this and other temples led religious services in the camps. Reopened after war as spiritual center and temporary hostel for returning evacuees. New temple built 1976 in area called "Little Tokyo." "For the past twenty years, it has served as a landmark, exemplifying the beauty of traditional Japanese architecture in the midst of the high-rise buildings of central Los Angeles."

Sunday Services (10:00 am), Dharma school, and other youth programs for infants through college age (focus on both Buddhist education and social interaction). Biannual seminars in spring and fall on various subjects, primarily to do with relevance of Shin Buddhism to everyday life. No formal meditation or rituals are taught, but services incorporate traditional chanting, considered a form of verbal meditation. Publish monthly newsletter, *The Way*, in English and Japanese.

Branch centers in Berkeley, Covina, and Newport Beach (Costa Mesa)—see separate entries.

Founder/Guru	Shinran Shonin; First priest in U.S. Rev. Junjyo Izumida
Teachers	Rev. Noriaki Ito, Rev. Gyoko Saito, Rev. Kenjun Kawawata
Opening Times	9:30 am–5:30 pm Mondays–Saturdays; 9:30 am–3:00 pm Sundays
Residents	None
Festivals	Obon
Facilities	See above
Accommodation	None
Food	None
Booking	Contact center
Fees	Contact center
Expected Behavior	Contact center

How to Get There   Corner of Third St. and Central Ave. Nearest freeways
are 101, 110, and 5.

International Buddhist Meditation Center (Zen–Vietnamese)
928 South New Hampshire Avenue
Los Angeles, CA 90006
Tel: (213) 384–0850
Fax: (213) 386–6643
E-mail: nunk123@ix.netcom.com
Web site: http://www.cpsc.suu.edu/users/henderso

Six houses (two-story) on residential street several miles west of downtown Los
Angeles. Bell tower with garden bell cast and sent from Vietnam just before the fall of
Saigon, fish pond, aviary, and gardens. On campus with College of Buddhist Studies.
All activities run by American disciples of an Asian master for Americans in developing
an American Buddhist style. Founded 1970.

Daily practice. Sunday services include meditation, chanting, and Dharma talks
by resident monks. Classes include Beginning Meditation, Introduction to Buddhism,
Buddhist Techniques in Daily Life, Sanskrit & Pali Terminology, Asian Languages,
Sutra Study, and Women in Buddhism. Offers training of Buddhist monks (male and
female), ordination in lineage directly from the Buddha. Meditation retreats in
Vietnamese Zen style—six weekends per year. One-day retreats on such topics as
Women in Buddhism, Kwan Yin Bodhisattva, or Loving-Kindness. Three-month sum-
mer training. Memorial services.

Offers separate groups designed specifically for gays or lesbians: Gay Men's Buddhist
Group and Lesbian Zen Group. Community involvement, interfaith and inter-Buddhist
involvement. Meetingplace for Los Angeles Buddhist Peace Fellowship and Los Angeles
chapter of Sakyadhita—the International Association of Buddhist Women. Produce
Monthly Guide newsletter. Sunday shop with books and Buddhist paraphernalia.

Founder/Guru	Ven. Dr. Thich Thien-An
Teachers	Resident: Ven. Dr. Karuna Dharma—Abbess, Ven. An-min—Head Monk, Ven. Haranpola Shanti—Vice-Abbot, Rev. Kusala Ratna Karuna—Resident Monk, Ven. Dr. Haranpola Ratanasara—President of the College of Buddhist Studies
Opening Times	See program
Residents	8 monks, 30 laity
Festivals	Buddha's Birthday, Wesak, Ullambana Day
Facilities	Zendo, temple shrine room, class rooms, hall to hold 150 people, library, and residence rooms
Accommodation	Residency program $350/month including private room,

	shared kitchen, and bath. Shorter-term guests depending on availability of rooms—prorated on daily or weekly basis
Food	Vegetarian—only available during retreats and workshops. All 6 houses have full kitchen facilities
Booking	Call for information
Fees	Weekend retreats $125, 1-day retreats and workshops $40, college classes $125 each on a quarterly basis, other activities donation requested
Expected Behavior	No smoking inside houses or rooms, zendo behavior includes quiet, respectful attitude, residency requires cooperative attitude
How to Get There	North of the 10 (Santa Monica Freeway). Near Wilshire and Vermont—30 minutes from LAX.

International Zen Institute of America (Zen–Rinzai)
Headquarters of International Zen Institute of America (IZIA)
P O Box 491218
Los Angeles, CA 90049
Tel: (310) 472–5707

Founder of IZIA, Ven. Gesshin Prabhasa Dharma resident here. Contact center for further details.

Kanzeonji Non-Sectarian Buddhist Temple (Zen–Soto and Hatha Yoga)
944 Terrace 49
Los Angeles, CA 90042
Tel: (213) 255–5345
Fax: (213) 254–5204

Two houses facing each other in the city. Zendo with regular abbot, two monks, and ashram with about fifty Hatha Yoga students a week. Temple founded 1989.

Daily zazen and daily Hatha Yoga. Sesshins offered. Quarterly news journal, *The Spiritual.*

Founder/Guru	Rev. Ryugen Watanabe, Abbot
Teachers	Abbot and 2 monks
Opening Times	Contact center
Residents	2 monks and 1 laity
Festivals	None
Facilities	Zendo, ashram, library, gift shop, office
Accommodation	By arrangement and donation
Food	Vegetarian by donation

Booking	1 week in advance
Fees	By donation
Expected Behavior	Following Temple rules
How to Get There	Exit Ave. 52 from Pasadena Hwy. Turn left, left on Figueroa, right on Ave. 50, left on El Paso, left on Cleland, right on Terrace 49.

Kewanee Mountain Zen Center (Shaolin Zen)
4315 Kewanee Street
Los Angeles, CA 90032
Tel: (213) 628–3449

With views over Los Angeles. Associated with **California Buddhist University, Shaolin Buddhist University,** and **California Buddhist University's Zen Garden** (see separate entries).

Founder/Guru	Dr. Chia-Ho Chan
Teachers	Contact center
Opening Times	Contact center
Residents	None
Festivals	Contact center
Facilities	Shrine room, dojo, library, study room, and meditation room
Accommodation	None
Food	None
Booking	Contact center
Fees	Classes $100 for 3 months
Expected Behavior	No smoking, alcohol, or dancing
How to Get There	Map for all 3 centers available from the Student's Bookstore (see California Buddhist University).

Los Angeles Karma Thegsum Choling (Tibetan–Karma Kagyu)
Affiliation: Karma Triyana Dharmachakra, New York
3586 Tacoma Avenue
Los Angeles, CA 90065
Tel: (213) 222–0479

Founded 1978 by 16th Gyalwa Karmapa.
    Regular practice Sundays and Fridays. Special teaching events by visiting lamas. Lama Dudjom Dorje visits regularly. Interviews and meditation instruction by appointment.

Los Angeles Nichirenshu Beikoku Betsuin (Nichiren Shu)
Affiliate: Nichiren Propagation Center
2801 E 4th Street
Los Angeles, CA 90033
Tel: (213) 262–7886
Fax: (213) 262–4602

Resident priest—Rev. Shokai Kanai. See **Nichiren Propagation Center,** Oregon.

Los Angeles Shambhala Center (Tibetan–Kagyu/Nyingma)
Affiliation: Shambhala International
8218 W Third Street
Los Angeles, CA 90048
Tel: (213) 653–9342
E-mail: joelwach@earthlink.net
Web site: http://scow.gslis.ucla.edu/students_a-1/czachary/HTML/ShCen.html
International web site: http://www.shambhala.org

City center with over seventy members. Founded 1971.

Sitting practice and instruction in Buddhist and Shambhala traditions, Vajrayana practice for members with appropriate transmissions. Ongoing Monday night classes in Buddhist practice and study. More advanced courses less frequently for senior students. Quarterly weekend meditation retreats at the center and at Shambhala. Local quarterly newsletter; Shambhala International publishes the *Shambhala Sun*.

Founder/Guru	Chogyam Trungpa Rinpoche
Teachers	Resident: senior students of Rinpoche; visiting: many lineage teachers
Opening Times	Sunday 9:00 am–noon; Wednesday and Thursday 7:30–9:30 pm for public meditation; Monday evenings for Buddhist classes; other times for specific programs
Residents	None
Festivals	Contact center
Facilities	2 shrine rooms and a library
Accommodation	None
Food	None
Booking	Not necessary
Fees	Classes usually $10, public meditation free of charge
Expected Behavior	Contact center
How to Get There	Contact center

Reiyukai America (Reiyukai)
2741 Sunset Boulevard
Los Angeles, CA 90026
Tel: (213) 413–1771
Fax: (213) 413–5417
E-mail: rykam@wavenet.com

Two buildings, one for administration and one with meditation hall seating around seventy-five. Office in Los Angeles opened 1972. "Friendly and willing to talk with anyone."

Group recitation on first and third Thursdays of month in English and second Sunday of month in Japanese. Retreats: sports dojo for young people four times a year.

InterConnection published monthly.

Founder/Guru	Kakutaro Kubo and Kimi Kotani
Teachers	No teachers, only lay people
Opening Times	9:00 am–5:00 pm daily
Residents	3 laity
Festivals	Contact center
Facilities	Shrine room, study room
Accommodation	None
Food	None
Booking	Not applicable
Fees	None
Expected Behavior	Not applicable
How to Get There	Exit Hollywood Freeway at Rampart Blvd. from north; Benton Way from south. North on Benton Way to Sunset Blvd., turn left and go $1/4$ of a block—they are on the north side of the street at 2741.

Rigpa (Tibetan–Nyingma)
Affiliation: Rigpa Fellowship
Los Angeles, CA
Tel: (310) 274–1651

Contact: Jane Florentinus. See **Rigpa National Office,** California, for details.

Rinzai-ji Zen Center (Zen–Rinzai)
Main center for Rinzai-ji sangha
2505 Cimarron Street

Los Angeles, CA 90018-2020
Tel: (213) 732–2263

Contact center for details.

Shaolin Buddhist Meditation Center (Shaolin Zen)
3165 Minnesota Street
Los Angeles, CA 90031
Tel: (213) 225–4631

Shaolin Temple and study center. Associated with **California Buddhist University, Kewanee Mountain Zen Center,** and **California Buddhist University's Zen Garden** (see separate entries). *The Shaolin Monastery* published quarterly.

Founder/Guru	Dr. Chia-Ho Chan
Teachers	Contact center
Opening Times	Contact center
Residents	None
Festivals	Contact center
Facilities	Shrine room, dojo, library, study room, and meditation room
Accommodation	None
Food	None
Booking	Contact center
Fees	Classes $100 for 3 months
Expected Behavior	No smoking, alcohol, or dancing
How to Get There	Map for all 3 centers available from the Student's Bookstore (see California Buddhist University)

Zen Center of Los Angeles (Zen–Soto)
Lineage of Yasutani Roshi, Koryu Roshi, and Maezumi Roshi
923 South Normandie Avenue
Los Angeles, CA 90006-1301
Tel: (213) 387–2351
Fax: (213) 387–2377

Although a Soto temple, they include full koan practice in English. Main center composed of four contiguous structures with large grassy backyard and onsite parking in the center of Los Angeles. Residents housed in adjoining apartment buildings. Resident community of twenty-seven for the teaching, training, and practice of priests and laypeople in Zen Buddhism with approximately two hundred visitors per week. Established in 1969 by Hakuyu Taizan Maezumi, Roshi. Thousands of students have trained here, including all twelve of Maezumi Roshi's successors.

Daily sitting practice with Daisan (interview with Nyogen, Sensei). Morning and evening sutra chanting service. Ango, Shuso Hossen, memorials, and marriages. All of the foregoing suitable for newcomers. Meditation instruction every Sunday morning 8:30 am to noon, followed by lunch. Introduction to Zen Buddhist practice 9:00 am–5:00 pm one Saturday per month. Ongoing Kuroda lecture series and guest lecture series on various topics. Courses: Aspects of Zen Practice five Saturday mornings for $1^1/_2$ hours; Jukai: Taking the Buddhist Precepts five weeks $1^1/_2$ hours each for those interested in exploring the possibility of taking the precepts; weekly sutra study group. Monthly seven-day sessions and thirty-day sesshin twice a year. Monthly *Sangha Letter* and monthly *Calendar*. Bookstore onsite.

Zen Mountain Center, Mountain Center, California, is their mountain retreat center. Affiliated groups across the States and worldwide.

Founder/Guru	Hakuyu Taizan Maezumi, Roshi
Teachers	Resident: William Nyogen Yeo, Abbot
Opening Times	Contact center
Residents	27
Festivals	Obon, Hana Matsuri, Parinirvana, New Year, Buddha's Enlightenment (December 8)
Facilities	Kaisando, Godo, library, bookstore, zendo, kitchen, sangha house
Accommodation	Various—dorms and apartment available for serious active Zen practitioners on advance notice
Food	Vegetarian—free to participants
Booking	Varies: classes 1 week; sesshins 2–3 weeks preferably. Deposits required
Fees	Sesshin $30 per day for members; $50 for non-members. Meditation instruction $10; Introduction to Zen Practice $50
Expected Behavior	Smoking outside only; observe ZCLA statement of right conduct; be kind
How to Get There	Contact center.

Los Gatos Zen Group (Zen–Rinzai)
16200 Matilija Drive
Los Gatos, CA 95030-3033
Tel: (408) 354-7506

Zendo in private house founded by lay group in 1963. "This is a lay group providing support and instruction, if requested, in meditation and attention practice with emphasis on application in everyday life and workplace."

Zazen on Sundays and monthly weekend retreats. Private instruction. All suitable for newcomers.

Founder/Guru	Shoen Ando—Hakuyu Maezumi, Roshi
Teachers	Resident: Arvis Joen Justi
Opening Times	Contact center
Residents	None
Festivals	None
Facilities	Zendo
Accommodation	None
Food	Not applicable
Booking	Not applicable
Fees	None
Expected Behavior	5 precepts, no smoking
How to Get There	Please phone for directions

Dhammakaya International Society of California (Theravada–Thai)
Affiliation: Wat Phradhammakaya, Thailand
5950 Heliotrope Circle
Maywood, CA 90270
Tel: (213) 771–7435 or (213) 771–7436
Fax: (213) 771–7437
E-mail: dhammakaya@aol.com

Monastery established 1993. Church and house on 0.7 acres in Hispanic residential city. Around a hundred visitors a week. Buddhism and meditation class daily 6:30–8:30 pm. Three-day intensive meditation retreat course every fourth weekend. *Light of Peace* publication available.

Founder/Guru	Ven. Dhammajayo Bhikku
Teachers	Resident: Ven. Sudhivaro Bhikku, Ven. Vijjesako Bhikku
Opening Times	8:30 am daily
Residents	7 monastics, 10 laity
Festivals	New Year, Maka Puja, Visaka Puja
Facilities	Shrine room, study room, and meditation room
Accommodation	Contact center
Food	Wholefood
Booking	For retreats: 7 days in advance, no deposit
Fees	$50 for outing retreat only—rest dana
Expected Behavior	No smoking and 8 precepts
How to Get There	Freeway 710 exit.

Buddhist Compassion Relief Tzu Chi Foundation
206 E Palm Avenue

Monrovia, CA 91016
Tel: (818) 305–1188
Fax: (818) 305–1185

Contact center for details.

Sozenji Buddhist Temple of Montebello (Zen–Soto)
3020 West Beverly Boulevard
Montebello, CA 90640
Tel: (213) 724–6866

Converted Christian church building in residential suburbs 10 miles east of downtown. Fifty visitors/month. Founded 1971 by Soto Zen missionary, Rev. Shuyu Kurai of Mie Prefecture, Japan. "Approximately eighty families are members—mostly first-, second-, and third-generation Japanese-American. Son of Rev. Shuyu Kurai took over as head priest in 1986. Japanese cultural and community center approach."

Zazen sittings Wednesdays 7:30–8:30 pm. Weekly classes in Chigiri-e (Japanese paper craft), Shodo (Japanese calligraphy), Dharma Yoga, Taiko (Japanese drumming), Zazen meditation, Soroban for children (abacus), and batik art.

Founder/Guru	Rev. Shuyu Kurai from Japan
Teachers	Resident: Rev. Shuichi Thomas Kurai
Opening Times	Contact center
Residents	None
Festivals	Obon
Facilities	Buddha hall, Reihaido (memorial tablet) room, meditation room
Accommodation	None
Food	None
Booking	None
Fees	$10 per sitting
Expected Behavior	Not applicable
How to Get There	From downtown LA, 60 Freeway east, exit Garfield Ave., south, west on Beverly.

Zen Mountain Center (Zen–Soto)
P O Box 43
Mountain Center, CA 92561
Tel: (909) 659–5272
Fax: (909) 659–3275 (Call first)
E-mail: zmc@interserv.com

Mountain retreat site of the Zen Center of Los Angeles. Set on 160 acres of wilderness in the San Jacinto Mountains at 5,500 foot elevation approximately a hundred and twenty miles east of Los Angeles. Founded 1979.

Zen and related retreats; year-round program. Sesshin every month; ninety-day intensive in the summer; sixty-day winter intensive; subjects include Tai Chi, yoga, ecology, indigenous arts. Zen meditation includes koan study and shikantaza, Zen services, chanting, etc. All activities suitable for beginners. Bookstore and stitchery.

Founder/Guru	Hakuyu Taizan Maezumi Roshi
Teachers	Resident: Charles Tenshin Fletcher Sensei and Ann Seisen Fletcher (husband-and-wife teaching team)
Opening Times	Year-round
Residents	4 monastics and 10 laity
Festivals	None
Facilities	Zendo, Buddha hall, dormitory, cabins
Accommodation	Dormitory-style from $30 per night (depending on program)
Food	Vegetarian included in price
Booking	1 week in advance, deposit needed
Fees	From $30 per day
Expected Behavior	As appropriate
How to Get There	$2^1/_2$ hours east of Los Angeles

Kannon Do Zen Meditation Center (Zen)
292 College Avenue
Mountain View, CA 94040
Tel: (415) 903–1935

Contact center for details.

Mount Baldy Zen Center (Zen–Rinzai)
P O Box 429
Mount Baldy, CA 91759
Tel: (909) 985–6410
Fax: (909) 985–4870
E-mail: mbzc@aol.com

Old Boy Scout camp with cabins located on forest service land at 6,500 feet on pine-laden slopes. Established 1971 as a monastic-style facility to complement **Rinzai-Ji Zen Center** (see separate entry). Provides the opportunity for students to immerse themselves in strict Zen practice.

Summer (July–September) and winter (December–March) intensive training periods, called seichus, and less formal training periods in between. Eight week-long Dai sesshins/year. Daily zazen and work practice for residents (not open to public). Visitors' day many Saturday mornings. Zen weekends for beginning students. Center rented out to other groups during spring and fall. Bi-annual newsletter.

Founder/Guru	Joshu Sasaki Roshi (Kyozan Joshu Roshi)
Teachers	Resident: Joshu Sasaki Roshi (Kyozan Joshu Roshi)
Opening Times	Year-round
Residents	4 monastics and 6 laity
Festivals	None
Facilities	2 zendos, sutra hall, library
Accommodation	Visitors not involved in daily schedule: single cabin $40/night; guest cabin $80/night. Dormitory cabin for students involved in daily schedule
Food	Primarily wholefood/vegetarian, but donations of other foods
Booking	6 months in advance for sesshins. Deposit only for sesshins.
Fees	Seichu $190/week, sesshin $350, Seikan $100/week
Expected Behavior	None
How to Get There	Transportation to and from Ontario airport, bus and train depots can be provided by advance arrangement.

Shasta Abbey (Zen–Soto)
Headquarters of the Serene Reflection Meditation Tradition (Order of Buddhist
    Contemplatives)
3724 Summit Drive
Mount Shasta, CA 96067-9102
Tel: (916) 926–4208
Fax: (916) 926–0428
Web site: http://www.OBCON.org

In mountains of northern California on sixteen acres of evergreen forested land. Buildings include ceremony hall, monks' meditation hall, guest house. Living and working quarters for monks and large vegetable garden. Seminary for Buddhist priesthood. Founded 1970.

Teachings on Soto Zen and Mahayana Buddhist practice. Instruction in serene reflection meditation and Buddhist precepts, especially as applied to daily life. Weekly lectures and instruction for local congregation. Monthly introductory weekend retreat. Week-long retreats during summer. Other special retreats and traditional Buddhist festivals throughout the year. Newcomers and beginners welcome to introductory retreats, tours, and meditation instruction. *Journal of the Order of Buddhist Contemplatives* four times a year for $20/year.

Operate mail-order service providing extensive range of Buddhist meditation supplies. Phone or fax (916) 926–6682. For catalog, send $3 (refundable with first purchase) to **Shasta Abbey Buddhist Supplies** at above address.

Founder/Guru	V. Rev. Keido Shisan Koho Zenji
Teachers	Resident: Senior monks
Opening Times	9:30 am–12:30 pm and 2:30–5:30 pm. Closed for business matters on days of the month which end with a 4 or a 9 (e.g., January 4, May 29)
Residents	Around 40 monastics and 2–10 laity
Festivals	See current calendar
Facilities	Guest house: meditation hall, common room, and 20 private rooms. Monastery: large meditation hall and ceremony hall
Accommodation	Guest house
Food	Lacto-vegetarian—cost included in retreat fees
Booking	10 days notice if possible, deposit requested
Fees	Weekend retreats $80, week-long retreats $150
Expected Behavior	Strict—contact Abbey
How to Get There	Off Interstate 5—easy access by car, bus, and train.

California Vipassana Center, Dhamma Mahavana (Vipassana)
Affiliation: Vipassana Meditation Centers in the Tradition of S. N. Goenka
P O Box 1167
North Fork, CA 93643-1167
Tel: (209) 877–4386
Fax: (209) 877–4387
E-mail: Mahavana@aol.com

A hundred and nine acre retreat facility at three thousand feet in spectacular setting in old Mono Indian town near Yosemite National Park in foothills of Sierra Mountains; capacity a hundred and twenty-five. Established 1983.

For further description see **Vipassana Meditation Center,** Massachussetts.

Bay Zen Center (Zen)
Affiliation: Ordinary Mind Zen School
5600A Snake Road
Oakland, CA 94611
Tel: (510) 482–2533
Fax: (510) 482–9531

Residential area close to San Francisco in lower level of teacher's house. Lay practice.

Zazen and daisan—Mondays and Wednesdays 6:00 am; Tuesdays and Thursdays 7:15 pm; Saturdays 8:30 am. Monthly one- to six-day sesshins. Lectures, services (weddings and funerals). Beginners and newcomers may call for an appointment for zazen instruction. Quarterly newsletter.

Founder/Guru	Charlotte Joko Beck
Teachers	Resident: Diane Eshin Rizzetto (Dharma successor to Joko)
Opening Times	See zazen times above
Residents	Teacher
Festivals	Various throughout year
Facilities	Zendo
Accommodation	None
Food	None
Booking	6 weeks in advance for sesshins
Fees	Retreats: $25/day members, $30/day non-members
Expected Behavior	5 precepts
How to Get There	Contact center

California Diamond Sangha (Zen)
Affiliation: Diamond sangha
Oakland, CA
Tel: (510) 531–5779

See **California Diamond Sangha** in Santa Rosa, California, for details.

Fruitvale Zendo (Zen)
4001 San Leandro Street, # 1
Oakland, CA 94601
Tel: (510) 532–5226
E-mail: utapipig@ix.netcom.com

Very small zendo (sits five) at the corner of 40th and San Leandro in Fruitvale neighborhood.

Led by Greg Fain, whose home temple is Berkeley Zen Center and teacher is Sojun Mel Weitsman Roshi. Practice times vary according to Greg's schedule, and it is important that you contact him first if you are interested in sitting zazen here.

Ati Ling (Tibetan–Nyingma)
Affiliation: Chagdud Gonpa Foundation
P O Box 90
Oakville, CA 94562
Tel: (707) 944–1907
Teacher is Tulku Jigme Tromge Rinpoche. Contact center for details.

Ojai Valley Dharma Center (Tibetan–Karma Kagyu)
P O Box 1472
Ojai, CA 98024

Contact center for details.

Rissho Kose-kai of San Francisco (Rissho Kosei-kai)
1031 Valencia Way
Pacifica, CA 94044
Tel: (415) 359 6951
Fax: (415) 359 5569
E-mail: SFKosei@ix.netcom.com

Community of 150 in formerly Christian church in scenic city near San Francisco. Opened 1979. "Our main dojo is in being with the family and in the workplace, not in church, which is only a place for training. At church, we teach each other how to apply readings of the Lotus Sutra to daily life."

Meditation and sutra recitation daily at 9:30 am followed by Hoza at 9:30 am. Sunday Service 9:30 am–noon. Monthly Basic Buddhism seminar. Lotus Sutra seminar first and third Monday of the month at 7:00 pm. One-day retreats twice a year, mainly comparative study of religion and deepening understanding of Buddhism. Newsletter, *Everyday Buddhism*, every two months. Books and pamphlets on Buddhism.

Founder/Guru	Nikkyo Niwano founder, Nichiko Niwano president
Teachers	Minister: Keiji Kunitomi
Opening Times	9:00 am–2:00 pm
Residents	None
Festivals	New Year's Day, Foundation Day, Buddha's Birthday, Obon service, Founder's Birthday, Bodhi Day
Facilities	Main hall, library, and study room
Accommodation	None
Food	None
Booking	None
Fees	Not applicable
Expected Behavior	No smoking
How to Get There	Hwy. 1 south from San Francisco, turn left at Crespi Drive, then left at La Milada Drive and left onto Valencia Way, turn right and 1 block from there.

Palo Alto Dharmadhatu (Tibetan–Kagyu/Nyingma)
Affiliation: Shambhala International

Henry Polard, Coordinator
260 Fernando
Palo Alto, CA 94306
E-mail: henry@netcom.com

See International headquarters, **Shambhala Center,** Halifax, Nova Scotia, Canada.

Palo Alto Karma Thegsum Choling (Tibetan–Karma Kagyu)
Affiliation: Karma Triyana Dharmachakra, New York
P O Box 60793
Palo Alto, CA 94306
Tel: (415) 967–1145
E-mail: pema@dewachen.palo-alto.ca.us

Founded by 16th Karmapa. Weekly program and special events. Contact center for details.

Rigpa (Tibetan–Nyingma)
Affiliation: Rigpa Fellowship
Palo Alto, CA
Tel: (415) 366 3344

Contact: Lotte Grimes. See **Rigpa National Office,** California, for details.

Soka Gakkai International (SGI-USA) (Nichiren)
San Fernando Valley Area Regional Center
P O Box 4369
14840 Nordhoff Street
Panorama City, CA 91402-4369
Tel: (818) 830–1336
Fax: (818) 830–1334

See **Soka Gakkai International** National Offices & Center, Santa Monica, California, for more details.

Seiganzan Myoshinji Temple (Nichiren)
2631 Appian Way
Pinole, CA 94564-2202
Tel: (505) 222–8372
Fax: (505) 222–9969

Modern architecture in Japanese tradition. Officially opened 1984. "Peaceful, serene." Monthly Japanese and English general study meetings. Publish *Nichiren Shoshu* (monthly), *Shinyo* (quarterly), and *Nichiren Shoshu News* (monthly).

Founder/Guru	Nichiren Daishonin
Teachers	Contact center
Opening Times	9:00 am–7:00 pm daily
Residents	2 monastics, 1 laity, and 3 children
Festivals	Oeshiki Ceremony, Go Ho'on Oro Ceremony, Okyo-bi Ceremony, and Mo Kushi-e Ceremony
Facilities	Auditorium, small library, study room
Accommodation	Hotel opposite
Food	None
Booking	Not applicable
Fees	Not applicable
Expected Behavior	Basic human respect
How to Get There	From San Francisco take Highway 80 east toward Sacramento; continue through Berkeley, Richmond and take Appian Way exit. Turn right and after lights go 200 yards and make a left into temple grounds.

Abhayagiri Buddhist Monastery (Theravada–Thai Forest Tradition)
16201 Tomki Road
Redwood Valley, CA 95470
Tel: (707) 485–1630
Fax: (707) 485–7948

Two-bedroom house with good-sized meditation hall on two hundred and fifty acres of mountains and woods. Branch monastery of Amaravati in England. Residents live in meditation huts in forest, guests in campers or tents. Opened 1996.

No formal classes for visitors. Dhamma talks Saturday night and each evening of the four phases of the moon when there is also an all-night meditation vigil. Guests may arrange a stay of up to one week on their first visit and participate in the daily services and activities of the monastery on an equal basis with the residents. Two formal pujas a day. Quarterly newsletter.

Founder/Guru	Ajahn Chah
Teachers	Resident: Ajahn Amaro and Ajahn Visuddhi
Opening Times	Tea 5:30 pm; evening chanting/sitting 7:30 pm
Residents	3 monastics and 3 laity
Festivals	Contact center
Facilities	See above
Accommodation	Tents or campers on a dana basis

Food	Relies on donations of food from the lay community—generally vegetarian
Booking	Several days notice appreciated
Fees	No fees—dana basis
Expected Behavior	8 precepts, including no eating after midday
How to Get There	Off Route 101 north of Ukiah. Call for details.

Rosemead Buddhist Monastery (Basic Buddhism–multitraditional)
7833 Emerson Place
Rosemead, CA 91770
Tel: (818) 280–1213 or (818) 288–1210
Fax: (818) 280–9077
E-mail and web site: planned

Temple with outbuildings with two hundred visitors a week. Established 1985 by American and Asian immigrant Buddhists interested in bringing together the various ethnic groups and traditions present in larger Buddhist community in America. "Basic Teachings, multi-ethnic, multi-lingual; no specific tradition; open to all, active English speaking classes and programs."

Offers Chinese/Vietnamese services, and Vipassana instruction and regular practice twice weekly. Meditation, Dharma study, sutra study, and retreats held on Sundays. Insight Meditation Retreat bimonthly. Annual short-term ordination. Annual ministers ordination. For monastic training, inquire through abbot. Monthly *Common Sense* magazine. Sells books in English and Chinese.

Founder/Guru	Founding Abbot: Ven. Chao Chu
Teachers	Resident: Rev. Sam Haycraft, Rev. Aureliano Nava
Opening Times	8:00 am–6:00 pm daily
Residents	Abbot
Festivals	Vesak and Bodhidharma Day
Facilities	Shrine room, library, meditation hall, classrooms
Accommodation	If requested
Food	Vegetarian
Booking	Contact center
Fees	Nominal donation
Expected Behavior	5 precepts, self discipline, follow temple rules
How to Get There	Approximately 12 miles east of downtown Los Angeles; 2 blocks south of I-10.

ABS Temple at Sacramento (Theravada)
1715 Lisbon Avenue

West Sacramento, CA 95605
Tel: (916) 371–8535
E-mail: abs@slip.net

Training temple for American Buddhist Seminary (ABS) (see separate entry). Students will work with Buddhist community implementing theoretical knowledge gained at ABS into practice.

House with facilities for meditation and other public religious activities—shrine room, study room, and meditation room—with two resident monks.

Open 9:00 am–9:00 pm daily; Sunday service for general public 10:00 am.

City of the Dharma Realm (Pure Land and Ch'an)
Affiliation: Dharma Realm Buddhist Association
1029 West Capitol Avenue
West Sacramento, CA 95691
Tel & Fax: (916) 374–8268

Nunnery and training center for women novices and Bhikshunis. Lay men may attend shorter retreats and are referred to monasteries in Mendicino County and elsewhere. Spanish-style buildings. Over two hundred rooms for retreat purposes. On seventeen acres, building was a well-known hotel in 1950s. Opened 1993.

Services on Saturdays and Sundays open to public. Classes open to public include sutra study. Winter retreat period over last December and first two-three weeks of January with one week of Pure Land Dharma Door practice followed by three weeks of Ch'an. Rains Retreat for sangha members. Publish monthly newsletter.

Founder/Guru	Ven. Hsuan Hsu
Teachers	Contact nunnery
Opening Times	8:00 am–5:00 pm daily
Residents	Approximately 20 ordained Bhikshunis and novice nuns and 5 lay women
Festivals	As Buddhist calendar for Buddhas and Bodhisattvas
Facilities	2 Buddha halls, meditation facilities
Accommodation	$30/day; special allowances for those contributing their services to the temple (i.e., work/study)
Food	Vegetarian (strict)
Booking	2 weeks in advance
Fees	Usually $30/day
Expected Behavior	5 precepts for laity; monks/nuns adhere to precepts they have received. Clothes must be modest, perfumes avoided. No smoking, drinking, drug taking, television, or radio.
How to Get There	Shuttles from Sacramento airport (15 minutes away). From San Francisco or Oakland, take 80 East to

Sacramento, get off at Jefferson Blvd. exit. Turn left and turn right at first traffic light (Merkely Ave.). Road veers to left, down half a block on the right is a black iron gate.

Lion's Roar Mandala
3550 Watt Avenue
Suite 2
Sacramento, CA 95821
Tel: (916) 481–0424

Steve Walker resident lama. Contact center for details.

Sacramento Nichiren Buddhist Church (Nichiren Shu)
Affiliate: Nichiren Propagation Center
5191 24th Street
Sacramento, CA 95822
Tel & Fax: (916) 456–8371

Resident priest—Rev. Kenjo Igarashi. See **Nichiren Propagation Center,** Oregon.

Vietnamese Buddhist Association of Sacramento
Kim Quang Pagoda (Vietnamese)
3119 Alta Arden Expressway
Sacramento, CA 95825
Tel: (916) 481–8781
Fax: (916) 488–6510

Residential property remodeled as a temple with Buddha hall and meditation hall. Fifteen-foot Kwan Yin statue in a pond. Center with a hundred members; for special holidays five hundred to one thousand attend. "After 1975, many of us—Vietnamese—came to Sacramento to settle. As the community grew, a spiritual need emerged. We founded this association in 1976, and in 1981 Venerable Thich Thien Tri came and resided at our facility. Under his guidance as spiritual leader, we practiced Buddhist traditions." Center is mostly used by the Vietnamese community, although a few Westerners visit.

For English-speaking members, meditation and sutra learning class on Wednesdays. Contemplation day, starting Saturday and ending Sunday, with chanting, Dharma talks, and meditations.

> *Founder/Guru*   See above
>   *Teachers*   Resident: Ven. Thich Thien Tri
> *Opening Times*   8:00 am to 10:00 pm

Residents	1 monk, many laity
Festivals	All main Buddhist holidays
Facilities	Buddha hall, ancestors hall, meditation hall, living quarters, dining hall
Accommodation	Contact center
Food	Strictly vegetarian—no onion, no garlic, no dairy
Booking	Not necessary
Fees	Donations welcome
Expected Behavior	No smoking or drinking; 5 precepts
How to Get There	From 80 Business, exit Arden Way (east), then Alta Arden Expressway—pagoda is on the left with a big arch saying, "Chua Kim Quang."

Purple Lotus Society (Chinese–True Buddha School)
636 San Mateo Avenue
San Bruno, CA 94066
Tel: (415) 952–9513
Fax: (415) 952–9567
Web site for True Buddha School: http://www.ee.ucla.edu/~yang/truebuddha.html

Temple occupies two-story building in downtown San Bruno. Across the street is the Buddhist gift store and publication department. The Purple Lotus University is across the San Francisco Bay in a residential area in Union City. Was founded in 1987 by Vajra Master Samantha Chou, an emanation of the Purple Lotus Bodhisattva, starting in her small apartment and expanding to three buildings. University in Union City, CA, open in 1997.

Daily schedule: 7:30 am Shakyamuni practice and 5:00 pm Padmakumara practice (except Tuesdays and Saturdays). Saturday 8:00 pm group cultivation and Dharma talk. Tuesdays 8:00 pm (when Master Samantha Chou is in town) Bardo ceremony. First Sunday every month 10:00 am questions and answers for Western practitioners. Frequent Bardo and fire ceremonies to relieve participants' negative karma. Classes and courses are given on how to perform practice on a one-on-one basis. Once the University is open, college courses will be given on all aspects of Buddhism, feng shui, Chi Gong, etc. Fire Ceremony Retreat once every two years. Quarterly *Purple Lotus Journal* is a Tantric Buddhist, feng shui, and Taoist magazine featuring the works of Grand Master Lu. Free subscription by calling (415) 589–9559. Many pamphlets and books also available.

Amitabha Enterprises—Buddhist gift and statue shop at 629 San Mateo Ave., San Bruno, CA 94066.

Purple Lotus Publishing—Publishes *Purple Lotus Journal* and books at 627 San Mateo Ave., San Bruno, CA 94066.

Founder/Guru	Grand Master Sheng-yen Lu (Living Buddha Lian-Shen)
Teachers	Vajra Master Samantha Chou
Opening Times	9:00 am–5:00 pm
Residents	9 monastics and 12 lay people
Festivals	Contact center for schedule
Facilities	Shrine room, meditation room, dining room, kitchen, library, children's room, and Buddhist gift store
Accommodation	$10 per night for those who have taken refuge
Food	Chinese for a donation
Booking	Not necessary
Fees	By donation
Expected Behavior	5 precepts, no smoking
How to Get There	From the 101 Freeway take the San Bruno West exit (which is 1 mile north of the San Francisco Airport exit). At the 2nd traffic light, take a left on San Mateo Ave. Go two blocks to 636.

Rigpa (Tibetan–Nyingma)
Affiliation: Rigpa Fellowship
San Diego, CA
Tel: (619) 755–3941

Contact: The Hudsons. See **Rigpa National Office,** California, for details.

San Diego Dharma Study Group (Tibetan–Kagyu/Nyingma)
Affiliation: Shambhala International
c/o Paul & Brenda Wegener
3920 Goldfinch Street
San Diego, CA 92103
Tel & Fax: (619) 298–4279

See International headquarters, **Shambhala Center,** Halifax, Nova Scotia, Canada.

San Diego Karma Thegsum Choling (Tibetan–Karma Kagyu)
Affiliation: Karma Triyana Dharmachakra, New York
1236 Missouri Street
San Diego, CA 92109-2661
Tel: (619) 483–5028

Contact center for more information.

Vajrarupini Buddhist Center (Tibetan–Gelug)
Affiliation: New Kadampa Tradition
P O Box 420128
San Diego, CA 92142
Tel: (619) 692–1591
E-mail: vajrarup@adnc.com
Web site: http://www.adnc.com/web/vajrarup

General programs held in a quiet house in convenient location in city.

Weekly General Program classes provide overview of essential practices of Mahayana Buddhism for new and experienced meditators. Foundation program (two classes/week) for those wishing to deepen their knowledge and experience of the Dharma—correspondence course also available. Day courses on such subjects as the Buddhist view of death and dying or thangka painting. One-day and weekend retreats throughout the year. Pujas open to all three times a week. Monthly Mahayana precepts days observed. Quarterly newsletter.

Founder/Guru	Ven. Geshe Kelsang Gyatso
Teachers	Resident: Gen Kelsang Tubpa
Opening Times	Phone in advance
Residents	1 monastic, 2 laity
Festivals	Buddha's Enlightenment Day, Je Tsongkhapa Day, Celebration of Buddha's Turning the Wheel of Dharma Day, Celebration of Buddha's Return from Heaven
Facilities	Meditation room and small library
Accommodation	None
Food	None
Booking	Day courses—5 days in advance. Weekend courses/retreats—minimum 3 week in advance with 25% deposit
Fees	$10 per class or $160 per semester. Weekends $70–130 including meals
Expected Behavior	No intoxicants, including alcohol and tobacco. No meat or fish to be consumed on premises. No taking of any life.
How to Get There	Contact center

Faith is, above all, open-ness—an act of trust in the unknown.

Alan Watts *On the Taboo Against Knowing Who You Are*

Zen Center of San Diego (Zen)
Affiliation: Ordinary Mind Zen School
2047 Felspar Street
San Diego, CA 92109
Tel: (619) 273–3444

Head is Charlotte Joko Beck, founder of Ordinary Mind Zen School. Contact center for more details.

Aro Gar (Tibetan–Nyingma–Aro gTér)
Affiliation: Sang-ngak-cho-dzong of Great Britain
San Francisco, CA

See **Aro Gar** in New York for details. In San Francisco, telephone (510) 865–1394.

Buddhist Church of San Francisco (Pure Land–Jodo Shinshu)
Affiliation: Buddhist Churches of America
1881 Pine Street
San Francisco, CA 94109
Tel: (415) 776–3158
Fax: (415) 776–0264

Western-style three-story building in central San Francisco which includes chapel, gymnasium, kitchens, and classrooms. Outstanding altar and chapel in Jodo Shin Hongwanji style. Stupa containing holy relics donated by King of Siam (Thailand) in 1935. Between a hundred and a hundred and fifty visitors a week. Founded 1898; at current location since 1927.

Weekly Dharma services. Weekly and periodic family services. Study sessions. Personal consultations. Weekly and monthly lectures and study classes. Courses in Jodo Shin Buddhism, Mahayana Buddhism, Theravada Buddhism, History and Doctrine of Religions, and Japanese culture. Occasional retreats. Fund-raising and cultural activities.

Monthly newsletter and special commemorative publications.

Founder/Guru	Spiritual Head: Abbot Koshin Ohtani of Nishi Hongwanji, Japan
Teachers	Resident minister, lay leaders
Opening Times	Contact center
Residents	Minister
Festivals	Obon, Buddha Day
Facilities	Chapel, library, classrooms, and stupa
Accommodation	None
Food	None

Booking	Not applicable
Fees	Not applicable
Expected Behavior	Contact center
How to Get There	Central San Francisco

Buddhist Churches of America (Jodo Shinshu)
National Headquarters of Buddhist Churches of America
1710 Octavia Street
San Francisco, CA 94109
Tel: (415) 776–5600
Fax: (415) 771–6293

Administrative headquarters of hundreds of independent churches and branches, mostly on the Pacific Coast. Contact this center for details.

Diamond Way Buddhist Center (Tibetan–Karma Kagyu)
110 Merced Avenue
San Francisco, CA 94127
Tel: (415) 661–6467
Fax: (415) 665–2241
E-mail: kclsf.best.com
Web site: http://www.diamondway.org

Eight lay residents and extended sangha of twenty, one of eleven groups in the USA who are part of a worldwide network in the Karma Kagyu tradition.

Monday 8:00 pm Chenrezig meditation in English, Wednesday 8:00 pm Guru Yoga on the 16th Karmapa guided in English, Sunday 10:00 am Green Tara Prayer and Ngondro. Quarterly Ngondro, Phowa, and Chenrezig retreats. Magazine is *Buddhism Today*, an international publication.

Founder/Guru	Founder: 17th Gyalwa Karmapa, Thaye Dorje; Spiritual Director: Lama Ole Nydahl
Teachers	Resident: Jesper Jorgensen
Opening Times	Contact center
Residents	8 lay
Festivals	Contact center
Facilities	Meditation room
Accommodation	Not applicable
Food	Not applicable
Booking	Contact center
Fees	Contact center
Expected Behavior	Contact center
How to Get There	Contact center

Gay Buddhist Fellowship (Mixed traditions)
2261 Market Street, #422
San Francisco, CA 94114
Tel: (415) 974–9878

Organization supporting Buddhist practice in the gay men's community. Members from all three main traditions. Mailing list of six hundred names; active membership of 100. Rent space on an as-needed basis at present, but have plans to establish own center in the near future. Governed by a Steering Committee with a consensus style of management. Founded 1991 primarily as a support group for gay men who were Buddhist, but since developed into more complex and far-reaching organization.

Offer workshops and classes on a regular basis, including Foundations of Buddhism; Relationships and the Dharma; HIV Disease and Practice. Four monthly Saturday and Sunday morning meetings which include a period of sitting meditation and Dharma talk (for larger community). Sponsor one-day sittings on a regular basis. Sponsor an annual weekend retreat at a local rural practice place and plan to do more retreats with various themes in the future. Newcomers welcome at all GBF functions.

Also sponsor various other socially engaged activities. Members prepare meals for people at a local family homeless shelter; support people with HIV disease; have a Gay Prisoner's Dharma Project; potlucks, picnics, etc. General outreach and networking in the larger gay community. Publish monthly newsletter which includes GBF schedule of events, local Dharma calendar, articles of interest to the gay Buddhist community, and general information about the organization and its programs.

Founder/Guru	Founded by a group of lay and ordained practitioners
Teachers	Conscious choice of the membership to have no formal teachers or gurus. Teachers and monks are members.

Gold Mountain Monastery (Pure Land and Ch'an)
Affiliation: Dharma Realm Buddhist Association
800 Sacramento Street
San Francisco, CA 94108
Tel: (415) 421–6117

All Dharma Realm Buddhist Association branch monasteries are open to the public and have morning, afternoon, evening ceremonies, and sutra lectures every day as well as their own special programs. All activities are led by fully ordained monks or nuns.

Harbor Sangha (Zen)
Affiliation: Diamond sangha
c/o Hamilton Methodist Church
1525 Waller Street

San Francisco, CA 94117
Tel: (415) 241–8807
E-mail: jbobrow@aol.com or gregharr@aol.com

Own zendo in local Methodist church. About fifteen regular participants, all lay. Established 1989.

Zen meditation 6:30–9:00 pm Mondays. Hold various events throughout the year, from picnics and other social gatherings to introductions to Zen and meditation, to talks from various figures from Zen community. Host various retreats throughout year— seven-day sesshins biannually, one-day sittings monthly, yearly outdoor hiking retreat (Mountains and Rivers sesshin).

Founder/Guru	Joe Bobrow
Teachers	Joe Bobrow
Opening Times	Mondays 6:30–9:00 pm
Residents	None
Festivals	None
Facilities	Zendo, interview room
Accommodation	None
Food	None
Booking	Not necessary
Fees	$30/month suggested donation for regular members; $25 1-day retreats; around $200 sesshins
Expected Behavior	Contact center
How to Get There	1 block south of Haight St. in Haight/Ashbury district, near Golden Gate Park. Enter church in the front and walk to the back, through a door on the right. Zendo at top of flight of stairs.

Hartford Street Zen Center Issanji (Zen–Soto)
   (One Mountain Temple)
57 Hartford Street
San Francisco, CA 94114
Tel: (415) 863–2507

Victorian house in the Castro district. Small Zendo in the heart of gay area of San Francisco. Founded 1982 and dedicated as Zen temple in 1988.

Monday to Friday morning zazen 5:45–6:20 am followed by service at 6:20–6:45 am; evening zazen followed by served at 6:00–6:40 pm. Saturday zazen 9:10–10:00 am; Dharma talk 10:00 am followed by tea and discussion. Introduction to zazen and Zendo practice forms at 8:00 am by appointment on Saturdays. Dinner for the community on Monday nights after zazen—suggested donation five dollars. Abbot Zenshin available for *dokusan* (practice interviews) to answer questions and discuss student's practice by appointment.

Quarterly newsletter.

Founder	Issan Dorsey Roshi
Teachers	Resident: Abbot Zenshin Philip Whalen
Opening Times	See session times above
Residents	1 monk/nun and 1 lay person
Festivals	Contact center
Facilities	Zendo
Accommodation	None
Food	None
Booking	See text above
Fees	Donation appreciated
Expected Behavior	5 precepts
How to Get There	In center of town

Ratnashri Sangha (Tibetan–Drikung Kagyu)
2118 Hayes Street
San Francisco, CA 94117
Contact: Cindy Chang
Tel: (415) 688–8210
Fax: (415) 673–1100
E-mail: lamapema@ix.netcom.com
Web site: http://www.churchward.com/drikung

Contact center for details.

San Francisco Buddhist Center (Friends of the Western Buddhist Order)
37 Bartlett Street
San Francisco, CA 94110
Tel: (415) 282–2018
Web site: http://www.bluelotus.com/sfbc/sfbc.htm

Victorian house with very large first-floor extension in Mission District of San Francisco. Around 50 visitors per week. Good quiet meditation hall and good introduction and instruction in all practices. Aim to serve the local community by providing a place dedicated to the development of positive human values. Founded 1992 and still being remodeled.

Full program of courses, drop-in classes, and retreats—sittings and classes every weekday. Meditations offered include Mindfulness of Breathing, Walking Meditation,

Metta Bhavana, Seven Fold Puja, and Chanting. Weekly Tuesday Introductory Night 7:00–9:00 pm and weekly Thursday Friends Night 7:00–9:30 pm. Five-week introductory courses in meditation and in Buddhism on Wednesday evenings. Afternoon introductory meditation course. Weekend and longer retreats throughout the year, for example, retreats for men, retreats for women, ten-day winter and summer retreats, meditation, and study of Buddhist texts. FWBO publishes quarterly *Dharma Life* magazine.

Founder/Guru	Ven. Sangharakshita
Teachers	Members of the FWBO
Opening Times	7:00 am morning meditation and 7:00 pm evenings
Residents	2 Order members and 4 Mitras (equivalent to a novice)
Festivals	Wesak, Dharma Day, Sangha Day, Parinirvana Day, Padmasambhava Day
Facilities	Shrine room, library, and reception
Accommodation	None
Food	None
Booking	Contact center
Fees	Suggested donations for activities
Expected Behavior	Contact center
How to Get There	BART to 24th St./Mission, Buses 14 or 26, Bartlett St. at 21st Street, good parking on Bartlett St.

San Francisco Dharmadhatu (Tibetan–Kagyu/Nyingma)
Affiliation: Shambhala International
1630 Taraval Street
San Francisco, CA 94116
Tel: (415) 731–4426
E-mail: dasolman@slip.net

See International headquarters, **Shambhala Center,** Halifax, Nova Scotia, Canada.

San Francisco Nichiren Buddhist Church (Nichiren Shu)
Affiliate: Nichiren Propagation Center
1570 17th Avenue
San Francisco, CA 94122
Tel: (415) 665–4063

See **Nichiren Propagation Center,** Oregon.

San Francisco Zen Center (Zen–Soto)

300 Page Street
San Francisco, CA 94102
Tel: (415) 863–3136
Fax: (415) 431–9220
Web site: http://bodi.zendo.com

One of three practice locations—see also **Green Gulch Farm** and **Tassajara Zen Mountain Center**.

Urban temple in large three-story Julia Morgan building. Established 1969.

Wide variety of classes in Buddhism, including koan study, abhidharma, sutras, etc. Residential and nonresidential courses and classes offered. Monday to Friday: 5:25 am zazen, kinhin, service, and soji; 5:40 pm zazen and service. The Saturday morning program at 6:30–12:00 am may be joined either for a full morning of practice or any part of it and it includes breakfast and lunch. Meditation instruction for newcomers is given at 8:45 am Saturdays.

Residential guests may be part of the Guest Program, Guest Student Program, a Zendo Student, Practice Period Resident, or Resident. Publishes *Windbell* biannually and has bookstore.

Founder/Guru	Shunryu Suzuki Roshi
Teachers	3 resident abbots: Mel Weitsman, Norman Fischer, and Blanche Hartman. Senior resident teacher: Reb Anderson. Other priests and lay teachers lecture and assist in the teaching.
Opening Times	Contact center
Residents	About 50
Festivals	None
Facilities	Zendo, Buddha Hall (ceremony hall), library, classrooms, and study center
Accommodation	Contact center for details
Food	Vegetarian
Booking	Varies on availability—deposit required
Fees	$30 on up for classes for members; $15 per day as guest student and on up as full guest
Expected Behavior	16 Bodhisattva precepts (Mahayana)
How to Get There	Limited parking space, so you are encouraged to contact the center for carpooling facilities.

Saraha Buddhist Center (Tibetan–Gelug)
Affiliation: New Kadampa Tradition
3145 Geary Boulevard, # 515
San Francisco, CA 94118-3300
Tel & Fax: (415) 585–9161
E-mail: saraha@ix.netcom.com

Rented venues at several locations—San Jose, Los Gatos, Marin, and San Francisco. Founded 1991. "Variety of programs suited to the beginner or those with more experience to combine study and practice into a personal program."

General Program (meditation classes, talk, and meditation), Foundation Program (systematic study with meditation), day and weekend courses. Day retreats once or twice monthly on Lamrim, purification, Medicine Buddha, ten-day and month-long retreats. Bookstore selling books by Geshe Kelsang Gyatso, ritual items, statues, audio-tapes of teachings, and guided meditations, etc.

Founder/Guru	Geshe Kelsang Gyatso
Teachers	Resident: Gen Kelsang Togden
Opening Times	Contact center
Residents	2 monks, 1 nun, 3 laity
Festivals	Contact center
Facilities	Temporary residential facilities including gompa and library
Accommodation	None
Food	None
Booking	For special events only
Fees	General Program/meditation classes $10 suggested donation; Foundation Program $50/month 2 sessions per week
Expected Behavior	5 precepts
How to Get There	Please call

Soka Gakkai International (SGI-USA) (Nichiren)
San Francisco Area Regional Center
2450 17th Street
San Francisco, CA 94110-1442
Tel: (415) 255–6007
Fax: (415) 255–6079

See **Soka Gakkai International** National Offices & Center, Santa Monica, California, for more details.

Sokoji-Soto Mission (Zen–Soto)
1691 Laguna Street
San Francisco, CA 94115
Tel: (415) 346–7540
Fax: (415) 346–0355

Contact center for details.

Tse Chen Ling Center for Tibetan Buddhist Studies (Tibetan–Gelug)
Affiliation: Foundation for the Preservation of the Mahayana Tradition
4 Joost Avenue
San Francisco, CA 94131
Tel: (415) 339–8002
Fax: (415) 333–3261
e-mail & Web site: tclcenter@aol.com

In Glen Park neighborhood of city center. Storefront space with bookstore, meditation hall, and small office. Around a hundred visitors a week.

Early morning sittings three times a week. Meditation in Spanish language biweekly. Ongoing meditation programs; introductory level courses (Western Lamrim); initiations and commentary on Tantric practices; specific Tibetan practices (Tsog, Praises to Twenty-one Taras, Healing Buddha, Shantideva's Guide to Bodhisattvas Way of Life, Ganden Lageyma Practice and Commentary); visiting lamas and Rinpoches from around the world; advanced philosophy and psychology; mind training. Classes meet weekly, biweekly, or monthly and run from four to twelve sessions. Retreats are offered at two sister centers in the Santa Cruz mountains (about $1^1/_2$ hours away)— **Vajrapani,** Boulder Creek, CA, and **Land of Medicine Buddha,** Soquel, CA (see separate entries). Publish bimonthly newsletter.

Founder/Guru	Lama Yeshe and Lama Zopa
Teachers	Resident: Ven. Geshe Kalsang Wangdu; Ven. Robina Courtin; visiting: many Tibetan teachers
Opening Times	For evening programs almost daily and during the day for weekend programs
Residents	None
Festivals	Contact center
Facilities	Gompa, bookstore/library, and office
Accommodation	None
Food	None
Booking	Not necessary
Fees	Suggested donation $10 per meeting; members are not requested to donate
Expected Behavior	5 precepts
How to Get There	Please refer to newsletter

Yeshe Nyingpo Center Orgyen Dorje Den (Tibetan–Nyingma)
Affiliation: Pacific Region Yeshe Nyingpo–Tashi Choling
410 Townsend Street, Suite 406
San Francisco, CA 94107
Tel: (415) 495–0915

See **Pacific Region Yeshe Nyingpo–Tashi Choling,** Oregon.

Zen Group of San Francisco (Zen–Soto)
470 14th Street, #1
San Francisco, CA 94103 (subject to change)
Tel: (415) 553–8171
E-mail: Dominique.Zuni@Dana.com
Web site: http://www.cwi.nl/~gruau

Disciple of Master Kosen Thibaut, Dominique Zuni arrived California 1996 and is in early stages of developing center. At time of writing was looking for permanent premises—check web site for update. "Strong emphasis on the correct posture, no benches, chairs, etc."

Zazen Mondays and Wednesdays 6:30 am; Tuesdays and Thursdays 7:00 pm; Saturdays 9:00 am. Sewing of rakusu and kesa; kusen (oral teachings) during zazen. All-day zazen. Sesshins and retreats with masters from Europe. All activities open to newcomers; thirty-minute introduction given by appointment.

Founder/Guru	Master Taisen Deshimaru
Teachers	Resident: Doninique Zuni. Visiting: Master Kosen Thibaut, Master Barbara Richeaudeau, and others
Opening Times	See zazen times above
Residents	Contact center
Festivals	Contact center
Facilities	Dojo
Accommodation	Contact center
Food	Guen Mai (rice soup) served after morning zazen
Booking	Contact center
Fees	$3–4 per session; $20–30 per month
Expected Behavior	In the dojo, follow the rules of the dojo.
How to Get There	Contact center

Gold Sage Monastery (Pure Land and Ch'an)
Affiliation: Dharma Realm Buddhist Association
11455 Clayton Road
San Jose, CA 95127
Tel: (408) 923–7243

All Dharma Realm Buddhist Association branch monasteries are open to the public and have morning, afternoon, evening ceremonies and Sutra lectures every day as well as their own special programs. All activities are led by fully ordained monks or nuns.

Medicine Buddha Healing Center (Tibetan–Gelug)
Affiliation: Foundation for the Preservation of the Mahayana Tradition

6809 Chiala Lane
San Jose, CA 95129
Tel: (408) 777–8648
Fax: (408) 257–6155
E-mail: 102451.1422@compuserve.com
Web site: http://www.mbh.com

House with around fifty visitors a week. Very high lama, Ribur Rinpoche, is resident teacher. Contact center for schedule of events.

Founder/Guru	Lama Zopa Rinpoche
Teachers	Ribur Rinpoche resident; many Geshe visit
Opening Times	8:00 am–6:00 pm
Residents	4 monks
Festivals	Contact center
Facilities	Gompa, library, study room
Accommodation	Not applicable
Food	Vegetarian
Booking	Contact center
Fees	No charge
Expected Behavior	No smoking
How to Get There	1 hour south of San Francisco

San Jose Myoukakuji Betsuin (Nichiren Shu)
Affiliate: Nichiren Propagation Center
3570 Mona Way
San Jose, CA 95130
Tel: (408) 246–0111
Fax: (408) 246–3543

Resident minister—Bishop Ryusho Matsuda. See **Nichiren Propagation Center, Oregon.**

Ring of Bone Zendo (Zen)
Affiliation: Diamond sangha
P O Box 510
North San Juan, CA 95960

Contact center for details.

Soka Gakkai International (SGI-USA) (Nichiren)

San Diego Area Regional Center
800 Los Vallecitos Boulevard, Suite # C & D
San Marcos, CA 92069
Tel: (619) 591–9738
Fax: (619) 591–9504

See **Soka Gakkai International** National Offices & Center, Santa Monica, California, for more details.

Soka Gakkai International (SGI-USA) (Nichiren)
Santa Ana Area Regional Center
1500 Brookhollow Drive
Santa Ana, CA 92705
Tel: (714) 444–9580 or (714) 444–9575
Fax: (714) 444–9577

See **Soka Gakkai International** National Offices & Center, Santa Monica, California, for more details.

Mahakankala Buddhist Center (Tibetan–Gelug)
Affiliation: New Kadampa Tradition
1B North Alisos Street
Santa Barbara, CA 93103
Tel & Fax: (805) 965–1813
E-mail: contact center

Smallish house with gompa ten minutes from beach and surrounded by mountains. Small residential community and extended community of between fifty and hundred visitors/week. "The center is open to the public to come and use the meditation room, chat, have a cup of tea, or use the library." Founded 1994.

Meditation classes (General program) Mondays, introducing basic Buddhist meditation and explaining mainly Lamrim. More in-depth study classes (Foundation program) Sundays. Day and weekend courses every four-six weeks on subjects such as how to reduce anger, how to use meditation recitation, and how to use meditation to heal or improve all relationships. Retreats throughout year on subjects such as purification retreats, devotional retreats, Lamrim retreats, or on specific practices.

Classes held in Santa Monica Wednesdays 7:15–9:15 pm at Unitarian Universalist Community Church, Forbes Hall, 1721 Arizona Ave. (on 18th St.), Santa Monica, CA 90404.

> *Founder/Guru*   Geshe Kelsang Gyatso Rinpoche
> *Teachers*   Resident: Gen Kelsang Lekma (English nun)

Opening Times	9:00 am–7:00 pm (call before)
Residents	2 nuns and 1 director
Festivals	Not yet
Facilities	Gompa
Accommodation	None
Food	Vegetarian available during courses
Booking	Good to book a week in advance
Fees	$8–10/class; $30 day courses; $4/session retreats
Expected Behavior	No smoking, drugs, or alcohol allowed on premises
How to Get There	Take 1010 Freeway and the Milpas exit (144). Center is very near Follow your Heart health food store off Milpas St., is behind 1A North Alisos St. and has large avocado tree in front yard.

Rigpa (Tibetan–Nyingma)
Affiliation: Rigpa Fellowship
Santa Barbara, CA
Tel: (805) 687–5323

Contact: Angelika Berger. See **Rigpa National Office,** California, for details.

Santa Barbara Buddhist Priory (Zen–Soto)
Affiliation: Serene Reflection Meditation Tradition
1115 Tunnel Road
Santa Barbara, CA 93105
Tel & Fax: (805) 898–0848

House in Mission Canyon in foothills above town. Priest/monk and parish church for lay community. Started 1979 as branch of **Shasta Abbey,** California (see separate entry).

Meditation instruction Wednesdays 6:30 pm. Dharma classes Sundays 1:30–4:00 pm. Daily meditation and services Tuesday through Sunday. Two retreats monthly on Sundays 6:00 am–4:00 pm; one weekend retreat monthly 4:00 pm Friday to 4:00 pm Sunday. For retreats, previous instruction in Serene Reflection meditation required. *Santa Barbara Buddhist Priority News and Events Calendar* published six times annually. Small gift shop with Buddhist supplies.

Founder/Guru	Keido Chisan Koho Zenji and Rev. Master Jiyu-Kennett
Teachers	Rev. Jisho Perry, MOBC
Opening Times	See schedule above
Residents	1 monastic and 1 laity

Festivals	Buddha's Birth, Enlightenment, and Death; festivals for Bodhisattvas: Maitreya, Avalokiteshwara, Samantabhadra, Manjusri, Achalanatha, Nagyaarajyuna, Kshtigarbah, Bhaisajyagur, Great Masters Bodhidharma, Dogen and Keizen, and many more
Facilities	Meditation/ceremony hall, shrine room, library/guest room, gift shop/laundry room, office, and living quarters
Accommodation	Overnight during retreats—space is limited
Food	Vegetarian by donation
Booking	For retreats only
Fees	By donation
Expected Behavior	To follow Priory rules—contact center for further information
How to Get There	Follow Mission St. up to Old Santa Barbara Mission. Follow Mission Canyon Road up the hill to Tunnel Road.

Santa Barbara Karma Thegsum Choling (Tibetan–Karma Kagyu)
Affiliation: Karma Triyana Dharmachakra, New York
534 Arroya Avenue
Santa Barbara, CA 93109
Tel: (805) 569–9440

Contact center for current schedule of events and information on meditation instruction.

Rigpa Fellowship Office for North America (Tibetan–Nyingma)
National Office for the Rigpa Fellowship
The Spiritual Care for Living and Dying Program
P O Box 607
Santa Cruz, CA 95061-0607
Tel: (408) 454–9103 Rigpa National Office; (408) 454–9352 The Spiritual Care for
    Living and Dying Program
Fax: (408) 454–0917 for all activities on this site

Provides support to members and students across North America through the Rigpa Study and Practice Program, Rigpa Publications, and the Spiritual Care for Living and Dying Program. Rigpa Fellowship is affiliated with Rigpa, an international network of centers and groups under the guidance of Sogyal Rinpoche. "Having lived and taught in the West for more than twenty years, Sogyal Rinpoche has developed a profound insight into the modern mind. His rare gift for communication cuts through cultural, religious, and psychological barriers to reveal the essential truths of the Buddha's teachings. The ease, humor, and warmth with which he teaches open the hearts and minds of his audience to an intensely personal experience of their own true nature. All this, as well as the remarkable success of *The Tibetan Book of Living and Dying* ... has made Rinpoche one of the most popular interpreters of Tibetan Buddhism in the modern world, considered by many senior Tibetan masters as having a special role to play in the future of Buddhism, both in the West and in the East." Sogyal Rinpoche places great emphasis on the training of students and offers retreats of up to three months in length, some of which take place at the Rigpa Retreat Center in France.

Facilities include **Rigpa San Francisco Bay Area Center** (see separate entry), which offers a full program of graduated courses of study and practice.

Network of other locations in the U.S. and Canada—see separate entries. Please contact the Rigpa National Office for the latest information about the Rigpa Study and Practice Program, including retreats and courses at Rigpa centers and local study groups.

The Spiritual Care for Living and Dying Program, a project of Rigpa Fellowship, is an international education and service program benefiting people from all walks of life and religious orientation who are facing death or suffering the crises of life. It enriches and supports the work of professional and trained volunteer caregivers in the fields of healthcare and human services.

Rigpa Publications publishes and makes available a wide variety of books, tapes, videos, and study materials, including **Rigpalink,** a monthly tape subscription service. On this site: Tel: (408) 454–9242, orders: (800) 256–5262.

Founder/Guru	Sogyal Rinpoche; Spiritual Directors: Sogyal Rinpoche and H.E. Dzogchen Rinpoche
Teachers	Resident: Trained instructors who are Sogyal Rinpoche's students; Visiting renowned teachers from all Tibetan traditions in a spirit of Rime and as well as from Theravada and Zen.
Opening Times	Not applicable
Residents	Not applicable
Festivals	Contact center
Facilities	Varies according to center
Accommodation	Not applicable
Food	Not applicable
Booking	Not applicable
Fees	Evening courses: $5–15; weekends $50–150; 10-day retreats $500–800 including meals and lodging; work-study opportunities sometimes available
Expected Behavior	Not applicable
How to Get There	Not applicable

Santa Cruz Zen Center (Zen–Soto)
113 School Street
Santa Cruz, CA 95060
Tel: (408) 457–0206

Zendo and resident's home in a coastal resort/university town. Autonomous but main-taining links with the San Francisco Zen Center and Tassajara Zen Mountain Center, where the teacher was trained. Serves a nonresidential lay community. Founded in the 1970s.

Six morning meditations a week with service, six evening meditations a week (with service on Wednesdays), New Year's Eve zazen and ceremony, weekly zazen instruction and orientation, practice period twice a year. Several six-week series of classes per year on Mindfulness practice. Weekly lecture by the resident teacher, guest teacher, or senior student (average attendance about twenty-five). Traditional Soto Zen retreats: one-day sesshins six times a year; weekend sesshins three times a year; five-day sesshins twice a year. All programs are open to newcomers, but they recommend beginning with zazen instruction. Quarterly *Sangha Newsletter*.

Founder/Guru	Kobun Chino Roshi (taught by Shunryu Suzuki Roshi)
Teachers	Resident: Katherine Tanas
Opening Times	As per session times above
Residents	Resident teacher
Festivals	New Year's Eve
Facilities	Zendo, small library, dokusan room
Accommodation	None
Food	None
Booking	Not necessary
Fees	$7 per class; $30 per day retreats
Expected Behavior	No smoking
How to Get There	Downtown Santa Cruz, on the hill next to the mission

Drikung Kagyu Center (Tibetan–Drikung Kagyu)
P O Box 3291
Santa Monica, CA 90408
Tel: (818) 993–5658
Fax: (808) 993–3258
E-mail: jamyang@aol.com

No fixed premises; community of seventy-five. Founded late 1980s. Meditation, Chenrezig, and Lamrim weekly. Phowa biweekly. Courses in Abhidharma, Prajnaparamita, Madhyamika, Dharma History, and Five Books of Maitreya. Various meditation retreats such as Bodhicitta, Phowa, Illusory Body, Bodhisattva practice, etc.

Founder/Guru	Khenpo Konchog Gyaltsen
Teachers	Khonchog Gyaltsen, Lama Sonam Jorphel, Ayang Rinpoche, and others visit
Opening Times	Varies—please call or e-mail

Residents	None
Festivals	Contact center
Facilities	Shrine rooms in various residences
Accommodation	None
Food	None
Booking	Contact center
Fees	Contact center
Expected Behavior	5 precepts, general respect
How to Get There	Contact center

Los Angeles Yeshe Nyingpo Center (Tibetan–Nyingma)
Affiliation: Pacific Region Yeshe Nyingpo–Tashi Choling
c/o Suzanne Soehner
1112 Montana, # 4
Santa Monica, CA 90403
Tel: (213) 395–0072
See **Pacific Region Yeshe Nyingpo–Tashi Choling,** Oregon.

Ordinary Dharma (Zen–Vietnamese)
Affiliation: Community of Mindful Living
Santa Monica, CA

See **Manzanita Village,** California.

Santa Monica Zen Center (Zen–Soto and Rinzai)
Affiliation: White Plum Sangha of Taizan Maezumi Roshi
1001B Colorado Boulevard
Santa Monica, CA 90403
Tel: (310) 572–9070
Fax: (310) 394–5105

Simple high-ceilinged, sky-lit space zendo in former art gallery ten blocks from Pacific Ocean. Training center with over fifty members. Founded 1994. "The center is known for its ecumenical approach to all religions and attitude of inclusiveness of all peoples. A Catholic mass is sometimes offered as well as Jewish rituals on certain holy days of those religions."

Zazen daily 5:00–6:00 am; Wednesdays 7:30–9:00 pm; Sundays 8:00–11:30 am. Beginner's instruction Sundays 8:00–9:00 am. Weekly study group in selected Buddhist writings. Weekly Zen Dancing—movement workshop. Zen meditation for beginners weekly. Introduction to Zen practice monthly. Period Zen and the World Religions. Weekend training program, Zen Life Intensive: levels I, II, and III, bimonthly. Center prepares senior students to be Zen meditation instructors through The Lotus training program. Bimonthly three- to five-day sesshins in city center and occasionally at mountain retreat center.

Founder/Guru	Taizan Maezumi Roshi
Teachers	Rev. William Yoshin Jordan and Rev. Elisabeth Jikan Hartnett
Opening Times	Call for schedule
Residents	None
Festivals	Contact center
Facilities	Meditation hall, study room, and social room
Accommodation	May sometimes be arranged in members' homes
Food	Vegetarian during sesshins
Booking	Up to 1 week in advance for sesshins and intensives. 25% deposit.
Fees	Suggested donation of $35/day for sesshins. Other classes by donation
Expected Behavior	In accord with awareness of 16 precepts and respect for different points of view
How to Get There	From east of Santa Monica, take I-10 west-bound and exit at Lincoln Blvd. In Santa Monica, right onto Lincoln Blvd., then right at first light onto Colorado Blvd. Center is 3 blocks on left.

Soka Gakkai International-USA (SGI-USA) (Nichiren)
Affiliation: Soka Gakkai International
National Offices & Center
SGI-USA
525 Wilshire Boulevard
Santa Monica, CA 90401
Tel: (310) 260–8900
Fax: (310) 260–8917
E-mail: sgiusa@aol.com
Web site: http://www.sgi-usa.org

Founded 1960 as Nichiren Shoshu of America (NSA), this national center oversees organizational administration and communications, and has meeting facilities for SGI-USA activities.

Monthly activities include introductory, discussion, and study meetings on Buddhism and its application to daily living.

"The SGI-USA community believes that religion exists to serve humanity, and that Buddhism exists to enable all human beings to awaken to and fully utilize their potentials to create peace, happiness, and prosperity. Central to the SGI-USA community is its network of grassroots activities. There, as in the personal religious practice, the emphasis is on the practical application of Buddhist principles, i.e., to live mean-ingfully and make constructive contributions to the world around us. From neighbor-hood discussion groups to exhibits on the urgent global issues humanity faces, the aim is to evoke the individual's creativity to deal with personal and global dilemmas."

Publish *The World Tribune*, a weekly newspaper chronicling organizational activ-ities, personal experiences, and perspectives, and *Living Buddhism* (originally *Seikyo Times*), a monthly magazine of study material and essays. Bookstores at national and regional centers offer books and accessories for Buddhist practice. Addresses for region-al centers are listed in the relevant states.

Opening Times   Business hours and guest reception 9:00 am–5:00 pm
Monday–Friday. Activities by appointment.

Soka Gakkai International (SGI-USA) (Nichiren)
Los Angeles Area Regional Center
1212 7th Street
Santa Monica, CA 90401-1606
Tel: (310) 458–3850 or (310) 451–4422
Fax: (310) 451–8092

See **Soka Gakkai International** National Offices & Center, Santa Monica, California, for more details.

Soka Gakkai International (SGI-USA) (Nichiren)
Santa Monica Area Regional Center
2601 Pico Boulevard
Santa Monica, CA 90405-1915
Tel: (310) 829–1005
Fax: (310) 828–3164

See **Soka Gakkai International** National Offices & Center, Santa Monica, California, for more details.

California Diamond Sangha (Zen)
Affiliation: Diamond sangha
        Centers in Santa Rosa and Oakland
P O Box 2972
Santa Rosa, CA 95405
Tel: (707) 763–9466 (Santa Rosa) and (510) 531–5779 (Oakland)
Fax: (707) 588–8730
Web site: http://www.dnai.com/~kudzu/cds/index.html

Two city centers and a retreat center in the countryside. Has a community of seventy-five and several hundred participants at special events. "Exclusively lay practice, emphasis on koan practice, interest in the arts and psychology." Founded 1987.

Zazen, dokusan, koan study, and family practice. Weekly Community night with meditation and Dharma talk. Classes in Introduction to Zen, workshops on Zen and psychology, Zen and the arts, etc. Special events with guest teachers and speakers. Monthly Buddhism Study Group. Women's Institute for a Native Buddhist Practice have at least one event each month. Six sesshins a year, monthly zazenkai and periodic special retreats. Publish bimonthly newsletter and *Blind Donkey*, journal of the Diamond sangha biannually.

Founder/Guru	John Tarrant, Roshi, Dharma Heir of Robert Aitken
Teachers	Resident: John Tarrant, Daniel Terragno, Joan Sutherland, David Weinstein, Amie Diller, and Noelle Oxenhandler
Opening Times	Please call for details
Residents	None
Festivals	Not applicable
Facilities	Dojo, retreat space
Accommodation	During sesshins and special retreats only (retreat fees including food and lodging)
Food	Vegetarian during events only
Booking	2 weeks in advance; 10% deposit
Fees	Non-member: zazenkai, workshops, and special events $35; sesshins $170–390; talks $15
Expected Behavior	Follow retreat rules
How to Get There	Please call for directions

Rigpa (Tibetan–Nyingma)
Affiliation: Rigpa Fellowship
Santa Rosa, CA
Tel: (916) 874–2765

Contact: Annie Eichenholz. See **Rigpa National Office,** California, for details.

Zen Wind (Zen)
P O Box 4176
Santa Rosa, CA 95402
Tel: (707) 939–7023

An exclusively lay organization without temples, centers, monasteries, or professional clergy. Groups meet regularly in the homes of practitioners under the guidance of an authorized teacher. Founded in 1985 by Tundra Wind, who studied Zen in Korea and Japan.

Introduction to Zen course once a week for six weeks offered two or three times a year. Meditation retreats twice a year. Weekly meditation groups. Self-publishes books and music—ask for a list.

Founder/Guru	Tundra Wind
Teachers	7 qualified teachers
Opening Times	Not applicable
Residents	Not applicable
Festivals	None
Facilities	Not applicable
Accommodation	May be arranged on an individual basis in the home of a practitioner as a guest
Food	Vegetarian during retreats
Booking	One month in advance
Fees	Introduction to Zen: $40; Retreats: $60 to $80
Expected Behavior	Retreats: silence, no reading or disruptive behavior
How to Get There	Location varies; please write for details

Green Gulch Farm (Zen–Soto)
1601 Shoreline Highway
Sausalito, CA 94965
Tel: (415) 383-3134
Fax: (415) 383-3128 (no reservations by fax)

One of three practice locations—see also **San Francisco Zen Center** and **Tassajara Zen Mountain Center**.

Numerous buildings in a long valley surrounded by Golden Gate National Recreation area in Marin County (short walk from the ocean). Residential and community temple which support itself as an organic farm and garden and as a conference and workshop center with an active guest program.

Special program for the public on Sundays. The Mountain Gate Study Center offers a variety of classes in Buddhist philosophy and practice. Classes held Sunday mornings and Monday and Tuesday evenings. Sessions of six weekly classes five times a year. Traditional Zen meditation retreats of one, five, or seven days are held frequently. They suggest you begin with an introductory sitting. Tea classes in the Urasenke tradition offered weekly as well as organic gardening classes. Two seven- to eight-week practice periods each year beginning in October and February and a three-and-a-half-week practice period in January. Guest students may stay from five days to six weeks.

Subjects for retreats and workshops include such titles as watercolor and zazen, various cooking workshops, sensory awareness, Buddhism and Christianity, Buddhism and Judaism. Various gardening workshops/classes.

Center is also available for meetings and conferences.

Founder/Guru	Shunryu Suzuki Roshi
Teachers	3 resident abbots: Mel Weitsman, Norman Fischer, and Blanche Hartman. Senior resident teacher: Reb Anderson. Other priests and lay teachers lecture and assist in the teaching.
Opening Times	Contact center
Residents	At least 50—little distinction between priest and lay—all are monks
Festivals	None
Facilities	Traditional Japanese teahouse, contact center for other details
Accommodation	Residential facilities for about 35
Food	Vegetarian—produces some of its own organic produce
Booking	Varies on availability—deposit required
Fees	$15 per day as guest student and on up as full guest
Expected Behavior	16 Bodhisattva precepts (Mahayana)
How to Get There	Contact center

Stone Creek Zendo (Zen–Soto)
P O Box 1053
Sebastopol, CA 95473
Tel: (707) 829–9808

Small rural zendo about $1^1/_2$ hours north of San Francisco, open to all and centered on zazen. Modest single-story building with Zen sitting hall and kinhin porch; it has wheelchair access. "Emphasis of practice here is on zazen as a fundamental activity of life, and on practicing the Dharma as confronting and living out the full reality of one's life." Established 1996.

Morning and evening zazen four days a week. Weekly Dharma talk and discussion. Monthly introduction to zazen. Weekly study group on texts and on practice topics. Monthly one-day sittings and periodic collecting-the-mind retreats (sesshins) and beginners' retreats. Formal Zen meals (Oryoki) in retreats; instruction and bowls provided. Jisho Warner is an ordained disciple of Rev. Tozen Kaiyama and also trained under Dainin Katagiri Roshi.

Founder/Guru	Jisho Warner
Teachers	Resident priest: Jisho Warner
Opening Times	Write, fax, or call for schedule
Residents	None
Festivals	None
Facilities	See above

Accommodation	None
Food	None
Booking	Contact zendo for information
Fees	Contact zendo for information
Expected Behavior	To follow simple zendo forms; no smoking
How to Get There	Write or call for directions

Sonoma Valley Dharma Study Group (Tibetan–Kagyu/Nyingma)
Affiliation: Shambhala International
P O Box 614
Sonoma, CA 95476
Tel: (707) 935-3610
E-mail: jjacobs@vom.com

See International headquarters, **Shambhala Center,** Halifax, Nova Scotia, Canada.

FPMT Central Office (Tibetan–Gelug)
Affiliation: Foundation for the Preservation of the Mahayana Tradition
P O Box 1778
Soquel, CA 95073
Tel: (408) 476-8435
Fax: (408) 476-4823
E-mail: 76734.3620@compuserve.com Holly Ansett

Not actually a center, but central organization for association of over eighty centers worldwide. Coordinates and works with member centers. Contact this office for up-to-date information on the nearest FPMT center to you.
   This office publishes *Mandala Magazine,* the FPMT bimonthly journal.

KTC Santa Cruz (Tibetan–Karma Kagyu)
Affiliation: Karma Triyana Dharmachakra, NY
P O Box 1527
Soquel, CA 95073
Tel: (408) 423-5539
E-mail: sandyc@cabrillo.campus.mci.net

Small local sangha and membership is pending an interview with the resident lama.

Land of Medicine Buddha (Tibetan–Gelug)
Affiliation: Foundation for the Preservation of the Mahayana Tradition
5800 Prescott Road

Soquel, CA 95073
Tel: (408) 462–8383
Fax: (408) 462–8380
E-mail: 75671.3307@compuserve.com
Web site: http://www.vena.com/synergy/1mb

Buildings decorated in the style of a Tibetan village with prayer wheels and statues along paths and hiking trails. Situated on fifty-five acres of forest and meadowland adjoining the Forest of Nisene Marks, a few miles south of Santa Cruz. Residential staff of approximately fifteen, Buddhist and non-Buddhist. Founded as a place to make available the essence of the Buddha free from the trappings of cultural dogma. "Our approach to learning transcends national and cultural barriers, incorporating healing traditions from around the world, including Chi Gong, meditations, Tibetan Buddhism, nutritional therapy, visualization techniques, and purification practices."

Traditional Tibetan Buddhist retreats and variety of classes and events. Individual retreatants welcome per space available. Facility available to rent for conferences and workshops.

Founder/Guru	Lama Thubten Yeshe and Lama Zopa Rinpoche
Teachers	Contact center
Opening Times	Contact center
Residents	15 staff
Festivals	Contact center
Facilities	2 large meeting rooms, dining hall, pool, sauna, bookstore/gift shop, campgrounds, rooms for up to 50 people (sharing)
Accommodation	Single $40, double $70, triple $90, group rental $30/person/night based on 3 sharing
Food	Vegetarian: breakfast $5, lunch $8, dinner (only during programs) $7
Booking	For groups, 3–6 months in advance, 25% deposit
Fees	Generally by donation with fee for room and board
Expected Behavior	5 precepts; no smoking; eating of meat only under special circumstances
How to Get There	Hwy. 1 south from Santa Cruz. Porter St./Bay Ave. exit and turn left under freeway. Right onto Main St. until it merges into Glen Haven Rd. Prescott Rd. is another half mile farther on the right. Follow it to the end, cross the wooden bridge, turn left, and follow the signs for Land of Medicine Buddha.

Ocean Eyes Zen Center (Zen–Korean)
Affiliation: Kwan Um School of Zen
11582 Ale Lane

Stanton, CA 90680-3535
Tel: (714) 894–0177 Zen center, (714) 373–0803 residence
Fax: (714) 894–0177
E-mail: DoChong1@aol.com

Founded 1993 to serve Orange County community, residential center in six-bedroom house in heart of city with zendo and dojo attached.

Zazen practice as opening times below. Introduction to Zen workshop on third Monday of every month. One- to three-day retreats four times a year. Quarterly magazine, *Only Go Straight*.

Founder/Guru	Contact center
Teachers	Abbot: Paul Lynch, Poep Sa; Bob Moore, Ji Do Poep Sa Nim visit
Opening Times	Monday-Friday 6:00–6:30 am; Mondays 7:00–9:30 pm, Thursdays 7:00–8:00 pm
Residents	6 laity
Festivals	Buddha's Birthday, Buddha's Enlightenment Day
Facilities	See above
Accommodation	On individually negotiated basis
Food	Vegetarian
Booking	Contact center
Fees	Members $30/day, non-members $40/day
Expected Behavior	5 precepts
How to Get There	Between 22 and 91 Freeways off Beach Blvd.

Sagely City of Ten Thousand Buddhas (Pure Land and Ch'an)
Main Center of Dharma Realm Buddhist Association
P O Box 217
2001 Talmage Road
Talmage, CA 95481-0217
Tel: (707) 462–0939
Fax: (707) 462–0949
E-mail: craig@pacific.net

More than seventy buildings with over two thousand rooms located in Ukiah Valley about two hundred and forty miles north of San Francisco. Occupies an area of four hundred and eighty-eight acres of which about eighty acres are landscaped, the rest being meadows, orchards, and forests. Between one hundred and two hundred people attend daily ceremony. Established in 1976. Houses Dharma Realm Buddhist University, University Library, Buddhist Text Translation Society, Ordination Hall, primary and high schools.

Classes from elementary school up to university and sangha and laity training. Most courses are on Buddhist practice and studies, Buddhist text translation, Chinese culture, etc. Sunday group discussion, includes meditation, Tai Chi, and Buddhism in daily life. Three-day to three-week retreats most months include meditation, chanting, and lectures. Monthly journal *Vajra Bodhi Sea*. Bookstore.

Founder/Guru	Ven. Master Hsuan Hua
Teachers	Resident: Bhikshu Heng Lyu, Bhikshu Heng Sure; visiting: Bhiskshu Heng Bin, Bhikshu Heng Yuen
Opening Times	8:00 am–6:00 pm daily
Residents	80–100 monastics, 150 laity
Festivals	Buddha's birthday
Facilities	See above
Accommodation	Suggested donation $30/day or $100 per week
Food	Vegetarian restaurant on campus
Booking	5 days to 2 weeks in advance
Fees	Based on donation, no fixed fee
Expected Behavior	No eating meat or fish, no smoking, no alcohol, 5 precepts preferred
How to Get There	Highway 101 from San Francisco, exit Talmage Road, then east until you see the gates.

Khyung Dzong of California (Tibetan–Bon)
Affiliation: Ligmincha Institute, VA
P O Box 1607
Temple City, CA 91780-1607
Tel: (818) 248-1828
E-mail: Alicia8000@aol.com

Contact center for details.

Metta Forest Monastery (Theravada–Thai Forest Tradition)
P O Box 1409
Valley Center, CA 92082
Tel: (619) 988-3474

Small monastery with five to seven monks and lay community. Simple buildings in avocado orchard bordering on Indian reservation in the hills of northern San Diego County. Founded 1990 "with the intention of providing an environment where people of all nationalities can practice the Dhamma in an atmosphere of solitude. Authentic atmosphere of Thai forest monastery in an American setting."

Chanting sessions twice daily followed by group meditation sessions with instruction. Group meditation retreats on major weekends in the spring and summer, i.e., Memorial Day, Independence Day, Labor Day. Year-round opportunities for individual retreats.

Founder/Guru	Phra Ajaan Suwat Suvaco
Teachers	Resident: Thanissaro Bhikku
Opening Times	Year-round
Residents	5 monks, 4 laity
Festivals	Magha Puja, Visakha Puja, Asalha Puja
Facilities	Meditation hall, library, dormitory, tent platforms, and walking meditation paths under the trees in the orchard
Accommodation	Dormitory-style rooms in guest house, payment by donation
Food	1 potluck meal daily by donation
Booking	Contact center
Fees	Voluntary donations
Expected Behavior	Visits of 1 week or less, 5 precepts; others 8 precepts. All visitors expected to participate fully in group meditation and work schedule
How to Get There	North from Escondido on Valley Parkway to Valley Center. Cole Grade Road, McNally Rd., Moutama Rd. No public transport.

Manzanita Village (Zen–Vietnamese)
Affiliation: Community of Mindful Living
P O Box 67
Warner Springs, CA 92086
Tel & Fax: (619) 782–9223
Ordinary Dharma in Los Angeles: (310) 394–6653

Adobe zendo. Residential retreat center accommodating forty bordering national forest. Environmentally conscious living with some straw-bale construction rustic and deliberately simple. Also city practice center, Ordinary Dharma, in Santa Monica, CA. Manzanita Village started 1983 and Ordinary Dharma practice center 1983. Informal affiliation with Spirit Rock Center and Vipassana Meditation Community.

Ongoing classes Vipassana and Zen in the tradition of Thich Nhat Hanh. Sutra study and application of Dharma to daily life. Retreats of two days' to two months' duration. Aikido and Iaido classes.

Christopher Reed has received Dharmacarya transmission as a teacher from Thich Nhat Hahn. Michele Benzamin-Masuda holds Aikido and Iaido rankings and is an ordained member of the Order of Interbeing.

Founder/Guru	Christopher Reed and Michele Benzamin-Masuda
Teachers	Resident as founders and various visit from

	Plum Village and from local Theravada centers
Opening Times	By arrangement
Residents	5
Festivals	None
Facilities	Shrine room, dojo, library, study room, and meditation room
Accommodation	Dormitory-style, or camping in your own tent
Food	Vegetarian, organic when possible
Booking	For retreats, minimum 2 weeks in advance, 1 month preferred
Fees	Various
Expected Behavior	5 precepts. No meat, alcohol or drugs
How to Get There	Bus from San Diego daily—contact center for further details

I am he who goes his own way;

I am he who has counsel for every circumstance;

I am the sage who has no fixed abode.

I am he is unaffected whatever befall....

I am the madman who counts death happiness;

I am he who has naught and needs naught.

The Message of Milarepa

Vajrayana Foundation (Tibetan–Nyingma)
Pema Osel Ling
2013 Eureka Canyon Road
Watsonville, CA 95076
Tel: (408) 761–6266
Fax: (408) 761–6284
E-mail: vajrapol@scruznet.com
Web site: http://www.scruznet.com/~yeshenyi

Teacher is Lama Tharchin Rinpoche. Pema Osel Ling is a separate body on the same grounds. Has affiliates in Hawaii; Palo Alto; Little Rock, Arkansas; Baton Rouge, Louisana; Seattle, Washington; Santa Barbara and San Rafael. Contact center for details.

Watsonville Buddhist Temple (Jodo Shinshu)
423 Bridge Street
Watsonville, CA 95076
Tel: (408) 724–7860
Fax: (408) 722–3366

Contact center for details.

Zen Center of Willets (Zen)
Affiliation: Ordinary Mind Zen School
2085 Primrose
Willets, CA 95490
E-mail: elihu_smith@RedwoodFN.org

Teacher is Elihu Genmyo Smith. Contact center for details.

Spirit Rock Meditation Center (Vipassana)
P O Box 909
Woodacre, CA 94973
Tel: (415) 488–0164
Fax: (415) 488–0170
E-mail: srmc@spiritrock.org
Web site: http://www.spiritrock.org

Beautiful West Coast environment on 412 acres of land. Center has five hundred visitors per week—non-sectarian lay community who live and work in the world. Will begin construction of own residential facility spring 1997.

Meditation classes three times a week and daylong retreats every weekend. Residential silent Vipassana retreats monthly of three to twenty days. Retreats may focus on various topics, including Beginning Vipassana, Teen Weekend, Gay and Free, Family Practice Day, Meditation and Inquiry, Awakening Body and Mind, Wild & Wise: Celebrating Women in Buddhist Practice, Cultivating Gratitude. Newsletter twice a year.

Founder/Guru	Contact center
Teachers	Collective of local laypeople, including Jack Kornfield; visiting American and European Vipassana teachers
Opening Times	Not applicable
Residents	Non-residential staff of 10
Festivals	See schedule
Facilities	Large meditation hall
Accommodation	Contact center

Food	Vegetarian
Booking	4 months in advance for residential retreats
Fees	Residential retreats $50/day room and board. Daylong retreats $30/day with lunch
Expected Behavior	5 precepts
How to Get There	Contact center for details

The adept in Zen is one who manages to be human with the same artless grace and absence of inner conflict with which a tree is a tree ... He is all of a piece with himself and with the natural world, and in his presence you feel that without strain or artifice he is completely "all here"—sure of himself without the slightest trace of aggression.

Alan Watts *This is IT and Other Essays on Zen and Spiritual Experience*

COLORADO

The Boulder Shambhala Center / Karma Dzong (Tibetan–Kagyu/Nyingma)
USA Headquarters of Shambhala International
1345 Spruce Street
Boulder, CO 80302
Tel: (303) 444–0190
Fax: (303) 443–2975
E-mail: sc@indra.com

Urban center with large building for practice and study. Community of five hundred adults and over two hundred children. In Boulder foothills of the Rocky Mountains in a beautiful town surrounded by nature parks, ski resorts, etc. Includes three spiritual gates: Vajrayana Buddhism, Shambhala Training (nonsectarian), and Nalanda Arts and Education.

Open house Sunday 10:30 am to noon. Daily sitting meditation Monday to Friday 5:30–6:30 pm and Sunday 9:00 am–noon and 2:00–5:00 pm. Meditation instruction available on request. Path of Meditation seminar for newer meditators Friday evenings and Saturdays. Fairly continuous classes on all levels of Buddhism and of Shambhala training, contemplative arts, workshops, and seminars. Children's celebrations, classes, and retreats. Individual retreats, month-long group meditation retreats twice a year, and various other retreat programs. Three-year retreats at monastery at Cape Breton, Canada. Advanced seminars, leadership conferences, and right livelihood programs. Shammata Vipassana for advanced students, Vajrayogini and Chakrasamvara sadhana, Vajrakilaya practice, etc. *Shambhala Mirror,* monthly newsletter focused on local happenings in the community.

Founder/Guru	Chogyam Trungpa Rinpoche, succeeded by Sakyong Mipham Rinpoche
Teachers	Resident: senior students of Chogyam Trungpa; visiting: Khandro Rinpoche, Trangu Rinpoche, Khenpo Tsultrim Gyamtso, and others
Opening Times	1:00–6:30 pm Monday to Friday; 9:00 am–5:00 pm Sunday
Residents	None
Festivals	Shambhala Day, Nyida days, Solstice Celebration, Children's Day, Trunpa Parinirvana, Valshaku
Facilities	Major shrine room, auxillary shrine rooms
Accommodation	None
Food	None
Booking	Some seminars require advanced booking
Fees	Seminars $120–160; classes $15–60

Expected Behavior   Decent, no smoking
How to get there   Downtown Boulder

Namo Buddha Seminar (Tibetan)
1390 Kalmia Avenue
Boulder, CO 80304-1813
Tel: (303) 449–6608
Fax: (303) 440–0882

Co-ordinates the activities of Thrangu Rinpoche, a master of Mahamudra meditation, but who teaches all kinds of meditation. He gives seminars on Buddhism around the world, with the main seminars being in Nepal in March, Scotland in summer, and Vancouver and Big Bear (outside Los Angeles) in the fall. They also publish twenty-two books by Thrangu Rinpoche. Anyone interested can receive their free newsletter detailing Rinpoche's activities and receive a list of his books. Center also in England.

Founder/Guru   Thrangu Rinpoche
Facilities   Bookstore for Thrangu Rinpoche's books

Ratna Shri Sangha (Tibetan–Drikung Kagyu)
3565 Martin Drive
Boulder, CO 80303
Tel: (303) 494–2435 Mark Steiner
Web site: http://www.churchward.com/drikung

Contact center for details.

Rigpa (Tibetan–Nyingma)
Affiliation: Rigpa Fellowship
Boulder, CO
Tel: (303) 545–6518

Contact: Liz Acosta. See **Rigpa National Office,** California, for details.

Rocky Mountain Vipassana Association (Vipassana)
Affiliation: Vipassana Meditation Centers in the Tradition of S. N. Goenka
c/o Judi Sammons
760 NW Birch Street
Cedaredge, CO 81413
Tel: (970) 835–8295

Organizes one or two ten-day courses yearly at a rented site in rural western Colorado; organizes periodic ten-day courses at rural camp facilities in Montana, Utah, Idaho, and in the mountains east of Boulder; sponsors group sittings for experienced students and periodic one-day self-courses for experienced students. Established 1989. For further description see **Vipassana Meditation Center,** Massachussetts.

Karma Thegsum Tashi Gomang (Tibetan–Karma Kagyu)
Affiliation: Karma Triyana Dharmachakra, New York
P O Box 39
Crestone, CO 81131
Tel: (719) 256–4694 or (719) 256–4695
Fax: (719) 256–4266

House near village of Crestone with two hundred acres of wilderness with a forty-one-foot Tashi Gomang Stupa and two adobe retreat cabins and a community of ten. "Incredible stupa—seven years under construction containing a 100,000 tsa-tsas—took nearly one month to consecrate with help of eight Lamas."
    Group sitting practice and Green Tara on full and new moons. Buddhist study group. Courses on Buddhist meditation and philosophy. Weekend meditation retreats one to three times annually. All open to newcomers.

Founder/Guru	H.H. 16th Gyalwa Karmapa
Teachers	Karma Kagyu Lamas visit
Opening Times	Contact center
Residents	None
Festivals	Losar
Facilities	Shrine room, small library
Accommodation	In project house: single $25, double $35. Retreat cabin: $20/day or $120/week
Food	None
Booking	As early as possible. Deposit required for some courses
Fees	Weekend seminar approximately $60. Evening teaching $8–10. Does not include meals or lodging
Expected Behavior	No drugs, firearms, smoking, or alcohol
How to get there	$3^1/_2$ hours south of Denver; $3^1/_2$ hours north of Santa Fe

Denver Shambhala Center (Tibetan–Kagyu/Nyingma)
Affiliation: Shambhala International
718 East 18th Avenue
Denver, CO 80203

Tel: (303) 863–8366
E-mail: takseng@aol.com

See International headquarters, **Shambhala Center,** Halifax, Nova Scotia, Canada.

Lotus in the Flame Temple (Zen)
Denver Zen Center
Affiliation: Diamond sangha
1233 Columbine Street
Denver, CO 80206
Tel: (303) 333–4844
Fax: (303) 333–7844
E-mail: dzcenter@aol.com

Full schedule of lay Zen training, including introductory seminars, daily zazen, teisho, samu, chanting, ceremonies, Tai Chi, yoga, community services, sesshins, and zazenkais. Anyone who has completed introductory seminar may practice at the center. Sesshins open to those not affiliated with Denver Zen Center after telephone interview. Offer Monastery Without Walls—a program of intense training in Zen within the life of a householder living in the community at large.

Founder/Guru	Robert Aitken Roshi
Teachers	Resident: Ven. Danan Henry Sensei, Dharma Heir of Philip Kapleau Roshi and training with Robert Aitken Roshi
Opening Times	Contact center
Residents	Contact center
Festivals	Contact center
Facilities	Contact center
Accommodation	Contact center
Food	Contact center
Booking	For sesshins, 1 month in advance
Fees	Sesshins $35/day
Expected Behavior	Contact center
How to get there	Contact center

Soka Gakkai International (SGI-USA) (Nichiren)
Colorado Area Regional Center
1450 N Speer Boulevard
Denver, CO 80204-2536
Tel: (303) 893–0430
Fax: (303) 825–7336

See **Soka Gakkai International** National Offices & Center, Santa Monica, California, for more details.

Fort Collins Dharma Study Group (Tibetan–Kagyu/Nyingma)
Affiliation: Shambhala International
Fred Meyer
Fort Collins, CO 80521-2147
Tel: (970) 224–2156

See International headquarters, **Shambhala Center,** Halifax, Nova Scotia, Canada.

Dorje Khyung Dzong Shambhala Retreat Center (Tibetan–Kagyu/Nyingma)
Affiliation: Shambhala International
288 Country Road 626
P O Box 131
Gardner, CO 81040
Tel: (719) 746–2264
Fax: (719) 746–2997
E-mail: 74764.3550@compuserve.com

Quite remote retreat center with seven cabins used by practitioners of various different traditions of meditation. At 8,200 feet on 440 acres of pine and juniper forest in Huerfano Valley of southern Colorado. Founded 1972.

For solitary retreats only—no group programs offered. Open to those practicing an authentic meditation who are willing to follow the set guidelines—probably not suitable for newcomers. Two resident directors are meditation instructors trained in Buddhist meditation and able to assist most retreatants. "We provide an opportunity for practitioners to do a retreat in a simple way, free from the distractions of the world. Each cabin is isolated, but the mian house and a common shower house are just a short walk away. Cabins do not have electricity or running water. Each cabin has propane cook stove and lights, wood-burning stove for heat, and access to water from our spring."

Make ground juniper for ritual use, which is sold at Ziji Bookstore in Boulder, Colorado.

Founder/Guru	Ven. Chogyam Trungpa Rinpoche
Teachers	Resident Directors: Bruce and Melissa Robinson
Opening Times	All year-round
Residents	2 directors with a dog and a cat
Festivals	Losar, Midsummer's Day, Buddha's Birthday, and Milarepa Day
Facilities	Library of books and tapes

Accommodation	Limited space in main house at $5 for food
Food	Self-catering—Directors shop for long-term retreatants
Booking	At least 2–3 months in advance, 3–6 months for school holidays and summer
Fees	$25/day retreatants, $20 students/seniors
Expected Behavior	No alcohol or drugs, music, or crafts
How to get there	I-25 from Denver to Walsenburg, 28 miles from exit. Pick up from Colorado Springs, Pueblo Airport, or Walsenburg bus station can be arranged.

Orgyan Rigjed Ling (Tibetan–Nyingma)
Affiliation: Chagdud Gonpa Foundation
c/o Steve Glazer
808 E Geneseo Street
Lafayette, CO 80026
Tel: (303) 604–2537

Contact center for details.

Amitabha Foundation, Colorado (Tibetan–Nyingma and Drikung Kagyu)
10810 W 29th Avenue
Lakewood, CO 80215
Tel: (303) 674–1784 (John Welch)
Fax: (303) 237–3011
E-mail: loisjohn@ix.netcom.com

Located in the Cherry Creek area of city in basement of a business. Between five and twenty practitioners. "We are a small community who are connected, as are other communities, with Yogi Lama and Penor Rinpoche. Ayong Rinpoche organized us for practice and for project fund-raising."

Meet on new and full moons to complete vows, *Amitabha Tsog*, and *Achi Chokyi Drolma*. Invite various teachers to lead classes. Ten-day Phowa course when Ayang Rinpoche visits (usually annually).

Biannual newsletter.

Founder/Guru	Ayang Rinpoche
Teachers	Ayang Rinpoche visits annually, Ani Tsering (nun) visits quarterly
Opening Times	Contact center
Residents	None
Festivals	None
Facilities	Shrine room

Accommodation	Not applicable,
Food	Not applicable
Booking	Not applicable
Fees	Contact center
Expected Behavior	Contact center
How to get there	Contact center

Colorado Mountain Zen Centers (Zen)
Box 49
Ouray, CO 81427
Tel: (970) 325–4440

No fixed premises. Offer classes and sesshins. Founded by Michael Wise.

Rocky Mountain Shambhala Center (Tibetan–Kagyu/Nyingma)
Affiliation: Shambhala International
4921 County Road, 68-C
Red Feather Lakes, CO 80545-9505
Tel: (970) 881–2184 or (303) 466–1897
Fax: (970) 881–2909
E-mail: 75347.52@compuserve.com

See International headquarters, **Shambhala Center,** Halifax, Nova Scotia, Canada.

*In reality Buddhism is neither pessimistic nor optimistic. If compelled to label
it in this way at all we should borrow a word from George Eliot and call it
melioristic, for though asserting that conditioned existence is suffering it
also maintains, as the Third Aryan Truth teaches, that suffering
can be transcended.*

Sangharakshita, *The Three Jewels*

CONNECTICUT

Living Dharma Center (Zen–Soto and Rinzai)
Harada-Yasutani-Kapleau lineage
P O Box 513
Bolton, CT 06040
Tel: (860) 742–7049
Tel & Fax: (413) 259–1611

See **Living Dharma Center,** Massachussetts, for further details.

Center for Dzogchen Studies (Tibetan–Dzogchen, Nyingma/Kagyu)
847 Whalley Avenue
New Haven, CT 06515
Tel: (203) 387–9992

Rents two floors directly above a minimart overlooking a busy intersection. In a large valley below a glacier-cut mountain. Large park, gas station, and small fast-food joints across the street. Chose an urban environment to be accessible to a wide variety of people and to give practitioners the opportunity to integrate awareness practice with all other experiences. Primary emphasis is maintaining presence in daily life. Ten to fifteen locals and thirty to thirty-five active practitioners visit each week. Also around thirty practitioners from New York, Vermont, Massachussetts, and Maryland visit occasionally for individual or group retreats. Established 1994.

Introduction to Dzogchen Sundays 10:00–12:00 am and Wednesdays 7:00 pm. Guided sitting sessions for ongoing practitioners five times a week. Retreats for ongoing practitioners: one-day on one Saturday a month; three-day on Memorial Day, Labor Day, and New Year's weekends; and individual retreats. Period book courses. Padme Karma Rinpoche is involved in all activities. Individual sessions with him can be scheduled. Monthly newsletter with calendar of events, stories, poetry, summaries of talks and classes, discussion on Dzogchen practice, and articles on traditional Chinese medicine.

Founder/Guru	Padma Karma Rinpoche
Teachers	Resident: Padma Karma Rinpoche, Lama Tamara Wolfson
Opening Times	8:00 am–10:00 pm, 7 days a week
Residents	1 monk, 1 nun, and about 3 laity
Festivals	Contact center
Facilities	Large meditation room, shrine room, extensive library, and community room

Accommodation	Dormitory space for retreats; residential space occasionally available
Food	Organic wholefood vegetarian meals according to traditonal Chinese nutritional guidelines during retreats; otherwise, self-catering
Booking	Contact center
Fees	Courses $45, talks $10 by donation, 1-day retreats $45, 3-day retreats $145, 8-day retreats $360
Expected Behavior	Contact center
How to get there	From Whalley Ave., go approximately 2 miles, pass cemetery on right. Right at the Jackson Marvin hardware store onto Tour Ave. to park.

New Haven Shambhala Center (Tibetan–Kagyu/Nyingma)
Affiliation: Shambhala International
319 Peck Street
New Haven, CT 06513
Tel: (203) 776–2331
E-mail: 76771.2264@compuserve.com

Building was factory for children's toys, now converted into an office building. Yoga studio and massage therapist nearby. In New Haven since early 1980s; this location since August 1996. Around twenty members.

Offer classes on subjects related to meditation practice quarterly, running once a week for five to six weeks. Weekend programs on such subjects as meditation and leadership, lineage, and devotion. Shambhala Training Levels I, II, and III on an annual basis. Shamatha meditation instruction on request, usually on Sundays during sitting practice. All activities open to newcomers. Newsletter every few months.

Founder/Guru	Chogyam Trungpa Rinpoche
Teachers	Various visit
Opening Times	Sundays 10:00 am–1:00 pm and otherwise according to schedule
Residents	None
Festivals	Usually with **New York Shambhala Center**
Facilities	Shrine room, reception, meditation instruction room
Accommodation	None
Food	None
Booking	Not necessary, although encourage pre-registration for programs with discounts
Fees	5-week class $25, weekend program approximately $45–75
Expected Behavior	Contact center

> *How to get there*   Off exit 6 of Interstate 91 in New Haven. Left at end of
> ramp, cross State St., left onto Peck, left after 2nd build-
> ing into parking lot; behind Yoga Studio.

New Haven Zen Center (Zen)
193 Mansfield Street
New Haven, CT 06511
Tel: (203) 787–0912
Fax: nhzc@aol.com

Contact center for details.

DISTRICT OF COLUMBIA

The Buddhist Vihara (Theravada)
Affiliation: Bikkhu Training Center, Dhammayatanaya Maharagama, Sri Lanka
5017 16th NW
Washington, DC 20011
Tel & Fax: (202) 723–0773

Large house in downtown Washington, near Rock Creek Park and Carter Barron
Stadium. First Sri Lankan temple in United States. Established 1964.
    Classes in Sutta study 7:00–9:00 pm Fridays, Dhamma discussion 7:00–9:00 pm
Tuesdays, and Sunday school. Meditation classes 3:00 pm Sundays (service up to 4:00
pm), 7:00–9:00 pm Wednesdays and Saturdays, and 9:00 am–4:00 pm every third
Saturday. Courses in Buddhism, philosophy, and meditation. Quarterly newsletter.

Founder/Guru	Most Ven. Madhine Pannaseeha Mahanayaka Thero
Teachers	4 resident monks
Opening Times	9:00 am to 9:00 pm
Residents	4 monks
Festivals	Vesak, Katina, Sangamitta, New Year festivals
Facilities	Study room, meditation room
Accommodation	None
Food	Vegetarian by donation
Booking	Membership $25 per year
Fees	By donation
Expected Behavior	No smoking, 5 precepts
How to get there	Bus 52 or 54 from downtown Washington to 16th St. Get off by Rock Creek Park/Carter Barron Football Stadium. Vihara is on right just before stadium between Pallatin and Parraget Aves.

Rigpa (Tibetan–Nyingma)
Affiliation: Rigpa Fellowship
Washington, DC
Tel: (202) 332–2371

Contact: Martha Sigg. See **Rigpa National Office,** California, for details.

Vajrayogini Buddhist Center (Western Buddhist Tradition)
Affiliation: New Kadampa Tradition
3209 Cleveland Avenue NW
Washington, DC 20008
Tel & Fax: (202) 338–3701

Large detached house short walk from National Cathedral. Resident community of eight to ten; fifty regularly attend. Daily meditation schedule, weekly puja, initiations/empowerments about three times a year. Offer general classes on Buddhist thought and practice. Foundation program more in-depth study of Buddha's sutra teachings. Day and weekend courses. Monthly day, weekend, week or longer retreat on various Buddhist practices/meditations.

Founder/Guru	Ven. Geshe Kelsang Gyatso Rinpoche
Teachers	Resident: Kadam Morten Clausen
Opening Times	Call for details
Residents	3 monks, 1 nun, 7 laity
Festivals	Contact center
Facilities	Meditation room with shrine and reading room/library attached
Accommodation	Negotiable
Food	None
Booking	None
Fees	$10/class, $3 students ; courses/retreats vary
Expected Behavior	No smoking
How to get there	From Connective Ave., take Calvert to Cleveland.

See directly into mind and manifest original nature.
from Albuquerque Zen Center brochure

FLORIDA

Morikami Zen Group (Zen–Soto)
Affiliation: see below
c/o Mitchell Cantor
801 Bridgewood Place
Boca Raton, FL 33434
Tel & Fax: (561) 483–6680
E-mail: mitchcan@aol.com

Two-room house, Japanese style, on grounds of Morikami Japanese Museum and gardens, Delray Beach, Florida. Affiliated with **Sagaponack Zendo** (see separate entry), which in turn is affiliated with the **Zen Community of New York** (see separate entry) of Tetsugen Glassman.

Group of fifteen to twenty-five meet two mornings a week for zazen and one afternoon/evening for zazen and study of Buddhist literature. One-and-a-half-day retreats every four to six weeks.

Founder/Guru	Contact center
Teachers	Visiting: Peter Muryo Matthiessen, Sensei
Opening Times	Monday and Friday 7:00–8:00 am and Wednesday 5:45–7:30 pm
Residents	None
Festivals	Mitchell Cantor
Facilities	See above
Accommodation	None
Food	None
Booking	None
Fees	Dana—contributions
Expected Behavior	Contact center
How to Get There	Morikami Museum, off Powerline Road, Delray Beach, Forida

Tubten Kunga Center (Tibetan–Gelug)
Affiliation: Foundation for the Preservation of the Mahayana Tradition
7970 Little Lane
Boca Raton, FL 33433
Tel: (561) 391–1075
Fax: (561) 392–3318
E-mail: 104754,3141@compuserve.com

Meet in private homes—approximately 20 participants.

Weekly meditations following various Lamrim topics 9:10–11:00 am Wednesdays. Regular classes at Palm Beach Community College 8:30–9:45 am Mondays and 9:00–11:00 am Tuesdays during term time on topics such as Reincarnation—Fact or Fiction; Meditation for Contentment; and Enlightened Psychology—Tibetan Buddhism. Retreats periodically.

Founder/Guru	Founder: Lama Thubten Geshe; Spiritual Director: Lama Thubten Zopa Rinpoche
Teachers	Founder
Opening Times	See above
Residents	None
Festivals	None
Facilities	Not applicable
Accommodation	Perhaps at local homes
Food	Not applicable
Booking	For PBCC before session starts
Fees	Private home by donation; college nominal school fees
Expected Behavior	No smoking, 5 precepts
How to Get There	Contact center

Parbhawatiya Buddhist Center (Tibetan–Gelug)
Affiliation: New Kadampa Tradition
c/o Iben Clausen
633 Drake Lane
Dunedin, FL 34698
Tel: (813) 733–0971
Fax: (813) 733–3539

Contact center for details.

Soka Gakkai International (SGI-USA) (Nichiren)
Florida Area Regional Center
20000 SW 36th Street
Fort Lauderdale, FL 33332-1929
Tel: (954) 349–5200
Fax: (954) 349–5201

See **Soka Gakkai International** National Offices & Center, Santa Monica, California, for more details.

Jacksonville KKSG (Tibetan–Karma Kagyu)
Affiliation: Karma Triyana Dharmachakra, New York

1059 Park Street
Jacksonville, FL 32204
Tel: (904) 389-1317
E-mail: artdieties@aol.com

Study sessions on variety of Buddhist subjects. Has hosted Karma Kagyu Lamas for public talks and weekend seminars. Founded 1986 by Ven. Khenpo Karthar Rinpoche.

Jacksonville Zen Sangha (Zen–Rinzai)
1212 Fourteenth Avenue North
Jacksonville Beach, FL 32250
Tel: (904) 721–1050
Fax: (904) 725–8561
E-mail: zlewis@osprey.unf.edu (Zenrin R. Lewis)

Practice held at seven different locations around Jacksonville—Unitarian Universalist Church; University North Florida; FCCJ Kent Campus; Chua Hai-duc; Jacksonville University; Mandarin Community Club; and Kichu-an Arlington.

Zen sittings once or twice a week at each of above locations and weekend sesshins twice a year, spring and fall. Sangha led by Zenrin (was resident monk at Dai Bosatsu Zendo Kongo-ji, New York).

Publishers of *Book of the Zen Grove*, second edition, comprising phrases which are an important part of Rinzai Zen koan practice. Payment by donation.

Bodhi Tree Dhamma Center (Theravada/Vipassana)
11355 Dauphin Avenue
Largo, FL 33778-2903
Tel: (813) 392–7698

Urban residence with meditation hall set on an acre of ground with areas for outdoor walking meditation, and a specimen of the sacred Bodhi tree. Weekly sitting, Hatha Yoga, and Vipassana retreats. Quarterly three-day Vipassana retreats in the Burmese style. Traditional Theravada puja. Retreat flyers and weekly schedule available. Bookstore and mail order catalog. Opened 1985 and now affiliated with **Dhammachakka Meditation Center** in Berkeley, California, and **Bhavana Society** in West Virginia.

Founder/Guru	Ven. U Silananda
Teachers	Visiting from **Bhavana Society,** West Virginia, **Insight Meditation Society,** Massachussetts (see separate entries), Amarvati Monastery in England, and Ven. U Silananda
Opening Times	As per schedule

Residents	None
Festivals	Vesak
Facilities	Meditation hall
Accommodation	Home, meditation hall, and camping
Food	Ovo-lactic vegetarian
Booking	2 weeks in advance
Fees	3 days $100
Expected Behavior	Noble silence, 5 and 9 precepts
How to Get There	From I-275 heading south, take exit 18 and head west for about 9 miles on State Road 688, which becomes Ulmerton Road to 113th St. or from I-275 heading north, take exit 16, head north for about 1.2 miles on Roosevelt Blvd., and then west for abut 7.5 miles on 688 (Ulmerton Rd.) to 113th St. From Ulmerton Rd., turn south for one mile, then west on Walsingham for about 0.3 miles, then south on Dauphin.

Drikung Kagyu Tibetan Meditation Center (Tibetan–Drikung Kagyu)
258 S Clearwater-Largo Road
Largo, FL 34640
Tel: (813) 593–5854 (Jim Hayes)
E-mail: 1257@msn.com (Jim Hayes) or weekends trinley@churchward.com (Jack
    Churchward)
Web site: http://www.churchward.com/drikung

Contact center for details.

International Zen Institute of Florida (Zen–Rinzai)
Affiliation: International Zen Institute of America
3860 Crawford Avenue
Miami, FL 33133
Tel: (305) 448–8969

Urban center in Coconut Grove, a suburb of Miami with about twenty attendees a week. Consists of those wishing to seriously pursue meditation while continuing to live and work as members of society. Established 1989.

Daily early morning and evening zazen. Introductory classes twice a month. Weekend nonresidential retreats once a month. Generally a five- to seven-day residential retreat once a year. Several seminars. New and full moon celebrations. Newsletter four times a year.

Founder/Guru   Ven. Gesshin Prabhasa Dharma Roshi

Teachers	Resident: Rev. Hank Soan Poor, Lay Zen Minister
Opening Times	Monday to Friday 5:00 am
Residents	None
Festivals	Contact center
Facilities	Zendo
Accommodation	None
Food	Vegetarian during retreats
Booking	For annual retreat, 2 months in advance $100 deposit
Fees	Seminars $90, 5-day retreat $325
Expected Behavior	Silence
How to Get There	Contact center

Padmasambhava Buddhist Center
Affiliation: Padmasambhava Buddhist Center, New York
1039 Churchill Circle North
West Palm Beach, FL 33405
Tel: (407) 586–9941

Contact center for details or see **Padmasambhava Buddhist Center,** New York.

Gainesville Dharma Study Group (Tibetan–Karma Kagyu)
5785 Rudolph Avenue
St. Augustine, FL 32084
Tel & Fax: (904) 461–8401

Meets Sunday afternoon at Florida School of Massage, US 441 South, Gainesville. Between fifteen and forty visitors a week, sixty lay members, one monk. Founded in 1989. Devoted to maintain a friendly family atmosphere and to stay away from politics and conflict.

Sadhana 1:30 pm for initiates only. General meeting 2:00–4:00 pm with Samatha meditation and teachings on Mahayana texts as well as abidharma for beginners, mantra recitation, and general prayers. Courses in abidharma: five skandhas, six realms, twelve nidanas, etc; compassion and wisdom teachings. Courses repeat on a two-year cycle. Occasional seminar during the week. Retreat program planned. Occasional newsletter.

Founder/Guru	Khenpo Karthar Rinpoche (guru)
Teachers	Visiting: Frances H. Norwood, Lama Tsuldon
Opening Times	See above
Residents	None
Festivals	None

Facilities	Shrine room 50 ft. x 60 ft.
Accommodation	Possible at homes of members
Food	None
Booking	Phone
Fees	Not normally—contributions welcome
Expected Behavior	Behave decently and create no strife
How to Get There	East side of US 441 S on south side of Gainesville just north of Payne's Prairie

Gainesville KKSG (Tibetan–Karma Kagyu)
Affiliation: Karma Triyana Dharmachakra, New York
5785 Rudolph Avenue
St. Augustine, FL 32084
Tel: (904) 461-8401

Meets Sundays and Wednesdays at Florida School of Massage.

St Augustine Dharma Study Center (Tibetan–Karma Kagyu)
Affiliation: Karma Triyana Dharmachakra, New York
35 San Carlos Avenue
St. Augustine, FL 32084
Tel: (904) 829–6034
Fax: (904) 829–1952
E-mail: tvogler@aug.com

Residence of Buddhist couple.
   Weekly shamatha/Vipassyana sitting open to public. Weekly Chenrezig sadhana for members. Quarterly classes using KTD Woodstock three Yanas curriculum involving practice, instruction, and discussion, for both introductory and experienced practitioners. Host Kagyu Lamas visiting Florida centers for public and membership access. Have hosted cultural tours of Tibetan performance troupes. Quarterly *Sangha News*.

Founder/Guru	Khenpo Kharthar Rinpoche, Abbot of KTD
Teachers	Contact center
Opening Times	Not applicable
Residents	2
Festivals	None
Facilities	Contact center
Accommodation	None
Food	None
Booking	Contact center
Fees	$30 for 6-week KTD Curriculum course

Expected Behavior   Contact center
How to Get There   Contact center

Tampa Karma Thegsum Choling (Tibetan–Karma Kagyu)
Affiliation: Karma Triyana Dharmachakra, New York
820 S MacDill Avenue
Tampa, FL 33609
Tel: (813) 870–2904
E-mail: tdm@ix.netcom.com

Sessions held at local church. Weekly practice and study meetings Tuesdays. Has hosted distinguished Kagyu Lamas. Meditation instruction and practice by appointment; call (813) 961–0559. Founded 1985 by Ven. Khenpo Karthar Rinpoche.

Bookstore sells practice materials. Listing available for those wishing to order by mail.

GEORGIA

American Academy of Religion (Study of all religions)
1703 Clifton Road, NE G5
Atlanta, GA 30329
Tel: (404) 727–7928
Fax: (404) 727–7959
E-mail: tadams@emory.edu

Largest academic learned society of religion in North America with approximately eight hundred members studying the diversity of religious phenomena and practice, including Buddhism. Not a confessional organization or a study center. Primary focus is to provide professional services to professors of religion and theology at the universities, seminaries, and colleges in the U.S., Canada, and abroad.

Atlanta Shambhala Center (Tibetan–Kagyu/Nyingma)
Affiliation: Shambhala International
1167 Zonolite Place
Atlanta, GA 30306
Tel: (404) 873–9846
E-mail: 73054.1730@compuserve.com

See International headquarters, **Shambhala Center,** Halifax, Nova Scotia, Canada.

Atlanta Soto Zen Center (Zen–Soto)
1404 McLendon Avenue NE
Atlanta, GA 30307
Tel: (404) 659–4749

In Candler Park area of city. Two hundred members, fifty of them active. Plan to extend teachings into the community. Has affiliate center in Charleston, South Carolina. Founded 1960s.

Evening services daily (Monday–Friday and Sunday 7:30–8:30 pm; Saturdays 6:00–7:00 pm). Morning services Tuesdays, Thursdays, and Fridays 7:00–8:00 am. More formal service Sundays 8:00–10:30 am including dokusan and Dharma talk. Newcomers' sessions Sundays 10:00–11:00 am. Public lecture series on history of Zen. Weekend sesshins bimonthly, seven-day sesshin once a year. Newsletter, *Dharani*.

Founder/Guru	Michael Zenkai Taiun Elliston-Roshi
Teachers	Founder is superintendent
Opening Times	See session times above
Residents	None
Festivals	None
Facilities	Contact center
Accommodation	None
Food	None
Booking	Not applicable
Fees	By donation
Expected Behavior	Zazen etiquette will be taught
How to Get There	Near Candler Park Marta Station

Atlanta Zen Group (Zen)
Affiliation: Rochester Zen Center, New York
5141 Northside Drive North West
Atlanta, GA 30327
Tel: (770) 955-4321

Private house in wooded residential area, with twelve members. Zazen once a week, all-day sittings occasionally. Established 1973.

Founder/Guru	Roshi Philip Kapleau
Teachers	Visiting: Sensei Bodhin Kjolhede
Opening Times	For sessions only
Residents	1 lay
Festivals	Vesak
Facilities	Zendo

Accommodation	None
Food	None
Booking	Contact center
Fees	Contact center
Expected Behavior	No smoking, 5 precepts
How to Get There	Exit 15 off perimeter Expressway 285

The Zennist—Dark Zen—The Teachings of Mystical Zen Buddhism (Zen)
P O Box 15061
Atlanta, GA 30333
E-mail: zennist@teleport.com and zenmar@aol.com
Web site: http://www.teleport.com/~zennist/zennist.html

Prime publication is *The Zennist,* a newsletter commentary on Zen mysticism and its interaction with contemporary Zen, at $20 for 12 issues a year or $2 sample issue. Formerly called Buddhist Mind Institute.

"Ever wondered what happened to the mysticism in Zen Buddhism? We did, and also started to question why the sutras are not being taught, why Dogenism is placed over the Buddha's teachings, and why Zen is more psychological rather than mystical." Aims to help students who feel they have learned nothing at Zen centers and advanced students wanting to push forward with their learning "rather than sit in the remedial beginners class over and over."

Would like to build a network of Buddhist mystics, scholars, and teachers to promote the mystical aspect of Buddhism and perhaps in the future create an actual institute.

Soka Gakkai International (SGI-USA) (Nichiren)
Georgia Area Regional Center
5831 Riverdale Road
College Park, GA 30349-6201
Tel: (770) 996–5178
Fax: (770) 996–6978

See **Soka Gakkai International** National Offices & Center, Santa Monica, California, for more details.

You live in illusion and in the appearance of things. There is a reality. You are the reality. If you wake up to that reality, you will know that you are nothing, and being nothing, you are everything.

Kalu Rinpoche quoted in a brochure from Kagyu Thegchen Ling, Hawaii

HAWAII

Soto Mission of Aiea (Zen–Soto)
P O Box 926
99-045 Kauhale Street
Aiea, HI 96701
Tel: (808) 488–6794
E-mail: thase@pixi.com

Contact center for details.

Hilo Nichiren Mission (Nichiren Shu)
Affiliate: Nichiren Propagation Center
24 Makalika Street
Hilo, HI 96720
Tel & Fax: (808) 959–8894

Resident priest—Rev. Gakugyo Matsumoto. See **Nichiren Propagation Center,** Oregon.

Daihonzan Chozenji (Zen–Rinzai)
International Zen Dojo
3565 Kalihi Street
Honolulu, HI 96819
Tel: (808) 845–8129
Fax: (808) 841–5977

Contact center for details.

Diamond Sangha (Zen)
Affiliation: Diamond sangha
2119 Kaloa Way
Honolulu, HI 96822
Tel: (808) 946–0666

Branch of **Palolo Zen Center** (see seperate entry). Contact center for details.

Honolulu Dharma Study Group (Tibetan–Kagyu/Nyingma)
Affiliation: Shambhala International
Philip Bralich, Coordinator

1555 Pohaku Street, #A508
Honolulu, HI 96817-2836
Fax: (808) 944–3912
E-mail: bralich@hawaii.edu

See International headquarters, **Shambhala Center,** Halifax, Nova Scotia, Canada.

Honolulu Myohoji Mission (Nichiren Shu)
Affiliation: Nichiren Propagation Center
2003 Nuuanu Avenue
Honolulu, HI 96817
Tel & Fax: (808) 537–2854

Resident priest—Rev. Eijo Ikenaga. See **Nichiren Propagation Center,** Oregon.

Jamyang Choling Institute for Buddhist Women (Tibetan–nonsectarian)
400 Hobron Lane, #2615
Honolulu, HI 96815
Fax: (808) 944–7070 (Karma Lekshe Tsomo, Director)
E-mail: tsomo@hawaii.edu

Nonresident organization to promote education, monastic training, and meditation practice among nuns and laywomen of the Tibetan tradition. Six monastic schools for women in India and plans for a residential center in Hawaii. "These are the first full-time intensive programs for women of the Tibetan tradition; provide teacher training for women from all parts of India, Nepal, Bhutan, Tibet, Mongolia; vegetarian; incorporate meditation, and leadership training."
    Videotape and slide presentations given on request to elicit support for education programs in India. Opportunities for volunteer services in India in summer. Brochure published annually.

Kagyu Thegchen Ling (Tibetan–Kagyu)
26 Gartley Place
Honolulu, HI 96817
Tel & Fax: (808) 595–8989

House in residential neighborhood of city in a beautiful mountain pass valley with view of the sea. About fifty visitors a week. Founded 1974.
    Weekly meditations and pujas such as Chenrezig, Tara puja, Milarepa puja, etc. Classes: Shinay (Shamata) Meditation Saturday mornings—quarterly; Introduction to Tibetan Buddhism; The Jewel Ornament of Literature, and The Seven-Point Mind

Training (last four available as translation permits). Resident Lamas available for personal instruction. All activities suitable for newcomers. Quarterly newsletter, *The Empty Mirror*.

Founder/Guru	H.E. Kalu Rinpoche
Teachers	Resident: Lama Karma Rinchen, Lama Wangchuk. Visiting: Kagyu high Lamas
Opening Times	Please call outside events program
Residents	2 Lamas, 2 lay
Festivals	Contact center
Facilities	Shrine room, bookstore
Accommodation	As available at $15 per night. Not suitable for long stays unless a resident's room is available
Food	Residents' responsibility
Booking	Phone for details
Fees	Contact center
Expected Behavior	No smoking, respectful quiet behavior

Nichiren Mission of Hawaii (Nichiren Shu)
Affiliation: Nichiren Propagation Center
33 Pulelehua Way
Honolulu, HI 96817
Tel: (808) 595–3517
Fax: (808) 595–6412

Resident: Bishop Joyo Ogawa and Rev. Dairyo Tomikawa. See **Nichiren Propagation Center,** Oregon.

Palolo Zen Center (Zen–Soto and Rinzai)
Affiliation: Diamond sangha
2747 Waiomao Road
Honolulu, HI 96816
Tel: (808) 735–1347
Fax: (808) 735–4245
E-mail: hsangha@aloha.net

Country ambiance on borders of city. Facilities for forty retreatants. Founded 1959. Robert Aitken Roshi retired 1996, and Dharma Heir, Nelson Foster, became principal teacher in 1997.

Daily morning and evening zazen. Monthly Dharma classes. One- to eight-day retreats several times a year. Orientation for newcomers every month. Publish monthly newsletter.

Founder/Guru	Anne and Robert Aitken
Teachers	Robert Aitken Roshi until 1997, then Nelson Foster
Opening Times	Contact center
Residents	3 laity
Festivals	None
Facilities	Dojo, residence hall, teacher's residence, and office
Accommodation	Shared bedroom and bathroom facilities $25/day room and board, participation in work and zazen schedule required.
Food	Vegetarian
Booking	Contact center
Fees	Contact center
Expected Behavior	No alcohol or drugs; no smoking on grounds
How to Get There	Taxi—no public transportation within 1.25 miles. Visitors with cars should request map.

Sakyadhita International Association of Buddhist Women (Nonsectarian)
400 Hobron Lane, #2615
Honolulu, HI 96815
Fax: (808) 944–7070
E-mail: tsomo@hawaii.edu

Nonresidential. "The only active international Buddhist women's organization; has made a tremendous impact on improving the status, education, and practice conditions for women in the last ten years." Established after the first International Conference on Buddhist Nuns in Bodhgaya, India, in 1987. Its aims were "to create a network of communications among the Buddhist women of the world, to promote understanding among the different Buddhist traditions, to encourage and educate women as teachers of Buddhadharma, to provide guidance and assistance for Buddhist nuns and those aspiring to ordination, to conduct research into the Buddhist texts, especially as they relate to Vinaya (monastic disciple) and women's issues, and to foster world peace through the practice of the Buddha's teachings." Membership of 550, mailing list of 1800.

International conferences every other year on topics of interest to Buddhist women. Conferences have been held in India, Thailand, Sri Lanka, Ladakh, and Cambodia. National and local programs occasionally and periodic retreats at national or local level.

Sakyadhita newsletter published bi-annually. Videotapes available and books through Snow Lion Publications: *Sakyadhita: Daughters of the Buddha* and *Buddhism through American Women's Eyes*.

Founder/Guru	Ven. Ayya Khema, Ven. Karma Lekshe Tsomo, Dr. Chatsumarn Kabilsingh
Food	Vegetarian at conferences

Booking   A few months ahead
Fees   Conference registration about $50. Board and lodging variable, but very reasonable
Expected Behavior   5 precepts, no smoking

Soka Gakkai International (SGI-USA) (Nichiren)
Hawaii Area Regional Center
2729 Pali Highway
Honolulu, HI 96817
Tel: (808) 595–6324
Fax: (808) 595–6378

See **Soka Gakkai International** National Offices & Center, Santa Monica, California, for more details.

Yuk Fut Monastery (Pure Land)
3348 Mooheau Avenue
Honolulu, HI 96816
Tel: (808) 734–3021
E-mail: ylchang@hawaii.edu (Yu-Ling)

House with shrine, library, and study/meditation room. Founded mid 1970s by the resident Abbess, Rev. Suey Miu.

Morning and evening chanting, Sunday morning Buddha chanting assembly, meditation, sutra studies, etc. No fees for practices.

Puunene Nichiren Mission (Nichiren Shu)
Affiliate: Nichiren Propagation Center
9 Ani Street
Kahului, HI 96732
Tel: (808) 871–4831
Fax: (808) 871–2799

Resident priest—Rev. Chishin Hirai. See **Nichiren Propagation Center,** Oregon.

Zen Center of Hawaii (Zen)
Affiliation: White Plum sangha
P O Box 2066
Kamuela, HI 96743
Tel: (808) 885–6109

Fax: (808) 885–2009
E-mail: zch@aloha.net

House of Robert and Juna Althouse in beautiful country setting on Big Island of Hawaii, just outside the town of Waimeo. Two affiliate groups in Hilo area and Kona that have regular weekly sitting schedule at a public place. Various modes of social action as part of practice. Openly work with other groups and organizations. Street retreats and yearly march or walk for nonviolence.

Zazen, yoga, and Tai Chi classes. Monthly sesshins from three to ten days long. Plan to offer class on precepts. Weekly meditation schedule at three different locations: Waimea, Hilo, and Kona. Newsletter, *Muddy Waters*, sent out every other month which includes program of events.

Founder/Guru	Taizan Maezumi Roshi
Teachers	Robert Joshin Althouse
Opening Times	As per program
Residents	Family
Festivals	Contact center
Facilities	Zendo
Accommodation	Small guest room
Food	Usually vegetarian
Booking	1 month in advance
Fees	Retreats usually $25 per day including room and board
Expected Behavior	Common sense
How to Get There	Phone for directions for all 3 locations

Honseiji Temple (Nichiren Shoshu)
44-668 Kaneohe Bay Drive
Kaneohe, HI 96744
Tel: (808) 235–8486

Contact center for details.

Garden Island Sangha (Zen)
Affiliation: Diamond sangha
6585 Waipouli Road
Kapaa, HI 96716
Tel: (808) 822–4794
E-mail: indi@aloha.net

Old Hawaiian-style building surrounded by tropical flowers, mountain, and waterfall— small intimate group. Zendo holds ten. Sitting group of four started 1990. Zazen and chanting and occasional zazenkais.

Teachers	Teacher from Palolo Zen Center visits
Opening Times	Sunday 7:30–10:00 am
Residents	None
Festivals	None
Facilities	Zendo
Accommodation	For occasional zazenkais only
Food	Vegetarian
Booking	Write for schedule
Fees	$25/day for zazenkai
Expected Behavior	No drinking or smoking; in accordance with the Dharma
How to Get There	Write for directions

Kagyu Thubten Choling (Tibetan)
Affiliation: Lama Tenzin, Box 1029, Paia, Hawaii 96779 and Lama Wangmo,
    17 Acer, Southpoint, Big Island, Hawaii
6458B Kahuna Road
Kapaa, HI 96746
Tel: (808) 823–0949

Remote quiet river and jungle setting with vegetables gardens. Lama Tashi teaches in English and is connected to all Tibetan Buddhist meditation and retreats in Hawaii. He also runs a small business.

Classes held on Wednesdays 7:00–9:00 pm. Offers all Tibetan Buddhist Mahayana and Vajrayana practices, empowerments, shamanistic rituals, and preparation (taking four months) for three-year, three-month, three-day retreat. Public and children invited to all activities.

Founder/Guru	Kalu Yangtsi Rinpoche of Sonada Monastery, Lama Rinchen, 26 Gartley Place, Honolulu, HI
Teachers	Resident: Lama Tashi MacLaine; Lama Rinchen and Lam Tenzin visit
Opening Times	Contact center
Residents	2 laity
Festivals	Tara Dance and festival annually
Facilities	Shrine room and meditation room
Accommodation	B&B $50/night
Food	Breakfast free
Booking	1 week in advance
Fees	$10 per day on Maui
Expected Behavior	No smoking, 5 precepts
How to Get There	Contact center

Shantideva Center (Tibetan–Gelug)
Affiliation: Foundation for the Preservation of the Mahayana Tradition
HCR 4660
Keaau, HI 96749
Tel: (808) 966–6877

Contact center for details.

Daifukuji Soto Mission (Zen–Soto)
Box 55
Kealakekua, HI 96750
Tel: (808) 322–3524

Contact center for details.

Vajrayana Foundation Hawaii (Tibetan)
Affiliation: Vajrayana Foundation, California
P O Box 6780
Ocean View, HI 96737-6780
Tel: (808) 939–9889
Fax: (808) 393–8490
E-mail: vfh@ilhawaii.net

Retreat sanctuary for short- and long-term individual retreats. General teaching programs throughout the Hawaiian islands and two yearly retreats with Lama Tharchin Rinpoche, programs with Lama Yeshe Wangmo. Please contact Lama Yeshe Wangmo to arrange a visit or personal retreat.

Founder/Guru	Lama Tharchin Rinpoche
Teachers	Resident: Lama Yeshe Wangmo
Opening Times	Contact center for program
Residents	None
Festivals	None
Facilities	Contact center
Accommodation	For retreatants only

Nechung Dorje Drayang Ling (Tibetan–nonsectarian)
P O Box 250
Pahala, HI 96777
Tel: (808) 928–8539
Fax: (808) 928–6271
E-mail: nechung@aloha.net

Thirty acres in Wood Valley, Kau District at 2,000 foot elevation in a forested area with three buildings/complexes: main temple with library, residents' quarters, office, and gift/bookstore; retreat facility with meditation hall, private and dormitory quarters for twenty-five; and staff/administrative director's house. Close to black sand beaches and Volcano National Park. Started 1973 in an old Japanese Temple—buildings are unique as of three Buddhist sects: Nichiren, Shingon, and Hongwanji, in beautifully landscaped grounds. Special focus on being nonsectarian—head Lamas and main lineage Lamas of all schools of Tibetan Buddhism teach here, including H.H. the Dalai Lama. Provide facilities for other religious, secular, and community groups to hold their own programs.

Daily chanting and meditation mornings and evenings. Weekend seminars, retreats, courses of study ranging from one month to one year, and a summer institute. Subjects range from Foundational Buddhist Philosophy to sutra and Tantra trainings at all levels. Topics include Dzogchen and Mahamudra, Ngondro (preliminary practices), Stages of the Path, Samatha, and Vipassana meditation. Newsletter, *Drayang*, twice yearly. Small gift/bookshop.

Founder/Guru	Ven. Nechung Rinpoche
Teachers	Lamas of all Tibetan lineages visit
Opening Times	Contact center
Residents	1 monk and 2 laity
Festivals	Monthly lunar days, Buddha's Enlightenment Day, etc.
Facilities	2 temple rooms for meditation and teachings, excellent library of books and videocassettes
Accommodation	$20/night dormitory; $35/night single; $45/night double; groups of over 15 $18/night
Food	Vegetarian for groups if requested at $25/day for 3 meals
Booking	Groups—Deposit of $100–500 depending on length of program. Individuals—50% deposit. Booking can be made prior to arrival
Fees	Retreats/courses roughly $50–$100/day including room and board
Expected Behavior	No smoking, drinking, or intoxicants of any kind. Mindful behavior and awareness of other guests/residents and the environment
How to Get There	Hilo nearest airport, near town of Pahala.

Karma Rimay O Sal Ling (Tibetan–Karma Kagyu)
Maui Dharma Center
P O Box 1029
Paia, Maui
Hawaii 96779
Tel: (808) 579–8076
Fax: (808) 575–2044

E-mail: krosl@maui.net
Web site: http://www.maui.net/-krosl

Has two sites—an urban town center and a country retreat center, both founded 1974.

Town center: Registered church with resident teacher, board of directors, and between 75 and 125 visitors a week in a popular tourist windsurfing town. Small house fashioned to look like Japanese-style teahouse with shrine room and six guest and resident rooms.

Country retreat center: For individual retreats and small group retreats once or twice a month. In quiet countryside overlooking the ocean with small, humble rooms for individual retreats.

Twice daily service with prayer and meditation. Weekly meditation sitting and oral teaching given by resident teacher and translated into English. Five monthly services according to lunar calendar. Quarterly newsletter.

Founder/Guru	Ven. Kalu Rinpoche
Teachers	Resident: Ven. Lama Tenzin, and many visit
Opening Times	6:30 am–7:00 pm daily
Residents	Teacher and 5 laity
Festivals	Contact center
Facilities	Shrine room, library, and bookstore
Accommodation	Guest rooms $20/night. Shrine room space $15/night
Food	Included in retreat costs. Others provide their own.
Booking	1 month if possible. Deposits encouraged
Fees	Vary
Expected Behavior	No smoking, drugs, or alcohol
How to Get There	From Kahului Airport take Hana Hwy. to Paia town. Right on Baldwin Ave. to Hikina Place, turn left and look for 9 Hikina Place.

Rissho Kosei-kai of Hawaii (Rissho Kosei-kai)
2280 Auhuhu Street
Pearl City, HI 96782
Tel: (808) 455–3212
Fax: (808) 455–4633

House on a hill in a residential area. Established as first overseas branch of Rissho Kosei-kai 1959. Three hundred and fifty members.

Sunday services and runs a day care program for people with Alzheimer's three days a week with volunteer caretakers.

Publish magazines such as *Everyday Buddhism*, *Dharma World*, and *Newsletter*.

Founder/Guru	Founder: Rev. Nikkyo Niwano. President:

	Rev. Nichiko Niwao
Teachers	Minister: Rev. Mitsuyuki Okada (resident)
Opening Times	8:00 am–3:00 pm
Residents	Minister
Festivals	Bon Service/Bon Dance, Matsuri in Hawaii
Facilities	Main and small chapel, Hoza room, office, and small library
Accommodation	None
Food	None
Booking	Not applicable
Fees	Not applicable
Expected Behavior	Not applicable
How to Get There	From Waikiki side, take freeway H1, exit Pearl City, and go to Pacific Parisade, where the church is.

Maui Zendo (Zen)
Affiliation: Diamond sangha
c/o Patti Burke
2860 Liholani Street
Pukalani, HI 96768

Contact center for details.

Wahiawa Nichiren Mission (Nichiren Shu)
Affiliate: Nichiren Propagation Center
2112-B Puu Place
Wahiawa, HI 96786
Tel & Fax: (808) 621–6161

Resident priest—Rev. Eiyu Yoshiki. See **Nichiren Propagation Center,** Oregon.

> *The most profound teaching in Buddhism is to practice.*
>
> Milarepa quoted in a flyer of KKSG Minneapolis, Minnesota

ILLINOIS

Northwest Chicago Zen Group (Zen)
P O Box 3362
Barrington, IL 60011
E-mail: sander7@uic.edu (Susan Palmer Andersen)

Spiritual Director: Myoyu Anderson Sensei. Contact center for details.

Chagdud Gonpa Chicago (Tibetan–Nyingma)
Affiliation: Chagdud Gonpa Foundation
1632 South State Street, Suite A
Belvidere, IL 61008
Tel: (815) 544–6464 (member's office phone number)
Fax: (815) 547–5550

Meets in house and Quang Minh Temple, 4429 North Damen Ave., Chicago. Started 1993.
　　Activities include regular group practices Sundays 2:30–4:30 pm, Nyingma Vajrayana teachings/empowerments and meditations, and teachings about Great Perfection. Short weekend retreats three–four times a year; longer retreats planned from 1996.

> *Founder/Guru*　Chagdud Tulku Rinpoche
> *Teachers*　Founder and others visit

Amitabha Buddhist Society at SIUC (No school or affiliation)
322 West Walnut Street, Apt. #2
Carbondale, IL 62901
(Address subject to change—check web site for recent information)
Tel & Fax: (618) 457–2756
E-mail: amadeus@siu.edu
Web site: http://www.siu.edu/~abs

Student organization of around twenty members who meet usually at president's house. Purpose is "to explore the true meaning of Buddhist philosophy among the students at Southern Illinois University." Membership open to SIUC students expressing active interest in this purpose. Officially founded 1992.
　　Meet 7:00–10:00 pm Fridays. Activities include meditation, Buddhist study and discussion, and usually one field trip to another Buddhist organization per semester.

Founder/Guru	Master Shuan Hui of Taiwan while studying at SIUC
Teachers	Master Ge Zu, Master Zen Quang, and Master Hie Hwea visit
Opening Times	Not applicable
Residents	Not applicable
Festivals	Not applicable
Facilities	Library, meditation room, study, meeting room
Accommodation	None
Food	None
Booking	Not applicable
Fees	Not applicable
Expected Behavior	Behavior should not disturb others' learning
How to Get There	Check web site or e-mail for directions

Prairie Zen Center (Zen)
Affiliation: Ordinary Mind Zen School
P O Box 1702
Champaign, IL 61824
Tel: (217) 384–8817
Web site: http://luca.cba.uiuc.edu/PZC/PZChome.html

Rented house with room for about twenty-five retreatants. Planned move in 1997 to larger premises. Established 1991 by students of Charlotte Joko Beck.

Sitting and taped Dharma talk Sundays 10:00 am–noon and Tuesdays 7:30–9:30 pm; sitting and service Saturdays 8:00–8:45 am. Introduction to Zen meditation on second through last Sunday of each month. Monthly intensive Saturday afternoon to Sunday noon. Five-day sesshin three times a year. Newsletter published three–five times a year.

Founder/Guru	Students of Charlotte Joko Beck
Teachers	Elihu Genmyo Smith of Zen Center of Willets, California, Dharma Heir of Joko Beck
Opening Times	See practice times above
Residents	None
Festivals	None
Facilities	Zendo
Accommodation	During sesshins at Zen center
Food	Vegetarian during sesshins
Booking	Usually one month before sesshins
Fees	$150 sesshin; monthly membership $10
Expected Behavior	Silence during sittings and sesshins. Full participation for all activities during sesshins

*How to Get There*Champaign accessible by air, train, or interstate highway
Buddhist Temple of Chicago (Jodo Shinshu)
1151 W Leland
Chicago, IL 60640
Tel: (312) 334–4661

Contact center for details.

Bul Sim Sa Buddhist Temple (Bo Moon Order)
5011 N Damen
Chicago, IL 60625
Tel: (773) 334–8590
Fax: (773) 334–8597

Located on top floor of three-story building. Temple and Bo Moon Order founded 1978
by Bup Choon Seok Su Nim.

Teaches Buddhism, Korean music, and math for children under fifteen years 9:00
am–noon Saturdays. Zen for Korean speakers 3:00–6:00 pm Sundays. Buddhist talk for
everyone 11:00 am–1:00 pm Sundays. Weekly newsletter.

Founder/Guru	Priest: Bup Choon Seok
Teachers	Resident is priest
Opening Times	Daily
Residents	3 nuns
Festivals	Buddha's Birthday
Facilities	Library, meditation center, and youth center
Accommodation	For 200 guests
Food	Purely vegetarian and no green onion, onion, or garlic
Booking	Not necessary
Fees	None
Expected Behavior	No smoking
How to Get There	Call center

Chicago Karma Thegsum Choling (Tibetan–Karma Kagyu)
Affiliation: Karma Triyana Dharmachakra, New York
1311 W Arthur Street
Chicago, IL 60626
Tel: (312) 743–5134
E-mail: RobertB938@aol.com

Small membership includes senior students available to answer questions and lend support. Has a meditation hall and library. Founded late 1970s.

Practice Sundays 10:00 am and Wednesdays 7:00 pm. Host about two lama visits a year. All sessions open to beginners and free of charge. Free meditation instruction available at any practice session or by appointment.

Chicago Shambhala Center (Tibetan–Kagyu/Nyingma)
Affiliation: Shambhala International
7331 North Sheridan Road
Chicago, IL 60626
Tel: (773) 743–8147
E-mail: NormChapmanMD@msn.com

See International headquarters, **Shambhala Center,** Halifax, Nova Scotia, Canada.

Harmony Zen Center (Zen)
Mailing: 4524 North Richmond
Chicago, IL 60625
Attention: Richard Brandon
Tel: (312) 583–5794

Contact center for details.

Midwest Buddhist Temple (Jodo Shinshu)
Affiliation: Buddhist Churches of America
435 W Menomonee Street
Chicago, IL 60614
Tel: (312) 943–7801
Fax: (312) 943–8069

Japanese-style temple roof and concrete building located in the city. Three hundred and fifty pledged family members. Formally founded 1944.

Sundays: 8:00 am Zenshin meditation; 10:00 am Dharma school for children; 10:45 am adult sangha; 11:45 am service in Japanese for adults. Public Dharma talk three times a year. Monthly newsletter.

Founder/Guru	Late Rev. Gyodo Kono
Teachers	Resident Minister: Rev. Koshin Ogui, Sensei
Opening Times	Office hours: 9:00 am–3:00 pm Monday to Friday
Residents	1 Sensei
Festivals	Obon, Ginza Bazzar
Facilities	Main Dharma hall, 12 classrooms for school, 3 offices

Accommodation	None
Food	None
Booking	None
Fees	Pledge system according to individual income
Expected Behavior	Sincerity
How to Get There	Corner of Hudson and W. Menomonee

Nichiren Buddhist Temple of Chicago (Nichiren Shu)
Affiliate: Nichiren Propagation Center
4216 N Paulina Street
Chicago, IL 60613
Tel & Fax: (773) 348–2028

Resident priest—Rev. Sensho Komukai. See **Nichiren Propagation Center,** Oregon.

Padmasambhava Buddhist Center
Affiliation: Padmasambhava Buddhist Center, New York
2040 North Mohawk Street
Chicago, IL 60614
Tel: (312) 951–8010
Fax: (312) 951–8224

Contact center for details or see **Padmasambhava Buddhist Center,** New York.

Quan Am Tu Buddhist Temple
5545 N Broadway
Chicago, IL 60640
Tel: (312) 271–7048

Contact center for details.

Ratnashri Sangha of Chicago (Tibetan–Drikung Kagyu)
525 Stratford Place, Apt. 579
Chicago, IL 60657
Tel: (773) 296–4575
E-mail: plars@aol.com
Web site: http://www.churchward.com/drikung

City center group of about fifteen people meeting twice weekly in member's apartment.
Founded 1994. "We just have a small group here in Chicago, but we're part of the larger

Drikung Kagyu organization in the U.S., with its center in Frederick, Maryland, and often receive visits and teachings from Lamas in that lineage."

Discussion group Thursday nights. Group practice of Lama Chopa (basic Vajrayana technique) from Drikung Kagyu lineage Sunday mornings. *Dharma Wheel* published by main Drikung Kagyu U.S. center (**Tibetan Meditation Center**) in Maryland (see separate entry); call (301) 473–5750.

Founder/Guru	Khenpo Konchog Gyaltshen Rinpoche
Teachers	Khenpo Konchog Gyaltshen Rinpoche and other Drikung Lamas visit
Opening Times	Not applicable
Residents	None
Festivals	None
Facilities	See above
Accommodation	None
Food	None
Booking	Not applicable
Fees	Contact center
Expected Behavior	No specific rules, but observing the 5 precepts would be appreciated
How to Get There	Stratford Place can be accessed from Lakeshore Drive

Rigpa Chicago (Tibetan–Nyingma)
Affiliation: Rigpa Fellowship
Chicago, IL
Tel: (312) 409–2906

See **Rigpa National Office,** California, for details.

Soka Gakkai International (SGI-USA) (Nichiren)
Illinois Area Regional Center
1455 South Wabash Avenue
Chicago, IL 60605-2806
Tel: (312) 913–1211
Fax: (312) 913–0988

See **Soka Gakkai International** National Offices & Center, Santa Monica, California, for more details.

Wat Prasriratanamahadhatu of Chicago (Theravada)

4735 N Magnolia Avenue
Chicago, IL 60640
Tel: (773) 784–0257

Single-family three-story house with one acre of land in uptown community of Chicago. Founded 1992 by group of Thais, Laotians, and Cambodians living in Illinois and surrounding states. Member of the Council of Thai Bhikkus in USA from 1995. "A Buddhist Center welcoming all kinds of people regardless of nationality or religion."

Offers Buddhism course and Thai language classes every Monday, Tuesday, and Sunday. Meditation retreat first weekend of the month (Samatha Bhavana and insight meditations). Publish journal on Buddhist holy days and for ceremonies and festivals.

Founder/Guru	Ven. Ratana Thongkrajai (Thai Buddhist monk)
Teachers	Ven. Ratana Thongkrajai, Ven. Boonmee Chanchiew, Ven. Samrang Deemun, Ven. Somthawin Grongthong, Ven. Yart Pansoi, Ven. Pramoun Srisomsak
Opening Times	8:00 am–10:00 pm
Residents	6 monks and 1 layman
Festivals	Holy days: Magha Puja Day, Visakha Puja Day, Asalha Puja Day, Buddhist Lent Day, and Lent Ending Day. Festivals: Happy New Year Day, The Songkran Day, Kathina Ceremony
Facilities	Study room, meditation room, chanting room
Accommodation	None
Food	Nonvegetarian
Booking	None
Fees	Free of charge
Expected Behavior	No smoking, 5 precepts
How to Get There	From downtown Chicago, take North Lakeshore Drive, then exit at W Wilson Ave. about 4–5 blocks. When you see N. Magnolia Ave., turn right for about a block.

Zen Buddhist Temple (Zen)
Affiliation: Buddhist Society for Compassionate Wisdom
1710 West Cornelia Avenue
Chicago, IL 60657-1219
Tel: (312) 528–8685
Fax: (312) 528–9909

Buddhist temple in large, four-story Masonic temple built in 1915 with seventy or more members and upwards of sixty visitors a week. Building purchased 1992 and formal opening fall 1992, since when much renovation has taken place.

Public meditation services Sundays 9:30 am and 5:00 pm. Members sittings

Wednesdays 6:30–9:30 pm and Sundays 6:00–8:00 am. Introductory meditation courses in either a five–Tuesday evening or Friday evening through Saturday afternoon format. Saturday morning meditation workshop for those wishing to meditate in chairs. These last three run five–six times through the year. Annual spring and fall lecture series on three to five consecutive Saturday afternoons on such subjects as Buddhism in Everyday Life. Concurrently, Ven. Samu Sunim gives a Thursday evening lecture series on Buddhist sutras and doctrine. One and two silent meditation retreats and three- to five-day Yongmaeng Chongjin (intensive meditation retreats) throughout the year. Two-month summer retreats for those interested in staying in the temple for training.

Maitreya Buddhist Seminary is a three-year seminary program designed to train Buddhist priests and Dharma teachers and is open to all people who sincerely desire to undertake the training of discipleship for the spread of the Way of Buddha in the West. Publishes *Spring Wind—Buddhist Cultural Forum* biannually. Buddhist bookstore stocks a wide range of books and other Buddhist articles.

Founder/Guru	Ven. Samu Sunim
Teachers	Resident teacher as Founder plus others
Opening Times	To the public during Sunday services, other times by appointment
Residents	1 monk and 2 Dharma students/staff (contact person: Irjo Mark Gemmill)
Festivals	Year End and New Year's Day Services. Buddha's Enlightenment Day all-night sitting and Buddha's Birthday celebrations
Facilities	Meditation/Buddha hall, urban retreat center, bookstore, social/dining hall, dormitory
Accommodation	Day, week and month rates from $30/day to $450/month
Food	Vegetarian. All meals included in accommodation
Booking	1 month's notice and 25% deposit
Fees	Courses from $60–$140; retreats $50–$60 per day
Expected Behavior	Keep silence, concentrate your mind, be grateful and happy in this moment of your life
How to Get There	From I-90/94, exit at Addison and drive east to Lincoln Ave. Turn right (south), one block to Cornelia Ave., turn left, temple is second building from the corner.

Tilopa Buddhist Center (Tibetan–Gelug)
Affiliation: Foundation for the Preservation of the Mahayana Tradition
443 N Edward Street
Decatur, IL 62522
Tel: (217) 425–0803
Fax: (217) 423–0986
E-mail: tilopafpmt@aol.com

Second-floor apartment in city center where about ten people meet weekly. Started as study group 1994 and became FPMT center 1995. Resident monk: Ven. Thubten Kunga.

Holds daily practice and meditation instruction and Monday night study and practice group. Four–five visiting teachers a year. Special events occasionally. Celebrate Tsongkhapa's Birthday, Dalai Lama's Birthday, Buddha's Birthday, Tibetan New Year, Return of Buddha from Heaven.

Northwest Chicago Zen Group (Zen–Soto)
1433 E Walnut
Des Plaines, IL 60016
Tel: (847) 298–8472
E-mail: sander7@uic.edu (Susan Palmer Andersen)

Rent space from Unitarian Universalist Church—fully wheelchair accessible. Small group of practitioners. Established 1994.

Weekly Zen meditation. Two- to seven-day sesshins about three times a year. Newcomers welcome to all activities. Newsletter several times a year.

Founder/Guru	Honorary founder: Hakuyu Taizan Maezumi, Roshi
Teachers	Susan Myoyu Andersen, Sensei
Opening Times	7:30–9:00 pm Tuesdays
Residents	None
Festivals	None
Facilities	See above
Accommodation	None
Food	None
Booking	Preregister for sesshins; no advance booking for weekly sittings
Fees	Donations welcome
Expected Behavior	Contact center
How to Get There	Contact center

Heaven, the ultimate goal of so many faiths, since it is a mode of contingent and hence of transitory existence, is accounted no more than a pleasant interlude in a pilgrimage fundamentally of more serious import.

Sangharakshita, *The Three Jewels*

Buddhist Council of the Midwest (All)
2400 Prairie
Evanston, IL 60201
Tel: (847) 869–4975

Umbrella organization for Buddhist groups in the Chicago metropolitan area, established about 1982/83 as a way of setting up communications and providing publicity for
Buddhist organizations in the Midwest. No permanent address—monthly meeting
place rotates among member temples.

Meditation instruction at time of Visakha festival in May or June. Meditation
retreats once or twice a year. Membership $50/year for small temples/centers, $100/year
for large temples/centers.

Lakeside Buddha Sangha (Zen–Vietnamese)
Affiliation: Community of Mindful Living, lineage of Thich Nhat Hanh
P O Box 7067
Evanston, IL 60201
Tel & Fax: (847) 475–0080

Rented meditation hall. Approximately a hundred members. "Very warm, tolerant,
openhearted sangha which practices right speech and deep listening." Founded 1991.

Regular Introduction to Practice Series on sitting and walking meditations, the
use of gathas, basic Buddhist sutras, family practice, etc. Beginners should call in
advance.

Zen Buddhist Temple of Chicago (Zen–Soto)
Affiliation: Soji-ji Temple and Monastery, Japan
Temple location: 608 Dempster Street
Evanston, IL 60202
Mailing: 865 Bittersweet Drive
Northbrook, IL 60062
Tel: (847) 272–2070
Fax: (847) 272–3898

Located in busy commercial area of Evanston, a suburb of Chicago, this is the oldest
continuously operated Zen temple in the USA. Sesshins held in quiet, wooded area.
Founded 1949; present Abbot appointed Dharma successor 1970. "Besides carrying on
tradition of Shikantaza, emphaiss given to instruction and practice of Taoist philosophy
and practice (including Tai Chi Chuan) in order to deepen understanding of Soto Zen
Buddhism."

Three meditation services per week—10:00 am and 2:00 pm Sundays; 7:00 pm
Wednesdays. Instruction given at these services, emphasis on shikantaza. One-day

sesshin first Saturday of each month. Three-day sesshins in late winter, summer, and fall. All services suitable for newcomers.

Audiotapes of teishos given during zazen services available. Meditation supplies available for sale at cost.

Founder/Guru	Rev. Soyu Matsuoka Roshi
Teachers	Abbot: Rev. Kongo Langlois Roshi
Opening Times	See service times above
Residents	2 priests, 5 disciples
Festivals	Spring O'Higan, Hannamatsuri (Wesak), O'Bon, Fall O'Higan, and Bodi Day
Facilities	Meditation room
Accommodation	During sesshins only at private residence; cost included in sesshins' price
Food	Only during 3-day sesshins when flexible diet available
Booking	Reasonable notice; 50% deposit nonrefundable
Fees	1-day sesshin $30; 3-day sesshin $80; meditation service $5
Expected Behavior	Not applicable
How to Get There	Near intersection of Dempster and Chicago Ave. in Evanston. From Chicago, take Edens Expressway (I-94) north to Dempster St. eastbound exit and go east to 608 Dempster.

Togmay Sangpo Center (Tibetan–Gelug)
Affiliation: Foundation for the Preservation of the Mahayana Tradition
P O Box 1594
Lombard, IL 60148
Tel & Fax: (708) 629–9185

Contact center for details.

INDIANA

Buddhist Society
617 Stewart Center
Purdue University
West Lafayette, IN 47906
E-mail: buddhism@expert.cc.purdue.edu

Around ten frequent participants meet in university. Founded 1992 by students.

Weekly meeting 7:30 pm Fridays consisting of lectures (by students), discussion, and sitting meditation.

Indianapolis Zen Group (Zen–Korean)
Affiliation: Kwan Um School of Zen, Indiana
Tel: (317) 274–6879 (Paul Dubin)

See **Furnace Mountain,** Kentucky.

Louisville KKSG (Tibetan–Karma Kagyu)
Affiliation: Karma Triyana Dharmachakra, New York
1031 Cliffwood Drive
New Albany, IN 47150
Tel: (812) 944–5545

Introductory teachings and meditation instruction as well as regular shamata and tonglen practice.

IOWA

Des Moines Meditation Group (Vipassana)
Affiliation: Mid America Dharma Group
Mail: Charles W. Day
3333 Grand Avenue, #264
Des Moines, IA 50312
Tel: (515) 255–8398

Meet in members' homes. Began 1993. "All meditators welcome, beginners or experienced, in any tradition."
Meet Tuesday evenings and last Sunday of the month. Practice includes sitting and walking meditation and tapes and reading of Buddhist teachings. Sponsor retreats in cooperation with Mid America Dharma Group, Kansas City, Missouri. Charles Day is facilitator.

Jalandhara Meditation Center (Tibetan–Gelug)
627 South Governor Street
Iowa City, IA 52240
Tel: (319) 338–8755

Started 1986 when Ven. Lobsang Namgyal came to Iowa City and a group of students met with him weekly for three years until his return to India. Currently has ten to fifteen active members.

Meditation twice a week. Weekly study group reads text from Tibetan Buddhist Tradition and has discussion. Visiting Tibetan teachers lecture about five–six times per year.

Founder/Guru	Ven. Lobsang Namgyal
Teachers	See above
Opening Times	Sundays 9:00–10:00 am, Thursdays 7:00–8:00 pm
Residents	None
Festivals	None
Facilities	Home of one of members
Accommodation	None
Food	None
Booking	Not applicable
Fees	Call or write in advance to check on requested donation for any particular visiting teacher
Expected Behavior	No smoking, drinking, or drug use; behavior that is respectful to the Dharma teacher and teachings
How to Get There	Contact center

Mokyoji (Zen–Soto)
P O Box 331
New Albin, IA 52160
Tel: (507) 542–4968

Monastery and retreat center for the **Minnesota Zen Meditation Center,** Michigan, (see separate entry). Two hundred and sixty acres in southeast Minnesota near the Mississippi River.

KANSAS

Kansas City Dharmadhatu (Tibetan–Kagyu/Nyingma)
Affiliation: Shambhala International
2302 South Feree
Kansas City, KS 66103
Tel: (913) 677–4835
E-mail: gmmass@aol.com

See International headquarters, **Shambhala Center,** Halifax, Nova Scotia, Canada.

Mindfulness Meditation Foundation (Nonsectarian)
3061 Merriam Lane
Kansas City, KS 66106
Tel: (913) 432–7787 x 109
Fax: (913) 432–9242

No fixed premises—meet weekly at a Community Center. Emphasis on being non-sectarian and being more inclusive and less exclusive. Invite teachers of various lineages to teach. Founded 1995.

Meet Thursdays 6:30–7:15 pm meditation instruction (Shamatha Vipassana), 7:30–8:30 pm Dharma class on basic Buddhism. Retreats two–three times a year on various topics. Quarterly newsletter.

Founder/Guru	Chuck and Mary Stanford are founders
Teachers	Various teachers visit for retreats
Opening Times	Not applicable
Residents	None
Festivals	None
Facilities	Not applicable
Accommodation	None
Food	None
Booking	Not applicable
Fees	1 day retreat $35, yearly subscription to newsletter $15
Expected Behavior	None
How to Get There	Not applicable

Manhattan Zen Group (Zen–Soto)
c/o Rappoport
320 S Delaware Street
Manhattan, KS 66502

Group of six–ten people meeting regularly for Soto tradition zazen practice at private home or local community education center. Invite recognized teacher to lead weekend retreat once or twice a year. Some attend retreats at and/or are members of Minneapolis Zen Center. No fees or dues, no resident teacher, and no permanent meditation facility. Occasional introductory instruction in Zen philosophy and practice and sitting periods three times a week.

There is no enlightenment outside of everyday life.
Thich Nhat Hanh, *Zen Keys*

KENTUCKY

Furnace Mountain, Inc. (Zen–Korean)
Affiliation: Kwan Um School of Zen
P O Box 545
8640 Hardwicks Creek Road
Clay City, KY 40312-0545
Tel: (606) 723–4329

Timber-framed temple built in a modified Korean style, surrounded by low mountains and headwaters of the Appalachian foothills according to Sino-Korean principles of geomancy (feng-shui). Includes a teahouse for informal meals, meetings, and recreation; two multi-roomed log buildings; and three log cabin hermitages. Vegetable garden supplies significant portion of community's produce. Room for ten residents and fifteen additional retreatants. Set in uniquely beautiful landscape auspicious for meditation practice. Six hundred acres of woodland—visitors welcome to hike and camp. Founded in 1986.

Meditation instruction and classes on practice forms. Practices offered include: Keeping a question, Mantra practice, Koan practice, chanting, prostrations, and Clear Mind meditation (just sitting). One-day introductory workshops twice a year. Offers monthly retreats of one to five days and winter retreat of three months. These are intensive silent retreats following the forms of Korean Zen Buddhism. Chanting retreats two or three times a year, as well as opportunities to go on retreat at international centers in Seoul, Korea, and Providence, Rhode Island. Publishes a newsletter, *Black Turtle*, three times a year.

Affiliates: Dae Mun Community, Off the Avenue Studios, 1546 Knowlton St., Cincinnati, OH 45223, contact Fran Turner (513) 271–0834; Indianapolis Zen Group, contact Paul Dubin (317) 274–6879.

Founder/Guru	Zen Master Dae Gak
Teachers	As founder
Opening Times	Contact center
Residents	6 monastics and 2 laity
Festivals	Buddha's Enlightenment Day, Buddha's Birthday celebrated jointly with Lexington Vietnamese Buddhist Association
Facilities	Temple for formal practice, outdoor Buddha shrine, meditation room, library/media room, Kwan Yin shrine
Accommodation	Single and double rooms. During retreats: non-members $35/day, members $25/day. Other times: non-members $25/day, members $15/day. Includes meals and laundry if

	longer than a week
Food	Vegetarian. Advance notice needed for special dietary requirements. Organic produce used as much as possible
Booking	1 week in advance, no deposit necessary
Fees	See *Accommodation*
Expected Behavior	No illegal drugs or alcohol, no indoor smoking, retreats are silent
How to Get There	1 hour southeast of Lexington on the Bert T Combs Mountain Parkway. Write for map with directions.

Lexington Shambhala Center (Tibetan–Kagyu/Nyingma)
Affiliation: Shambhala International
315 W Maxwell Street
Lexington, KY 40508
Tel: (606) 225–4183
E-mail: Shelley Heinz: mheinz1@ukcc.uky.edu

See International headquarters, **Shambhala Center,** Halifax, Nova Scotia, Canada.

Just as, monks, the mighty ocean is of one taste—the taste of salt—so, monks,
this Dhamma is of one taste—the taste of freedom.

The Buddha

LOUISIANA

Dhongak Tharling Dharma Center (Tibetan–Nyingma)
3621 De Saix Boulevard
New Orleans, LA 70119
Tel & Fax: (504) 948–6721
Fax: (504) 948–6720
E-mail: tharling@ix.netcom.com

No residential facility as yet. Fifty-five members. Puja twice weekly, instruction on puja sadhanas. Occasional retreats on such subjects as Empowerments of Konchog Chiidu and Shitioes of Rigdzen Jyaltson Nyingpo. Tsoks on Guru Rinpoche Day and Dakini

Day. All activities open to newcomers. Newsletter with calendar three times a year.

Founder/Guru	Ven. Lama Ngawang Tsultsim Rinpoche
Teachers	Resident as founder, visiting: Ven. Lama Ngawang Tenzin Tulku and Ven. Lama Kushok Tulku
Opening Times	See calendar
Residents	1 lama and 1 practitioner and temple-keeper
Festivals	See above
Facilities	Shrine room, library, and lama room
Accommodation	Call to schedule a visit
Food	Not applicable
Booking	Contact center
Fees	Donation requested. Retreats approximately $150–175 per week non-residential
Expected Behavior	Respectful
How to Get There	Call before visiting

New Orleans Zen Temple (Zen–Soto)
Affiliation: Association Zen Internationale
American Zen Association Building
748 Camp Street
New Orleans, LA 70130-3702
Tel: (504) 523–1213
Fax: (504) 523–7024
E-mail: aza@gnofn.org

Converted four-story warehouse in Arts District of downtown New Orleans. Founded in 1983 after Master Deshimaru asked Master Robert Livingston, one of his closest disciples, to go the U.S. to open a Zen dojo and teach True Zen. "Zen training is combined with life in the New Orleans community for our ethnically diverse sangha of monks, nuns, ordained lay persons, and non-ordained students. Most of the residents are students or have jobs in the community, some work full- or part-time for the Temple."

Daily Zen practice (zazen, kinhin, ceremony, samu) as well as weekly introductions to the practice for beginners and new students and a monthly Day of Zen Practice. Quarterly three- to seven-day sesshin. Quarterly newsletter, occasional books published.

Run **New Orleans Zen Temple Store** at same address for Zen practice materials and artwork.

Founder/Guru	Robert Livingston Roshi
Teachers	Resident teacher as founder; various European and Japanese Zen masters visit
Opening Times	As scheduled

Residents	2 monks, 3 ordained lay students, and 1 non-ordained student
Festivals	Not applicable
Facilities	Dojo, workshop, art studio, exercise room, sewing room, library, living quarters
Accommodation	Private or semi-private room $20/night including practice and genmai, not including lunch and dinner
Food	Gen-Mai (traditional Zen breakfast of rice/vegetable soup) $1; non-vegetarian Italian, French, or Japanese meals often using wholefood ingredients—lunch $4, dinner $3, Saturday lunch $7
Booking	For most events payment in full at least 1 week in advance. After that late fees may apply.
Fees	Introductions $20; general practice $5/day or $50/month (members); Day of Zen Practice $50; sesshin $100–250. Discounts for members, full-time students and unemployed
Expected Behavior	Simple temple rules—"All other natural human behaviors are accepted."
How to Get There	From interstate, take any downtown exit and find Camp St. (parallel and between St. Charles and Magazine). Temple between cross streets of Julia and Girod.

Whatever conduces to purity, that is my teaching.

Whatever conduces to freedom, that is my teaching.

Whatever conduces to decrease of wordly gains and acquisitions, that is my teaching.

Whatever conduces to simplicity, that is my teaching.

Whatever conduces to contentment, that is my teaching.

Whatever conduces to individuality, that is my teaching.

Whatever conduces to energy, that is my teaching.

Whatever conduces to delight in good, that is my teaching.

The Buddha

MAINE

Brunswick Dharma Study Group (Tibetan–Kagyu/Nyingma)
Affiliation: Shambhala International
98 Maine Street
Brunswick, ME 04011
Tel: (207) 729–1496 (home number of Eunice St. John,
    center co-ordinator)
E-mail: mcep@mint.net

Not a residential center. Small shrine room in an office building which serves a community of about thirty members within a forty-mile radius of Brunswick. Practice and classes also held in Portland, Farmington, China, and Ellsworth. Established in 1985 by students of Chogyam Trungpa Rinpoche.
    Sitting meditation every Sunday 9:00 am–noon. Regular classes according to Shambhala programs. Shambhala training weekends three or four times a year. Call for information on training opportunities. Group Ngondro practice once a month. Tantra class meets once a month for Tantrikas and Sadhakas. Brochure of scheduled classes and events published three times a year.

Founder/Guru	Chogyam Trungpa Rinpoche
Teachers	Contact center
Opening Times	As program of events
Residents	Not applicable
Festivals	None
Facilities	Shrine room for about 20
Accommodation	None
Food	Not applicable
Booking	Not applicable
Fees	approximately $30 for 5-week course of classes
Expected Behavior	Not applicable
How to Get There	About 38 miles northeast of Portland Maine on Route 95

Belfast, Maine FWBO (Friends of the Western Buddhist Order)
c/o Bill Horton
Box 1870
Freedom, ME 04941
Tel: (207) 589–3168

Contact center for details.

Center for the Awareness of Pattern (Zen–Soto)
P O Box 407
Freeport, ME 04032
Tel: (207) 865–3396
Fax: (207) 865–1213

Family therapy training center which bases its training on a foundation of Zen thought and practice. House and restored garage which serve as the zendo, located on a peaceful side street. Opened in 1981.

Bi-weekly Zen sittings first Thursday and third Sunday of the month open to the public, with discussion and instruction before each session. Summer workshops and open discussions on many subjects throughout the year. Two-year training in family therapy, new students joining each fall. Journal, *Pattern Gatherings*, issued sporadically. Auxillary zazen practice group in Montclair, New Jersey—contact this center for information.

Founder/Guru	Phoebe Jiko Snover Prosky, MSW
Teachers	Resident as founder. Visiting: Sandra Coleman, PhD, and John Flynn, PhD, MSW
Opening Times	For open Zen sessions
Residents	1
Festivals	None
Facilities	Zendo
Accommodation	Not on site
Food	None
Booking	Not necessary
Fees	Zazen practice by donation. Family therapy training $1500/year. Workshop prices vary.
Expected Behavior	Being perfectly still during practice
How to Get There	From center of Freeport, north on Rte. 1 from exit 19. Pass LL Bean on your left and turn left immediately after the building onto Cushing Ave. Center is the 3rd building on the right: 10 Cushing Ave.

Palermo Forming Dharma Study Group (Tibetan–Kagyu/Nyingma)
Affiliation: Shambhala International
P O Box 4
Palermo, ME 04354
E-mail: 73123.102@compuserve.com

See International headquarters, **Shambhala Center,** Halifax, Nova Scotia, Canada.

Morgan Bay Zendo (Zen and Vipassana)
P O Box 188
Surry, ME 04684
Tel: (207) 667–7170 or (207) 374–9963 or (207) 667–5428

Zendo and separate building complex with retreat facilities for up to thirty people. Incorporated 1985, formerly known as Moonspring Hermitage. "Very quiet country setting near Acadia National Park. We work together as a lay group collectively and all decisions are made by our board of directors, several of our board have lived as monastics in other centers. At the present time, we are retreat-oriented, but hope to have longer training periods in the future."

Introductory classes at University of Maine. One-day workshops spring and summer. One or two Vipassana retreats, one- to five-day Zen or Ch'an retreats. Publish a newsletter.

Founder/Guru	Contact center
Teachers	Sheng Yen, Arinna Weissman, and Ruben Habito
Opening Times	Contact center
Residents	None
Festivals	Wesak, New Year's Day
Facilities	Meditation hall, meeting hall, 5 cabins, and 1 small rental house
Accommodation	Cabins, camping
Food	Self-catering, vegetarian
Booking	1 month in advance for retreats
Fees	$75–100 for 3-day retreat
Expected Behavior	5 precepts, no smoking
How to Get There	Within 20 miles of Acadia National Park and Bar Harbor (see brochure for map)

MARYLAND

Baltimore Shambhala Center (Tibetan–Kagyu/Nyingma)
Affiliation: Shambhala International
11 East Mount Royal Avenue
Baltimore, MD 21202
Tel: (410) 747–2422
E-mail: glntryridr@aol.com

See International headquarters, **Shambhala Center,** Halifax, Nova Scotia, Canada.

Vikatadamshtri Buddhist Center (Western Buddhist Tradition)
Affiliation: New Kadampa Tradition
Baltimore, MD
Tel: (410) 750–6163
Fax: (202) 338–3701
E-mail: vyogini@nmaa.org

Residential center planned for 1996. Has twenty attendees regularly. Established 1995.
Weekly classes in Baltimore.

Founder/Guru	Ven. Geshe Kelsang Gyatso Rinpoche
Teachers	Resident: Kelsang Sangkyong
Opening Times	Call for details
Residents	Contact center
Festivals	Contact center
Facilities	See above
Accommodation	Negotiable
Food	None
Booking	None
Fees	$7/class, $3 students
Expected Behavior	No smoking
How to Get There	From Connective Ave., take Calvert to Cleveland.

Ratna Shri Dharma Center (Tibetan–Drikung Kagyu)
9301 Gambrill Park Road
Frederick, MD 21702
Tel: (301) 473–5750
E-mail: DEmmer8@aol.com
Web site: http://www.churchward.com/drikung

Contact center for details.

Soka Gakkai International (SGI-USA) (Nichiren)
Maryland and DC Area Regional Center
4603 Eastern Avenue
Mount Rainier, MD 20712-2407
Tel: (301) 779–3255
Fax: (301) 779–4954

See **Soka Gakkai International** National Offices & Center, Santa Monica, California,
for more details.

Kunzang Palyul Choling (Tibetan–Nyingma)
18400 River Road
Poolesville, MD 20837
Tel: (301) 428–8116
Fax: (301) 428–8245
E-mail: kpc@tara.org
Web site: http://www.tara.org

Large white house in sixty-five-acre wildlife sanctuary with meditation gardens, nine stupas, and walking trails. "Primary distinction is resident lama, who is first Western woman to be recognized as incarnate lama (tulku). Unique ability to teach from wisdom mind in our common language, with her full empathy and understanding of the Western culture which produced us."

Classes range from extensive Sunday teaching program to children's peace curriculum, one-day workshops such as Stabilizing the Mind, multi-week Foundational Buddhist Thought, and ongoing Dharma in Depth series. Migyur Dorje Institute offers seven-year curriculum and three-year retreat. Frequently hosts visits from teachers of the Nyingma tradition. Individual and group retreats. Publishes *Vajra Voice* quarterly, *News & Notes* monthly, and *Front Page* weekly.

Runs two businesses: **Tara Enterprises,** producing Buddhist images and fine artistic collectibles, and **Ladyworks,** manufacturers of patented hair care products. Tara Enterprises, Tel: 1-(800) 775 TARA, c/o KPC. Ladyworks, PO Box 605, Poolesville, MD 20837, Tel: (301) 916–3500 or 1-(800) 428–9877, Fax: (301) 916–3029.

Founder/Guru	H.H. Padma Norbu (Penor) Rinpoche
Teachers	Resident: Jetsunma Ahkon Norbu Lhamo; Khenpo Tsewang visits
Opening Times	Year-round
Residents	32 monastics and 150–200 laity
Festivals	According to Tibetan Buddhist calendar
Facilities	Meditation, teaching and community rooms, library
Accommodation	None
Food	Friday dinner and Sunday lunch $3–5—vegetarian and nonvegetarian
Booking	Contact center
Fees	Sundays and Wednesdays free; special courses vary widely.
Expected Behavior	No smoking, modest dress
How to Get There	Capital Beltway (495) to River Rd. exit, 14 miles to "T" at Bretton Woods Country Club. Turn left. Center is $3^1/_2$ miles on left.

Avatamsaka Hermitage (Pure Land and Ch'an)
Affiliation: Dharma Realm Buddhist Association

11721 Beall Mountain Road
Potomac, MD 20854-1128
Tel: (301) 299–3693

All Dharma Realm Buddhist Association branch monasteries are open to the public and have morning, afternoon, and evening ceremonies and sutra lectures every day as well as their own special programs. All activities are led by fully ordained monks or nuns.

Salisbury Dharmadhatu (Tibetan–Kagyu/Nyingma)
Affiliation: Shambhala International
104 West Chestnut Street, 2nd Floor
Salisbury, MD 21801
Tel: (410) 341–0941
E-mail: cossairt@shore.intercom.net

See International headquarters, **Shambhala Center,** Halifax, Nova Scotia, Canada.

Mahayana Sutra and Tantra Center—Washington DC (Tibetan–Gelug)
Affiliation: Mahayana and Sutra Center, Howell, New Jersey
1917 Rookwood Road
Silver Spring, MD 20910
Tel: (301) 585–4575 or (703) 503–5487

Small center based in member's house in suburb—classes also held at member's house in Fairfax, Virginia. MSTC established 1975 in New Jersey and incorporated 1980.

Restricted Tantra classes (prior initiation needed); Ganden Lhagyama (Guru Yoga) meditation class; sutra reading and discussion classes; Tibetan language taught as needed; class on Essence of Refined Gold text. Khensur Rinpoche teaches periodically on range of subjects such as Lamrim, debate, logic, abhidharma, madhyamaka philosophy, and some Tantric practices. Occasional meditation practice retreats held in Fairfax.

Newsletter published once or twice a year.

Founder/Guru Khensur Rinpoche Geshe Lobsang Tharchin
Teachers Designated senior students teach locally

Sakya Phuntsok Ling Center for Tibetan Buddhist Studies and Meditation
(Tibetan–Sakya)
608 Ray Drive
Silver Spring, MD 20810
Tel: (301) 589–3115

E-mail: sakya@erols.com or shiwa@aol.com
Web site: http://members.aol.com/shiwa/sakya.html

With around thirty visitors a week, "The center's aim is to help those interested in Buddhism come into contact with great spiritual masters and to train those interested in personal study and practice. The Sakya Center is also active in translation projects and in liaison with other Buddhist and spiritual communities."

Meditation classes for novices and experienced meditators. Buddhist philosophy for beginners, advanced students. Children's classes in basic Buddhism. Periodic weekend retreats.

Founder/Guru	Contact center
Teachers	Resident: Lama Kalsang Gyaltsen
Opening Times	Contact center
Residents	Contact center
Festivals	Contact center
Facilities	Shrine room, library area
Accommodation	Contact center
Food	Contact center
Booking	Contact center
Fees	Contact center
Expected Behavior	Contact center
How to Get There	Contact center

Shambhala Center of Washington, DC (Tibetan–Kagyu/Nyingma)
Affiliation: Shambhala International
8719 Colesville Road, # 210
Silver Spring, MD 20910
Tel: (301) 588–8020
E-mail: slh27@aol.com

Located on second floor of a three-story building with an interior designed by sangha architect. Offer introductory classes on Buddhism Tuesdays and Thursdays 7:00 pm, Sunday mornings, and third Sunday of the month in the afternoon. Instruction in shamatha and vipashyana. Intermediate classes. Sadhana of Mahamudra twice monthly. Classes in the Shambhala arts of kyudo, ikebana, dance, movement, etc. Shambhala training, weekend programs to introduce meditation as part of daily life. Advanced Buddhadharma studies offered as month-long meditation programs (called dathuns) at retreat centers. Retreats at other Shambhala centers including **Karme Choling,** Vermont, and **Rocky Mountain Shambhala Center,** Colorado (see separate entries). *Shambhala Center News* published monthly for members and friends. *Shambhala Sun* newspaper bimonthly by subscription through Shambhala International or by single copy in the bookstore.

Founder/Guru	Vidyadhara Chogyam Trungpa Rinpoche; now led by Sakyong Mipham Rinpoche
Teachers	Visiting teachers of Shambhala International
Opening Times	See times for introductory classes above
Residents	None
Festivals	Shambhala Day (Tibetan New Year), Midsummer's Day, Milarepa Day, parinirvanas for the Vidyadhara, Vajra Regent, H.H. Karmapa, H.H. Khyentse Rinpoche, Jamyong Kontrul Rinpoche, Vesak
Facilities	Main shrine room, Tantra shrine room for individual practice and feasts, Shambhala meditation hall, Miyako Kyudojo off-site, meditation instruction rooms, community room
Accommodation	Local hotels or program visitors in members' homes
Food	None
Booking	Telephone, pre-registration not required
Fees	$8 per class, $125 per weekend
Expected Behavior	No smoking on premises, 5 precepts on retreats only
How to Get There	3 blocks from Silver Spring (Red Line) subway stop. Doorbell at street level answered at public meditation times

International Meditation Center—USA (Theravada)
Affiliation: International Meditation Center
438 Bankard Road
Westminster, MD 21158
Tel: (410) 346–7889
Fax: (410) 346–7133
E-mail: IMCUSA@compuserve.com

Located on eight acres of rolling hills in rural Maryland and comprises The Dhamma Yaung Chi Ceti Pagoda, a large Dhamma hall for meditation, dormitory, kitchen, and dining room. Founded 1984, premises bought 1989, Pagoda built 1991, and other new buildings added 1994. Affiliated with the five other IMCs around the world: Yangon in Myanmar, Wiltshire in England, Austria, and Sydney and Perth in Australia.

Ten-day residential retreats in Vipassana Meditation offered six–eight times a year. Meditation and other activities available for those who have done at least one retreat, and the facilities are available at all times for these people. Newsletter published four times a year and about twenty-five booklets and books published privately or in cooperation with BPS in Sri Lanka.

Founder/Guru	Sayagyi U Ba Khin
Teachers	Resident: Michael Kosman, Craig Storti. Visiting: Mother Sayamagyi Daw Mya Thwin, Sayagyi U Chit Tim

Opening Times	Continuously
Residents	1 lay
Festivals	Not applicable
Facilities	See text above
Accommodation	Dormitories—no charge for old students. Center supported by donations
Food	Vegetarian included in accommodation prices
Booking	At least 1 week in advance, deposit $50
Fees	$300–350 for 10-day retreat including board and lodging—teaching is free
Expected Behavior	New students: 5 precepts. Old students: 8 precepts. No smoking in any building, noble silence throughout retreats, stay on property
How to Get There	Nearest towns are Westminster and Hanover. Nearest city: Baltimore. Nearest train station: Baltimore. Nearest airport: BWI.

MASSACHUSETTS

Living Dharma Center (Zen–Soto and Rinzai)
Harada-Yasutani-Kapleau lineage
P O Box 304
Amherst, MA 01004
and P O Box 513
Bolton, CT 06040
Tel: (860) 742–7049
Tel & Fax: (413) 259–1611

Has two locations for weekly meditation and monastery for seven-day sesshins in Rhode Island. Around a hundred members. Founded 1972 in New York State, current location since 1980. "We go to the root core of Zen Buddhist practice, beyond any attachments to cultural/arbitrary (e.g., ritualistic) trappings.... We employ the traditional koan system in our teachings."

Weekly zazen practice 7:30–9:45 pm Tuesdays in Amherst, 7:00–9:15 pm in Connecticut. Workshop on fundamentals of Zen practice in spring and fall. Occasional lectures and regular weekly lecture by Richard Clarke, usually commentaries on traditional Zen texts. Seven-day sesshins in April, July, and December. One-day retreats about once a month in New England and irregularly in Switzerland. Quarterly newsletter, *The Sangha News*.

Founder/Guru	Richard Clarke

Teachers	Resident: Richard Clarke
Opening Times	See zazen times above
Residents	None
Festivals	Jukai ceremony in November
Facilities	Zendos in Amherst and Connecticut, monastery in Rhode Island
Accommodation	During residential retreats only
Food	Lacto-vegetarian
Booking	Retreats for experienced students only—book 1 month in advance.
Fees	Retreats $55–35 per day including board and lodging
Expected Behavior	No smoking and especially sincerity, respect for others, and zazen experience for retreats
How to Get There	Contact center for detailed instructions

Barre Center for Buddhist Studies (Theravada/Eclectic)
149 Lockwood Road
Barre, MA 01005
Tel: (508) 355–2347
Fax: (508) 355–2798

Two buildings in the countryside, one a tastefully renovated two-hundred-year-old farmhouse containing the administrative offices, library, kitchen, and dining hall; the other is a new hall seating a hundred with fourteen single rooms for overnight stay. Started 1990 as an adjunct of the **Insight Meditation Society,** Massachusetts (see separate entry).

One-day, weekend, five-day, and two-week classes and programs on Buddhist history, teachings, and meditation (all residential except one-day). Biannual newsletter published jointly with the International Meditation Society.

Teachers	Diverse group of lay and ordained teachers visit
Opening Times	Contact center
Residents	Lay residents
Festivals	Contact center
Facilities	Library, meditation hall, reading room
Accommodation	14 single rooms for course participants only
Food	Contact center
Booking	Contact center
Fees	Contact center
Expected Behavior	Contact center
How to Get There	Contact center

Insight Meditation Society (Theravada)
1230 Pleasant Street
Barre, MA 01005
Tel: (508) 355–4378
Fax: (508) 355–6398

Wooded rural setting in central New England. Main building is a Georgian mansion (circa 1912) housing dormitory and meditation hall with additions dating from 1950s–1960s and one major dormitory with forty-nine single rooms added in 1995. Capacity for a hundred retreatants run by staff community of about twenty-five. "One of the leading Vipassana retreat centers in the Western world."

Offers meditation retreats (mostly Vipassana) from two- or three-day weekend courses to many nine-day courses. Annual three-month course in the fall. All retreats in silence. Biannual newsletter published jointly with the **Barre Center for Buddhist Studies** (see separate entry).

Founder/Guru	Not applicable
Teachers	Diverse group of lay and ordained teachers visit
Opening Times	Closed January
Residents	18 lay
Festivals	Contact center
Facilities	See above
Accommodation	For retreatants only
Food	Ovo-lacto-vegetarian—cost included in course fees
Booking	Contact center
Fees	2-day weekend $95; 9-day course $265; 3-month course $2,250. Average daily rate $30
Expected Behavior	Noble silence, 5 precepts
How to Get There	Call for instructions—details given on registration.

Kurukulla Center (Tibetan–Gelug–FPMT)
P O Box 628
Astor Station
Boston, MA 02123-0628
Tel: (617) 628–1953
Fax: (617) 536–1897
E-mail: persyn@law.harvard.edu or sr@math.bu.edu

City center four-bedroom apartment which is also residence for Geshe Tsulga. "Very unique situation to have a resident Geshe, a fully qualified teacher of the Tibetan tradition." Started 1987.

Center offers instruction in meditation/practice, group practices/pujas, weekly Introduction to Buddhist Philosophy and Meditation, and a variety of courses based on the Lamrim (Graduated Path to enlightenment) taught by Ven. Geshe Tsulga. Also offers classes in Lojong teachings, logic (Geshe-type studies), and Tibetan language. Retreats several times annually at Milarepa Center, Vermont ($1^1/_2$ hour drive away). Publishes newsletter and FPMT publishes *Mandala* magazine.

Founder/Guru	Lama Thubten Zopa Rinpoche
Teachers	Resident: Geshe Tsulga and various visiting
Opening Times	As program of events
Residents	Non-residential
Festivals	Contact center
Facilities	Contact center
Accommodation	None
Food	None
Booking	Contact center
Fees	$10/class non-members. Membership includes all classes for $40/month or $25/month for students
Expected Behavior	Contact center
How to Get There	Best to call for directions

Mr. Loman McClinton (Nichiren Shu)
Affiliate: Nichiren Propagation Center
17 Abbotsford Street
Boston, MA 02121
Tel: (617) 442–8088

See **Nichiren Propagation Center,** Oregon.

Rigpa (Tibetan–Nyingma)
Affiliation: Rigpa Fellowship
Boston, MA
Tel: (617) 489–0170

Contact: Pam Russell. See **Rigpa National Office,** California, for details.

> *The underlying principle of all religions is one. We can commune on the deepest level and link hands with people of any religion, as long as they adhere to this fundamental principle and do not quibble over minor differences.*
>
> Nikkyo Niwano, founder of the Rissho Kosei-kai

Soka Gakkai International (SGI-USA) (Nichiren)
Massachusetts Area Regional Center
7 Harcourt Street
Boston, MA 02116-6439
Tel: (617) 536–3820
Fax: (617) 536–1357

See **Soka Gakkai International** National Offices & Center, Santa Monica, California, for more details.

World Shim Gum Do Association, Inc. (Zen)
American Buddhist Shim Gum Do Association, Inc.
Shim Gwang Sa
Main center for both World Shim Gum Do Association, Inc. and American Buddhist
 Shim Gum Do Association, Inc.
203 Chestnut Hill Avenue
Brighton, MA 02135
Tel: (617) 787–1506
Fax: (617) 787–2708
E-mail: simgumdo@tiac.net

A hundred-year-old church on an acre of land including formal Zen landscape designed by Founding Master Chang Sik Kim and a vegetable garden. The World Shim Gum Do Association has thousands of members worldwide, and the American Shim Gum Do Association has around a hundred and fifty members.

Meditation class followed by Dharma talk by Founding Master on first Friday of every month open to public. Ongoing classes, retreats, and residential training program in the art of Shim Gum Do, which means "Mind Sword Path," a complete martial arts system combined with Zen meditation. "Shim Gum Do training is very unique. Zen Master Chang Sik Kim is a living legend. He has served as and continues to serve as the vehicle which has brought the timeless art of Shim Gum Do to our planet. The training works on many levels helping to develop a clear mind and also to open up energy stems within the body. The Founding Master is in residence and oversees all the teaching at the center." The practice also includes traditional bowing, chanting, meditation, and Dharma discourses. Published two books by Founding Master.

Founder/Guru	Zen Master Chang Sik Kim
Teachers	Resident: Founding Master and USA Head Master Mary Jeanette Stackhouse (Abbot)
Opening Times	Contact center
Residents	14 lay students
Festivals	Contact center
Facilities	2 Dharma halls and living quarters

Clear Light Society (Zen style with special emphasis on retreats)
P O Box 306
Brookline, MA 02146
Tel: (617) 734–2939
Fax: (617) 734–2939 and (617) 522–0099
E-mail: clear@tiac.net
Web site: http://www.clearlightsociety.org

Retreat center on the southern coast in Maine; private house or university setting in city of Boston; branch sitting group in New Hampshire. "Our specialty is working with the dying and their families, not only during the weeks and months prior to death, but also at the moment of death itself. Practitioners who have gone through years of study under Ms Shelton's direction personalize a program in harmony with the belief system of each client. These special meditative forms pioneered by Ms Shelton respond to the fundamental need of discovering the way to 'peaceful heart, clear mind.' " Founded 1977.

Offer daily morning meditation practice, weekly evening Zen class and open house with sitting and talk, Moment of Death Training Weekend at least four times a year in Maine. Incremental six-month advanced training for those wishing to become a certified Clear Light practitioner. Zen-style three-day retreats monthly. Two- or three-week retreat in May. One-week Holiday retreat December 26–31.

Boston: Zen morning service and weekly open house with sitting and talk.

Founder/Guru	Patricia Shelton
Teachers	Patricia Shelton
Opening Times	Not applicable
Residents	None
Festivals	None
Facilities	Shrine room
Accommodation	By arrangement
Food	Vegetarian included in price of retreat
Booking	Moment of Death retreat: deposit 2 weeks in advance
Fees	Moment of Death retreat: sliding scale $135–175 for weekend plus accommodation
Expected Behavior	Not applicable
How to Get There	Please call for directions

What is this? Do you know? If you understand, there is no eyes, no ears, no nose, no tongue, no body, no mind. Never appear, never disappear. No name, no form.... Then what? Go drink tea.

Zen Master Seung Sahn quoted in a Cambridge Zen Center, Massachusetts, flyer

Boston FWBO (Friends of the Western Buddhist Order)
23 Irving Terrace, Apt. 23
Cambridge, MA 02138
Tel: (617) 567–7345
E-mail: Vajramati@aol.com

Contact center for details.

Cambridge Insight Meditation Center (Vipassana)
331 Broadway
Cambridge, MA 02139
Tel: (617) 491–5070
Fax: (617) 491–5070
E-mail: contact center

Renovated three-story Victorian house in city center with Japanese-style garden and walking path. Welcome people of all religious, nonreligious, and philosophical persuasions. Membership of over two hundred and fifty, and many more use center. Incorporated 1985. "CIMC is unique in that it is located in the heart of Cambridge, and its programs focus on the needs of an urban constituency, in the midst of their busy daily lives. CIMC's main emphasis is on the integration of meditation practice and daily life, and in that regard, serves as a model of a 'new breed' of meditation centers for students of insight meditation in the United States and Europe."

Tuesdays evenings and some Wednesdays at noon, beginners' drop-in classes for ongoing instruction and practice in insight meditation. Courses on variety of subjects and for different experience levels: Introduction to Vipassana Meditation four times a year; Fundamentals of Buddhism practice group for more experienced students; Anapanasati practice group for yogis with at least one year's daily formal practice; Old Yogis practice groups for yogis with at least three years' experience; other topics for practice groups have included Metta, wise speech, relationships, conscious aging, and three trainings. One-, two-, and three-day retreats. Seven-day nonresidential retreat twice a year.

Founder/Guru	Larry Rosenberg
Teachers	Resident: Larry Rosenberg, plus other full- and part-time teachers and visiting teachers from several different traditions for Wednesday evening talk
Opening Times	Office: Monday–Friday 9:00 am–5:00 pm. For members: 7:00 am–10:00 pm daily except retreat days
Residents	Founder's family and 3 laity
Festivals	None
Facilities	Large meditation hall; large basement for walking meditation and Wednesday lecture; interview room; small apartment for individual retreats

Accommodation	No—telephone for details of local hotels and B&Bs
Food	Vegetarian/vegan during retreats
Booking	At least 3 weeks in advance with payment in full
Fees	Drop-ins $5; Courses $135 for 8 sessions; financial aid available; reduced rates for members
Expected Behavior	No smoking in house and garden and street shoes to be removed in house. 5 precepts and no conversation during retreats.
How to Get There	Short walk from Central Square. Easy access via bus and subway. Call for details.

Cambridge Zen Center (Zen)
Affiliation: Kwan Um School of Zen
199 Auburn Street
Cambridge, MA 02139-3828
Tel: (617) 576-3229
E-mail: cambzen@aol.com

Residential Zen center in four city townhouses that are connected to form one big building in heart of city. Close to Harvard and MIT and half a mile from Charles River. Also own a separate apartment building. "The community feeling here is very strong and helps to make CZC a very welcoming and friendly Zen center." Founded 1973.

Daily morning and evening practice free and open to public. Monthly retreats. Monday evening meditation instruction; Thursday night Dharma talks with questions and answers. Six- to eight-week classes on Zen meditation also offered at Cambridge, Boston, Brookline, and Interface Centers for Adult Education. Two–three monthly Zen meditation retreats. One-day Christian-Buddhist retreats two or three times a year. CZC newsletter once a month.

Founder/Guru	Zen Master Seung Sahn
Teachers	Resident: Jane McLaughlin and Mark Houghton
Opening Times	Contact center
Residents	2–4 monastics, 18–25 laity, and 2–5 children
Festivals	Buddha's Birthday and Buddha's Enlightenment Day
Facilities	Meditation room, library, and garden. 40-room house with communal kitchen, etc.
Accommodation	$20 per night private/shared depending on availability
Food	Vegetarian, included in room price
Booking	1 week in advance for short term; residents are place on waiting list
Fees	Daily practice and introductory classes free of charge; retreats $40/ day non-members, $25 members

Expected Behavior	No smoking, alcohol, or meat on premises
How to Get There	Contact center

Dzogchen Foundation (Tibetan–Dzogchen)
P O Box 734
Cambridge, MA 02140
Tel: (617) 628–1702
E-mail: 75377.1175@compuserve.com
Web site: http://www.kei.com/homepages/surya/dzogchen

Organized 1991 to preserve and transmit to Westerners the Dzogchen teachings. Meditation group with Dharma talk and question-and-answer session Monday 7:30–9:30 pm. Vajrayana practice group concentrating on Ngondro Saturdays. Lama Surya Das teaches fifteen–twenty meditation retreats a year of one day to one month in duration around the States. Sell audio- and videotapes of teachings and books by Lama Surya Das.

Sakya Institute (Tibetan–Sakya)
P O Box 391042
Cambridge, MA 02139
Tel & Fax: (617) 492–2614

Offers regular courses on mind training, abhidharma, and madhyamika. Retreats on common and uncommon foundation and Yidam practice regularly.

Founder/Guru	Lama Migmar Tseten
Teachers	Contact center
Opening Times	Visiting: H.H. Sakya Trizin, H.E. Lhogye Trichen, H.E. Ludhing Khenpo
Residents	Contact center
Festivals	Usual Tibetan Buddhist festivals
Facilities	Shrine room, meditation room
Accommodation	Contact center
Food	Contact center
Booking	Contact center
Fees	Contact center
Expected Behavior	5 precepts
How to Get There	Contact center

Dzogchen Community in America Inc—Tsegyalgar (Tibetan–Dzogchen)
Affiliation: International Dzogchen Community

P O Box 277
Conway, MA 01341
Tel: (413) 369–4153
Fax: (413) 369–4165
E-mail: 74404.1141@compuserve.com

Main seat of practice for the International Dzogchen Community in America, has a community practice center, administrative offices, the Shang Shung Institute—a Tibetan cultural study center—and Shang Shung Editions are housed in the old grammar school in the town of Conway. Community land for collective and personal retreats is nearby in the county of Buckland. Namkhai Norbu Rinpoche usually visits about once every two years. The community was established in 1982.

Weekly practices, practice weekends, and work weekends are ongoing. Retreats several times each year for community practice and retreats with visiting Lamas. A teacher training program is being conducted by Chogyal Namkhai Norbu. Publish: *The Mirror*, the newspaper of the International Dzogchen Community and a local Tsegyalgar bimonthly newsletter with a calendar of events—both by subscription. Shang Shung Editions books sold by mail order.

Founder/Guru	Chogyal Namkhai Norbu
Teachers	Chogyal Namkhai Norbu, visiting Yantra Yoga and Vajra Dance teachers
Opening Times	Year-round
Residents	Caretaker
Festivals	Contact center
Facilities	Community center and retreat property
Accommodation	Dormitory—$5 per night plus work arrangement
Food	Kitchen facilities
Booking	Arranged with caretaker
Fees	Retreat fees as announced
Expected Behavior	Considerate
How to Get There	Mass. Route 91 to Conway/S. Deerfield exit 24/25, Rte. north to Conway, ask for the old grammar school.

> *Those who practice mindful living will inevitably transform themselves and their way of life. They will live more simply and have more time to enjoy themselves, their friends, and their natural environment, and to offer joy to others and alleviate other's suffering.*
>
> Thich Nhat Hahn quoted in the Webpage of the Community of Mindful Living.

Falmouth Dharma Study Group (Tibetan–Kagyu/Nyingma)
Affiliation: Shambhala International
Cindy Wright, Coordinator
Box 714
Falmouth, MA 02541-0714
Tel: (508) 457–9527

See International headquarters, **Shambhala Center,** Halifax, Nova Scotia, Canada.

Dharmakaya Center
Massachusetts Buddhist Association (MBA) (Chinese)
319 Lowell Street
Lexington, MA 02173
Tel & Fax: (617) 863–1936 (contact person Sam Chan)

House in residential area, with community of around a hundred members. Founded in 1986 by a few engineers. The MBA purchased and moved to current facility 1992. Mostly Chinese-speaking with limited English.

Dharma lectures, meditation classes, sutra reading, Pure Land practice, and chanting. Meditations offered are Anapana, Insight, and Dynamic (rhythmic movement). Weekly classes at weekends, mostly Sundays. Ten-week Introduction to Buddhism course. One- and two-day retreats in meditation and Buddha's Recitation. Monthly newsletter in Chinese

Founder/Guru	Herman Yang and Leo Tsai
Teachers	Visit from other centers
Opening Times	Weekends 10:00 am–4:00 pm and sometimes on weekdays
Residents	1 lay person
Festivals	Buddha's Birthday
Facilities	Shrine room, meditation room, and library
Accommodation	Visitors should contact them in advance—no formal facilities
Food	Vegetarian meal on Sunday afternoon—suggested donation $3
Booking	Contact center
Fees	All regular events free of charge. Special events and workshops suggested donation of $5
Expected Behavior	No smoking or alcohol
How to Get There	From Boston and neighborhood, take I-28 exit 32A to south (Middlesex Turnpike). Continue to Lowell Street.

Boston Shambhala Center (Tibetan–Kagyu/Nyingma)
Affiliation: Shambhala International
515 Centre Street
Newton, MA 02158
Tel: (617) 965–2827 or (617) 965–8919 for Shambhala training

Urban center with two hundred nonresidential members, with one building with three shrine rooms, classroom, and offices. Facilities include parking lot; near restaurants and not far from public transport; and some child care.

Offer classes three nights a week for beginners and intermediates in Buddhist philosophy, practice, and history. Also arts: Japanese flower arranging, Japanese archery and calligraphy, and art theory from a Dharma perspective. Hold weekend intensive workshops, and intensive sitting meditation weekends in Buddhist and Shambhala training, and weekend retreats. Newcomers start with sitting meditation. Monthly open house free and open to public. Publish bimonthly community newsletter and calendar.

Founder/Guru	Chogyam Trunpa Rinpoche
Teachers	Visiting Sakyong Mipham Rinpoche and others
Opening Times	Evenings 7:00–11:00 pm and 9:00–12:00 am Sundays
Residents	None
Festivals	Contact center
Facilities	See above
Accommodation	None
Food	Tea, coffee, and cookies
Booking	Phone and leave message
Fees	$45 for 5-week class; $100 for weekend
Expected Behavior	Contact center
How to Get There	3 blocks south of Newton Corner at the corner of Wesley and Centre Street

Sang Ngag Ling (Tibetan–Nyingma)
Affiliation: Chagdud Gonpa Foundation
c/o Cheryl Conner
68 Larchmont Avenue
Newton, MA 02168
Tel: (617) 332–0327
Meggin Sullivan
9 Fairfield Street
Cambridge, MA 02138
Tel: (617) 492–5370

Contact center for details. Teacher is Chagdud Tulka Ripoche.

Tibetan Meditation Center (Tibetan–Drikung Kagyu)
34 Adams Street
Newton, MA
Tel: (617) 332–1835 (Lorraine Binder)
E-mail: jdean@mvinc.com
Web site: http://www.churchward.com/drikung

Contact center for details.

Northampton Dharmadhatu (Tibetan–Kagyu/Nyingma–Shambhala International)
518 Pleasant Street, # 2
Northampton, MA 01060
Tel: (413) 584–6415

Situated on the edge of town in a valley surrounded by the Berkshire Mountains. Affiliate of Vajradhatu International for twenty years. There are five colleges in the area. Thirty members, ten–twenty visitors a week.

Introductory-level meditation courses at least once a season. Mahayana courses including tonglen, slogan practice, maitri practice, and teachings on the Transcending Madness text. Shambhala training once every six months. Vajrayogini and Chakrasamvara feasts. Newsletter once a season.

Founder/Guru	Chogyam Trungpa Rinpoche
Teachers	Visiting: Drukpa Yongzin Rinpoche
Opening Times	9:30–12:30 am Sundays
Residents	None
Festivals	Contact center
Facilities	Shrine room and small library
Accommodation	Contact center
Food	Contact center
Booking	Contact center
Fees	Contact center
Expected Behavior	Contact center
How to Get There	Contact center

Massachusetts Budhi Siksa Society (Chinese)
53–55 Massachusetts Avenue
Quincy, MA 02169
Tel: (617) 773–7745
Fax: (617) 770–3859

Traditional Buddhist temple with around a hundred visitors a week. Grand opening

July 1996. "We are a traditional Buddhist temple and we practice Buddhism and cele-brate Buddhist festivals in a traditional way. We don't emphasize any particular Buddhist sect's theories but we encourage Pure Land Buddhism. Our temple is just like a big family with warm, enthusiastic, and caring members."

Weekly meditation classes are alternately in English and in Chinese. Most Buddhist workshops are taught in Mandarin/English. Publish journal, *Lun Yin*, every few months.

Founder/Guru	Sik Kuan Yin
Teachers	None
Opening Times	9:00 am–5:00 pm daily
Residents	Monk sometimes
Festivals	All major Buddhist festivals: Sakyamuni Memorial Day, Birthday of Amitabha Buddha, Birthday of Kuan Yin and other major Bodisattvas
Facilities	Large shrine room (300 people), small shrine room (60 people), library
Accommodation	Not applicable
Food	Vegetarian (no eggs). Lunch on Sundays free for everyone.
Booking	Not applicable
Fees	Not applicable
Expected Behavior	No smoking
How to Get There	From Boston: Highway 93S, take exit 12, follow Quincy signs and drive along Wollaston Beach until the very last traffic light and turn left. On Washington Street, go three blocks and turn left. From New York: Highway 93N, take exit 18, follow the Quincy signs, and turn right at the intersection of Newport Ave. and Granite St. Turn left at the first traffic light, turn right at the second light, and turn right again at the third light. Drive for about two miles on Washington St., and the temple is on the right-hand side. Public transport: Take the Red Line to Quincy Center Station and then bus 220, 221 or 222.

Vipassana Meditation Center (VMC), Dhamma Dhara (Vipassana)
Affiliation: Vipassana Meditation Centers in the Tradition of S. N. Goenka
P O Box 24
Shelburne Falls, MA 01370-0024
Tel: (413) 625–2160
Fax: (413) 625–2170
E-mail: VmcDhara@aol.com
Web site: http://www.dhamma.org

Rural retreat complex with individual meditation cells on a hundred and eight acres in the hills of western Massachusetts; winter capacity sixty-four students; summer capacity two hundred and fifty.

S. N. Goenka has taught ten-day or longer Vipassana meditation courses since 1969. VMC was the first center outside of India. Intensive silent retreats held regularly and are open to the general public (see web site for information and introductory materials). Courses conducted by authorized assistant teachers using taped instructions by S. N. Goenka, which have been translated into over thirty-five languages. No charges for courses, even for food and accommodation—all expenses are met by donations from those who, having completed a course and experienced the benefits of the practice, wish to give others the same opportunity. Teachers, assistant teachers, and other staff volunteer their time; they receive no remuneration.`

Retreats offered: ten-day Vipassana meditation (suitable for newcomers), twice monthly at centers and less frequently at associations and foundations; periodic three-day and short children's courses (suitable for newcomers); periodic advanced ten-, twenty-, and thirty-day courses focusing on the Satipatthana Sutta.

A typical Vipassana retreat involves: taking the five precepts; working to concentrate the mind by focusing attention on the natural breath at the entrance of the nostrils, and when this is established, Vipassana technique proper—exploring mental and physical nature by moving attention systematically throughout the body, dispassionately observing the physical sensations that naturally occur—"this ever-deepening introspection sets in motion a process by which the past conditioning of the mind is eliminated layer by layer." Course concludes with practice of Metta Bhavana.

Publish *Vipassana Newsletter* three times annually which is sent to all "old students." Centers and associations publish periodic regional newsletters sent to local old students. A separate company, **Vipassana Research Publications of America (VRPA),** is the North American locus for publications (books and cassettes), allowing centers and course sites to be free of any commercialism. **Vipassana Research Institute (VRI)** publishes books on Vipassana and the Buddha's teachings in several Indian languages and in English. All VRI publications and other related books and videocassettes are available from VRPA and its affiliate, **Pariyatti Book Service,** both at: VRPA, P O Box 15926, Seattle, WA 98115; Tel: (800) 829–2748; Fax: (206) 522–8295; E-mail: info@vrpa.com and website: http://www.vrpa.com.

Affiliates: **California Vipassana Center,** California, **Southwest Vipassana Meditation Center,** Texas, **Northwest Vipassana Center,** Washington, **Foundation Vipassana Foundation,** Quebec, Canada, **Vipassana Foundation,** British Columbia, Canada, and **Rocky Mountain Vipassana Foundation,** Colorado (see separate entries).

Founder/Guru	Founder and Spiritual Director: S. N. Goenka
Teachers	Numerous assistant teachers on a guest basis
Opening Times	Not applicable
Residents	Residential managers only
Festivals	None
Facilities	Vary at different retreat centers, generally including

meditation hall, dormitories, dining room, kitchen, bathing facilities, office, and walking areas. VMC has pagoda building with individual meditation cells.

Accommodation	For retreatants only
Food	Vegetarian
Booking	Contact center
Fees	See above
Expected Behavior	5 precepts, no smoking, adherence to timetable, vegetarian diet
How to Get There	Generally provided at registration by each center or association

Khandarohi Buddhist Center of Massachusetts (Tibetan–Gelug)
Affiliation: New Kadampa Tradition
34 Avon Street
Somerville, MA 02143
Tel: (617) 628–2648

Teacher: Gen Kelsang Lekmon. Branches of Khandarohi Center in Connecticut and Harvard, Massachusetts. Contact center for details.

Rangrig Yeshe Center (Tibetan–Nyingma)
P O Box 1167
Stockbridge, MA 01262
Tel: (413) 528–9932
Fax: (413) 448–7595

Countryside center with around fifty visitors a week, founded in 1990.

Offers teachings and retreats on Buddhist subjects and Dzogchen. Buddhist meditation. Suitable for beginners and advanced practitioners.

Founder/Guru	Ven. Shyalpa Tenzin Rinpoche
Teachers	Resident: Ven. Shyalpa Tenzin Rinpoche
Opening Times	Contact center
Residents	None
Festivals	Contact center
Facilities	Shrine room, library, meditation room
Accommodation	Guest room available
Food	None
Booking	Not applicable
Fees	None
Expected Behavior	No smoking
How to Get There	$2^1/_2$ hours from New York City and Boston

MICHIGAN

Ann Arbor KTC (Tibetan–Karma Kagyu)
Affiliation: Karma Triyana Dharmachakra, NY
614 Miner Street
Ann Arbor, MI 48103
Tel: (313) 761–7495
Fax: (313) 668–1009
E-mail: mannikka@umich.edu

House on west side of town in a very quiet, old neighborhood close to downtown and the University of Michigan. Ideal location for practice. Registered as a church with the city. Large shrine room open to members at all times. Has eight registered members, but between fifty and two hundred people may attend on a Rinpoche's visit. Founded as affiliate of **Karma Triyana Dharmachakra,** New York, (see separate entry) in 1978.

Shamatha Sunday morning 10:00–11:00 am and Chenrezig Sunday morning 11:00–11:45 am. Closed meditations on Medicine Buddha and Ngondro for those who have received the initiation. Dharma discussions Wednesdays 7:30–8:30 pm. At least one *nyun-nye* retreat per year.

Founder/Guru	Khenpo Karthar Rinpoche
Teachers	Visiting Tibetan monks from KTD
Opening Times	See above
Residents	Contact center
Festivals	Contact center
Facilities	Shrine room with capacity for 75–100
Accommodation	None
Food	None
Booking	Usually not required
Fees	Varies greatly—6-week meditation class $60
Expected Behavior	No smoking or drinking inside center
How to Get There	Off Miller Road between Fountain and Seventh

Crazy Cloud Hermitage (Tibetan–Nyingma)
Mailing: 7101 W Liberty
Ann Arbor, MI 48103
Tel: (313) 741–1084
E-mail: dalef@umich.edu

"Founded in 1990 by students of the Western-born spiritual master, Prem Pranama, Crazy Cloud is a community with a single common goal—to uncover the inherent wisdom and compassion which resides within you... Five acres of land provides space for weekly public Satsang, a meditation hall, outdoor meditation gardens, organic vegetable and herb gardens, and children's play areas." Students also in the Indianapolis area, Chicago, and on the East Coast.

Deep Spring Center for Meditation & Spiritual Enquiry (Mixed)
3455 Charing Cross Road
Ann Arbor, MI 48108
Tel: (313) 971–3455
E-mail: info@DeepSpring.org

Purpose is to offer nondenominational spiritual teachings on nonduality and to teach and support the deepening of nondual awareness through the practice of meditation— teach meditation and encourage spiritual inquiry. Although teachings derive from Buddhism and emphasis is on such elements as taking the precepts, it is not formally a Buddhist center and no religious ritual is offered. Foundation practice insight meditation (Vipassana). Presently rent facilities, but are in process of building a meditation hall and office space. Local sangha of about sixty and extended sangha of a hundred and twenty.

Four weekly classes for students of all levels, and continuing classes and introductory classes (latter co-sponsored with University of Michigan). Teacher training program and special sittings and classes for senior students. No channeling in meditation classes. Weekly program involves about sixty people. Retreats attended by those from farther away. Two local residential weekend retreats a year (with optional Monday continuation) and one of ten days. Additional one- or two-day retreats for ongoing students only. All emphasize Vipassana with pure awareness practices akin to Dzogchen also taught. Publish *Deep Spring Newsletter* three times a year and four books with teachings from Aaron (spirit channeled by Barbara Brodsky).

Barbara Brodsky (guiding teacher) also offers retreats throughout United States; some under Deep Spring co-sponsorship.

Founder/Guru	Founder and guiding teacher: Barbara Brodsky
Teachers	As founder and John Orr visits; director David Brown
Opening Times	Contact center
Residents	Founder
Festivals	Contact center
Facilities	See above
Accommodation	Short-term housing by sangha members, approximately $140/weekend, $350 for 10 days
Food	Vegetarian; try to meet all dietary needs
Booking	Retreats fill about 1–2 months in advance
Fees	Dana basis
Expected Behavior	Contact center

How to Get There   Nearest airport Detroit—will help provide transportation. Amtrak stops in Ann Arbor, and transportation to retreats from the station can be provided for a small fee.

Zen Buddhist Temple (Zen)
Affiliation: Buddhist Society for Compassionate Wisdom
1214 Packard Road
Ann Arbor, MI 48104-3814
Tel: (313) 761–6520
Fax: (313) 995–0435

Buddhist temple near the University of Michigan, consisting of large house with yard and garden with a hundred and ten members in a residential neighborhood. Opened 1981.

Public meditation services Sundays 9:30 am and 5:00 pm. Members' sittings Wednesdays 6:30–9:30 pm and Sundays 6:00–8:00 am. Introductory meditation courses in either a five–Thursday evening or Friday evening through Saturday afternoon format. Saturday morning Meditation Workshop for those wishing to meditate in chairs. These last three run five–six times through the year. Annual spring and fall lecture series on three–five consecutive Saturday afternoons on such subjects as Buddhism in Everyday Life. One-, two-, and three-day silent meditation retreats throughout the year. Family services, Peace Camp for Children, and runs Right Livelihood Fund.

Maitreya Buddhist Seminary is a three-year seminary program designed to train Buddhist priests and Dharma teachers and is open to all people who sincerely desire to undertake the training of discipleship for the spread of the Way of Buddha in the West.

Temple News produced quarterly. Buddhist bookstore stocks a wide range of books and other Buddhist articles.

Founder/Guru	Ven. Samu Sunim
Teachers	Resident teacher as founder plus others
Opening Times	To the public during Sunday services, other times by appointment
Residents	Rev. Sukha Linda Murray (resident teacher and contact person)
Festivals	Year End and New Year's Day services. Buddha's Enlightenment Day all-night sitting and Buddha's Birthday celebrations
Facilities	Meditation/Buddha hall, bookstore, dormitory, workshop, and organic garden
Accommodation	Daily, weekly, and monthly rates from $30/day to $450/month

Food	Vegetarian. All meals included in accommodation
Booking	1 month's notice and 25% deposit
Fees	Courses from $60–$140; retreats $50–$60 per day
Expected Behavior	Keep silence, concentrate your mind, be grateful and happy in this moment of your life
How to Get There	On Packard Road between State and Stadium Streets

Heart Center Karma Thegsum Choling (Tibetan–Karma Kagyu)
Affiliation: Karma Triyana Dharmachakra, New York
315 Marion Avenue
Big Rapids, MI 49307
Tel: (616) 796–2398
(616) 696–2944—mail order bookstore and KTD Dharma Goods
800 TIBETAN—information line for KTD organization
E-mail: ktd@thenewage.com
Web site: http://www.thenewage.com

Serves the greater KTD community with many special projects, including the transcription, editing, and distribution of the teachings of Ven. Khenpo Karthar Rinpoche. Operate KTD Dharma Goods, a mail-order service specializing in providing texts and practice materials from the Karma Kagyu tradition and mail-order bookstore. Assist Dzogchen Ponlop Rinpoche in the preparation of a draft curriculum for the KTD community. Staff the Buddhist information line listed above. Facilities include Heart Center house, which provides accommodation for visiting Lamas and scholars as well as several residents, plus a separate shrine building and stupa. Host regular lama visits and teachings by Lamas. Founded 1982.

Nothing on a regular basis—call for an update. In the past hosted seminars on variety of topics including Family Dharma weekends and a Tibetan Astrology Conference. Produce *Sangha Newsletter* for the KTD organization and various publicity brochures.

Founder/Guru	Ven. Bardor Tulku Rinpoche and Ven. Khenpo Karthar Rinpoche as representatives of H.H. the 17th Karmapa guide the center. Founded by Michael Erlewine at Khenpo Rinpoche's request.
Teachers	As founders and other Lamas of the Karma Kagyu lineage visit 2–3 times a year
Opening Times	Not applicable
Residents	Directors/coordinators Michael and Margaret Erlewine
Festivals	Not applicable
Facilities	Separate shrine seats about 30
Accommodation	For visiting teachers or occasional residential

	programs only
Food	Not applicable
Booking	Not applicable
Fees	Not applicable
Expected Behavior	Not applicable
How to Get There	1 hour north of Grand Rapids on U.S. 131

Traipitra Sarnsethsiri (Vipassana)
2427 Hunt Club Drive
Bloomfield Hills, MI 48304
Tel: (810) 644–7403

Independent Vipassana teacher teaching from home and at other Buddhist centers in the USA and Europe.

Mrs. Traipitra Sarnsethsiri was born Thailand 1939 and moved to USA 1966. She started Vipassana practice 1974 and has studied in Thailand, Burma, and the USA. Authorized to teach by Achan Sobin 1985. Part of home converted for teaching. Lectured and led meditation retreats in USA, Europe, and Thailand.

Detroit Zen Center (Zen–Rinzai–Korean)
Tel: (313) 366–7738
Fax: (313) 366–7940
E-mail: Mandalla1@aol.com

House attached to 5,000-square-foot hall in a multicultural urban setting. Community of four with 50 outside members practicing Korean Rinzai Zen in an American context. Run "Our Homes," which renovates homes for low-income people. Founded in 1990.

Classes in Zen meditation and Taoist Yoga (Sun-do). Sun-do retreats periodically include overview of Oriental medicine, energy analysis for body typing, breathing and posture, diet and nutrition. Seven-day Zen sesshin every other month, and two-day Zen weekend every other month. Residential training for Dharma teachers. Precept ceremony and training with five and ten precepts.

Founder/Guru	Sahn Bul Sunim
Teachers	Hyunoong Sunim visits
Opening Times	Daily from 6:00 am
Residents	1 monk and 3 lay
Festivals	Buddha's Birthday and Lunar New Year
Facilities	Meditation room and yoga room
Accommodation	Room for 4 guests; $30/day and $600/month includes room, board, and fees

Food	Vegetarian, animal foods as required for medicinal purposes
Booking	1 week in advance, $25 deposit
Fees	7-day retreat $150, 6-week introduction to Zen $125, 2-day retreat $35, 8-week introduction to Sun-do $120
Expected Behavior	Typical Zen center conduct
How to Get There	Contact center

Tam Quang Temple—Clear Mind Temple (Zen–Vietnamese)
For information, write to: Tom Holmes
2923 Memory Lane
Kalamazoo, MI 49006
Tel: (616) 344–0836
Fax: (616) 387–3389
E-mail: Holmest@wmich.edu

Vietnamese community of several hundred; English-speaking community around twenty-five at monthly retreat. Founded 1985 to serve Vietnamese community in west Michigan area. Vietnamese and English program offered.

Monthly mindfulness half-day retreats for English-speaking community. Sunday morning services and occasional special meetings for Vietnamese community. Newcomers welcome at monthly retreat. New Year's festival held annually in October as a special ceremony honoring Bott Quan Te Am (Kwan Yin).

Abbess Thich Nu Thanh Luong and sister Thich Nu Dien Thien are the nuns in residence and lead both Vietnamese and English services. Sister Thanh Luong spent several years at Plum Village, France, studying with Thich Nhat Hahn.

MINNESOTA

KKSG Minneapolis (Tibetan–Karma Kagyu)
Affiliation: Karma Triyana Dharmachakra, Woodstock, New York
4301 Morningside Road
Edina, MN 55416
Tel: (612) 926–5048

Established 1991 to support those who want to learn, practice, and study the in the lineage of Tibetan Karma Kagyu. The center has a beautiful shrine room.

Tuesdays 7:00 pm sitting meditation with study; Fridays 7:30 pm Chenrezig with study; Sundays usually Green Tara Puja and Ngondro with free practice period in afternoon. Offer Medicine Buddha practice monthly. Tibetan language classes, Nyungne retreats, meditation instruction available on a regular basis. Beginners always welcome.

Call for current calendar and to have flyer mailed to you.

Founder/Guru	Spiritual head: H.H. the 17th Gyalwa; Abbot Ven. Khenpo Karthar Rinpoche head of KTD
Teachers	As above and Bardor Tulku Rinpoche
Opening Times	As program above
Residents	Contact center
Festivals	Contact center
Facilities	Contact center
Accommodation	Contact center
Food	Contact center
Booking	Contact center
Fees	By donation
Expected Behavior	Contact center
How to Get There	Contact center

Clouds in Water Zen Center (Zen–Soto)
Minneapolis, MN
Tel & Fax: (612) 798–5821
E-mail: cloudsnh2o@aol.com
Web site: http://freenet.msp.mn.us/people/angelus/buddhism

Started 1992. It is a community of engaged mindfulness, looking for permanent premises 1996. Currently about 50 attendees weekly. "All welcome!"

Offer meditation Sundays mornings, monthly Saturday one-day sittings, trainings, talks, and retreats, Zen introductory program Wednesday evenings, weekly study group, and individual sessions with teacher available.

Founder/Guru	Mike Dosho Port
Teachers	Mike Dosho Port and Judith Byakuren Ragir
Opening Times	As program of events
Residents	Teachers
Festivals	None
Facilities	Contact center
Accommodation	None
Food	None
Booking	Contact center
Fees	Contact center
Expected Behavior	Contact center
How to Get There	Various locations, contact center

Minneapolis Shambhala Center (Tibetan–Kagyu/Nyingma)

Affiliation: Shambhala International
c/o Connie Brock
Minneapolis, MN 55405
Tel: (612) 874–6341
E-mail: Rich Griffiths: griffith@win.bright.net

See International headquarters, **Shambhala Center,** Halifax, Nova Scotia, Canada.

> *Enlightenment is not some good feeling or some state of mind. The state of mind*
> *that exists when you sit in the right posture is, itself, enlightenment.*
> *If you cannot be satisfied with the state of mind you have in*
> *zazen, it means your mind is still wandering about.*
>
> Shunryu Suzuki Roshi quoted in Muddy Water, newsletter of the Zen Center of Hawaii, Hawaii

Minnesota Zen Meditation Center (Zen–Soto)
3343 East Calhoun Parkway
Minneapolis, MN 55408-3313
Tel: (612) 822–5313
E-mail: mnzenctr@aol.com

Three-story Spanish-style building on Lake Calhoun has membership of two hundred. Established 1972 by a small group who invited a founder from San Francisco. Acquired land for **Mokyoji,** Iowa (see separate entry) to be a monastery in 1979. City center is a community of lay practitioners.

Offer daily zazen schedule, Saturday lecture, classes, and Buddhist studies program. Introduction to Zen Buddhism three times a year, zazen instruction four times per month, introductory retreats four times a year, sesshins about once a month, practice period of six weeks in August–September. Publish bi-monthly newsletter. Zafu and Zabuton business.

Founder/Guru	Dainin Katagiri Roshi
Teachers	Various
Opening Times	Contact center
Residents	None
Festivals	None
Facilities	Zendo, Buddha hall, and library
Accommodation	None
Food	Vegetarian during retreats and sesshins
Booking	2–4 weeks in advance, deposit required
Fees	Sesshins $30/day and classes $15/evening
Expected Behavior	No smoking, no perfume—incense not burned

How to Get There	4 blocks west of Hennepin Avenue off I-94 exit for Mennepin Ave. On east side of Lake Calhoun.

MISSISSIPPI

Starkville Zen Dojo (Zen–Soto)
Affiliation: New Orleans Zen Temple
231 Santa Anita Drive
Starkville, MS 39759
Tel: (601) 324–3622

Dojo in private residence. Between five and ten members of local sangha.
Zazen 6:00–7:00 am Tuesdays to Fridays, 10:00–11:30 am weekends, 7:00–8:00 pm Tuesdays and Thursdays. Periodic sesshins, usually one day, consisting of zazen, kinhin, samu, and simple ceremony.

Founder/Guru	Not applicable
Teachers	Tony Bland
Opening Times	See zazen times above
Residents	None
Festivals	Contact center
Facilities	Dojo
Accommodation	Can be arranged
Food	None
Booking	Negotiable
Fees	Negotiable
Expected Behavior	Practice zazen
How to Get There	Contact center

MISSOURI

Columbia Zen Center (Zen)
Check web site for current contact information
1405 East Walnut Street
Columbia, MO 65201
Tel: (573) 442–8401
Web site: http://www.coin.missouri.edu/community/spirit/zen

Group meets in a chapel designed by Eero Saarinen on the Stephens College campus. Sitting group of approximately fifty with five to twenty-five at any one sitting. Current sitting times available on web site. All-day sits about every six weeks. Occasional visits from teachers. Newsletter to members every six weeks to two months by e-mail if possible.

Wat Phrasriratanaram (Theravada–Thai)
The Buddhist Temple of Greater St Louis
890 Lindsay Lane
Florissant (St Louis), MO 63031
Tel: (314) 839–3115 or (314) 837–9717
Fax: (314) 839–3115

Converted church with congregation of about three hundred families. Founded 1983 to service Thai community of greater St Louis and to teach Buddhism to general public and insight meditation to all. Teaching center of Thai culture, tradition, and language.

Vipassana/insight meditation class every Saturday 7:00–8:30 pm. Daily insight meditation with the monks 6:00–7:00 am and 7:00–8:00 pm. Introductory Buddhism and General Buddhism on request. One-day retreat with insight meditation masters about once a year. Monthly Thai Food Fair.

Quarterly journal, *Sri Ratanasarn*.

Founder/Guru	H.E. Phra Monkolthepmolee
Teachers	Resident: Ven. Phramaha Lai Kosaro, Ven. Phramaha Woei Signkhan, Ven. Dr. Phramaha Nikhom Panyang
Opening Times	9:00 am–6:00 pm
Residents	3 monks and 1 laity
Festivals	Kathin and Songkran
Facilities	Shrine room, meditation room, and library
Accommodation	None
Food	Thai Food Fair first Sunday of each month
Booking	Not applicable
Fees	Free, but accept donations
Expected Behavior	No smoking, dress politely
How to Get There	From I-270, go north onto Lindbergh Boulevard for $1^1/_2$ miles, passing Washington Street. Turn left onto Lindsay Lane for half mile. Temple is on south side.

American Buddhist Center at Unity Temple on the Plaza (American Buddhist)
707 West 47th Street
Kansas City, MO 64112
Tel: (816) 561–4466 x 143

Affiliated with Unity Temple on the Plaza with 1,300-seat auditorium and 300-seat chapel which is urban and south of downtown Kansas. Hosts eighty to a hundred visitors weekly. Founded 1996 with focus on teaching meditation and a sitting community, connecting with other Buddhist groups, and presenting major teachers. Serves a diverse community of people from all walks of life. "Our center is reflective of the synthesis that is evolving as the different Buddhist traditions have taken root here and is developing a philosophy to meet the needs of Americans."

Weekly Vipassana and Zen sitting groups, topic meeting, and Sunday morning sitting. Daylong Vipassana retreat monthly and book study. Often monthly special event with prominent Buddhist teacher speaking. All suitable for newcomers.

Founder/Guru	Ben Worth
Teachers	Various visit
Opening Times	8:00 am–5:00 pm weekdays
Residents	None
Festivals	None
Facilities	Classrooms, chapel, and auditorium
Accommodation	None
Food	None
Booking	"First come, first served"
Fees	Dana
Expected Behavior	No smoking, 5 precepts
How to Get There	Contact center

Mid America Dharma Group (Therarada–Thai Forest Tradition)
P O Box 414411
Kansas City, MO 64141-4411
Tel: (913) 685-3430
Web site: http://www.geocities.com/Athens/3712/index.html

Organize retreats, no fixed premises—utilize facilities of famous monasteries and retreat houses in the Midwest. Started 1983 in Topeka, Kansas. "We have no residential teacher, so we use the sangha-as-teacher model to supplement visits by teachers from Spirit Rock and Insight Meditation Society."

Monthly classes in Vipassana meditation in Kansas City area. Four residential and two nonresidential retreats annually following traditional Vipassana format of **Insight Meditation Society**, Massachusetts, and **Spirit Rock Center**, California (see separate entries). At least one of the annual retreats is ten days, and the rest are weekenders. All activities suitable for newcomers.

Teachers	Mostly from Spirit Rock Center or Insight Meditation Society
Opening Times	Not applicable
Residents	None
Festivals	None
Facilities	See above

<table>
<tr><td>Accommodation</td><td>Varies</td></tr>
<tr><td>Food</td><td>Vegetarian</td></tr>
<tr><td>Booking</td><td>30 days in advance</td></tr>
<tr><td>Fees</td><td>Vary by facility and length of retreat</td></tr>
<tr><td>Expected Behavior</td><td>5 precepts, no smoking, no talking</td></tr>
<tr><td>How to Get There</td><td>Different locations</td></tr>
</table>

Soka Gakkai International (SGI-USA) (Nichiren)
Missouri Area Regional Center
1804 Broadway
Kansas City, MO 64108-2007
Tel: (816) 474–7973
Fax: (816) 842–9301

See **Soka Gakkai International** National Offices & Center, Santa Monica, California, for more details.

Missouri Zen Center (Zen–Soto)
220 Spring Avenue
St Louis, MO 63119
Tel: (314) 961–6138
E-mail: c/o Rick Grucza—ragrucza@biochem.wustl.edu
Web site: http://www.members.tripod.com/~mozencenter/mzc.html

House in a residential neighborhood with approximately a hundred members. Started twenty years ago.

Zazen Monday to Friday and Sunday mornings and Monday, Thursday, and Friday evenings. Day retreats at least twice a year. Beginners workshop, six-week introduction to meditation, and Zen. Monthly newsletter, *Dharma Life*.

<table>
<tr><td>Founder/Guru</td><td>Rosan Roshida, descendant of Katiguri Roshi</td></tr>
<tr><td>Teachers</td><td>Rosan Roshida; Dr. Yoshida visits for 2–3 months a year</td></tr>
<tr><td>Opening Times</td><td>See session times above</td></tr>
<tr><td>Residents</td><td>None</td></tr>
<tr><td>Festivals</td><td>Not applicable</td></tr>
<tr><td>Facilities</td><td>Sitting room, kitchen, and small library</td></tr>
<tr><td>Accommodation</td><td>Not applicable</td></tr>
<tr><td>Food</td><td>Not applicable</td></tr>
<tr><td>Booking</td><td>Not applicable</td></tr>
<tr><td>Fees</td><td>Donations—$25 suggested for beginners' course</td></tr>
<tr><td>Expected Behavior</td><td>Contact center</td></tr>
<tr><td>How to Get There</td><td>Call for directions or visit the web site</td></tr>
</table>

MONTANA

Open Way Sangha (Zen–Vietnamese)
Affiliation: Community of Mindful Living
P O Box 7281
Missoula, MT 59807-7281
Tel: (406) 549–9005 (voicemail box is #3)
E-mail: darwin@selway.umt.edu or conradrw@aol.com

Rents space for activities from the local Quaker congregation and various retreat centers. Missoula is a university town and major tourist destination in western Montana. About thirty core members, including four ordained Order members. Started 1989 by people inspired by Thich Nhat Hanh's USA tour that year. "Democratic consensus based rather than teacher-dominated. Zen lineage but nondenominational perspective."

Weekly events and periodic retreats. Dharma discussions Thursday evenings October–May and related program (Alaya) of classes on meditation, the Eightfold Path, the life of the Buddha, etc. Two or three major retreats of four to seven days each year—themes negotiated with master leading. Sunday evening meditation with additional monthly tea ceremony and discussion or precept recitation and discussion. Meditation instruction offered one Sunday each month. Newcomers always welcome. Quarterly publication, *News & Views*.

Founder/Guru	Tradition of Thich Nhat Hanh
Teachers	Resident and visiting Order members
Opening Times	Sunday and Thursday evenings
Residents	None
Festivals	None
Facilities	Share a sanctuary with the local Quaker congregation
Accommodation	None
Food	None
Booking	Not necessary
Fees	Between $100–135 for a 4-day weekend retreat
Expected Behavior	No smoking, 5 precepts
How to Get There	12th and Grant

Osel Shen Phen Ling(Tibetan–Gelug)
Affiliation: Foundation for the Preservation of the Mahayana Tradition
7222 Siesta Drive
Missoula, MT 59802
Mailing Address: P O Box 5932
Missoula, MT 59806

Tel: (406) 549–1707

Contact center for details.

Rocky Mountain FWBO (Friends of the Western Buddhist Order)
540 South Second West
Missoula, MT 59801
Tel: (406) 327–0034 (center); (406) 721–5047 (Linda Veum); (406) 543–1158
(Dharmachari Saramati) or (406) 549–4792 (Dharmachari Budhapalita)
Fax: (406) 721–5047 by prior arrangement only
E-mail: varasuri@ism.net

Meet in rented premises—more permanent center and right-livelihood business
planned. Between forty and fifty visitors a week. Started 1991 by husband and wife
Western Buddhist Order members. "We are a young and thriving center known for our
friendly atmosphere and we expect to grow tremendously in the next five years."

Six or more classes/gathering a week: Friends night, beginning meditation, basic
Dharma, open meditation and puja, women's group. Weekly study and practice meetings for more committed friends and Order members. Occasional intermediate-level
meditation or Dharma course. Introductory weekend retreat twice yearly; annual week
or ten-day retreat in summer. Meditations taught are Mindfulness of Breathing and
Metta Bhavana (development of loving-kindness).

Small bookstore selling books by **Windhorse Publishing** (main publishing house
of the FWBO).

Founder/Guru	Sangharakshita
Teachers	Resident and visiting Order members
Opening Times	Contact center
Residents	Not applicable
Festivals	Wesak, Dharma Day, Sangha Day, and Padmasambhava Day
Facilities	Rented space with shrine room, small bookstore, and kitchen
Accommodation	None
Food	Vegetarian or vegan during all activities
Booking	Contact center
Fees	On a dana basis—$20 contribution for introductory classes
Expected Behavior	5 precepts
How to Get There	Contact center

NEBRASKA

Kearney Zendo (Zen–Soto)
3715 Avenue F (P O Box 370)
Kearney, NE 68848
Tel: (308) 236–5650
Fax: (308) 237–1294
E-mail: mosig@platte.unk.edu

Small sitting group established 1984. Shares facilities with the Zen Shuri-Ryu Karate Kobudo Dojo in a 26-by-26-foot separate former two-car garage building. Has Buddhist altar, twenty-four sets of zafu/zabuton, and a library of five thousand volumes of books and videotapes.

Daily zazen and sutra chanting as well as classes in introduction to zazen practice, Okinawan Karatedo, and Okinawan Kobudo. All-day sittings on Bodhidharma Day and other special days; intensive sitting schedule during Rohatsu days; occasional sesshin led by a guest teacher. Dr. Mosig also teaches Eastern psychology at the University of Nebraska—Kearney where he is Professor of Psychology.

Founder/Guru	Dainin Katagiri-Roshi (1928–1990)
Teachers	Practice Director: Dr. Yozan Mosig
Opening Times	As program times
Residents	Practice Director
Festivals	Buddha's Birthday, Parinirvana, Bodhidharma Day, Dogen's Birthday, Dogen's Parinirvana Day, Katagiri-Roshi's Birthday, and Parinirvana Days.
Facilities	See above
Accommodation	None
Food	None
Booking	Not applicable
Fees	Not applicable
Expected Behavior	No smoking, drinking, or profanity; 5 precepts; no shoes on dojo floor
How to Get There:	Contact center

Nebraska Zen Center (Zen–Soto)
3625 Lafayette Avenue
Omaha, NE 68131-1363
Tel: (402) 551–9035

House in one of Omaha's oldest neighborhoods. Rev. Nonin Chowaney in Omaha since 1991, when present premises purchased and refurbished. Two full-time priests leading community of about twenty-five laity.

Morning and evening zazen and morning service. One- or two-day retreat most months and precept ceremony (Ryaku Fusatsu). Rohatsu Sesshin Dec 26–Jan 1. Rev. Chowaney teaches class in Buddhism at local university and ongoing Buddhist studies class at center. Offer three-day seminar each summer and Introduction to Zen Thursday evenings. Quarterly newsletter, *The Nebraska Monkey*.

Founder/Guru	Nonin Chowaney
Teachers	Resident: Nonin Chowaney
Opening Times	Contact center
Residents	Resident teacher and 1 nun
Festivals	Rohatsu
Facilities	Zendo, Buddha hall, library
Accommodation	For overnight, must request permission and follow schedule
Food	Vegetarian, mostly organic
Booking	Contact center
Fees	$25/day for all overnights and sesshins (low-income rates available)
Expected Behavior	No smoking
How to Get There:	I-80 north on 480, take north freeway, take Cuming St. exit, west to 38th St., north to Lafayette, east and first house on right.

NEVADA

Mojave Desert Zen Center (Zen)
Affiliation: Kwan Um School of Zen
Center: 919 Charleston Boulevard
Las Vegas, NV
Mailing: 901 El Camino Way
Boulder City, NV 89005
Tel: (702) 293–4222
E-mail: sittinzen@aol.com
Web site: http://www.cs.ucsb.edu/~raimisl/southwest.html

House in cul-de-sac that has around thirty visitors a week. Founded 1994; moved to current location 1996. "Las Vegas, with all the distinctive characteristics that only a gambling mecca could produce, provides a most interesting environment for finding our true self."

Sitting, chanting, bowing practice Tuesdays 9:00 am; Wednesdays 6:30 pm;

Sundays 9:00 am. Introduction to Zen first Saturday of each month. Evening Zen liter-ature workshop second Wednesday of each month. One-day retreats four times yearly. Three-day Yong Maeng Jon Jims (literally, "to leap like a tiger while sitting") three times a year. *Only Go Straight* quarterly; *Primary Point* twice yearly. Small bookstore selling Kwan Um School of Zen publications and meditation supplies planned 1996.

Founder/Guru	Zen Master Seung Sahn
Teachers	Resident: Thomas Pastor, Kwan Jok Poep Sa; Robert Moore, Ji Do Poep Sa Nim, visiting guiding teacher
Opening Times	See session times above
Residents	1 laity and monks/nuns of Kwan Um School as guests periodically
Festivals	Buddha's Birthday, Buddha's Enlightenment Day, Sangha Weekend
Facilities	Dharma room, study room
Accommodation	Kwan Um School of Zen members only: $40/night; $30 more than 1 night
Food	Vegetarian
Booking	60 days in advance; deposit determined by projected length of stay
Fees	Introduction to Zen $30; retreats $40/day; regular daily practice free
Expected Behavior	No smoking, alcohol, or drugs on premises. Full adherence to daily practice schedule
How to Get There:	3 miles due east via Russell Rd. from McCarran International airport, left on Lamb, left on Asmara, right on Chela.

NEW HAMPSHIRE

Barrington Zen Center (Zen)
7 Lois Lane
Barrington, NH 03825
Tel: (603) 664–7654

Unlimited space in large simple common building in a rural wooded setting next to a pond. Small local group with four to eight regular participants with regular schedule since 1994.

Offers traditional Zen practice, beginner's instruction on request, and daylong meditation on second Sunday of the month.

Founder/Guru	Contact person: Charter Weeks

Teachers	Looking for qualified teacher at time of writing
Opening Times	Contact center for practice times
Residents	None
Festivals	None
Facilities	Large zendo with unlimited seating
Accommodation	None
Food	None
Booking	Contact center
Fees	$20 for monthly retreat, otherwise free
Expected Behavior	Contact center
How to Get There:	Call for directions

Aryaloka Buddhist Retreat Center (Friends of the Western Buddhist Order)
14 Heartwood Circle
Newmarket, NH 03857
Tel & Fax: (603) 659–5456
E-mail: aryaloka@aol.com, vajramati@aol.com, aryadaka@aol.com
Web site: http://www.fwbo.org/ or http://bluelotus.com/sfbc/sfbc.htm (San Francisco)
    or http://web.mit.edu/benbr/www/FWBOHOME.HTM
    or http://www.ciens.ula.ve/~toro (in Spanish)

Two large geodesic domes and a barn on property housing a men's community; however, there are two residential communities, one for men, one for women. Large sangha of around forty attend on a regular basis. "We are known to offer a very friendly atmosphere in which we attempt to communicate what is essential in the practice of a Buddhist life without the cultural trappings of the Eastern forms." Established 1985.

Tuesday evening sangha nights. Weekly classes and discussion groups on Buddhist principles, monthly workshops on meditation practice, regular weekend retreats, and periodic retreats of a week to ten days. Courses on sutra study and on Sangharakshita's writings. Teach Mindfulness of Breathing (Anapansati) and Development of Friendliness (Metta Bhavana) meditations. Perform collective pujas. Quarterly magazine, *Dharma Life*, and *Lotus Realm* for Buddhist women.

Run Buddhist book distribution business handling book sales to individuals and educational institutions for **Windhorse Publications,** the FWBO publishing house. Hope to open vegetarian restaurant 1997/98.

The **Portland, Maine FWBO** can be contacted via this center.

Founder/Guru	Ven. Sangharakshita
Teachers	Members of the Western Buddhist Order
Opening Times	9:30 am–4:00 pm and for evening classes
Residents	8 men, 5 women, neither lay nor monastic
Festivals	Friends of the Western Buddhist Order Day, Wesak Day, Dharmachakra Day, Sangha Day, Padmasambhava Day,

	Parinvirvana Day
Facilities	Reception room, study rooms, shrine room and yoga/Tai Chi room used also for lectures
Accommodation	B&B at $15 per night
Food	Vegetarian, wholefood included in accommodation price
Booking	1/3 of retreat price deposit approximately 2 weeks in advance
Fees	4-week meditation course $40; day workshops $45; sangha nights $5; weekend retreats $80; week-long retreats $210
Expected Behavior	No smoking in Retreat Center buildings; no illegal drugs, firearms, or alcohol on property
How to Get There:	1$^1/_2$ hours north of Boston on Interstate 95 or 25 minutes drive from Portsmouth, NH

Seacoast NH Dharma Study Group (Tibetan–Kagyu/Nyingma)
Affiliation: Shambhala International
c/o Phyllis Murray
Tel: (603) 868–2636

See International headquarters, **Shambhala Center,** Halifax, Nova Scotia, Canada.

NEW JERSEY

Jizo-an Monastery/The Zen Society (Zen–Soto)
1603 Highland Avenue
Cinnaminson, NJ 08077
Tel: (609) 786–4150
Fax: (609) 786–2112
E-mail: jizoan@aol.com

House built in Japanese style and houses a community of twenty. "Jizo-An offers a comprehensive and traditional Zen practice for laypersons of all ages and religious backgrounds."

Zazen daily. Nonresidential lay student formal training, one-day workshop retreats, Chado—the Way of Tea (private lessons by appointment), tea gatherings, monthly one-day or weekend sesshins, sutra services, private hermitage retreats, private group retreats. *Kokoro* newsletter every three months.

Founder/Guru	Seijaku Stephen Reichenbach Roshi
Teachers	As founder

Opening Times	Contact center; closed week following third Sunday of each month and the month of August
Residents	1 monk and 1 layperson
Festivals	Obon
Facilities	Dojo, meditation room, and teahouse
Accommodation	Not applicable
Food	Vegetarian
Booking	2 weeks and deposit required
Fees	Contact center
Expected Behavior	No smoking, 5 precepts
How to Get There:	Contact center

Zen (Arts) Temple of Cresskill (Zen–Korean [Son])
185 6th Street
Cresskill, NJ 07626
Tel: (201) 567-7468
Fax: (201) 569-0831

Son Temple converted from Baptist church with Dharma hall seating a hundred people. Founded 1972 by Rev. Dr. Sun Ock Lee in New York City; moved to present location 1985. "Our center is the only place where Son Mu: Zen dance, meditation in movement practice is offered." Dr. Sun Ock Lee is "one of Korea's foremost traditional and modern dancers and choreographers."

Korean Son meditation and chanting based on teachings of Zen Master Songdhan in Korea. Daily practice. Son Mu—Zen dance/meditation in movement—classes, workshops, and retreats. Taught by Dr. Lee when she stays (she travels worldwide to teach), and classes by other qualified teachers are by appointment. These classes are available for beginners, artists, general public, and dancers.

Son Mu Ga: Zen Dance Company based at the Temple and tours, giving lectures, workshops, and performances.

Founder/Guru	Rev. Dr. Sun Ock Lee
Teachers	Founder, nuns and monks, and Zen Dance practitioners
Opening Times	Only during workshops, retreats, and by appointment
Residents	1–2 monastics and 3–5 laity
Festivals	None
Facilities	Meditation room
Accommodation	During retreats and workshops only
Food	During retreats and workshops only
Booking	By appointment only
Fees	Varies according to duration—3 days $150, 2 days $110
Expected Behavior	No smoking and wear comfortable clothing
How to Get There:	Contact center for details

Mahayana Sutra and Tantra Center (MSTC) (Tibetan–Gelug)
c/o Rashi Gempil Ling Buddhist Temple
47 East Fifth Street
Howell, NJ 07731
Tel: (908) 364–1824
Fax: 908 901–5940
E-mail: acip@well.com

Located in suburb in heart of Kalmyk-Mongolian community in Freewood Acres, MSTC has been kindly allowed to use the premises of Rashi Gempil Ling, the First Kalmyk Buddhist Temple, for its courses and retreats. Temple established 1952 by Kalmyk immigrants wanting to keep their tradition alive. They meet regularly on holy days and holidays to attend religious services chanted by resident Tibetan monks. About fifty regular attendees. MSTC established 1975 and incorporated 1980. Part of community including **MSTC of Washington,** District of Columbia, **Asian Classics Institute,** New York, and **MSTC of Connecticut** (see separate entries).

Offer basic and advanced meditation classes, teachings by the Lama, bi-weekly ceremonies and twice-weekly classes in Tibetan language, twice-monthly Tsechu for those with initiation, annual three-day retreat in August for those with prerequisite initiation (sometimes weekend retreat in July which offers this). Occasional newsletter.

Some translations not-for-profit from **Mahayana Sutra and Tantra Press,** 112 West 2nd Street, Howell, New Jersey 07731.

MSTC sangha run **Three Jewels Buddhist Bookstore,** which sells books, gifts, and teas, and books may be borrowed from Tara Lending Library, 211 East 5th Street, New York, New York 10003, Tel: (212) 475–6650.

Founder/Guru	Lama Khen Rinpoche Geshe Lobsang Tharchin
Teachers	Resident: Founder, Artemus Engle PhD, Geshe Michael Roach of Asian Classics Institute
Opening Times	During classes and retreats or by appointment
Residents	4 monks
Festivals	Not applicable
Facilities	Temple
Accommodation	In homes of local Dharma students during annual retreat where possible, or at local motels or campgrounds
Food	During retreat, vegetarian and nonvegetarian meals for $5–10 contribution per meal
Booking	Call in advance
Fees	No charge, but donations and reimbursements for practice and study materials encouraged
Expected Behavior	Since land and temple belong to Kalmyk-Mongolian community, all members and guests must be respectful of the premises
How to Get There:	Contact center for details

Buddhist Study Association of Greater New York, Inc. (Nonsectarian)
16 Stanford Avenue
West Orange, NJ 07052
Tel: (201) 736–8957
Fax: (201) 736–8957 *51

Founded by Anthony Bucci, the center's mission is to advance and teach basic
Buddhist meditation, philosophy, psychology, and spirituality. Endeavor to be source of
information about various Buddhist traditions and other Buddhist centers; for directing
institutions to Buddhist clergy, teachers, and volunteers for chaplain positions in institutional organizations; and of free books on Buddhism. Spiritual center with regular
meetings for study of Buddhist texts, meditation practice, and "the enjoyment of spiritual friendship."

> *You live in illusion and in the appearance of things. There is a reality.*
> *You are the reality. If you wake up to that reality, you will know that you are*
> *nothing, and being nothing, you are everything.*
>
> Kalu Rinpoche quoted in a brochure from Kagyu Thegchen Ling, Hawaii

NEW MEXICO

Albuquerque Karma Thegsum Choling (Tibetan–Karma Kagyu)
Affiliation: Karma Triyana Dharmachakra, New York
139 La Plata NW
Albuquerque, NM 87107
Tel: (505) 344–4661
E-mail: carpenter@apsicc.aps.edu

Active since 1981. Practice Sundays and Tuesdays. Meditation instruction by appointment.

Albuquerque Zen Center (Zen–Rinzai)
P O Box 4585
Albuquerque, NM 87196
Tel & Fax: (505) 268–4877
E-mail: seiju@swcp.com

Urban setting with plans to build larger meditation hall on new half-acre site which
will have two buildings for zendo and office/residence. Daily practice center with fifty

to a hundred and twenty people practicing each week. Focus is to provide a clear and frequent practice environment for the Albuquerque area residents who must adjust their ability to practice with respect for family and work obligations.

Sessions of zazen, kinhin, tea, and chanting 5:15 am and 7:30 pm weekdays, 8:00 am Saturdays. Buddhist ceremonies observed. Weekly beginners' introduction or by appointment. Month-long practice intensives each quarter. Daylong retreats monthly; weekend retreats quarterly; week-long retreats occasionally. Extended invitation to practice and etiquette quarterly. Weekly discussion group. Classes on Buddhism several times annually. All events are suitable for newcomers after beginners' orientation class. Marriage ceremonies, funerals, memorial services, and dedications are celebrated. Also offers hospitality for social events.

Quarterly newsletter by staff members.

Founder/Guru	Kyozan Joshu Saski Roshi spiritual leader; Kogan Seiju Mammoser founder
Teachers	Kogan Seiju Mammoser resident
Opening Times	5:00 am daily
Residents	Resident teacher
Festivals	Contact center
Facilities	Zendo, library/study room
Accommodation	None
Food	None
Booking	Notify center if you will be attending
Fees	Day sittings $25; weekends $50. Discounts available to members ($25 per month)
Expected Behavior	To be awake and responsible
How to Get There:	Half a block east of Yale and Garfield, midway between airport and University of New Mexico. Two blocks east of San Mateo and half a block south of Zuni.

> As stars, a fault of vision, a mock show, dew drop or a bubble, a dream,
> a lightning flash, or cloud, so should one view what is conditioned.
>
> *The Diamond Sutra*

Hidden Mountain Zen Center (Zen–Soto)
Affiliation: White Plum sangha
216 Ninth Street, NW
Albuquerque, NM 87102
Tel & Fax: (505) 248–0649

Located downtown in large house remodeled into a zendo and living quarters. Expect to acquire country property. Founded 1995 by students of the late Hakuyu Taizan Maezumi Roshi.

Offer zazen practice and services daily, aspects of Zen practice Saturday mornings, courses of koan study, and monthly meditation retreats (sesshins) of three–seven days. One- to three-month longer intensive practice periods (Ango). Mountain retreats with troubled adolescents. Quarterly newsletter, *Mountain Path*.

Founder/Guru	Hakuyu Taizan Maezumi Roshi
Teachers	Resident: Alfred Jitsudo Ancheta Sensei
Opening Times	Contact center
Residents	3 lay
Festivals	Contact center
Facilities	Zendo, living quarters, kitchen, library
Accommodation	$25 per day, $450 per month
Food	Vegetarian/wholefood served with retreats
Booking	30 days in advance
Fees	$35 per day, $25 for members
Expected Behavior	No smoking, 10 grave precepts
How to Get There:	Downtown Albuquerque, 1 block north of Central on Ninth

Daibutsuji—Dharma Mountain Zendo (Zen–Soto)
34 Oak Glen
Cloudcroft, NM 88317
Tel & Fax: (505) 687–2131

Mountain chalet building with zendo designed in Japanese style. In mountainous terrain in forest at eight thousand feet with hiking trails, horse riding nearby. Small Dharma center in the mountains which acts as headquarters for this area and to Las Cruces Zen Center. Established 1987 in Las Cruces and moved here to build permanent temple. Resident priests are trained in Japanese tradition, but conduct and ceremony slightly modified to better suit Western practitioners.

Shikantaza zazen 7:30 pm Wednesdays and 10:00 am Sundays. History, tradition, and techniques for Zen Buddhist practice offered to all who come. Four sesshins each year—spring, fall, O'Higen, Hannamatsuri, and Rohatsu.

No business, but equipped to design and fashion personal and zendo furniture and devices, e.g., Butsudan, incense burners, benches, etc.

Founder/Guru	Rev. Dr. Soyu Matsuoka Roshi
Teachers	Rev. Ken McGuire Roshi
Opening Times	Not applicable
Residents	2 priests
Festivals	Obon and Hannamatsuri
Facilities	Zendo, library, and study room

> *Accommodation*   Bring sleeping bag
> *Food*   Vegetarian and/or wholefood for donations
> *Booking*   2 weeks in advance
> *Fees*   Approximately $20 for 3-day sesshin
> *Expected Behavior*   No smoking, limit reading to library, keep discussions relevant
> *How to Get There:*   Call or fax for directions

Bodhi Mandala Zen Center (Zen–Rinzai)
Affiliation: Rinzai-ji; Joshu Sasaki lineage and Mount Baldy Center in Los Angeles,
  California
P O Box 8
Jemez Springs, NM 87025
Tel & Fax: (505) 829–3854

Contact center for details.

Las Vegas Vipassana (Vipassana)
Southwest Center for Spiritual Living
715 Sperry Drive
Las Vegas, NM 87701
Tel: (505) 454–1671

Weekly meeting. Contact center for details.

Apaya (Zen–Vietnamese)
Affiliation: Community of Mindful Living
1404 Cerro Gordo Road
Santa Fe, NM 87501
Tel: (505) 986–8518
Fax: (505) 986–8528
E-mail: upaya@rt66.com
Web site: http://www.rt66.com/~upaya

Retreat center of two adobe structures next to an adobe zendo in the foothills of the
Sangre de Cristo Mountains. Founded 1991.
    Retreats on such topics as Practices for Being with Dying; Building Community
in the Classroom; Mindfulness; Exchanging Self with Others; Wilderness Solitude
Insight Practice, Kindness of the Llamas; Mountain Walking; Women, Compassion
and Spirituality; and The Healing Brush (calligraphy). Zazen 5:30 pm Mondays to
Fridays.

> *Founder/Guru*   Joan Halifax

Teachers	Resident: Joan Halifax, many others visit
Opening Times	Not applicable
Residents	1 nun, 2 lay women
Festivals	Not applicable
Facilities	Zendo, office, dining hall, sauna, accommodation for 20 retreatants
Accommodation	For retreatants only
Food	Organic when possible and vegetarian for retreats
Booking	2 months in advance is best, deposit necessary
Fees	Vary, e.g., 2 days $230 plus $100 residency, 10 days $700 plus residency $300
Expected Behavior	5 precepts
How to Get There:	On eastern edge of Santa Fe

Center for Dzogchen Studies of Santa Fe (Tibetan)
Affiliation: International Shakyamuni Dzogchen Heart Lineage
329 Otero Street
Santa Fe, NM 87501
Tel: (505) 989–4206
E-mail: 103624.401@compuserve.com

Small adobe house within walking distance from historical downtown Santa Fe, at the foot of the Sangre de Cristo Mountains. At an elevation of seven thousand feet with remarkable desert mountain scenery, with incredible blue skies and outstanding sunsets—ideal for any form of awareness practice. Resident lama and five–ten practitioners. Began in 1995 as second Center for Dzogchen Studies in the U.S.

"The practice and teaching style uses the teacher/student/human communication element in combination with consistent awareness practice to discover each and every habitual pattern and limiting tendency as well as our own open and liberated hearts. Strongly emphasized and discussed is the usefulness and integration of practice with every activity of daily life."

Guided sitting awareness practice four times a week. Option to use the practice room at other times. Introduction to the teachings Sundays 2:00 pm, including instruction on sitting practice. Concentrated seminar courses on texts primarily from Dzogchen and Tibetan Buddhism—schedules vary. One-day Dzogchen retreats. Periodic workshops and teachings on specific areas of interest, e.g., health, gender, and ecology. Appointments recommended for meetings with Lama Pema Dzogtril.

Founder/Guru	Lama Pema Dzogtril
Teachers	Resident: Lama Pema Dzogtril, Padma Karma Rinpoche visits
Opening Times	Sunday–Friday 10:00 am–9:00 pm; Saturdays 8:00 am–9:00 pm

Residents	Resident teacher only
Festivals	Contact center
Facilities	Awareness practice room, small library, kitchen
Accommodation	None
Food	None
Booking	Contact center
Fees	Contact center
Expected Behavior	Contact center
How to Get There:	North on I-25, then St. Francis Drive exit. Turn right on Paseo de Peralta until the 4-way stop sign (Otero Street). Turn right up a steep hill and park. 329 is the fifth house on the right.

Gaden Foundation (Tibetan–Nonsectarian)
823 Don Diego
Santa Fe, NM 87501
Tel: (505) 989–9590
Fax: (505) 989–9519
E-mail: clpublish@aol.com

Organize Tibetan events such as monk tours; sponsoring lamas for teachings; organize political initiatives for a Free Tibet; organize lectures on Tibetan cultural/educational subjects. No permanent structure. Founded 1979 in New York City to organize weekly lectures at Office of Tibet and host events in all Tibetan Buddhist's great traditions for between 5 to 5,000 attendees. Encourages participation and co-hosting of events. Nondenominational center dedicated to perpetuating the Buddha's teachings. Plans to offer dialectics course in Tibetan Buddhism in 1998. Extensive tape library. Catalog available for books published by **Clear Light Publishers,** with whom affiliated.

Founder/Guru	The 98th Ganden Tripa, Jampal Zhanpen
Teachers	Wide range of teachers from all traditions
Opening Times	Not applicable
Residents	Not applicable
Festivals	Not applicable
Facilities	See above
Accommodation	Not applicable
Food	Not applicable
Booking	Not applicable
Fees	Not applicable
Expected Behavior	Contact center
How to Get There:	Not applicable

Karma Shenpen Kunchab Tibetan Buddhist Center (KSK) (Tibetan–Kagyu)
Affiliation: Kalu Rinpoche
751 Airport Road
Santa Fe, NM 87505
Tel: (505) 471–1152
Fax: (505) 471–5336 (also bookstore number)
E-mail: janet@rt66.com or cooper@lanl.gov

Small residential center with stupa/shrine room consecrated by Kalu Rinpoche 1986. Around fifty registered members. Land acquired 1982, expanded from three to six residences. Lama Karma Dorje resident since 1981. "Fabulous stupa/shrine room in traditional Tibetan style!" Started 1977.

Calm abiding and insight meditation Sundays 10:45 am. Chenrezig puja Sundays and Wednesdays 6:00 pm. Green Tara puja Sundays 8:30 am. Mahakala practice day before new moon 6:00 pm. Full moon meditations 6:00 pm. Instruction in calm abiding and insight meditation. Instruction in Chenrezig and Green Tara puja; Mahakala and Milarepa practice by appointment. Monthly talks/empowerments by visiting lamas from Kagyu tradition. Evening/weekend classes on other aspects of practice, such as Ngondro and Tonglen. Retreats occasionally offered on different premises. **Noble Truth Bookstore** on center grounds. Opening hours: Monday–Friday Noon–6:00 pm; Weekends 10:00 am–6:00 pm. Tel: (505) 471–5336.

Founder/Guru	Kalu Rinpoche
Teachers	Resident: Lama Karma Dorje; lay teacher: Fred Cooper. Many visit, such as Tai Situpa Rinpoche, Bokar Rinpoche, Khenpo Tsultrim Gyamtso, Lama Lodro, etc.
Opening Times	See session times above
Residents	7
Festivals	Contact center
Facilities	Stupa/shrine room, library, bookstore, meditation room, study room
Accommodation	None

Mountain Cloud Zen Center (Zen)
Affiliation: Diamond sangha
c/o Sandy Anderson
P O Box 5768
Santa Fe, NM 87502
Tel: (505) 988–4396

Contact center for details.

Southwest Sangha (Theravada)
Black Range Station
San Lorenzo, NM 88041
Tel: (505) 536–9847

Rock house and chapel built by Jesuit priest in 1930s on four acres in very remote desert environment at six thousand feet elevation. Started 1995 by Michael Freeman and Amy Schmidt.

Vipassana meditation. Sitting and walking practice 8:00 am–noon Saturdays. Occasional daylong sits. Offer space for individual retreats for experienced meditators, who should visit before doing their retreat.

Founder/Guru	Spiritual director: Bhante Gunaratana
Teachers	Resident: Michael Freeman and Amy Schmidt
Opening Times	Not applicable
Residents	3 laity
Festivals	Not applicable
Facilities	Historic chapel (formerly Catholic, now ecumenical), meditation room, 2 tent sites
Accommodation	Tent sites only until meditation huts/kutis built by 1999
Food	Vegetarian, non-dairy on request, for dana
Booking	Contact center
Fees	None—dana
Expected Behavior	5 precepts, no smoking, must sit twice daily with the community and be willing to help with work
How to Get There:	Please call for directions

NEW YORK

Albany Karma Thegsum Choling (Tibetan–Karma Kagyu)
Affiliation: Karma Triyana Dharmachakra, New York
P O Box 6545
Albany, NY 10565
Tel: (518) 374–1792
E-mail: RothW@global1.net

Members meet nearby. Contact center for more details.

Kinpu-an, Albany Affiliate of Zen Mountain Monastery (Zen–Soto/Rinzai)
4 Providence Place
Albany, NY 12202
Tel: (518) 432–4676

Urban lay practice center in a residential area. Established 1989.
    Formal periods of morning and evening zazen on weekdays. All-day and half-day meditation retreats held monthly. Eight Gate training: Zen meditation, face-to-face teaching, ethical and moral teachings, liturgy, work practice, body practice, academic, and art practice. Quarterly newsletter.

Founder/Guru	Roshi John Daido Loori
Teachers	Founder visits and senior MRO students
Opening Times	Contact center for program
Residents	6
Festivals	Contact center
Facilities	Zendo, office, kitchen
Accommodation	None
Food	None
Booking	Not necessary
Fees	None
Expected Behavior	Not applicable
How to Get There	Contact center

Temple of Enlightenment (Theravada, Mahayana, and Tibetan)
Affiliation: Buddhist Association of the United States, New York
3070 Albany Crescent
Bronx, NY 10463
Tel & Fax: (718) 884–9111
E-mail: bausny@aol.com
Twelve weekend services, lectures on Sundays, five one-day services. Open at weekends.

Brooklyn Buddhist Association (Zen and Pure Land)
Affiliation: International Zen Dojo Sogenkai
211 Smith Street
Brooklyn, NY 11201
Tel: (718) 488–9511
Fax: (718) 797–1073
E-mail: sjosephj@aol.com, bbajsk1@aol.com

Twenty-member zazen group based in Brooklyn downtown storefront. Founded in 1984 with Jikisinkan Aikido Dojo in founder's home, moving to current location to provide more space for sixty-member dojo. "Martial arts and Buddhist arts working together for realization of oneness."
Offers Rinzai-style zazen, Shintoitsu-style Aikido, Chozenji-style kyudo, and Zen therapy. Zazen four days a week, Aikido seven days a week, Dharma talks and discussions. One-week intensive retreat per year of Aikido and Zen arts (usually the last week of August) in a camp near Middletown, Connecticut.
Publish *Dojo* newsletter quarterly.

Founder/Guru	Not applicable
Teachers	Shaku Joseph Jarman
Opening Times	Daily—see program of events
Residents	None
Festivals	None
Facilities	Dojo
Accommodation	Visitors welcome for any donation
Food	None
Booking	Not necessary
Fees	Aikido $55 per month
Expected Behavior	5 precepts, no smoking
How to Get There	From Manhattan, take F train to Bergen St. exit. Turn right, walk 2 blocks.

"Some people," said Buddha, the master, "have accused me of uttering these words: When one attains the release called the Beautiful, and abides therein, at such a time he considers the whole universe as ugly.
But I never said these words. This is what I do say:
When one attains the release called the Beautiful, at such a time he knows in truth what Beauty is."

Samyuta and Digha Nikaya

Chakrasambara Buddhist Center (Tibetan–Gelug)
Affiliation: New Kadampa Tradition
361 17th Street
Brooklyn, NY 11215
Tel: (718) 788–4749
E-mail: chakra@advn.com

Apartment in Park Slope, Brooklyn. Class attendance between twenty and thirty. Established 1994. Daily meditation schedule. Weekly puja. Initiations/empowerments about three times a year. General classes on Buddhist thought and practice. Foundation program more in-depth study of Buddha's sutra teachings. Day and weekend courses. Monthly day, weekend, week, or longer retreat on various Buddhist practices/meditations.

Founder/Guru	Ven. Geshe Kelsang Gyatso Rinpoche
Teachers	Resident: Kadam Morten Clausen
Opening Times	Call for details
Residents	4 monastics, 4 laity
Festivals	Contact center
Facilities	Meditation room with shrine, library
Accommodation	Negotiable
Food	None
Booking	None
Fees	$10/class; courses/retreats vary
Expected Behavior	No smoking
How to Get There	Contact center

Buddhist Association of the United States (Theravada, Mahayana, and Tibetan)
Rd. 13, Route 301
Carmel, NY 10512
Tel: (914) 225–6470, (914) 225–6117, (914) 225–1819
Fax: (914) 225–0447
E-mail: bausny@aol.com

Name of the organization which operates **Chuang Yen Monastery** and **Temple of Enlightenment** (see separate entries) on the same site.

Chuang Yen Monastery (Theravada, Mahayana, and Tibetan)
Affiliation: Buddhist Association of the United States, New York
Rd. 13, Route 301
Carmel, NY 10512

Tel: (914) 225–1819, (914) 225–6117, (914) 225–0063, (914) 225–0084, (914) 228–4645, and (914) 225–6740
Fax: (914) 225–0447, (914) 225–6117, and (914) 225–6740
E-mail: bausny@aol.com

Chinese Tang Dynasty–style buildings built in woods on a hill. Facilities include Hall of Ten Thousand Buddhas; Kuan Yin Hall used for special ceremonies and events; dining hall also used as lecture and meeting hall; One Thousand Lotus Memorial Terrace with niches to hold cremated remains of the deceased, and the Tai-Hsu Hall. Functions as educational Dharma center in three main Buddhist traditions. Founded 1964, construction began 1979.

Great Buddha Hall contains the largest enclosed statue of the Buddha in the world and formally dedicated by the Dalai Lama in May 1997. "The ceremony, which will start on May 24 and continue through May 27, will include the Dedication of the Great Buddha Hall by the Dalai Lama, a World Peace Ceremony, performances by Chinese, Korean, Japanese, Thai, and Tibetan Buddhist groups, and many other ceremonies. Attendance is estimated at four thousand five hundred to five thousand people."

Resident monks are Mahayana, but organization invites teachers, practitioners, scholars, etc. from all main Buddhist traditions for classes, summer camps, meditation retreats, etc. Seven-day Ch'an retreats, seven-day chanting retreats, three-month winter retreat, seven-day Pure Land retreat, eleven one-day services, etc. Summer camp for beginners, retreats for practitioners.

Bimonthly magazine in Chinese sent to members and other Buddhist groups.

Founder/Guru	Rev. Shien-Min Shih
Teachers	See above
Opening Times	Contact center
Residents	5–10 monastics
Festivals	Contact center
Facilities	See above
Accommodation	For around 200
Food	Vegetarian lunch $5 on weekend for visitors or regular participants. Also food on retreats.
Booking	Contact center
Fees	Contact center
Expected Behavior	Contact center
How to Get There	From New York City: Take I-78 Major Deegan Expressway North, turn onto Sprain Brook Parkway. Take Exit 5 Route 100 (Central Avenue) North. Stay left until the second traffic light. Take Sprain Brook Parkway North, which continues onto Taconic Parkway North, take the Route 301 East exit (toward Carmel). The Monastery is approximately 1.7 miles on the left side of the road.

Institute for Advanced Studies of World Religions (All religions)
Associated with Buddhist Association of the United States, New York
Rd. 13, Route 301
Carmel, NY 10512
Tel: (914) 225–1445
Fax: (914) 225–1985
E-mail: iaswr@aol.com

Purpose is to provide information and services to assist in the teaching, study, and practice of religious ways of life. Maintains research library, publishes bibliographies, monographs, and translations of Asian religious texts. Will produce microfiche copies of scarce or requested materials at nominal charge. Encourages exchange of information and views among those involved in religious studies. Extensive library of seventy thousand books with materials in thirty-two Asian and eleven other languages, the bulk of which are Buddhist reference books including sutras in Chinese, Tibetan, Pali, and other languages. Large reading room. Information Services Department has files on planned or ongoing research and published works on Asian religious thought and practices, especially Buddhism. Files on Asian religious organizations and related data. Around a hundred visitors a week and more on special occasions. Founded 1972 by Dr. Chia Theng Shen; based at State University of New York at Stony Brook until 1989, when moved to current premises.

Open 9:00 am–5:00 pm weekdays; 2:00–5:00 pm Saturdays.

Vajiradhammapadip Temple (Theravada–Thai)
110 Rustic Road
Centereach, NY 11720-4070
Tel: (516) 471–8006
Fax: (516) 588–2482

On 4.98 acres of countryside approximately seventy miles from New York City—about one-hour drive. All festivals are held at this location. Maximum occupancy two thousand. See also **Vajiradhammapadip Temple** at Mount Vernon, NY.

Theravada meditation techniques taught every evening for newcomers and advanced students. Buddhist Sunday School: Thai language, Buddhist religion, customs and traditions. $25. Sundays September to July. Thai Classical Musical instruments: one-to-one teaching at $10 per one-hour lesson. September to July, Wednesdays to Sundays. Thai Classical Dance: September–July, free. Summer School: five days a week intensive study of Thai language, Buddhist religion, customs and traditions. $250. August to September. *Dhammapadip* journal published usually monthly, sometimes bimonthly.

Founder/Guru   Abbot: Ven. Phra Rajkittivedi

Teachers	See abbot above
Opening Times	Always open
Residents	11 monks, 2 laity
Festivals	New Year Day, Magha Puja Day, Sonkran Day, Visakha Puja Day, Asalha Puja Day, Khao Phansa (Buddhist rain retreat), Sarada Ceremony, Ok Pansa, Thot Kathin
Facilities	Shrine room, auditorium, library, study room, and meditation room
Accommodation	Free, but limited; phone in advance
Food	Whole food
Booking	Not applicable
Fees	See above
Expected Behavior	5 precepts, no smoking
How to Get There	Contact center

North Fork Sitting Group (Zen–Soto)
Affiliation: Sagaponack Zendo, New York
c/o George Kryzminski
P O Box 786
Cutchogue, NY 11935
Tel & Fax: (516) 734–7656

Affiliate of **Sagaponack Zendo,** New York (see separate entry).

Buffalo Forming Dharma Study Group (Tibetan–Kagyu/Nyingma)
Affiliation: Shambhala International
c/o Clifton J. Jackson III
1002 Charlesgate Circle
East Amherst, NY 14051
Tel: (716) 882–8271, work (716) 645–2765 x 1293
E-mail: cjackson@acsu.buffalo.edu

See International headquarters, **Shambhala Center,** Halifax, Nova Scotia, Canada.

Karuna Tendai Dharma Center (Tendai)
Autonomous affiliate of Japanese Tendai with direct lineage from Shoshin Ichishima
1525 Route 295
East Chatham, NY 12060
Tel & Fax: (518) 392–7963
E-mail: tendai1@aol.com

Japanese village–style temple in rural area. On former Shaker farmstead with thirty acres of wooded hills and pastures, surrounded by additional two hundred acres. Main house is 1820s Shaker farmhouse. Two barns, one converted to zendo with plans for hondo, and other buildings. Resident community of two–five; nonresident sangha of more than thirty. Founders are members of the Tamonin and Senzoji Temple communities in Japan. Monshin is Dharma son of Ichishima Shoshin. Couple trained for six years and returned to U.S. in 1994 to found Tendai temple here as "similar in feel to sacred mountain areas of Asia." Open to practices of all traditions and resource for Buddhists and non-Buddhists. "This Center is intended to operate as a small village Tendai temple, such as our temple in Japan. We do not attempt to be a monastery or convent, nor do we intend to be a large-scale program center. We emphasize the practices and teachings of Tien T'ai and Tendai Buddhism, which include viewing the three vehicles as one. Tendai is a Vajrayana school, as well as the root school of almost all modern Japanese traditions…. [Prefer participants to be integrated in larger community.] Children are welcome to participate with their parents. Additionally, we feel that North American Buddhism has matured to the point where it is possible for Buddhist teachings and practice to be a part of the larger community life."

Meditation service Wednesdays 6:30–9:30 pm with Dharma talk and pot-luck dinner—meditations include shikan (Shamatha and Vipashyana), moonlight, mandala Dharani, and mindfulness. Order of Interbeing meditations (based on Thich Nhat Hanh's 14 precepts) twice monthly. Meditation instruction provided, more advanced techniques provided on individual basis. Classes and lectures on Buddhist practice, philosophy, and lifestyle—range from discussion of primary text, sutras, and shastras, to teachings of specific masters, as well as social, political, and economic contexts of Buddhist development. Classes for all levels of experience. Longer courses on periodic basis to meet need of community and guests on Tendai practices and teachings or others such as mindfulness practices or Tibetan Buddhist meditation. Monthly retreats on mindfulness, training or gyo, and Zenski (combination of meditation and downhill skiing). Occasional newsletter, other materials planned. Also operates **Bodhi Tree Inn** on premises, B&B open to public.

Founder/Guru	Monshin (Paul) and Tamami Naamon
Teachers	Resident Paul Monshin Naamon; Shoshin Ichishima, Enshin Saito, and Dr. Barry Clark visit
Opening Times	Daily—residents usually available
Residents	Abbot, Tenzo (managing director), up to 4 monastics and up to 3 laity
Festivals	O-Higan, Obon, New Year, and others according to Buddhist calendar
Facilities	Zendo, library, gathering rooms, hondo, and walking meditation trails
Accommodation	4 guest rooms as doubles or dorm style. $75–100 per room

Food	Vegetarian, macrobiotic, and wholefoods depending on needs and arrangements
Booking	June–August busy; rest of year 1 week in advance. 50% deposit. Always call in advance
Fees	Weekend retreats approximately $150 all inclusive. Zenski $600/week. Classes and courses up to $100 depending on need and materials required
Expected Behavior	No smoking and no shoes in buildings. Appropriate and dignified behavior
How to Get There	Short drive from Taconic Parkway, Adirondack Northway, Massachusets Turnpike and New York State Thruway. Call or write for specific directions.

Peaceful Dwelling Project, Inc. (Zen–Soto)
2 Harbourview Drive (P O Box 3159)
East Hampton, NY 11937
Tel & Fax: (516) 324–3736
E-mail: peacefuldwell@hamptons.com

Small meditation room in light and airy house with garden with two ponds and many sitting areas, located near the ocean. Founded 1995 to offer retreats for people with chronic or life-threatening illness and for professional caregivers—most retreats are done on other premises. "We specialize in bringing Buddhist meditation practice to people of all faiths, especially those who are ill and those caring for them."

Open meditation 6:30–8:00 pm Tuesdays. Meditation for those who are ill 6:00–7:00 pm Thursdays. Women's meditation and discussion 4:00–5:30 pm last Sunday of month. Meditation 8:00–9:00 am Sundays. *Metta* (loving-kindness) 6:00–7:30 pm Mondays. Meditation instruction for those who are HIV+ 6:00–7:00 pm Thursdays. Monthly morning of mindfulness 8:00 am–noon Sundays. Courses about using meditation for emotional, spiritual, and physical healing for patients, professional caregivers, and clergy from other traditions. Offer workshops of three hours to a full day at any location requested, e.g., Day of Renewal retreats for professional caregivers, meditation workshops teaching several kinds of meditation and visualization for working with stress and pain, feelings of powerlessness and anger, developing compassion without being overwhelmed by grief, etc. Newsletter twice a year. Madeline Ko-i Bastis is a Zen priest and certified hospital chaplain and has worked at various medical centers.

Founder/Guru	Madeline Ko-i Bastis
Teachers	Founder is resident teacher
Opening Times	See program of events
Residents	1 monk
Festivals	Obon
Facilities	Meditation room

Accommodation	None
Food	Vegetarian included in retreat fee
Booking	2 weeks in advance, prepayment in full
Fees	To cover expenses only; donations gratefully accepted, e.g., Day of Renewal $25
Expected Behavior	Not applicable
How to Get There	From New York City, Long Island Expressway to exit 20, Rte. 27 to East Hampton. Bus or train from New York City to East Hampton

Ch'an Meditation Center (Ch'an)
Institute of Chung-Hwa Buddhist Culture
of the Dharma Drum Mountain Foundation
90-56 Corona Avenue
Elmhurst, NY 11373
Tel: (718) 592–6593
Fax: (718) 592–0717
E-mail: DDMBAny@aol.com

Two three-story brick buildings at urban center in metropolitan area of New York. Variety of ranch-style structures at country retreat facility in upstate New York (under construction 1996). Over two hundred visitors a week. Established 1978 primarily for Western students; since has become a place welcoming all, regardless of background, age, or ethnic origin. "The Center's founder and guru is the only Ven. Ch'an Master who teaches in the West. He travels between New York and Taipei twice a year to be Abbott of monasteries on both sides of the Pacific.... The Ch'an methods he teaches are easy to understand, traditional, yet flexible."

Offer evening sitting session weekly, all-day sitting Saturdays, Sunday morning sitting session, recitation group, chanting of Amitabha Buddha's name weekly. Repentance practice, chanting Buddha's name and repentance monthly, beginners' meditation class monthly. Introductory Ch'an meditation class weekly by appointment only, Sunday lecture on Buddhist sutras or scriptures, group meditation practice and lectures on either Ch'an practice or Ch'an scriptures both weekly. Vegetarian cooking class and Tai chi class twice yearly. Seminars on Buddhist studies conducted by visiting professors twice yearly. Ch'an meditation retreats: one-, two-, and three-day retreats monthly on an alternating basis; seven-day intensive four times a year. Monthly *Ch'an Newsletter*. Quarterly *Ch'an Magazine*. List of English publications by Ven. Master Sheng-yen.

Founder/Guru	Ven. Master Dr. Sheng-yen
Teachers	Resident: Ven. Guo-yuan, Ven. Guo-cho, Ven. Guo-gu and Stuart Lachs. Professors of Buddhist studies visit from various U.S. universities.

Opening Times	7 days a week
Residents	5 monastics, 1 laity
Festivals	Shakyamuni Buddha's Birthday and Lunar New Year Celebration
Facilities	Buddha Hall, library, meditation room, and retreat sleeping quarters
Accommodation	None
Food	Vegetarian included in retreat fees; Sunday lunch $3 suggested donation
Booking	For 7-day retreat, 3 months in advance; everything else at least 1 week in advance; fees to be paid in advance
Fees	Open lectures and most sitting sessions free of charge; classes and courses average $8–10/2-hour session; 1-day retreat $25 (9:00 am–8:00 pm including lunch and dinner)
Expected Behavior	On grounds of center: strictly vegetarian, no smoking, no drinking, no exchange of interest between members of opposite sexes, and strictly silent during retreats
How to Get There	Bus or subway from within New York City area.

Tzu Chi Foundation New York Branch
Affiliation: Buddhist Compassion Relief Tzu Chi Foundation, California
36-09 Main Street, #10B
Flushing, NY 11354
Tel: (718) 460–4590
Fax: (718) 460–2068
E-mail: tzuchiny@aol.com

Contact center for details.

Ithaca Dharma Study Group (Tibetan–Kagyu/Nyingma)
Affiliation: Shambhala International
Andrew Cove, Coordinator
P O Box 4912
Ithaca, NY 14852-4912
Tel: (607) 273–0837 Andrew

See International headquarters, **Shambhala Center,** Halifax, Nova Scotia, Canada.

White Cliff Sangha (Zen–Soto)
Affiliation: White Plum Sangha
Stefano Mui Barragato, Sensei
250 Grande Terrace
Kerhonkson, NY 12446
Tel: (914) 626–7374
E-mail: mui@pop.mhv.nrt

Lay community of six–eight members. Over six years in practice, Jukai and Tokudo train-ing. Sunday zazen and Wednesday evening koan study. One-day or weekend retreats when possible. Newcomers are welcome on Sundays especially, but Wednesdays also.

Gang Jong Namyal (Tibetan)
Box 169
Lew Beach,
Lew Beach, NY 12758
Contact center for details.

International Dai Bosatsu Zendo Kongo-ji (Zen–Rinzai)
HCR1 Box 171
Livingston Manor, NY 12758
Tel: (914) 439–4566
Fax: (914) 439–3119
E-mail: zen@daibosatsu.org
Web site: http://www.daibosatsu.org

Traditional Japanese Zen Buddhist monastery located in the Catskill Mountains—four-teen hundred acres surrounded by forest preserve. Temple and guest lodge are beside Beecher Lake, the highest lake in the Catskills. Two cottages for private retreats. Near hiking trails and the Beaverkill River. Between three hundred and five hundred attend retreats. Official opening 1996.

"Definitely the most traditionally Japanese of any Zen center in America, i.e., architecture, teaching style, way of life, art. Probably the only Zen center in America to have an active exchange with a Japanese temple with groups of monks visiting and par-ticipating in sesshins regularly." Marcia Kelly, author of *Sanctuaries*, said, "This is the most dramatic setting of any monastery I have visited."

Zazen and samu daily. Traditional Rinzai Zen training: two three-month training periods a year ($2500 for three months including room, board, and three sesshins); seven day sesshins six times a year ($500); five-day sesshin once a year ($375); two weekend sesshins per year ($225). Introduction to Zen weekends throughout the year ($150). Guests welcome for the night or longer stays. If they participate in the zazen and work schedule $50 per night; if not participating $75. Guest house $85 per night including meals. Groups of fifteen or more $65 per night per person. Guest season: February–beginning of December.

Founder/Guru	Eido Tai Shimano Roshi (also Abbot)
Teachers	Abbot; Spiritual Founders Soen Nakagawa Roshi and Nyogen Sensaki; General manager/senior student Jiro-san Fernando Afable
Opening Times	Contact center
Residents	15–25 ordained monks, nuns, and laypersons
Festivals	O-Bon
Facilities	Zendo, Dharma hall, dining hall, library, 20 guest rooms, guest lodge (sleeps 17), 2 retreat cottages
Accommodation	See above
Food	Ovolacto-vegetarian. Meals with residents formally in silence
Booking	Contact center
Fees	See above
Expected Behavior	Contact center
How to Get There	3 hours north of New York City via 87 or Palisades Parkway to Rte. 17 West. Exit 96/Livingston Manor or Shortline Bus Co. from Port Authority in Manhattan. Contact center for more detailed instructions.

Zen Mountain Monastery (Zen–Soto/Rinzai)
Main center of Mountains and Rivers Order
P O Box 197
South Plank Road
Mount Tremper, NY 12457
Tel: (914) 688–2228
Fax: (914) 688–2415
E-mail: dharmacom@mhv.net
Web site: http://www1.mhv.net/~dharmacom

Two hundred and thirty-five acres in the southern bowl of Tremper Mountain, bordered by the Beaverkill and Esopus streams. Designated as a nature sanctuary by board of directors. Main building large bluestone and wooden in Scandinavian Arts and Crafts style—buildings designated a state and national historic landmark 1994. Originally a Catholic retreat center in 1920s and later Lutheran summer camp. Purchased 1981 by ZMM. Three hundred formal nonresidential students; about four thousand people per year attend retreats or services. "Rather than ... increased secularization of practice and training, Roshi Daido Loori has chosen to preserve the rich transcultural religious heritage of Buddhism, emphasizing the subtle interplay of lay and monastic practice...."

Wide variety of programs and retreats for newcomers and more experienced practitioners. One-month to one-year residential trainings. Eight Gate training: Zen meditation, face-to-face teaching, ethical and moral teachings, liturgy, work practice, body practice, academic, and art practice. Annually 12 sesshins and two nine-day training intensives. Introduction to Zen retreat; Zen arts, environmental, and academic retreats.

Social action programs include statewide prison practice program and national prison practice support program, AIDS practice group, Green Dragon Society (environmental action group), and Annual Community Dinner.

Dharma Communications is their educational not-for-profit corporation dedicated to making the Dharma, particularly Zen, available to everyone. Publish quarterly *Mountain Record, The Practitioner's Journal,* and *The Dharma Communications Catalog,* which offers video- and audiotapes, books, art practice sets, Buddha figures, sitting and altar supplies. Extensive on-line services: *Cybermonk* (available at E-mail: address above) on-line senior student to answer questions on Zen practice and World Wide Web page (see above). Dharma Communications, P O Box 156, Mount Tremper, NY 12457; Tel: (914) 688–7993; Fax: (914) 688–7995.

Founder/Guru	Roshi John Daido Loori
Teachers	Roshi John Daido Loori, Sensei Bonnie Myotai Treace, and Dharma Teacher Geoffrey Shugen Arnold
Opening Times	Year-round
Residents	20–30 monastics and laity
Festivals	Contact center
Facilities	Zendo, Buddha hall, library, dining room/meeting hall, kitchen
Accommodation	Dormitory-style with semi-private and private room; gender segregated
Food	Vegetarian—cost included in cost of retreats and trainings
Booking	1 month in advance, $50 deposit
Fees	Weekend retreats $175–225; 7-day sesshin $250; residential training by application only at $575 per month
Expected Behavior	Follow the monastic code and schedule and be respectful and in harmony with the sangha
How to Get There	By bus from Port Authority Bus Terminal in New York City or from Boston. For instructions by car, contact the center.

Vajiradhammapadip Temple (Theravada–Thai)
75 California Road
Mount Vernon, NY 10552-1401
Tel: (914) 699–5778
Fax: (914) 667–1623

Private house in residential area approximately thirty minutes from New York City with maximum occupancy of two hundred and fifty. See also their main temple, **Vajiradhammapadip Temple** at Centereach, New York 11720-4070. Started 1965. Relocated here from West Bronx 1983.

Theravada meditation techniques taught every evening for newcomers and advanced students. Thai Classical Musical instruments: one-to-one teaching at $10 for one-hour lesson. September to July, Wednesday to Sunday. Summer School: five days a week intensive study of Thai language, Buddhist religion, customs and traditions. $250. August to September. *Dhammapadip* journal published usually monthly, sometimes bi-monthly.

Founder/Guru	Abbot: Ven. Phra Rajkittivedi
Teachers	See Abbot above
Opening Times	Always open
Residents	11 monks, 2 laity
Festivals	New Year Day, Magha Puja Day, Sonkran Day, Visakha Puja Day, Asalha Puja Day, Khao Phansa (Buddhist rain retreat), Sarada Ceremony, Ok Pansa, Thot Kathin
Facilities	Shrine room, auditorium, library, study room, and meditation room
Accommodation	Free, but limited; phone in advance
Food	Whole food
Booking	Not applicable
Fees	See above
Expected Behavior	5 precepts, no smoking
How to Get There	Contact center

American-Sri Lanka Buddhist Association Inc
(New York Buddhist Vihara) (Theravada–Sri Lankan)
84-32 124th Street
Kew Gardens
New York, NY 11415
Tel & Fax: (718) 849–2637

Sri Lankan Buddhist temple in a three-story row house in Queens. Association started 1980 and the Vihara began 1981 when the current Abbot was invited from the London Buddhist Vihara. Current building purchased 1986. A new building is under construction in Sri Lankan architectural style on a quarter acre in Queens which will be used for weekend meditation classes, retreats, public talks, etc. "All are welcome, open to everyone who would like to talk to us and seek for the Dhamma!"

Meditation class Wednesday evenings, daily morning and evening chanting, and meditation by monks in which the public can participate. Dhamma class for everyone including children Sundays. Theravada tradition, Samatha, and Vipassana meditation taught. Dana Sila and Bhavana practice offered. Sinhala and Pali classes. Retreats will be offered in the new building; the current one is too small and has no accommodation facilities.

Abbot also teaches meditation and Zen once a week for two hours at the New School for Social Research in Manhattan. Monks teach Sunday Dhamma classes fortnightly in New Jersey and in Staten Island and will accept invitations to talk from other organizations. Annual Vesak celebration according to Theravada tradition in the Vihara and also a public meeting and procession in the city. In 1995, over two thousand Buddhists and friends participated in the procession. The Federation of Korean Buddhist Temples also takes a major part in the Lotus Lantern Parade. **Dhamma Book Service** distributes Dhamma literature. Donations for shipping and postage thankfully accepted.

Founder/Guru	Ven. Kurunegoa Piyatissa—Maha Thero and Ven. G. Nanissara Thero
Teachers	6 resident monks and visiting monks
Opening Times	9:00 am–9:00 pm
Residents	6 monks
Festivals	New Year, Vesak, Posan, Esala, Sanghamitta Day, etc. Full moon days usually
Facilities	Shrine room, library, and monks' living quarters
Accommodation	None
Food	Nonvegetarian and vegetarian food is given at breakfast and lunch for no charge according to Buddhist custom
Booking	None
Fees	No fees
Expected Behavior	No smoking or alcohol. 5 precepts or higher appreciated.
How to Get There	From Kennedy airport, Vanwyck Station or Union Turnpike, take Q10 bus to Metropolitan Avenue (124th St). From Jamaica, Q54 bus to 124th St. From Brooklyn J train or Q56 bus. From Bronx, Q44 and change to Q54 at Sutphin Blvd. By car, take Vanwyck Expressway, exit 6 to Hillside Ave. and turn right to 124th St.

Aro Gar (Tibetan–Nyingma–Aro gTér)
Affiliation: Sang-ngak-cho-dzong of Great Britain
P O Box 247
Chelsea Station
New York, NY 10113-0247
Tel: (212) 439–4780; California (510) 865–1394

Community of twenty in the USA/Canada. Sang-ngak-cho-dzong is the name given by H.H. Dudjom Rinpoche to inspire the establishment of a Ngak-'phang sangha in the

West. Starting with a few people in Wales who asked Ngakpa Chogyam Rinpoche for teachings, it has grown into an international organization with sanghas in Britain, Europe, and North America. The USA/Canadian sangha is called Aro Gar.

Meet weekly for meditation in the homes of practitioners in both New York City and San Francisco—open to public. Ngakpa Chogyam Rinpoche and Khandro Dechen visit New York City and San Francisco twice yearly. At these times, offer evening, all-day, and weekend trainings. Weekend retreats available to public semi-annually.

Publish quarterly magazine, *Vision*, and yearly journal, *Hidden Word*. Affiliated with **Aro Books**, a publishing company.

Founder/Guru	H.H. Dudjom Rinpoche
Teachers	See above
Opening Times	New York City: Tuesday evenings; California: Wednesday evenings
Residents	None
Festivals	None
Facilities	None
Accommodation	None
Food	None
Booking	Call or write for teaching and retreat schedules
Fees	None
Expected Behavior	No smoking, 5 precepts
How to Get There	Contact center

The Asian Classics Institute (Tibetan–Gelug)
Affiliation: Mahayana Sutra and Tantra Center (MSTC), New Jersey
P O Box 20373
New York, NY 10009
Tel: (212) 475–7752

Classroom in Manhattan with class sizes from ten to a hundred. Primarily a teaching center. Offers a wide range of programs, including meditation instruction; drop-in lectures for the general public; long-term program of study for training Buddhist teachers and Tibetan translators; Tibetan language classes; extensive home study correspondence course; Buddhist monastery and nunnery for ordained Westerners (Diamond Abbey); and several international Buddhist research and translation projects. Meditation retreats rarely. Tsechu and Sojong twice per month.

Asian Classics Input Project collects, preserves, and digitally propagates ancient, endangered texts. It focuses on important classical Asian literature (preliminary goal of preserving the Kangyur and Tengyur collections which were preeminent in Asian philosophical thought from 500 BCE onward). The material is published and distributed in digital form—available on the Internet, more than ten thousand diskettes and

CD-ROMS, which have been sent to scholars, individuals, and institutions in fifty countries worldwide free of charge.

Diamond Abbey's monks and nuns live in New York City at separate locations. Especially active in social work and the translation and study of literature covering vinaya.

Founder/Guru	Geshe Michael Roach under spiritual direction of Khen Rinpoche Geshe Lobsang Tharchin
Teachers	Resident Director: Geshe Michael Roach
Opening Times	See program of events
Residents	10 monks and nuns
Festivals	Contact center
Facilities	Classroom and shrine room
Accommodation	None
Food	None
Booking	Not necessary
Fees	Voluntary donation
Expected Behavior	Not applicable
How to Get There	Contact center

The Buddhist Council of New York (Interdenominational)
c/o Ven. Kurunegoda Piyatissa
New York Buddhist Vihara
84-32 124th Street
Kew Gardens
New York, NY 11415-3303
Tel: (718) 849–2637 and (212) 781–1947
Fax: (212) 795–8146
E-mail: DimitriB@aol.com

Has no fixed premises but holds a meeting at least once a month at various Buddhist temples. Founded 1984 by Ven. Kurunegoda Piyatissa (New York Buddhist Vihara), Ven. Jomyo Tanaka (Mandala Center), and Mr Randolph Sunday (New York Dharmadhatu). Only interdenominational Buddhist organization in New York City which is truly ecumenical, open to all Theravada, Mahayana, and Vajrayana groups.

Main activities are an annual all-Buddhist Vesak Celebration (see **New York Buddhist Vihara** for more details) and monthly lectures at Columbia University. Can provide a list of Buddhist groups in the Greater New York area.

Chogye International Zen Center of New York (Zen)
Affiliation: Kwan Um School of Zen

400 E 14th Street, #2D
New York, NY 10009
Tel: (212) 353–0461

Daily Zen practice. Contact center for details.

Community of Mindfulness/NY Metro (Zen–Vietnamese)
Affiliation: Community of Mindful Living
P O Box 61
Planetarium Station
New York, NY 10024
Tel: (212) 501–2652 (information line)

Practitioners in the New York metropolitan area inspired by the teachings of Thich Nhat Hanh; resident teacher, Lyn Fine, ordained as Dharmacarya by him 1994.

Weekly sitting groups and study groups held in people's homes in Manhattan, Brooklyn, Queens, Long Island, New Jersey, and upstate New York. "Affinity" groups at time of writing were: being with children, being with illness and dying, and touching our roots (Buddhist-Jewish, Buddhist-Christian exchange). Monthly days of mindfulness. Guest teachers from other Buddhist traditions. Network with Buddhist Peace Fellowship and other local Buddhist groups. Monthly newsletter.

First Zen Institute of America (Zen)
113 East 30th Street
New York City, NY 10016
Tel: (212) 686–2520

Lay organization. Founded 1930.

Open to the public every Monday and Wednesday 7:30–9:30 pm for zazen. Weekend sesshin once a month from Saturday 9:00 am until Sunday 5:00 pm. No classes or courses are given. Publishes books and quarterly newsletter, *Zen Notes*.

Founder/Guru	Zen master Sokei-an Sasaki Roshi
Teachers	Contact center
Opening Times	See session times above
Residents	Contact center
Festivals	Contact center
Facilities	Contact center
Accommodation	Contact center
Food	Contact center
Booking	If you plan to come, please call
Fees	None

Expected Behavior   Contact center
How to Get There   Contact center

Horin Buddhist Center of Rissho Kosei-kai in New York (Rissho Kosei-kai)
306 East 38th Street
New York, NY 10016
Tel: (212) 686–2252
Fax: (212) 599–5691
E-mail: mail0082@pop.kdd.net
This center does not offer any Buddhist practice or studies, but is liaison office for the Rissho Kosei-kai, where Masamichi Kamiya represents the organization to the United Nations and promotes interfaith dialogue and cooperation in the USA—one of their main aims.

There are other RKK centers in Hawaii (see separate entry), Los Angeles, San Francisco (see separate entry), and New York.

Reverend Join Inoue (Nichiren Shu)
Affiliate: Nichiren Propagation Center
25 Tudor City Place, # 1006
New York, NY 10017
Tel: (212) 599–1510
Fax: (212) 599–1510

See **Nichiren Propagation Center, Oregon.**

Maitri Dorje (All traditions, with focus on Tibetan and Zen)
c/o Bill and Peter
16J Duane Street (Ph-F)
New York, NY 10013-3332
Tel & Fax: (212) 619–0656
E-mail: potala@juno.com

Members range in experience from no practice to fifteen–twenty years. Fifteen–thirty participants at monthly meetings. Founded 1993 by participants in Gay Pride parades who were senior students of Ven. Chogyam Trunpa Rinpoche. "We offer gays and lesbians a safe haven to explore Buddhism as it relates to themselves. We offer the possibility for them to practice silent meditation together (Shamata/Vipassana) and to learn of and discuss Buddhist practice from gay-friendly, gay and lesbian Buddhist practitioners. We hope to be useful, especially in showing that in Buddhism all beings are truly seen to be equal without discrimination for any reason, including 'lifestyle,' where loving-kindness and compassion for all are emphasized."

Monthly meetings open to all gay and lesbian Buddhists of all traditions held at New York Gay and Lesbian Community Center, 208 W 13th Street, New York, NY (in Greenwich Village). Study group under development at time of writing (1996). Monthly speakers/discussions (with meditation) on various topics related to inter-connection between being gay/lesbian and Buddhist by speakers from all Buddhist traditions. All-day sitting meditation two–three times a year. Usually biannual newsletter.

Founder/Guru	Advisory board members participate in Tibetan, Zen, and Shambhala meditation traditions
Teachers	With the guidance of Rev. Pat Enkio Ohara Roshi
Opening Times	Not applicable
Residents	None
Festivals	Participate as a group under own banner
Facilities	Not applicable
Accommodation	None
Food	None
Booking	Contact center
Fees	$2 for monthly meeting; contributions to cover mailing, retreats, etc. are optional
Expected Behavior	Loving-kindness and compassion
How to Get There	Bus or subway to W 14th Street in Manhattan

New York Buddhist Church (Jodo Shinshu)
331–332 Riverside Drive
New York, NY 10025
Tel: (212) 678–0305
Fax: (212) 662–4502

A historical building in a safe area with a big hall for up to a hundred people, dojo, smaller rooms for meditation. A hundred to a hundred and fifty members. Started in 1938 by Rev. Hozen Seki. The only Jodo Shinshu church in New York City. Statue of Shinran Shonin, which survived the atomic bomb in Hiroshima and was sent here in 1955.

Pure Land, Nembutsu, sutra chanting, walking meditation, and Naikan. Meditation Mondays, yoga Wednesdays, Tai Chi Sundays, and martial arts Mondays to Fridays. Beginners meditation occasionally. Occasional lectures on Buddhism and Shin Buddhism. Seminar and retreats twice a year. Newsletter every month.

Founder/Guru	Hozen Seki
Teachers	Rev. T. Kenjitsu Nakagaki Sensei
Opening Times	9:00 am–5:00 pm and by appointment
Residents	1 minister, 1 assistant minister, and a caretaker
Festivals	Obon, Hanamatsuri, Hoonko, Gotan-E, Higan, Nirvana Day, Bodhi Day, Peace Day

Facilities	Shrine rooms, dojo, multipurpose rooms, and library
Accommodation	None
Food	None
Booking	Not necessary
Fees	$10–30
Expected Behavior	No smoking, to respect the place
How to Get There	Subway #1 or #9, get off at 103rd Station. Bus #5 or #104

New York City Karma Thegsum Choling (Tibetan–Karma Kagyu)
Affiliation: Karma Triyana Dharmachakra, New York
412 West End Avenue, # 5N (Intercom #19)
New York, NY 10024
Tel: (212) 580–9282
E-mail: slrr1@aol.com
Established 1976 by H.H. the Gyalwa Karmapa. Weekday classes, evening practice sessions, and weekend seminars. Series of introductory classes and special events. Individual meditation instruction by appointment.

New York Shambhala Center (Tibetan–Kagyu/Nyingma)
Affiliation: Shambhala International
118 West 22nd Street, 6th Floor
New York, NY 10011
Tel: (212) 675–6544: Dharmadhatu; (212) 675–1231: Shambhala training & Nalanda
Fax: (212) 675–3090
E-mail: emirror@aol.com

See International headquarters, **Shambhala Center,** Halifax, Nova Scotia, Canada.

New York Zendo Shobo-ji (Zen–Rinzai)
223 East 67th Street
New York, NY 10021
Tel: (212) 861–3333
Fax: (212) 628–6968

Three-story renovated carriage house between Second and Third Avenues on the Upper East Side of Manhattan. Sixty full-time lay practitioners. Official opening was in 1968.
    Zazen five days a week for members. Beginners and first-time visitors are welcome for Thursday Public Night 7:00–9:00 pm. Buddhist Studies classes every other week during training periods. Zazen instruction given with two periods of zazen and occasional teisho (Dharma talks) given by the abbot. Occasional lectures, e.g., Zen and Psychology. All-day sittings five times a year. Weekend sesshins five times a year.

Publish *Newsletter of the Zen Studies Society* three times a year. Small store with meditation cushions, incense, books, etc.

Founder/Guru	Eido Tai Shimano Roshi (also Abbot)
Teachers	Eido T. Shimano Roshi; Director Aiho-san Yasuko Shimano
Opening Times	6:30–9:00 pm Wednesdays–Fridays; 1:30–4:00 pm Tuesdays; 9:30 am–noon Saturdays
Residents	None
Festivals	Segaki Festival and New Year's Eve
Facilities	2 zendos, Dharma hall, library, rock garden
Accommodation	Occasional stayover during retreats
Food	Vegetarian during retreats
Booking	For retreats: 2 months ahead, 50% deposit
Fees	Membership $40 monthly; Thursday Public Night $10 suggested contribution; all-day sittings $20; weekend sesshins $110; lower prices for members
Expected Behavior	No smoking, 5 precepts
How to Get There	Lexington Ave. subway, #6. Stop at Hunter College, walk to 67th St. between Second and Third Aves.

Orgyen Ling (Tibetan–Nyingma)
Affiliation: Chagdud Gonpa Foundation
c/o Chris Sarazen
1220 Park Avenue
New York, NY 10128-1708
Tel: (212) 794-2050

Contact center for details.

Padmasambhava Buddhist Center (Tibetan–Nyingma)
Headquarters of Padmasambhava Buddhist Centers worldwide
P O Box 1533
Old Chelsea Station
New York, NY 10011
Tel & Fax: (212) 683–4958

International organization with thirteen centers in the U.S., two in Russia, and two in India, including monastery (Sarnath) and retreat lands. Started in U.S. in 1985. This center in East Catskills Mountains.

Weekly membership meditation sessions. Monthly seminars, weekend empowerments and teachings. Classes in Tibetan Buddhist meditation, philosophy, and monastic training. These include retreats, transmissions and teachings, pujas and practices. Ten-day retreat in summer, all-weekend fall retreat.

Newsletter, *Pema Mandala*, three times a year.

Internet web page, books, tapes, and images available.

For other Padmasambhava Buddhist Centers in the USA, see entries for **Padmasambhava Buddhist Centers** in West Palm Beach, Florida, and Chicago, Illinois, or phone: New York City (212) 683–4958; San Francisco (415) 221–8316; Boulder, Colorado (303) 530–5025; Wilmington, Delaware (302) 655–3364; Orlando, Florida (407) 830-4458; Princetown, New Jersey (609) 924–6863; Maine (207) 923–3131; Whitleyville, Tennessee (615) 678–4462 or Madison, Wisconsin (608) 255–4588.

Founder/Guru	Khenpo Palden Sherab Rinpoche and Khenpo Tsewang Dongyal Rinpoche
Teachers	Resident as founders
Opening Times	Contact center
Residents	3 monastics and 7 laity
Festivals	Lunar on 10th and 25th day
Facilities	Shrine room and library
Accommodation	6 rooms at suggested donation of $15–20/night
Food	Vegetarian
Booking	Deposit 1–2 months in advance
Fees	$75 weekends; $350 10-day retreat
Expected Behavior	No smoking or alcohol
How to Get There	New York City to Rte. 17, get off at Roscoe and take Rte. 206 to Walton. Nine miles outside of Walton, in town of Tompkins.

Rigpa New York (Tibetan–Nyingma)
Affiliation: Rigpa Fellowship
New York, NY
Tel: (212) 831–7214

See **Rigpa National Office,** California, for details.

Soka Gakkai International (SGI-USA) (Nichiren)
New York Area Regional Center
7 East 15th Street
New York, NY 10003-3108
Tel: (212) 727–7715
Fax: (212) 727–7712

See **Soka Gakkai International** National Offices & Center, Santa Monica, California, for more details.

The Tibet Center (Tibetan–Gelug)
359 Broadway, 5th Floor
New York, NY 10013
Tel & Fax: (212) 966–8504

Medium-sized urban center on top floor of a Civil War–period commercial building in Tribeca. Abraham Lincoln sat for the portrait now used on the one-cent coin in a room in this center. In 1979 sponsored address of H.H. the Dalai Lama at Cathedral Church of St. John the Divine—5,000 attended. In 1991 sponsored The Kalachakra Initiation for World Peace in New York City given by H.H. the Dalai Lama—5,000 attended. Study comes mainly from the Lamrim teachings of the Gelugpa school, but also welcome visiting teachers from other Tibetan and non-Tibetan schools to offer the chance for comparative study. Atmosphere relaxed, informal, and friendly. Very international gathering. Founded 1975.

Tuesdays 6:00 pm Medicine Buddha (suitable for newcomers); Thursdays 7:30 pm Green Tara; Saturdays 11:00 am White Tara. Wednesday evening classes in basic Buddhism, a wide range of topics throughout the year. Occasional weekend nonresidential retreats for mantra recitation. Newsletter usually quarterly.

Founder/Guru	Ven. Khyongla Rato Rinpoche
Teachers	Founder is resident lama; many monks and lamas visit
Opening Times	See practice times above
Residents	None
Festivals	Buddha's Birthday, Dalai Lama's Birthday, First Turning of the Wheel, Descent from Heaven of the 33 Gods, Tsongkhapa Day
Facilities	Shrine room (exceptionally beautiful, used in Mandala House in the 1991 Kalachakra Initiation), library
Accommodation	None
Food	Tea, cookies (sometimes fruit and popcorn, etc.) during opening hours
Booking	Not necessary unless otherwise indicated
Fees	Donations welcome. Largest special events have modest suggested donation to cover expenses
Expected Behavior	No smoking in shrine room, normal "church" decorum is appropriate
How to Get There	On Broadway, 4 blocks south of Canal St. or 6 blocks north of City Hall. Subway to Canal Street, then walk to Broadway and Franklin or take the Broadway bus to White St.

Tibet House New York (Tibetan)
241 East 32nd Street
New York, NY 10016
Tel: (212) 213–5592
Fax: (212) 213–6408
E-mail: tibetkb@aol.com

Dedicated to preserving the living culture of Tibet. Work to preserve and present Tibetan art and culture in a Museum Without Walls; acquiring photographic archive and resource library, working with Internet and web sites to distribute information on Tibet and activities to preserve its culture; "share with the world Tibet's practical systems of spiritual philosophy, science of the mind, nonviolent approach to confrontations, and human development using intercultural dialogues in cooperation with educational, historical, and other cultural institutions."

Activities include ongoing classes in Tibetan language, art, history, medicine, and spiritual sciences taught by local scholars and visiting specialists (including lamas); international exhibitions, conferences, and publications. Quarterly newsletter, *The Tibet House Drum.*

The True Buddha Diamond Temple (Chinese–True Buddha School)
105 Washington Street
New York, NY 10006
Tel: (212) 732–5264
Fax: (212) 732–8478

Contact center for details.

Unitarian Universalist Buddhist Fellowship (New York Metro Chapter) (Non-creedal)
c/o Yvonne Groseil
New York, NY 10128
Tel: (212) 427–1696
E-mail: dorjay@aol.com

Unitarian Universalism is a non-creedal religious tradition, with American roots going back through Emerson and the Transcendentalists, emphasizing freedom of individual religious inquiry, the use of reason in religion, and tolerance of religious diversity. There is growing interest among this group in Buddhism. A continental Unitarian Universalist Buddhist Fellowship (UUBF) has been formed, and workshops sponsored by the UUBF have been presented at several recent annual General Assemblies of the

Unitarian Universalist Association. The New York UU Buddhist Fellowship is an affiliate of the UUBF and welcomes members and non-members of the UU who are interested in Buddhism's relevance to contemporary American religious and social concerns.

Meet irregularly at various local UU churches' meeting rooms. Founded 1987 as a study group, one of several UU groups interested in Buddhism. Provide an opportunity for people with a wide variety of interest and experience in Buddhism to come together for discussion, debate, and exchange information on books, teachers, etc. Offer information on the wealth of Buddhist classes, lectures, and centers in New York City. Function as a discussion group, visiting other centers occasionally, visiting museums or cultural events with a Buddhist perspective (such as Asia Society or Metropolitan Museum). Invite guest speakers or visiting scholars from various Buddhist groups. All events suitable for newcomers. Publish *The Wheel*, now semi-annual, will be quarterly in 1997.

Founder/Guru	Henry Wiemhoff
Teachers	Invited speakers
Opening Times	Contact them for program of events
Residents	None
Festivals	Vesak with New York Buddhist Council
Facilities	None
Accommodation	None
Food	None
Booking	None
Fees	None
Expected Behavior	Not applicable
How to Get There	Not applicable

Village Zendo (Zen–Soto)
Affiliation: White Plum Lineage
15 Washington Place, #4E
New York, NY 10003
Tel: (212) 674–0832
Fax: (212) 998–1898
E-mail: ohara@is.nyu.edu
Web site: http://westnet.com/~sarahd/zendo

Small flat in Greenwich Village with dedicated temple space and about forty visitors a week. Started 1986 as small sitting group, now grown to small temple. "We are concerned with urban practice. How do we live a balanced life in the midst of our space and time? We specialize in AIDS care and awareness."

Zazen 6:15–8:30 pm Mondays–Thursdays; Tuesday, Wednesday, and Friday 7:30–8:30 am. Study groups every Friday night on selected sutras. Introductory class as needed. Jukai classes monthly. Monthly one-day meditation retreats. Ad hoc weddings, memorials, etc. Quarterly newsletter

Founder/Guru	Bernard Tetsugen Glassman, Roshi
Teachers	Resident: Enkyo O'Hara
Opening Times	See zazen times above
Residents	1 monk, 1 laity
Festivals	None
Facilities	Meditation room
Accommodation	None
Food	Vegetarian at retreats
Booking	Not applicable
Fees	$3 per sitting, $20/day retreats
Expected Behavior	As appropriate
How to Get There	Downtown New York City

Zen Center of New York (Zen–Soto/Rinzai)
119 West 23rd Street, Room 1009
New York, NY 10011
Tel: (212) 642–1591
E-mail: dharmacom@mhv.net
Web site: http://www1.mhv.net/~dharmacom/nyc_fire.htm

Urban nonresidential center on the tenth floor in lower midtown Manhattan. Established in 1984. Current full-time teacher resident since 1995.

Meditation sessions Sunday and weekday mornings. Beginning instruction Wednesday evening and Sunday morning. Ango (three-month) and Saturday retreats twice a year. Introduction to Zen quarterly. Quarterly newsletter, *Fire Lotus*.

Founder/Guru	Roshi John Daido Loori
Teachers	Resident: Sensei Bonnie Myotai Treace
Opening Times	Contact center
Residents	None
Festivals	Contact center
Facilities	Zendo, office, kitchen
Accommodation	None
Food	None
Booking	Newcomers should call zendo answering service on (212) 642–1591
Fees	Open donation for visitors
Expected Behavior	Not applicable
How to Get There	On West 23rd Street between 6th and 7th Avenue.

Rochester Zen Center (Zen)
7 Arnold Park
Rochester, NY 14607
Tel: (716) 473–9180
Fax: (716) 473–6846

Zen Buddhist training center in two old houses, joined together, in an inner-city neighborhood. The two-acre property includes a landscaped garden and Buddha hall which is a remodeled carriage house. Center was donated a hundred and thirty five acre country estate (Chapin Mill) in June 1996, which will be developed as a rural retreat center. One of the longest-established Zen centers in the U.S. and one of the few that provides a full residential training program. Offers authentic Zen training in a Western context. Established 1966.

No formal classes offered as the emphasis is on zazen and work practice. Buddhist teachings daily. Dokusan offered (private instruction with teachers or senior students). Discussion groups on Buddhist themes. Regular all-day workshops to give a practical and thorough introduction to Zen. Two-, four-, and seven-day sesshins throughout the year for those who have done a workshop at the center or have some experience. Basic practice is zazen, which may take the form of breath practice, koan work, or shitantaza. Chanting and prostrations are part of daily life. Publish *Zen Bow* four times a year and *Zen Arrow* every few months.

Founder/Guru	Roshi Philip Kapleau
Teachers	Resident: Sensei Bodhin Kjolhede (spiritual director); Sensei Sanya Kjolhede and Sensi David Sachter
Opening Times	Wednesdays and Saturdays 8:00 am–12:30 pm; Sundays closed; rest of the week 8:00 am–3:30 pm
Residents	3 ordained priests and a lay staff of 15–20
Festivals	New Year; Vesak, Kannon Day, Bodhidharma Day, Thanksgiving—Jukai
Facilities	Zendo, library, Kannon room, Buddha hall
Accommodation	For those attending workshops—$15 per night
Food	Vegetarian lunch during workshops
Booking	Write or phone for introductory package, which includes a workshop registration form and dates for forthcoming workshops
Fees	Workshops $60, $45 students
Expected Behavior	In accordance with Buddhist environment. Training guidelines are provided for retreatants
How to Get There	15 minutes from Rochester airport and 5 from the station. Arnold Park is a small street running between East Ave. and Park Ave., on the east side of the city

Drikung Kagyu Enlightenment Institute (Tibetan–Drikung Kaygyu, also practice Nyingma)
P O Box 25577
Rochester, NY 14625
Tel: (716) 454–3844
Fax: (716) 442–7630
E-mail: info@dkei.com or Fhoward861@aol.com
Web site: http://www22.rpa.net/~tilley/kchakra.html

Founded 1986. Forty supporting members and many more at retreats. "Our center is unusual in the amount of activity it sponsors despite being run by volunteers and not having a lama in residence. Our involvement with the coming Kalachakra is a special blessing."

Regularly scheduled weekly and monthly practices. Free course, Introduction to Buddhism, two hours on six successive Sundays twice a year. Lamas invited for teachings and retreats. Practice Amitabha Buddha, Dudjom Tersar Ngondro, Drikung Kagyu Ngondro, Achi Chogyi Drolma, Phowa, the Vajrasattva of Rigdzin Tsewang Norbu, and monthly tsogs of Guru Rinpoche and Yeshe Tsogyel. Hosting and organizing first Kalachakra to be given by the Nyingma in the U.S. July 1997 in Rochester. Newsletter four times a year. Sell handmade Tibetan carpets, incense, and reproductions of two special thangkas.

> *True Zen means sitting quietly in the right posture. Zen means setting the mind at rest, concentrating intuition and reasoning together. Zen is not some special state, it is our normal condition, silent, peaceful, awake, without agitation.*
>
> Taisen Deshimaru

Empty Hand Zendo (Zen)
The Meeting House
624 Milton Road
Rye, NY 10580
Tel: (914) 921–3327

Held in the Quaker Meeting House, which is an antique chapel (built 1835) in a suburb of New York—"quite small, a bit in need of repair and very simple." Sixty or more participants. "Strong practice—zazen is the main focus. Warm, sensitive community of lay practitioners ranging from ages 14 to 75!"

Meditation 7:30 pm Monday, Wednesdays, and Saturdays; 7:30–9:00 pm Saturday mornings (except on Retreat Days). Introductory evening Wednesdays. Monthly study group offered on various topics of basic Buddhist teaching. Annual class in preparation for Jukai—receiving the Buddhist precepts. Monthly one-day meditation retreats 9:00 am–5:00 pm Saturdays. Two or three weekend sesshins per year at rented conference center.

Founder/Guru	Rev. Susan Ji-on Postal (student of Maurine Myo-on Stuart Roshi of Cambridge Buddhist Association)
Teachers	Resident: as founder; guests from various Zen centers several times a year
Opening Times	See session times above
Residents	None
Festivals	Buddha's Birthday, Hungry Ghosts Ceremony
Facilities	Meditation hall
Accommodation	At homes of sangha members
Food	Vegetarian, whole grain, simple included in retreat fee
Booking	Contact center
Fees	1-day retreat $25, 3-day sesshin $140
Expected Behavior	No smoking, 5 precepts, silence, simple plain clothing, no shorts or tank tops
How to Get There	I-95 to Exit 19 (Playland Parkway). At first light, turn right onto Milton Road, continue past Firehouse to Meeting House on right.

> *What we are today comes from our thoughts of yesterday, and our present thoughts build our life of tomorrow: our life is the creation of our mind.*
>
> The Dhammapada

Sagaponack Zendo (Zen–Soto)
Affiliation: Zen Community of New York
P O Box 392
Bridge Lane
Sagaponack, NY 11962
Tel: (516) 537–0178 or (516) 324–3736

Large renovated house with Zendo that seats twenty-four in a large well-landscaped private property within walking distance of Atlantic Ocean. Four monastics, forty lay members. Sitting geared for lay practitioners. Founded 1984.

Meditation and discussion group 4:30–6:30 pm Mondays. Meditation 7:00–7:40 am

Tuesdays–Fridays. Service followed by meditation 7:30–8:30 am Saturdays. Monthly one-day retreats 6:00 am–5:00 pm.

Founder/Guru	Tetsugen Glassman Roshi
Teachers	Resident: Peter Muryo Matthiessen, Sensei
Opening Times	See session times above
Residents	None
Festivals	None
Facilities	Meditation room
Accommodation	None
Food	Vegetarian included in cost of retreats
Booking	2 weeks in advance
Fees	$25/day for retreats
Expected Behavior	Contact center
How to Get There	From New York City, Long Island Expressway to exit 70; Sunrise Hwy. (Rte. 27) to Montank Hwy. to Bridgehampton. Bus from New York City

Suffolk Institute for Eastern Studies, Inc. (Zen)
330 Moriches Road
St. James, NY 11780
Tel: (516) 584 6085

Primarily an Aikido school renting space from a karate school. "Meditation is taught once each week; primarily training in the Buddhist practice of Mindfulness."

Woodstock Karma Thegsum Choling (Tibetan–Karma Kagyu)
Affiliation: Karma Triyana Dharmachakra, New York
P O Box 645
Shady, NY 12409
Tel: (914) 679–6028
E-mail: dmccarthy@mhv.net

As so close to **Karma Triyana Dharmachakra** (see separate entry), mostly operates within their activities. Also regular informal get-togethers at members' homes.
    Call for more information.

Albany Dharma Study Group (Tibetan–Kagyu/Nyingma)
Affiliation: Shambhala International
Slingerlands, NY 12159

Tel: (518) 439–7618
E-mail: ewrook@aol.com

See International headquarters, **Shambhala Center,** Halifax, Nova Scotia, Canada.

Ithaca Zen Center (Zen)
56 Lieb Road
Spencer, NY 14883
Tel & Fax: (607) 272–0694
Daily sittings and monthly retreats.

Springwater Center for Meditative Inquiry & Retreats (Non-traditional, nonsectarian)
7179 Mill Street
Springwater, NY 14560
Tel: (716) 669–2141
Fax: (716) 669–9573
E-mail: spwtrctr@servtech.com
One very spacious plain building with large windows on two hundred acres of land. Retreat cabin in the woods for solitary retreats or use by families, couples, or friends. Originally called the Genesee Valley Zen Center, land bought and center built 1985 and name changed to Springwater Center. "The atmosphere is very simple, open, spacious. No tradition or meditation practice is imposed. There are no rituals or religious trappings. Very bare-bones approach. People free to do what they want, to explore their own rhythms. Quiet."

About ten silent retreats throughout the year with about thirty-five participants, eight of them led by Toni Packer and with possibility to meet her. Retreats schedules are optional. Visits possible outside of retreat times as guests or volunteers. All events suitable for beginners. Newsletter four times a year.

Founder/Guru	Toni Packer
Teachers	Resident: Toni Packer
Opening Times	Open throughout the year
Residents	About 7 staff
Festivals	No ceremonies
Facilities	Meditation room, exercise room
Accommodation	Shared rooms during retreats. Outside of retreats, single rooms at $16/night non-members. Volunteers pay nothing if they work full-time.
Food	Lacto-vegetarian $7.50 per day
Booking	7-day retreat $335 non-members including board and lodging

Fees	Full fee needed for retreats; outside of retreats, no deposit needed
Expected Behavior	No smoking or intoxicants, being generally considerate of others
How to Get There	Transportation provided from airport, train station or bus depot in Rochester

Syracuse Dharma Study Group (Tibetan–Kagyu/Nyingma)
Affiliation: Shambhala International
Bob Temple, Coordinator
218 Cambridge Street
Syracuse, NY 13210
Tel: (315) 471–1527
See International headquarters, **Shambhala Center,** Halifax, Nova Scotia, Canada.

Zen Center of Syracuse Hoen-ji (Zen–Rinzai)
266 West Seneca Turnpike
Syracuse, NY 13207
Tel: (315) 492–9773
Fax: (315) 478–1253
E-mail: schayat@mailbox.syr.edu

Three-story Federal-style building in city, which was an underground railroad station. Next to a creek with six acres of mostly wooded grounds. Center with forty visitors a week. Started by students of Syracuse University; abbot arrived 1976 and center moved to current site 1996. "Primarily lay center with members incorporating Zen practice into their daily life."

Zen meditation Tuesday 8:30–9:30 pm, Thursdays 6:00–8:00 pm, and morning service with taped talk Sundays 9:00 am–noon. Precepts classes weekly January to May. Dharma study 7:00 pm first Sunday of the month. Introduction to Zen Buddhism once or twice a year. Newcomers should call first. Spring and fall sesshins.

Quarterly newsletter. **Ho-enji Bookstore** is located in the center and sells books, incense, tapes, T-shirts, etc.

Founder/Guru	Nikyu Robert Strickland and Hogen Howard Blair
Teachers	Roko Sherry Chayat, Abbot
Opening Times	See meditation times above
Residents	3 laypeople
Festivals	Buddha's Birthday and Rohatsu
Facilities	Zendo, small library, 2 rooms for workshops
Accommodation	None
Food	None

Booking	Not necessary
Fees	3-day sesshin $75 non-members, $50 members. Introduction to Zen Buddhism $50 regular, $30 member or student.
Expected Behavior	No smoking or drugs, 5 precepts, arrive $1/2$ hour before start of session.
How to Get There	From I-81, north or south, get onto I-481 and take exit 1. Turn right off exit and go to Brighton Ave. Turn left onto W Seneca Turnpike, turn right to get to 266.

Kagyu Thubten Choling (Tibetan–Kagyu)
127 Sheafe Road
Wappingers Falls, NY 12590
Tel: (914) 297–2500
Fax: (914) 297–3843

Large main house for public events; guest house for private retreats. Facilities for three-year retreats. Property overlooks the Hudson River. Community of about fifteen. Founded 1979 by Ven. Lama Norlha, director of Kalu Rinpoche's East Coast Dharma Centers. Began the first three-year retreat in North America—4th in session 1996. "Traditional presentation of Tibetan Buddhism. Possible to follow a graded path from very beginning up through most advanced practices as given in three-year retreat."

Group chanting and meditation twice daily, 6:00 am and 6:00 pm. Morning session features prayers to Buddha Shakyamuni, Tara, and Medicine Buddha. Evening session is Chenrezig and Mahakala. Classes on request in Tibetan language, Torma, and traditional Buddhist musical instruments. Weekend seminars by resident lama on various topics of Tibetan Buddhism. Three-year retreats. Private retreats designed by the individual.

Founder/Guru	Kalu Rinpoche
Teachers	Resident: Ven. Lama Norlha; Khenpo Tsultrim Gyamtso and Tai Situ Rinpoche visit
Opening Times	Contact center
Residents	12 monastics, 3 laity
Festivals	Vajrayogini, Mahakala, Milarepa, Tara. Many fire offerings.
Facilities	Shrine room/meditation room, library
Accommodation	Members: dorm $400/month, $20/day; private room $450/month, $25/day; guest room $550/month, $30/day. Non-members: dorm $550/month, $30/day; private room $650/month, $35/day; guest room $700/month, $40/day.
Food	Vegetarian: breakfast $4, lunch $8, dinner $6
Booking	Please call in advance; interview needed if interested in residency

<table>
<tr><td>Fees</td><td>Varies, e.g., Lama Norlha's seminars $10/session members, $15 non-members</td></tr>
<tr><td>Expected Behavior</td><td>No smoking, drinking, or drugs. No TV, radio, or newspapers. 5 precepts</td></tr>
<tr><td>How to Get There</td><td>From New York City, take Metro North to New Hamburg stop (less than 2 hours). Call for details.</td></tr>
</table>

Kanzeon Zendo (Zen–Rinzai)
Box 80
Paul's Lane
Water Mill, NY 11976
Tel: (516) 537–1163

In the home of a member. Dedicated 1968 by Yasutani Roshi, Soen Roshi, and Eido Roshi. Very long-standing sitting group. Meet once a week. Contact center for more details.

New York Cho Gye Sa (Zen–Korean)
Affiliation: Kwan Um School of Zen
45-18 48th Avenue
Woodside, NY 11377
Tel: (718) 706–1749
Fax: 178 392–3011

Buddhist meditation and bowing practice, koan practice. Three-month meditation retreats.

<table>
<tr><td>Founder/Guru</td><td>Seung Sahn Nim</td></tr>
<tr><td>Teachers</td><td>Abbot: Myo Ji Hab Jang Su Nim</td></tr>
<tr><td>Opening Times</td><td>6:00 am–6:00 pm</td></tr>
<tr><td>Residents</td><td>2 monastics, 1 laity</td></tr>
<tr><td>Festivals</td><td>None</td></tr>
<tr><td>Facilities</td><td>2 Dharma rooms and meditation room</td></tr>
<tr><td>Accommodation</td><td>Small space</td></tr>
<tr><td>Food</td><td>Vegetarian on retreats</td></tr>
<tr><td>Booking</td><td>1 week in advance</td></tr>
<tr><td>Fees</td><td>$25/day</td></tr>
<tr><td>Expected Behavior</td><td>No smoking</td></tr>
<tr><td>How to Get There</td><td>Train to 46th and walk 3 blocks south.</td></tr>
</table>

Karma Triyana Dharmachakra (Tibetan–Karma Kagyu)
Headquarters for many affiliates

352 Meads Mountain Road
Woodstock, NY 12498
Tel: (914) 679–5906
Fax: (914) 679–4625
E-mail: office@kagyu.org or KTDWdstk@aol.com
Web site: http://www.kagyu.org

North American seat of H.H. Gyalwa Karmapa. Traditional Tibetan monastery in Catskill Mountains combining Tibetan design with Western architecture. Main shrine room of 2,400 square feet for major teachings and practices. Many other shrines including Tara shrine room for daily chanting and meditation practice. Founded 1978.

Daily practice schedule for staff and guests—5:00–6:00 am Green Tara, 5:00–6:00 am Mahakala, 7:00–8:00 am Chenrezig. From introductory Buddhism to advanced practices taught, including three-year retreat. Visitors may attend teachings and special events. Facilities for individual retreats.

Regular guided tours. Accommodations, including meals, available with advance reservation. Bookstore with wide variety of books and meditation materials. Over two dozen affiliates around the USA and Canada.

Founder/Guru	H.H. the Gyalwa Karmapa
Teachers	Resident senior lamas: Ven. Khenpo Karthar Rinpoche and Ven. Bardor Tulku Rinpoche; major lineage holders visit

NORTH CAROLINA

Chapel Hill Zen Group (Zen–Soto)
Affiliation: San Francisco Zen Center (SFZC)
Meeting: 5322 Highway 86
Chapel Hill, NC 27514
Mail: P O Box 16302
Chapel Hill, NC 27516
Tel: (919) 967–0861

Wheelchair-accessible temple located on two and a half acres outside Chapel Hill. Forty members, thirty to forty people a week. Began 1981 when several people moved to the area and began sitting together. In 1991 a priest trained at the SFZC was invited to lead the group.

Zazen three times a week, call for times for meditation instruction and orientation. Sutra chanting or sutra study twice a week, Dharma talk once or twice a month. Bodhisattva ceremony once a month, precepts ceremony (Jukai) once a year. Classes or study groups run for ten weeks several times a year on such subjects as Bodhisattva

Precepts, Mahasatipatthana Sutra, Diamond Sutra, and Dogen's Teaching. Yoga-Zen Meditation Posture Workshop once a year. Introduction to Zen Meditation Workshop four times a year. One-day meditation retreats once a month; three-day once a year and five-day once a year. Publish monthly newsletter.

Teachers	Resident: Tai Taku Pat Phelan, others from SFZC visit
Opening Times	During practice
Residents	None
Festivals	Buddha's Birthday, Buddha's Enlightenment, Segaki
Facilities	Meditation hall, kitchen, library/dormitory, interview room
Accommodation	Dorm space, bring bedding, donation requested
Food	Sesshin food—vegetarian
Booking	10 days minimum
Fees	Retreat $35 a day
Expected Behavior	Contact center
How to Get There	Highway 86 between I-40 (exit 266 and go $2^1/_2$ miles north) and I-85 (exit 165 and go $2^1/_2$ miles south)

Charlotte the True Buddhist Society (Chinese–True Buddha School)
1601 East 4th Street
Charlotte, NC 28204
Tel & Fax: (704) 370–0440

Based at a dry-cleaning business building in the center of the city. Has a hundred and fifty members. Founded 1990 as one of three hundred True Buddha Schools worldwide.

Group practice 11:00 am Sundays. Meditation taught and practiced every Sunday or by appointment. Offer free material on True Buddha School of Buddhism. *True Buddha News* published in Canada twice a month for worldwide distribution. *Chan Kuan News* published locally every two months in Chinese only. A hundred and twenty books written by Grand Master Lu and often translated into English.

Founder/Guru	Grand Master Lu
Teachers	Resident: Mrs Pauline Lee
Opening Times	10:00 am–5:00 pm Mondays–Saturdays; 11:00 am–3:00 pm Sundays
Residents	None
Festivals	See newsletter
Facilities	Contact center
Accommodation	Contact center
Food	Contact center

Booking	Contact center
Fees	Contact center
Expected Behavior	No smoking and respect for the Buddha
How to Get There	Contact center

Durham KTC (Tibetan–Karma Kagyu)

Affiliation: Karma Triyana Dharmachakra, New York
c/o 1408 Tyler Court
Durham, NC 27701
Tel: (919) 688–7509

Shrine in the private residence of a member in Research Triangle Park area with ready access to Duke University, North Carolina State University, and University of North Carolina. Ten regular members and number of affiliates. Founded early 1980s when founder visited at request of a senior student.

Meeting Wednesdays for text study, meditation, and discussion on mutually agreed topics. Chenrezig/amitabha practice and sitting and walking meditation Sundays. Four-week Introduction to Buddhism at least once a year. Host lama visits, retreats, and empowerments several times a year.

Founder/Guru	Guru: 17th Karmapa; Founder: Kenpo Karthar Rinpoche
Teachers	Visiting Tibetan teachers
Opening Times	During practice times
Residents	None
Festivals	None
Facilities	Shrine room and library
Accommodation	None
Food	None
Booking	Not applicable
Fees	Not applicable
Expected Behavior	Not applicable
How to Get There	Call for directions

> *Our ideas about what holiness is, that it is pious, bland, and meek, may make us blind to the dynamic and sometimes exuberantly playful manifestation of the enlightened mind.*
>
> Sogyal Rinpoche *The Tibetan Book of Living and Dying*

Durham Shambhala Center (Tibetan–Kagyu/Nyingma)
Affiliation: Shambhala International
1200 W Markham Avenue
Durham, NC 27701
Tel: (919) 286–1487
E-mail: gaylords@med.unc.edu

Located on third floor of office building and has twenty-five members. Affiliated 1978.
Basic sitting meditation 9:00 am–noon Sundays and 7:00–8:00 pm Wednesdays.
Meditation, contemplative arts, and Shambhala Training. Introductory weekend intensives on practice and study of Buddhism and Shambhala Training. Publish quarterly newsletter.

Founder/Guru	Chogyam Trungpa Rinpoche
Teachers	4 resident, and various senior teachers of Shambhala International visit
Opening Times	See session times above
Residents	None
Festivals	Shambhala Day, Vesak, Children's Day
Facilities	Shrine room, library/office, interview room, Tantrika shrine room
Accommodation	Not applicable
Food	Not applicable
Booking	Only for special events
Fees	$25 per course of 5 sessions approximately; regular practice sessions, no charge; other prices vary
Expected Behavior	Basic decency
How to Get There	3 blocks off Durham Expressway

Greenville Karma Thegsum Choling (Tibetan–Karma Kagyu)
Affiliation: Karma Triyana Dharmachakra, New York
P O Box 4243
Greenville, NC 27836
Tel: Bonnie Snyder (919) 756–8315
E-mail: snyderbml@aol.com

Founded early 1980s. Meet Sundays and Wednesdays for meditation practice and study.

North Carolina Zen Center (Zen–Rinzai)
283a Quartz Hill Road
Pittsboro, NC 27312
Tel: (919) 542–4234
Contact center for details.

Kadampa Center (Tibetan–Gelug)
Affiliation: Foundation for the Preservation of the Mahayana Tradition
7404-G Chapel Hill Road
Raleigh, NC 27607
Tel: (919) 859–3433
Fax: (919) 460–1769

Contact center for details.

It has been recognized even in the West (by Schopenhauer) that all great Art contains an element of self-transcendence akin to that which constitutes the quintessence of religion. When this element of self-transcendence is consciously cultivated in poetry, in music, or in painting and sculpture, instead of the element of mere sensuous appeal, Art ceases to be a form of sensuous indulgence and becomes a kind of spiritual discipline, and the highest stages of aesthetic contemplation become spiritual experiences.

Sangharakshita, *The Path of the Inner Life*

OHIO

Buddhist Dharma Center of Cincinnati (Mixed)
P O Box 23307
Cincinnati, OH 45223-0307
Tel: (513) 281–6453 (Michael Atkinson), (513) 541–1650 (Bonnie Beverage),
(513) 271–0384 (Fran Turner)
E-mail: michael.atkinson@uc.edu

Meditation hall in renovated artist's studio in old building full of studios. Twenty or so regular members; between twenty and sixty attendees for special programs. "Our center accommodates and nourishes various kinds of practice, from the ceremonially inclined practice of Zen to the ceremony-free practice of meditative inquiry and Vipassana. We enjoy having tea with one another as well as sitting together. The atmosphere is low-key and steady." Founded early 1980s.

Practice variety of styles of Buddhist meditation and also meditative inquiry. Every Sunday, early service in Kwan Um Zen school style and a later morning service of simple sitting and walking meditation common to all forms of Buddhism. Simple sitting service Tuesday nights. Introductory meditation instruction monthly. Four weekly classes twice a year for beginners and seasoned meditators on such topics as Tranquility and Insight, Meditation and Everyday Life, Spacious Mind/Open Heart, Exploring the Hsin-Hsin-Min. Special Sundays with visiting teachers, particularly in the Vipassana tradition two–three times a year. Zen Masters Keido Fukushima and Dae Gak Sunim hold yearly retreats sponsored by Buddhist Dharma Center.

Founder/Guru	Nonaligned; members work with teachers of different traditions
Teachers	Various visit: Jacqueline Mandell, Roshi Keido Fukushima, Dae Gak Sunim, etc.
Opening Times	See above
Residents	No
Festivals	No
Facilities	Meditation hall
Accommodation	No
Food	No
Booking	Not applicable
Fees	Weekend retreats and 4-week classes $35–$45. Other instruction on dana basis
Expected Behavior	No smoking
How to Get There	Please call for directions—"We will send you a map and a current schedule of activities."

Cincinnati Dharma Study Group (Tibetan–Kagyu/Nyingma)
Affiliation: Shambhala International
Allan Hundley
12 Burton Woods Lane
Cincinnati, OH 45229
Tel: (513) 281–8606

See International headquarters, **Shambhala Center,** Halifax, Nova Scotia, Canada.

Dae Mun Community (Zen–Korean)
Affiliation: Kwan Um School of Zen
Off the Avenue Studios
1546 Knowlton Street
Cincinnati, OH 45223
Tel: (513) 271–0834 (Fran Turner)

See **Furnace Mountain,** Kentucky.

Cleveland Dharma Study Group (Tibetan–Kagyu/Nyingma)
Affiliation: Shambhala International
Richard Dickinson, Coordinator
13302 Cormere Avenue, #703
Cleveland, OH 44120-1569
Tel: (216) 921–7256

See International headquarters, **Shambhala Center,** Halifax, Nova Scotia, Canada.

Columbus Dharma Study Group (Tibetan–Kagyu/Nyingma)
Affiliation: Shambhala International
Helen Thiry, Coordinator
2208 Arlington Avenue, #6
Columbus, OH 43221
Tel: (614) 267–5942

See International headquarters, **Shambhala Center,** Halifax, Nova Scotia, Canada.

Columbus Karma Thegsum Choling (Tibetan–Karma Kagyu)
Affiliation: Karma Triyana Dharmachakra, New York
228 South Grubb Street
Columbus, OH 43215

Tel: (614) 228–6546
E-mail: lmccart@magnus.acs.ohio-state.edu

Located in old Christian church just west of downtown with large shrine room, library, and bookstore. Twenty members, forty–fifty visitors a week.

Basic tranquility meditation Sundays 10:00–11:00 pm. Vajrayana practices Tuesdays and Thursdays 7:30–9:00 pm and on full moon day. Basic meditation instruction Sundays 10:00–10:30 am. Three–four week Beginning Buddhist classes every two months Sundays 11:30–12:30 pm. More advanced classes on Tibetan Buddhist practices or book studies every Sunday 11:30–12:30 pm. Two weekend retreats annually, usually for those who have taken refuge. Quarterly newsletter, *Bell and Damaru*.

Founder/Guru	Khenpo Karthar Rinpoche
Teachers	Members and visiting teachers
Opening Times	See practice times above
Residents	No
Festivals	Contact center
Facilities	See above
Accommodation	For donation; when teacher visiting $10/night suggested
Food	No
Booking	Contact center
Fees	Donation
Expected Behavior	No smoking and basic common sense
How to Get There	315 south or 715 to Rich/Town Street exit. East on Rich and first building on right is the center.

Cleveland Buddhist Temple (Jodo Shinshu and Zen)
Affiliation: Buddhist Churches of America
1573 East 214 Street
Euclid, OH 44117
Tel: (216) 692–1509
Fax: (216) 692–2012

Brick building with a hundred and fifty person capacity in main temple, social/dining area in the basement. Library in basement has selection of books in English and Japanese. Founded in 1945 by Japanese Americans who resettled in the Cleveland area after being discharged from internment camps and wanting a place to practice. Present location acquired 1968 and extensively remodeled. Rev. Koshin Ogui resident minister since 1977.

Dharma Services 10:30–11:30 am Sundays bimonthly; Beginner's Meditation Class 7:00–8:30 pm Tuesdays; Advanced meditation class 7–9:00 pm Wednesdays; Meditation class followed by pancake breakfast 9:00–11:30 am second Sunday of the month. Public talks, one-day seminars, and workshops regularly. Regular food bazaars with traditional Japanese and vegetarian cuisine. *The Bulletin of the Cleveland Buddhist Temple* published monthly and distributed to members of the temple and Zen Shin sangha.

Temple Treasures Bookstore supplies meditation aids.

Affiliated group, **Zen Shin Sangha** (see separate entry), uses same premises.

Founder/Guru	See above
Teachers	Resident minister: Rev. Koshin Ogui
Festivals	New Year's, Temple Anniversary service, Shonin Shinran's Memorial Day, Nirvana Day, Spring Equinox, Buddha's Birthday, Vishakha Day, Shonin Shinran's Birthday, O'Bon or Ullambana, Autumn Equinox, Buddha's Enlightenment, Year-End Service
How to Get There	At corner of East 214 Street and Euclid Ave.

Zen Shin Sangha (Zen and Jodo Shinshu)
Cleveland Buddhist Temple
1573 E 214 Street
Euclid, OH 44117
Tel: (216) 692–1509
Fax: (216) 692–2012

Uses premises of **Cleveland Buddhist Temple** (see separate entry). Between seventy and eighty regular members. Established 1978.

Zazen meditation and Nembutsu realization—Tuesdays 7:00–9:00 pm for beginners, Wednesdays 7:00–9:00 pm for advanced meditators. Courses in Zen Way and Nembutsu Way. One-, two-, and three-day retreats combined with Tai Chi, Shiatsu, and yoga classes. Weekly meditation classes at Cleveland Buddhist Temple and Midwest Buddhist Temple in Chicago. Public lectures and seminars on Chi Kung, Tai Chi, Hatha Yoga, Constructive Living Practice, Shiatsu massage, and other stress-management techniques. Seminars include vegetarian lunch and cost $35–45. Publish *Zen Shin* quarterly.

Founder/Guru	Rev. Koshin Ogui, Sensei of **Midwest Buddhist Temple,** Chicago, Illinois
Teachers	As founder
Opening Times	As Cleveland Buddhist Temple
Residents	As Cleveland Buddhist Temple
Festivals	No
Facilities	Temple, dojo, meditation hall
Accommodation	No
Food	No
Booking	No

Fees	Usually $35 for 1-day retreat
Expected Behavior	No smoking, no alcohol
How to Get There	As Cleveland Buddhist Temple

CloudWater Zendo (Zen and Pure Land)
21562 Lorain Road
Fairview Park, OH 44126
Tel: (216) 331–8374
E-mail: clevezen@aol.com

In half facility which used to house a beauty college and now renovated to reflect traditional Zen and Buddhist meditation halls in middle of typical suburb. Founded 1992 by senior Dharma Student of Rev. Koshin Ogui Sensei; current address since 1995. "We have a very 'organic' sangha, in that people come and go as they please without being expected to do anything unless this is their wish (training, contributing, etc.). We try to accommodate the busy lifestyles of Americans living in a major city so they may balance practice with family responsibility. Plus, we have a very good sense of humor."

Open practice on Tuesdays and Thursdays 6:00 pm and Wednesdays and Fridays 6:30 am and Saturdays 8:30 am. Introduction to Zen Tuesday and Thursday nights before formal meditation practice. Monthly Sunday Dharma services 9:30 am; weekend intensives and two or three yearly sesshins (senior sangha Zen retreats and open sangha retreats). Public lectures eight times a year on various Buddhist subjects. Everything suitable for newcomers.

Newsletter, *Clouds and Water*, quarterly.

Founder/Guru	Mike Shu Ho Bonasso
Teachers	Resident: Mike Shu Ho Bonasso
Opening Times	See practice times above
Residents	No
Festivals	Wesak, Bodhi Day, Buddha's Birthday, New Year's Day
Facilities	Dharma hall, zendo
Accommodation	No
Food	No
Booking	Not applicable
Fees	By contribution
Expected Behavior	No smoking, shoes off, respect the facility. Senior students take 5 or 10 precepts.
How to Get There	I-480 west to Clague Rd., north approx 1 mile to Lorain Rd., right (east) on Lorain. Zendo on north side next to bank.

Yellow Springs Dharma Center (Nondenominational)
502 Livermore Street
Yellow Springs, OH 45387
Tel: (513) 767–9919

Apartment in house near Antioch College and has connection with Antioch College and its Buddhist Studies Program. Formed by practitioners of Vipassana, Tibetan, and Zen who were part of Buddhist Peace Fellowship chapter. Membership of fifty-six. House rented 1993.

Forty-minute meditations periods every evening except Saturdays and three mornings a week. Zen meditation Saturday mornings; Vipassana Sunday mornings. Three Tibetan practices per month: Green Tara, Medicine Buddha, Chenrezig and amitabha. Discussion/study groups led by members on such subjects as History of Buddhism, Sogyal Rinpoche's Tibetan Way of Living, and Dying and Living. Invite teachers to lead weekend retreats. Four- to eight-day in wooded nature reserve owned by Antioch College in early June—type of retreat rotated according to three Buddhist schools represented. All activities suitable for newcomers. Publish monthly calendar.

Teachers	Many visit of different traditions
Opening Times	See practice times
Residents	1 to 4 lay in flat above center
Festivals	No
Facilities	Small meditation room, small library
Accommodation	Not usually
Food	No
Booking	Not necessary
Fees	Last retreat $240 for 8 days plus dana for teacher
Expected Behavior	5 precepts and no smoking
How to Get There	From Route 68 (Xenia Ave. in Yellow Springs), turn east on Davis St. Center is on corner of David and Livermore, brown house with prayer flags in front.

OKLAHOMA

Vien Giac Buddhist Temple (Zen)
5101 NE 36th Street
Oklahoma City, OK 73121-6516
Tel: (405) 424–0264 or (405) 749–1895
Fax: (405) 749–1895
E-mail: mindessence@thor.net
Web site: http://lawtonnet.com/buddhist

Chinese-style temple with red brick roofs, ten minutes from downtown. Chinese Vietnamese physical structure not too close to any neighborhood. Up to three hundred visitors a week and up to fifteen hundred people on major holidays. First temple built 1981 and new temple 1992.

Meditations from three traditions of Theravada, Pure Land, and Mahayana; Theravada and Pure Land for beginners and Zen for advanced meditators. Classes 10 am–noon Saturdays on such subjects as the Four Noble Truths, The Wheel of Life, Full Awareness of Breathing, Four Areas of Contemplation, The Diamond Sutra, Lotus Divine Laws Sutra, etc. Twenty-four-hour retreats every other month.

Founder/Guru	Group of Buddhists
Teachers	Resident: Kevin Kim and Ven. Thich Tri Hoa
Opening Times	10:00 am–3:00 pm Sundays
Residents	Ven. Thich Tri Hoa
Festivals	Many—contact center
Facilities	Shrine room, 4 class rooms
Accommodation	No charge, but accept donation
Food	Vegetarian, mostly free, but for group of over 20, $5 per person per meal donation requested
Booking	2 weeks in advance
Fees	$20 per person, free for those who can't afford it
Expected Behavior	5 precepts preferred
How to Get There	I-35 north, exit on NE 36. Go east for 3 miles, after 3 stop signs, the temple is on the right or NE corner of 36 and Bartel, west of Sooner Road.

OREGON

Pacific Region Yeshe Nyingpo—Tashi Choling (Tibetan–Nyingma)
P O Box 124
Ashland, OR 97520
Tel: (541) 488–0477
Fax: (541) 482–0117

"Mother center" near Ashland with affiliate centers in Portland, Oregon, Newport, Oregon, San Francisco, California, and Ensenada, Mexico.

Four-story temple-residence, thirty-four-foot statue of Buddha Vajrasattva and two twenty-foot statues of Tara in a mandala-style garden. Traditional-style Tibetan shrine room/temple with adjoining residence for Lamas. Addition for retreatants scheduled for completion 1997. Retreat center with five ordained sangha and twenty lay practitioners in mountains of south Oregon. "Devoted to preserving and transmitting the ancient Vajrayana Buddhist spiritual teachings, arts, and sciences."

Ongoing classes in town of Ashland and at temple on various topics from sitting meditation to formal Ngondro practice. Daughter centers are located in cities and offer ongoing practice sessions as well as sponsoring empowerments and teachings by visiting Lamas. Contact each center for complete schedule of practices, retreats, teachings, and classes.

Founder/Guru	H.H. Dudjom Rinpoche
Teachers	Spiritual representative: Ven. Gyatrul Rinpoche
Opening Times	Contact center
Residents	5 monastics
Festivals	Contact center
Facilities	See above
Accommodation	See above and small rustic guest house
Food	Self-catering
Booking	Contact center
Fees	Contact center
Expected Behavior	Contact center
How to Get There	Contact center

Zen Community of Oregon (Zen–Soto/Rinzai)
P O Box 310
Corbett, OR 97019
Tel: (503) 282–7879; (503) 695–2122 (Retreat Center)
Fax: (503) 695–2188
E-mail: Jiyromm@aol.com

"Weekly Zen meditation in city at Dharma center, in southeast Portland neighborhood. Rural retreats held at Larch Mountain Zen Center (LMZC) in Columbia River Gorge. LMZC has guest accommodations for 35. Traditional Zen retreats of 2–8 days' duration held monthly. Classes and retreats focus on topics including fundamentals of Buddhism, beginner's retreats, the precepts, and intensive Zen practice." (Supplied by ZCO.)

Teachers	Resident: Jan Chozen Bays, Sensei
Opening Times	Contact center
Residents	2 monastics, 4 lay
Festivals	Contact center
Facilities	See above
Accommodation	Plenty of rooms at low cost
Food	Fresh vegetarian—lunch $5, dinner $8
Booking	Suggest 6 weeks in advance
Fees	Full week retreats $220–260
Expected Behavior	No alcohol, drugs, cigarettes, or other self-destructive behavior

How to Get There   Call for directions.

Corvallis Dharma Study Group (Tibetan–Kagyu/Nyingma)
Affiliation: Shambhala International
Randy Chakerian, Coordinator
1007 NW 31st Street
Corvallis, OR 97330-4447
Tel: (541) 758–4649

See International headquarters, **Shambhala Center,** Halifax, Nova Scotia, Canada.

Eugene Buddhist Priory (Zen–Soto)
Affiliation: Serene Reflection Meditation Tradition
P O Box 5369
Eugene, OR 97405
Tel: (541) 344–7377

Meet twice weekly for meditation plus service or chant. Newcomers are asked to start by attending orientation class held monthly. Contact center for more information.

Eugene Zendo (Zen–Soto)
Affiliation: Dharma Rain Zen Center, Oregon
3480 Potter Street
Eugene, OR 97405
Tel & Fax: (541) 341–1301
E-mail: Brox@oregon.uoregon.edu

Meet in private house and use larger facilities for retreats and evenings of Ecumenical Buddhist Meditation. Approximately twenty visitors a week. Small, nonhierarchical center. Aim to create Buddhist community in Eugene. Established 1988.

Zazen one evening a week. Reading and discussion of Buddhist texts one evening a week. Weekend retreats two or three times a year. Also affiliated with Buddhist Peace Fellowship (meetings monthly). Sponsor of Ecumenical Buddhist Meditation twice a year.

Founder/Guru	Kyogen Carlson
Teachers	Founder visits once a month and for retreats
Opening Times	Tuesdays 7:30–9:30 pm, monthly meetings and potlucks
Residents	1
Festivals	None
Facilities	Meditation room and library
Accommodation	None

Food	None
Booking	None
Fees	Donations accepted. Weekend retreats $25 suggested donation
Expected Behavior	No smoking during events. Expect members to do precept practice
How to Get There	I-5, 30th Street/Lane Community College exit, turn left on Potter St.

Kempon Hokke Kai (Nichiren–Kempon Hokke Shu)
Affiliation: Hosshoji Temple, Japan
P O Box 5874
Eugene, OR 97405
Tel & Fax: (541) 485–3522
E-mail: fujufuse@cris.com
Web site: http://www.cris.com/~fujufuse/hokkekai.htm

In the U.S., primarily linked by computer (Cyberspace Temple), but meet annually in various cities when priest from Japan visits. Lay tradition. Three hundred plus believers of Kempon Hokke Kai worldwide; a hundred thousand believers of Kempon Hokke Shu in Japan. "We pledge to remain true to the orthodox teachings of Nichiren, and to provide English-language materials to all believers who seek the truth of the Dharma of the Lotus Sutra…. Often we provide an alternative to those who have left various Nichiren 'cults'…. Our emphasis is individual practice only, and spreading the Lotus Sutra."

Plan to offer comprehensive courses from 1997—seminar/lecture series, probably in Portland, Oregon. Chanting is done at home mornings and evenings. On 28th of every month, all members of Kempon Hokke Kai chant for one hour from 6:00–7:00 pm Pacific Time. Publish monthly newsletters: *Kempon Hokke Vision* in English and *Hotoke No Hikari* in Japanese. Other writings available.

In Japan: Rev. Tetsujo Kubota, Hosshoji Temple, Shimoi ino, Futtsu-shi, Chi Ba-Ken, Japan 293; Tel: 0439 87 0962, Fax: 0439 87 7708.

Dharma Rain Zen Center (Zen–Soto)
2539 SE Madison
Portland, OR 97214
Tel: (503) 239–4846
Fax: (503) 239–5217
E-mail: kyogen@msn.com

Large house with library, offices, small zendo, residences, and Church building with large zendo, institutional kitchen, and lecture room. Run by married couple who are priests with Dharma Transmission. Zendo shared with another Zen, a Vajrayana, a

Vipassana, and a Sufi group (see details for each below). Lay temple with a hundred and fifty pledging members. Founded 1973 in Eugene, Oregon, and affiliated with Shasta Abbey until 1986.

Teaches Shikantaza meditation. Sunday morning practice includes meditation, sanzen (private interview), morning service (chanting and vows), and Dharma talk. Introductory workshops. Introductory to Intermediate Class series, open to all, no charge. Advanced study group for senior members. Introductory to intermediate day-long retreats and private retreats. Four sesshins per year and occasional weekend retreats. Very limited residential training. Everything open to newcomers except special retreats and classes. Dharma school for children. Bimonthly newsletter, *Still Point*. Also available online at http://www.teleport.com/~ryanjb/still point/sp.shtml.

Founder/Guru	Keido Chisan Koho Zenji
Teachers	Resident: Kyogen Carlson Sensei and Gyokuko Carlson Sensei
Opening Times	Contact center
Residents	Contact center
Festivals	Contact center
Facilities	See above
Accommodation	Short stays for established members only
Food	Contact center
Booking	Contact center
Fees	No
Expected Behavior	No smoking or alcohol
How to Get There	Contact center for detailed instructions.

Kagyu Changchub Chuling (Tibetan)
73 NE Monroe
Portland, OR 97212
Tel: (503) 284–6697

Contact center for details.

Jacqueline Mandell (Vipassana)
P O Box 2085
Portland, OR 97208-2085
Tel & Fax: (503) 790–1064

Independent teacher of Buddhist meditation, leadership consulting and coaching, and Team Spirit Certification Trainings. Team Spirit is an organizational model founded and developed by Barry Heermann and being used in a number of major companies in the USA.

Jacqueline Mandell has extensive experience leading large retreats, lectures, and personal consultations worldwide. In 1971 began Buddhist mediation practice in Bodh Gaya, India. Trained extensively with masters in three main Buddhist traditions. Authorized to teach Vipassana by Ven. Mahasi Sayadaw and further encouraged in teachings by Ven. Taungpulu Sayadaw. Continues own meditation practice and development in Vajrayana.

Nichiren Propagation Center (Nichiren Shu)
2031 SE Yamhill Street
Portland, OR 97214
Tel: (503) 232–8064
Fax: (503) 238–4767
E-mail: npc@imagina.com

Currently using a house owned by the Nichiren Buddhist Church of Portland, but planning to build new center by 2002. Administrated by the Nichiren-Shu Headquarters, Tokyo, Japan, which provides materials and holds seminars for lay members of Nichiren Buddhist Churches in North America. Founded 1991.

Dharma Conference once a year (usually June), which is a study seminar for lay members. Subjects are Lotus Sutra, History of Sakyamuni Buddha, History of Nichiren, and his doctrine. Each Nichiren Shu church offers different classes of study and practice. This church's priest is Rev. Ryuken Akahoshi.

Founder/Guru	Nichiren (1222–1282)
Teachers	Contact center
Opening Times	Contact center
Residents	No
Festivals	New Year's Service, Setsubun, Higan Service, Buddha's Birthday, Obon, Nichiren's Memorial Service, Bodhi Day
Facilities	Study room, hondo (main hall), office
Accommodation	No
Food	No
Booking	No
Fees	No
Expected Behavior	Contact center
How to Get There	I-84 west from Portland International Airport, exit at Downtown, Belmont St. East, right turn at 20th Street, left at Yamhill St.

Nichiren Shu Minori-kai (Nichiren Shu)
Affiliate: Nichiren Propagation Center
9449 S W 8th Drive
Portland, OR 97219

Tel: (503) 246–5316
Fax: (503) 246–0541

Resident priest—Rev. Zuigaku Kodachi. See **Nichiren Propagation Center,** Oregon.

Portland Sakya Center (Tibetan–Sakya)
P O Box 14201
Portland, OR 97293
Tel: (503) 238–8097 (resident teacher)
E-mail: anigt@teleport.com (Gilda Taylor)

Shared space with **Dharma Rain Zen Center** (see above). Twenty-five supporting members. Directed toward lay adults—senior students trained to become teachers. Founded 1989.

Weekly practice 7:00–9:00 pm Mondays varies on monthly rotation—Tara, Avalokiteshvara, or Calm Abiding meditation; one-day teaching/retreat monthly; occasional video series; sponsoring visiting teachers. Publish occasional newsletter.

Founder/Guru	Chogyi Tri Rinpoche; Spiritual Direction: H.H. Sakya Trizin and Jetsun Kusho Chimey Luding
Teachers	Resident: Ani Gilda Paldron Taylor
Opening Times	Contact teacher
Residents	No
Festivals	No
Facilities	See above
Accommodation	No
Food	No
Booking	Contact teacher
Fees	Contact teacher
Expected Behavior	Contact teacher
How to Get There	See **Dharma Rain** above

Portland Shambhala Center (Tibetan–Kagyu/Nyingma)
Affiliation: Shambhala International
Irene Lundquist, Coordinator
1110 SE Alder, Suite 204
Portland, OR 97214
Tel: (503) 231–4971
E-mail: parkerd@ohsu.edu

See International headquarters, **Shambhala Center,** Halifax, Nova Scotia, Canada.

Portland Vipassana Sangha
Contact: Robert Beatty (503) 223–2214
(uses Dharma Rain Zen Center premises—see details above)

Vipassana Sundays 7:00–10:00 pm; instruction for newcomers first Sunday of the month, 6:00 pm.

Portland Yeshe Nyingpo Center (Tibetan–Nyingma)
Affiliation: Pacific Region Yeshe Nyingpo—Tashi Choling
c/o Clark Hansen
3200 NW Skyline Drive
Portland, OR 97220-3815
Tel: (503) 292–4004

See **Pacific Region Yeshe Nyingpo—Tashi Choling,** Oregon.

Rigpa (Tibetan–Nyingma)
Affiliation: Rigpa Fellowship
Portland, OR
Tel: (503) 646–5771

Contact: Pam Holt. See **Rigpa National Office,** California, for details.

Newport Yeshe Nyingpo Center (Tibetan–Nyingma)
Affiliation: Pacific Region Yeshe Nyingpo—Tashi Choling
c/o Ann Goddard
5380 N Beaver Creek Road
Seal Rock, OR 97376
Tel: (503) 563 5729

See **Pacific Region Yeshe Nyingpo—Tashi Choling,** Oregon.

PENNSYLVANIA

Three Rivers Dharma Center (Tibetan–Drikung Kagyu)
100 Comrie Avenue
Braddock, PA 15104
Tel: (412) 351–6542 (John Bogaard)
Web site: http://www.churchward.com/drikung

Contact center for details.

Carnegie Shambhala Study Group (Tibetan–Kagyu/Nyingma)
Affiliation: Shambhala International
1584 Railroad Street, #2
Carnegie, PA 15106

See International headquarters, **Shambhala Center,** Halifax, Nova Scotia, Canada.

Won Buddhism of Philadelphia (Won Buddhism)
423 Abington Avenue
Glenside, PA 19038
Tel & Fax: (215) 884–8443

Christian Science church with changed altar. Has about seventy members. Started in 1987 in north Philadelphia and moved 1995 to current location. "People who visited our temple described that they had a comfortable time in it and they shared their practices with other participants."
    For English speakers: Saturdays 2:30–3:00 pm sitting meditation and chanting; 3:00–4:30 pm services including Dharma talk, members and guests presentation, recital of sutra, singing Dharma songs, and silent prayer. Services for Korean speakers on Sundays. Plan to offer sitting meditation for one hour every day from 1997. Annual retreat at other location, more planned. Priests do daily sitting meditation 6:00–7:30 am and evening prayer 9:30–10:00 pm, and members are encourage to participate in both. *Won Buddhism Newsletter* three times a year; *Won Buddhist Studies* once a year, both in English.

Founder/Guru	Sot'aesan Pak, Chungbin
Teachers	Resident: Bokim Kim, Sundo Ho, Hyunrin Paek
Opening Times	Contact center
Residents	3 priests
Festivals	Buddha's Birthday, Sot'aesan's Enlightenment;

<table>
<tr><td></td><td>Remembrance of Sot'aesan's Death; Celebration of Disciples' devotion, Won Buddhist Thanksgiving</td></tr>
</table>

Facilities	Meditation room and library
Accommodation	Small numbers of visitors
Food	Mostly vegetarian
Booking	Contact center
Fees	No fees, voluntary donations
Expected Behavior	No smoking or drinking at temple
How to Get There	Contact center

Philadelphia Shambhala Center(Tibetan–Kagyu/Nyingma)
Affiliation: Shambhala International
2030 Sansom Street, 3rd Floor
Philadelphia, PA 19103
Tel: (215) 568–6070 or (215) 568–6071
E-mail: phill62@ibm.net

See International headquarters, **Shambhala Center,** Halifax, Nova Scotia, Canada.

Plum Tree Zendo (Zen)
214 Monroe Street
Philadelphia, PA 19147
Tel: (215) 625–2601

Four-story house in the city with about a dozen supporting members. "Small, intimate setting; everyone made to feel welcome; we concentrate on meditation practice on maintaining an atmosphere conducive to and encouraging both seated meditation and bring awareness into daily life."

Focus on zazen practice. Tuesday, Wednesday, and Thursday mornings ($3) and evenings ($5); every first and third Sunday ($5); beginners' orientation Wednesday evenings; introductory workshops also offered. Scheduled workshops ($40) and one-day ($25), weekend ($100), and week-long ($300) retreats.

Founder/Guru	Rev. Genro Lee Milton
Teachers	Founder visits
Opening Times	See practice times above
Residents	1 nun
Festivals	Buddha's Enlightenment Day
Facilities	Meditation room, library/gathering room
Accommodation	Dormitory-style during retreats, gender-segregated, price included in retreat fees
Food	During workshops and retreats, price included in cost

Booking	Contact center
Fees	See above
Expected Behavior	Respectful, quiet and thoughtful, kind consideration of others
How to Get There	2 blocks south of South St., between 2nd and 3rd Streets; near the Delaware River in the south of city center.

Soka Gakkai International (SGI-USA) (Nichiren)
Pennsylvania Area Regional Center
2000 Hamilton Street, Suite 210
Philadelphia, PA 19130-3814
Tel: (215) 569–2144
Fax: (215) 569–2565

See **Soka Gakkai International** National Offices & Center, Santa Monica, California, for more details.

RHODE ISLAND

Kwan Um School of Zen (Zen)
Headquarters of Kwan Um School of Zen
99 Pound Road
Cumberland
Providence, RI 02864
Tel: (401) 658–1476
Fax: (401) 658–1188
E-mail: kwanumzen@aol.com

Contact center for details.

SOUTH CAROLINA

Columbia Dharmadhatu (Tibetan–Kagyu/Nyingma)
Affiliation: Shambhala International
2065 Blossom Street
Columbia, SC 29205
Tel: (803) 254–9048

See International headquarters, **Shambhala Center,** Halifax, Nova Scotia, Canada.

TENNESSEE

Clarkesville Forming Dharma Study Group (Tibetan–Kagyu/Nyingma)
Affiliation: Shambhala International
Jim Hartz, Coordinator
22 Lacy Lane
Clarkesville, TN 37043

See International headquarters, **Shambhala Center,** Halifax, Nova Scotia, Canada.

Delta Insight Group (Zen/Tibetan/Theravada)
Mailing: 715 N Auburndale
Memphis, TN 38107
Tel: (901) 327–2545 (Clark Buchner); (901) 278–0961 (Mark Muesse)
Fax: (901) 327–2545 *51
E-mail: muesse@rhodes.edu

Meet at Eastern Sun Yoga Studio. Community varies between twelve and twenty-five.
    Meditation Wednesdays 7:30 pm. Teaching/reading one Sunday morning per month. Instruction in meditation on weekends on request. Retreats. Newsletter planned 1997.

Founder/Guru	Mark Muesse/Clark Buchner
Teachers	None regular
Opening Times	See above
Residents	None
Festivals	None
Facilities	See above
Accommodation	None
Food	None
Booking	Not applicable
Fees	Minimal cost when offered. $150 approximately for 3-day retreat; $325 for 1 week
Expected Behavior	No smoking, 5 precepts
How to Get There	Eastern Sun Yoga Center is on Forrest Ave. in Memphis. From Highland Ave. at Summer Ave., go east to Sievier St., then south to Forrest and west on Forrest.

Nashville Zen Group (Zen)
Nashville, TN
Tel: (615) 255–7715 (Bill Compton)

Practice in small outbuilding connected with First Church Unity in room also used by other groups. "We offer a meditation room and practice style for anyone who wishes to meditate with a group. We try to be open to all styles of silent meditation while maintaining a basically Buddhist framework for practice."

Focus on mindfulness and shikantaza practices, although some members practice with koans. Zen Buddhist practice for lay practitioners Saturdays 7:30–9:00 am and 5:00 am on first Saturday of the month. Summer and winter three-day sesshins with Zen Master; spring and fall one-day sesshins without a teacher.

Founder/Guru	Steve Warren and Bill Compton
Teachers	George Bowman of Cambridge Buddhist Association visits
Opening Times	See session times above
Residents	None
Festivals	None
Facilities	See above
Accommodation	No formal accommodation
Food	Vegetarian on sesshins
Booking	Contact center
Fees	3-day sesshins $130 and 1-day sesshins $25
Expected Behavior	5 precepts and silence on sesshins
How to Get There	First Church Unity at 5125 Franklin Road about 1 mile north of Old Hickory Blvd. and Franklin Rd. in Nashville.

TEXAS

Empty Sky (Zen)
Affiliation: Diamond sangha
2100 North Spring Street
Amarillo, TX 79107
Tel: (806) 383–3764 or (806) 383–1811
Fax: (806) 383–6919
E-mail: bdrcesky@arnet.arn.net

Situated in semi-private wing of the Bishop DeFalco Retreat Center. Local sangha of about twenty.

Monthly orientation classes for both Zen and Christian contemplation. Monthly discussion group. Organize and give sesshins four or five times a year. Yearly intensive training session for students of their teacher. Publish monthly newsletter.

Founder/Guru	Contact center
Teachers	Resident: Patrick Hawk, Roshi
Opening Times	Contact Glenna Pitlock, Roshi's assistant for program

Residents	Permanent staff of 3; 0–10 lay residents
Festivals	None
Facilities	Zendo, library, study room, Zen garden
Accommodation	Single room with bath, 3 meals, $50–60 per day
Food	Vegetarian diet usually available
Booking	At least 1 month in advance, deposit necessary
Fees	7-night sesshin $305, 5-night $205
Expected Behavior	Mature adult behavior
How to Get There	Exit I-40 at Grand Ave. North to 21st Street, 2 blocks to the Retreat Center

Austin Shambhala Center (Tibetan–Kagyu/Nyingma)
Affiliation: Shambhala International
1702 South Fifth Street
Austin, TX 78704
Tel: (512) 443–3263
E-mail: blint@ccsi.com

See International headquarters, **Shambhala Center,** Halifax, Nova Scotia, Canada.

Dallas Karma Thegsum Choling (Tibetan–Karma Kagyu)
Affiliation: Karma Triyana Dharmachakra, New York
312 S Winnetka Avenue
Dallas, TX 75208-5901
Tel: (214) 948–3348
E-mail: Bill_Swanson@acd.org

Large house in Winnetka Hights Historic District of an old Dallas neighborhood. Large shrine room and space rented to members.
      Practice Sundays and Thursdays. Dharma discussions Tuesday evenings. Meditation instruction available. Schedule three or four visits by Lamas per year.

Maria Kannon Zen Center (Zen–Sanbo Kyodan)
P O Box 140662
Dallas, TX 75214-0662
Tel: (214) 361–1066
Fax: (214) 388 5254
E-mail: hcortes@flash.net, douglas@why.net, or hamric@omega.uta.edu

Uses Methodist church in inner city near Dallas Metroplex. Forty to fifty regular participants. "Open to persons with different religious backgrounds (Buddhist, Jewish,

Christian, etc.); emphasis on lay life and spirituality, and experience of realization in daily situations." Zazen four times a week. Introductory courses for beginners. Sesshins four times a year. *Maria Kannon Zen Center Newsletter* twice a year.

Founder/Guru	Ruben Habito
Teachers	Founder
Opening Times	Contact center
Residents	None
Festivals	Contact center
Facilities	Meditation hall
Accommodation	Not usually
Food	Vegetarian
Booking	1 month in advance for retreats
Fees	$50 per day approximately for retreats
Expected Behavior	Traditional prescriptions for meditation
How to Get There	Corner Haskell and Junius

Soka Gakkai International (SGI-USA) (Nichiren)
Texas Area Regional Center
2733 Oak Lawn Avenue
Dallas, TX 75219-4108
Tel: (214) 559–4115
Fax: (214) 559–2288

See **Soka Gakkai International** National Offices & Center, Santa Monica, California, for more details.

Southwest Vipassana Meditation Center, Dhamma Siri (Vipassana)
Affiliation: Vipassana Meditation Centers in the Tradition of S. N. Goenka
P O Box 190248
Dallas, TX 75219-0248
Tel: (214) 521–5258 for course information; (214) 932–7868 for meditation center
Fax: (214) 522–5973
E-mail: vip@onramp.net

Meditation center on twenty acres of agricultural land, twenty-five miles southeast of Dallas near Kaufman; capacity thirty-five students. Established 1990. For further description see **Vipassana Meditation Center,** Massachusetts.

Vajradakini Buddhist Center (Tibetan–Gelug)
Affiliation: New Kadampa Tradition

4915 Junius Street
Dallas, TX 75214
Tel: (214) 823–6385
Fax: (214) 823–6395
E-mail: dakini@waonline.com

Founded 1994.
   Full complement of classes and courses. Beginner, intermediate, and advanced studies available, all based on the teachings and books of Geshe Kelsang Gyatso. Courses vary from one evening to three years in length. One-day, weekend, and week-long retreats at the center and off-site. Classes held at the center, various sites around Dallas and in Austin, Texas—contact center for details. Publish newsletter bimonthly. Bookstore also selling practice items.

Founder/Guru	Geshe Kelsang Gyatso Rinpoche
Teachers	Resident: Gen Kelsang Dekyi
Opening Times	Contact center
Residents	Yes
Festivals	Many celebrated
Facilities	Contact center
Accommodation	None
Food	None
Booking	Contact center
Fees	Contact center
Expected Behavior	Contact center
How to Get There	Contact center

Diamond Way Buddhist Center (Tibetan–Karma Kagyu)
Affiliation: Under the 17th Karmapa, Thaye Dorje
804 Tall Pines
Friendswood, TX 77546
Tel: (281) 482–2926
Fax: (281) 482–2606

Meditation center south of Houston with core group of about thirty.
   Teaching and meditation Sundays 7:00 pm with Guru Yoga Meditation on the 16th Karmapa. Meditations and teachings in Houston at various locations on Tuesdays and Fridays. Phowa retreat every other year with Lama Ole Nydahl. Affiliate in San Francisco publishes *Buddhism Today*, a quarterly journal of articles from Karma Kagyu teachers.

Founder/Guru	Lama Ole Nydahl
Teachers	Visiting: Lama Ole Nydahl, Lopon Tschechu Rinpoche,

	Gyaltrul Rinpoche
Opening Times	Contact center
Residents	4 laity
Festivals	None
Facilities	Gompa
Accommodation	By invitation only
Food	None
Booking	Contact center
Fees	Contact center
Expected Behavior	Contact center
How to Get There	Contact center

Houston Dharma Study Group (Tibetan–Kagyu/Nyingma)
Affiliation: Shambhala International
Celeste Budwit, Coordinator
Houston, TX 77019
Tel: (713) 956–9269
E-mail: 103337.3145@compuserve.com

See International headquarters, **Shambhala Center,** Halifax, Nova Scotia, Canada.

Kyung Dzong Center (Tibetan–Bon)
Affiliation: Ligmincha Institute, Virginia
P O Box 54179
Houston, TX 77254-1791
Tel: (713) 523-7330
E-mail: eddy@hti.net (Edouard Philippe)
Web site: http://www.zenteknet.com/sangha

True Buddha Temple (Chinese–True Buddha School)
7734 Mary Bates Boulevard
Houston, TX 77036
Tel: (713) 988–8822
Fax: (713) 988–8488

My teaching is not a philosophy. It is the result of direct experience. The things I say come from my own experience. You can confirm them all by your own experience.... Only direct experience enables us to see the true face of reality.

Thich Nhat Hanh *Old Path White Clouds*

Former Calvary Church renovated to convert outside to Buddhist Temple in residential suburb. 23,000-square-foot building with day-care center, food court retreat, mausoleum (in progress 1996), main sanctuary for five hundred people. Organized by group of True Buddha practitioners 1991; moved to these premises 1996.

True Buddha Yoga practice classes on Sundays. Occasional Bardo Ceremony and Fire Ceremony. Monthly retreats on Fire Ceremony and mantra chanting. Monthly *True Buddha Newsletter*. Also offer *Purple Lotus Journal* and *True Buddha Newspaper* from affiliate temples. Sells books, thangkas, vajra bells, beads and religious mantra papers authorized by Grand Master Lu.

Founder/Guru	Grand Master Sheng Yen Lu
Teachers	To be appointed at time of writing
Opening Times	1:00–6:00 pm daily (will be extended)
Residents	2 laity
Festivals	Contact center
Facilities	Shrine room, library, activity hall, retreat/meditation room, classroom
Accommodation	From 1997 at about $10/day
Food	By donation
Booking	First come, first serve; no deposit
Fees	By donation
Expected Behavior	No smoking, 5 precepts
How to Get There	Mary Bates Blvd. is a cross street between Bellaire Blvd. and Beechnut, both off Sam Houston 8.

Rigpe Dorje Center (Tibetan–Kagyu)
P O Box 690995
San Antonio, TX 78269
Tel: (210) 342–3054
Fax: (210) 614–1172
E-mail: jsrpuck@texas.net

Rented office space in city, with small sangha. Founded 1990.

Weekly meditation Fridays 6:00–8:00 pm with Chenrezig sadhana practice and Shamatha/Vipashyana. Meditation instruction for new visitors. Organizes yearly week-long retreats based on Treasury of Knowledge teachings of Jamgon Kontrul Lodro Thaye—have been led by Dzogchen Ponlop Rinpoche and Khenpo Tsultrim Gyamtso Rinpoche. Ongoing study of teachings from previous retreats. Transcripts and tapes of teachings from previous retreats may be ordered.

Founder/Guru	Jamgon Kongtrul Rinpoche
Teachers	See above
Opening Times	Contact center

Residents	None
Festivals	None
Facilities	Meditation room
Accommodation	None
Food	None
Booking	Only for retreat, $50 deposit
Fees	Retreats $370 including room and board. Membership fee $25/month
Expected Behavior	No smoking or alcohol
How to Get There	2900 Mossrock, Ste 215, San Antonio, TX 78230. Mossrock is 1 block north of Loop 410 off Vance Jackson

San Antonio Shambhala Center (Tibetan–Kagyu/Nyingma)
Affiliation: Shambhala International
6233 Evers Road
San Antonio, TX 78230
Tel: (210) 647–1804
E-mail: dwgordon@tenet

See International headquarters, **Shambhala Center,** Halifax, Nova Scotia, Canada.

Wat Dhammabucha (Theravada)
6201 Sawyer Road
San Antonio, TX 78238-2206
Tel: (210) 521–7622 (8:00 am–1:30 pm) or (210) 520–5011
Fax: (210) 520–5042
E-mail: bucha@connecti.com
Web site: http://www.connecti.com/~bucha

Three stone-wall buildings with many trees. Recieves about sixty visitors a week. Established 1986 by Thai and Laos community to have a place for spiritual services in Southeast Asian Buddhist tradition.

Daily: 5:00 am chanting and meditation, 7:00 pm chanting and meditation. Have two other properties: Wat Sanghabucha in Pipecreek and Rock Spring Meditation Center which will be used for retreats from between 1999 and 2002.

Founder/Guru	See above
Teachers	3 resident monks
Opening Times	7:00 am–8:00 pm
Residents	3 monks and temple attendant
Festivals	Makabucha Day, Thai's Songkran Festival, Visakabucha

	Day, Asarahabuch Day, Sart Ceremony, End of Rains retreat, Kathin Ceremony
Facilities	Meditation room, service room, open air meditation patio, 3 small meditation houses
Accommodation	To be announced
Food	Wholefood
Booking	Not applicable
Fees	Not applicable
Expected Behavior	5 and 8 precepts
How to Get There	Out side loop 410, from Bandera Rd. to Sawyer Rd. At the end of Sawyer Rd. on your right is the sign for Wat Dhammabucha.

UTAH

Salt Lake City Forming Dharma Study Group (Tibetan–Kagyu/Nyingma)
Affiliation: Shambhala International
Stephen Coffin, Coordinator
1257 North 3100 East
Layton, UT 84040-3001

See International headquarters, **Shambhala Center,** Halifax, Nova Scotia, Canada.

Wat Dhammagunaram (Theravada)
644 E 10000 N
Layton, UT 84041
Tel & Fax: (801) 544–7616
E-mail: ThaiPal@aol.com

Chief incumbent is Thawatchai N. Puakta.

Kanzeon Zen Center Utah (Zen–Soto)
International Headquarters of Kanzeon sangha
1274 East South Temple
Salt Lake City, UT 84102
Tel: (801) 328–8414
E-mail: kanzeon@aol.com
Two frame houses and two brick apartment buildings in residential area near University of Utah. Strong emphasis on zazen.
    Formal zazen sittings two–four times daily. Soto Zen chanting services three times

a day during the two three-month training periods each year. Beginner and advanced zazen classes three times a week. Courses in Zen several times a year through the Division of Continuing Education at the University of Utah. Sesshins from three days to one month duration every one or two months. Summer program has recently included wilderness retreats. All activities open to newcomers, but new students are encouraged to take a four-week introductory course. *Kanzeon Sangha* newsletter published two or three times annually. Runs a stitchery called **Kanzeon Jade Thread.**

Founder/Guru	Dennis Genpo Merzel Roshi
Teachers	Resident: Founder, Anto Tenkei Coppens Sensei, Colin Gonin Fraser
Opening Times	Always open for meditators
Residents	15 monastics and 15 laity
Festivals	Buddha's Enlightenment—Rohatsu
Facilities	2 meditation halls, founder's shrine, private interview room, classroom, abbot's quarters, residents' facilities
Accommodation	Outside of Ango
Food	3 vegetarian meals a day during training periods. Breakfast and lunch $2; dinner $4
Booking	Contact center
Fees	Contact center
Expected Behavior	Wholehearted participation
How to Get There	Contact center for detailed instructions.

Shaolin Chi Mantis (Ch'an of Songshan Shaolin Temple)
P O Box 58547
Salt Lake City, UT 84158
Tel: (801) 595–1123

Teach Dharma and meditation for general public in churches and parks—contact center for current list of locations. Primarily a Shaolin Kung Fu school with instructors at various churches, rehabilitation centers, youth prisons, and women's shelters. "Shaolin is a way of life and not intended for monastic living. Our goal is to create more Bodhisattvas to live within society. A Temple is being planned for San Diego, but any location can suit our purposes. We enjoy teaching in the Temples of other denominations. Shaolin Chi Mantis is a modern version of the Buddhist Temple seen in the TV series *Kung Fu*, starring David Carradine. Martial arts are taught without violence, sparring, or wood breaking. Martial arts best describes our curriculum, where each student learns to love their self, their family, their friends, and all persons, animals, and things. Our focus on mind/body balance enables each student to easily develop their spiritual awareness. Our meditations are active and productive."

Classes four days per week in afternoons and evenings and include Ch'an Buddhism and meditation, Taoism, yoga, Shaolin Kung Fu, Taijiquan, Seven-Star Praying Mantis,

Taiji Praying Mantis, Chin Na, Push Hands, Combat Tai Chi, Staff, Sabre and other classical Chinese weapons. Curriculums include Chinese philosophy, world theology, psychology, and Chinese healing. Retreats seasonally on various topics or Master Zhen Shen-Lang may be hired for retreats in other locations in the U.S. and Canada.

Publish *Tai Chi Beginner* by Master Zhen Shen-Lang. **Shaolin Communications** produces music and audiobooks and publishes books and the newsletter *Shaolin Zen*. Other products include herbs and weaponry. **Shaolin Music** is a music publishing company. **Shaolin Film & Records** produces videos, cassettes, CDs, and artwork. **Tai Chi Youth** is a nonprofit corporation for youths at risk.

Founder/Guru	Master Zhen Shen-Lang
Teachers	Resident: Master Zhen Shen-Lang; visiting: Master Ru Jing Shi and Master Dou Wan Chun
Opening Times	Contact center
Residents	Not applicable
Festivals	Tai Chi Youth Tournament and San Diego Kung Fu Open
Facilities	Shrine/meditation room, Guan/Temple, study rooms, music studio, and yoga room
Accommodation	Will be available in new Temple
Food	Cantonese and Mandarin cuisine and eclectic dishes at restaurant prices. 3 meals for $10 to $20 per day
Booking	Varies—contact center
Fees	Monthly tuition $35/month; discounts available; some classes cost extra
Expected Behavior	Contact center for Basic Rules Sheet
How to Get There	Not applicable

Retreat is very useful, super useful. If you don't retreat you miss something, you become distant from Dharma unless you are super skillful and can make every action Dharma. Otherwise, in this twentieth century we need Dharma injections to keep it strong within us.

Lama Thubten Yeshe, 1981, quoted in a Vajrapani Institute brochure

VERMONT

Karme Choling (Tibetan–Kagyu/Nyingma)
Affiliation: Shambhala International
RR1 Box 3
Barnet, VT 05821
Tel: (802) 633–2384
Fax: (802) 633–3012
E-mail: Karmecholing@shambhala.org

Blend of New England, Tibetan, and Japanese design surrounded by 540 acres of meadows and woodlands. Six shrine rooms, including a meditation hall that seats two hundred, an azuchi or outdoor target range, and shrine for kyudo (Zen archery). Main building houses forty-five staff and offers variety of guest accommodation. Large organic vegetable garden, seven retreat cabins, tent sites, and guest house in town of Barnet. Founded 1970.

Sitting Meditation (Shamatha/Vipassyana) 7:00 am and 6:00 pm daily. Extensive program of activities in the three Shambhala gates, i.e., Vajradhatu for Buddhist study and training, Shambhala training (nonsectarian, nonreligious spiritual path), and The Nalanda Gate for cultural disciplines with a contemplative approach. Some are suitable for the public, and some for authorized students. Calendar produced twice a year. **Samadhi Cushions** produces meditation cushions on-site and also sells books, practice materials and gifts. Free catalog 1 (800) 331–7751.

Founder/Guru	Chogyam Trungpa Rinpoche
Teachers	Contact center
Opening Times	Visitors are welcome in the afternoons (check if it is not an open day)
Residents	45 plus some children
Festivals	Contact center
Facilities	See above
Accommodation	$25/day for basic accommodation, meals, and meditation instruction, plus $20 private room. 20% discount for Canadians, senior citizens, and students
Food	Nonvegetarian, vegetarian, or special diet available
Booking	Contact center
Fees	Varies—contact center
Expected Behavior	No smoking indoors, no alcohol in public areas, no music or TV (except on open days), no drugs.
How to Get There	1 hour north of White River Junction. Half mile west of exit 18 on I-91

Milarepa Center (Tibetan–Gelug)
Affiliation: Foundation for the Preservation of the Mahayana Tradition
Barnet Mountain
Barnet, VT 05821
Tel: (802) 633–4136
Fax: (802) 633–3808

Contact center for details.

St Johnsbury Dharma Study Group (Tibetan–Kagyu/Nyingma)
Affiliation: Shambhala International
Cathy Hinchey, Coordinator
P O Box 58
Barnet, VT 05821
Tel: (802) 633–4362

See International headquarters, **Shambhala Center,** Halifax, Nova Scotia, Canada.

Hanover Dharma Study Group (Tibetan–Kagyu/Nyingma)
Affiliation: Shambhala International
Herb Ferris, Greg Elder
HCR 71, Box 60
Windsor, VT 05089
Tel: (802) 674–6391

See International headquarters, **Shambhala Center,** Halifax, Nova Scotia, Canada.

Brattleboro Dharma Study Group (Tibetan–Kagyu/Nyingma)
Affiliation: Shambhala International
2 Flat Street
Brattleboro, VT 05301

See International headquarters, **Shambhala Center,** Halifax, Nova Scotia, Canada.

> *Since we are all Buddha by nature… every one of us possesses the potential for
> liberation, freedom, and enlightenment. That is quite clear.*
>
> H.E. Khentin Tai Situ Rinpoche in Lion's Roar, Issue One, Volume III—newsletter of KTD.

Sunray Meditation Society (Tibetan and Native American)
P O Box 269
Bristol, VT 05443
Tel: (802) 453–4610
Fax: (802) 453–3501
E-mail: sunray@sover.net

"International spiritual society dedicated to planetary peace, which offers ongoing programs of spiritual training, education and service. Our purpose is to being together people from all walks of life to share and apply, on the individual, family, community, and international levels, the ancient wisdom of peacemaking rooted in the Cherokee and Tibetan Buddhist traditions. Sunray also works with Native American and Tibetan communities to support and preserve their cultural and spiritual heritage.

"Sunray is rooted in Native American Earth wisdom and is also recognized as a Tibetan Buddhist Dharma center of the Nyingma and Drikung Kagyu schools. The Sunray practices embody these three ancient, intact spiritual lineages, whose common thread is teaching practical means to realize compassion and right relationship on Earth and throughout the family of life.

"Ven. Dhyani Ywahoo, Sunray's founder and spiritual director, is Chief of the Green Mountain Aniyunwiwa (Cherokee) and author of *Voices of Our Ancestors: Cherokee Teachings from the Wisdom Fire.*

"Sunray Community Meditation Circles meet around the world, organized by local community members. Visitors are always welcome. For more information, contact the Sunray office (802) 453–4610.

"The Peace Village is located in the Green Mountains of Vermont. This is a campground where summer teachings are held. Various Native American elders and Buddhist lamas give teachings."

Burlington Shambhala Center (Tibetan–Kagyu/Nyingma)
Affiliation: Shambhala International
236 Riverside Drive
Burlington, VT 05401
Tel: (802) 658–6795

See International headquarters, **Shambhala Center,** Halifax, Nova Scotia, Canada.

Zen Affiliate of Vermont (Zen–Soto/Rinzai)
Affiliation: Zen Mountain Monastery, Mountains and Rivers Order
54 Rivermount Terrace
c/o Bob Tokushu Senghas
Burlington, VT 05401
Tel: (802) 658–6466

Consists of three sitting groups with about forty members in Burlington, Montpelier, and Springfield, which each meet weekly for zazen. Formerly Zen Affiliate of Burlington, established 1984.

Burlington group meets Mondays 4:50–6:00 pm; contact Bob Tokushu/Dorrie Seishu Senghas on (802) 658–6466. Montpelier group meets Thursdays 4:50–6:00 pm; contact Michael Joen Gray on (802) 456–1983. Springfield group meets Thursdays 7:00 pm; contact Richard Ryoha Dunworth on (802) 228–2476. The affiliate gathers monthly for an all-day retreat, including zazen, chanting, services, oryoki, and taped Dharma discourse by John Daido Loori. Offers twice-yearly sesshin led by a MRO teacher. Publish bimonthly newsletter.

Founder/Guru	John Daido Loori
Teachers	See above
Opening Times	See practice times above
Residents	None
Festivals	Contact group
Facilities	Churches and students' homes
Accommodation	None
Food	See above
Booking	Contact group
Fees	Contact group
Expected Behavior	Contact group
How to Get There	Contact group

Rutland Dharma Study Group (Tibetan–Kagyu/Nyingma)
Affiliation: Shambhala International
Steve Butterfield, Coordinator
RR #1, #632
Cuttingsville, VT 05837
Tel: (802) 773–0909

See International headquarters, **Shambhala Center,** Halifax, Nova Scotia, Canada.

Manchester Dharma Study Group (Tibetan–Kagyu/Nyingma)
Affiliation: Shambhala International
Maggie Bernstein, Coordinator
P O Box 33
Manchester, VT 05254
Tel: (802) 362–3432
E-mail: (802) 362–3432

See International headquarters, **Shambhala Center,** Halifax, Nova Scotia, Canada.

Green Mountain Sangha (Theravada)
c/o Ann Barker
P O Box 78
East Middlebury, VT 05740
Tel: (802) 388–7329 and (802) 247–3479
Fax: (802) 388–6404
E-mail: asbarker@sover.net
Web site: http:/www.sover.net/~asbarker/sangha.html

Old farmhouse in Green Mountains on a remote, silent, secluded mountainside with flowers, ponds, and fields. Community of ten. Started 1991.

Dharma talks weekly on Theravada practice. Individual interviews on request. Beginners and more advanced practitioners welcome at everything. Quarterly silent one- or two-day retreats. Teachings in Theravada tradition, though participants welcome from any tradition.

Theravadanet—e-mail sangha. Reading, practice instruction, and guidance and detailed questions. Consists of about thirty members and a Theravada teacher—details at web site above.

Founder/Guru	Ann Barker
Teachers	Resident: Ann Barker
Opening Times	Contact center
Residents	None
Festivals	None
Facilities	Meditation room, working space, interview room
Accommodation	Farmhouse or tents free for overnight retreats. Otherwise, contact center for details of local country inns, motels, B&B.
Food	During retreats bring your own food; kitchen facilities available, except for 2 communal dinners on weekend retreats priced at $5
Booking	Depends on retreat
Fees	No charge
Expected Behavior	No smoking except on designed outdoor area; 5 precepts minimum, 8 precepts optional
How to Get There	For retreats, map can be faxed; for sittings, in Middlebury near Route 7

Vermont Zen Center (Zen)
Harada–Yasutani lineage via Roshi Philip Kapleau
P O Box 880
Shelburne, VT 05482
Tel: (802) 985–9746

Fax: (802) 985–2668
E-mail: vzc-graef@worldnet.att.net

Large house in semi-residential area on six acres pastoral land with river and several large gardens. Fifty members in Vermont; sister sanghas in Toronto (see **Toronto Zen Center,** Canada) and Costa Rica. Organizing small outreach group 1996. Established 1988; current premises since 1991, dedicated 1992 after building zendo and extensive landscaping. "Our center's small size makes it more personal than very large organizations. We hope that it is a warm and inviting place to practice."

Formal zazen Tuesdays and Thursdays 6:45–8:30 pm and Sundays 9:00–11:00 am. Informal sittings twice a week; chanting services once or twice a week; teisho weekly; dokusan and private instruction three times a week. Bimonthly introductory all-day workshops on Zen. No academic courses, but teisho by senior practitioners on aspects of Zen training. Twice-yearly Term Student programs of one to three months of intensified training activities. Periodic study/discussion groups. Four- to seven-day sesshins for experienced meditators on 4:00 am to 9:30 pm schedule with zazen, walking meditation, work training, chanting, and prostration. All-day sittings four times a year. Monthly newsletter, *Walking Mountains*. Sell some books.

Founder/Guru	Sensei Sunyana Graef
Teachers	Resident: Sensei Sunyana Graef
Opening Times	See sitting times above; always open to members
Residents	1 lay
Festivals	Kannon Day, Buddha's Parinirvana, Jukai, Vesan, Water Baby Observance, Bodhidharma Day, Hungry Ghost Ceremony, Oxfam Fast Day, Thanksgiving Ceremony, Buddha's Enlightenment, Home Purification Ceremonies, New Year's Eve Ceremonies
Facilities	Zendo, kannon area, small library
Accommodation	By special arrangement only
Food	Only at functions
Booking	Workshops, 2 days minimum; sesshins, 3 weeks; deposit required
Fees	Introductory workshops $45; membership $30–35 suggested contribution; sesshin $25/day members, higher nonmembers
Expected Behavior	No smoking, alcohol, or recreational drugs. Only vegetarian food on premises. Strive to observe 10 Cardinal Precepts in daily lives
How to Get There	Off Rte. 7 in Shelburne, turn onto Marsett Rd. Continue across small bridge, turn right immediately onto Thomas Rd., and Zen Center is $1/2$ mile down on right, tan house set back from street.

Virginia

Charlottesville Dharma Study Group (Tibetan–Kagyu/Nyingma)
Affiliation: Shambhala International
Charlottesville, VA 22901
Tel: (804) 295–7593
E-mail: jms5j@curry.edschool.virginia.edu

See International headquarters, **Shambhala Center,** Halifax, Nova Scotia, Canada.

Ligmincha Institute (Tibetan–Bon)
P O Box 1892
Charlottesville, VA 22903
Tel: (804) 977–6161
Fax: (804) 977–7020
E-mail: ligmincha@aol.com
Web site: http://www.comet.net/ligmincha

Practice center that also serves as administrative center for growing number of Bonpo Dharma centers in the West. Around twenty at each practice session; retreats draw between fifty and a hundred. Founded 1992. "We are the only representatives of Bon, the indigenous religion of Tibet, in the West, with close ties with the two Bon monasteries in exile.... The main focus of our practice is Dzogchen, the Great Perfection."

Regular meditation sessions and full schedule of residential retreats. Weekly practice sessions on Short Meditation Session in Six Parts (a Dzogchen practice) and the Bon Ngondro. Retreat topics vary according to the needs of practitioners, but common topics are: Introduction to Dzogchen, Dream Yoga, Sleep Yoga, Phrul Khor, Six Lokas Practice, and Ngondro. Also two retreat curriculums: seven-year program for training teachers and Experiential Transmission series, which reveals essential aspects of Dzogchen. Has translation program to publish texts from the Bonpo canon. Quarterly newsletter, *The Voice of Clear Light.* Back issues available on web site. Sell books and audiotapes relating to Dzogchen meditation and other practice materials through their newsletter and web site.

Two affiliate centers, **Khyung Dzong** and **Khyung Dzong of California** (see separate entries) and unofficial affiliate groups: San Francisco, Mark Dahlby, E-mail: mark&writers.com; Boston, Martin Lowenthal, E-mail: lowenthalm@aol.com; and Austin, Texas, Stephen Dignan, E-mail: stephen.dignan-next@attws.com.

Founder/Guru	Tenzin Wangyal Rinpoche
Teachers	Founder is resident teacher. Lopon Tenzin Namdak and Nyima Dakpa Rinpoche visit

Opening Times	Contact center
Residents	None
Festivals	Not applicable
Facilities	Meditation hall, library
Accommodation	Will help visitors arrange local accommodation
Food	None
Booking	2 weeks minimum for retreats
Fees	2-day nonresidential retreat $100 approximately. 1-week residential retreat $450 approximately.
Expected Behavior	No smoking within buildings
How to Get There	Call or e-mail for details

Unless your work is your meditation, your meditation is not meditation.

Sangharakshita

Mountain Light Zen Center (Zen–Soto)
6656 Mountain Light Place
Crozet, VA 22932
Tel: (804) 978–7770

Contact center for details.

Sai Sho An Zen Group (Zen–Rinzai)
11324 Pearlstone Lane
Delaplane , VA 20144
Tel: (540) 592–3701
Fax: (540) 592–3717
E-mail: tdavenport@aol.com

Small Zen sangha in rural/suburban community. Began meeting 1973—one of oldest Zen sanghas in South.

Meets in Emmanuel Episcopal Church Saturdays 7:00–9:30 am. Beginners and newcomers welcome. Church sponsors meditation meeting 6:30–7:00 pm Thursdays, followed by liturgy of Evensong. Special all-day sits and weekend sesshins throughout the year—often in conjunction with **Blue Ridge Zen Group** (see separate entry), Charlottesville.

Teachers	Tom Davenport (senior student of Joshu Sasaki Roshi)
Opening Times	See session times above
Residents	Not applicable
Festivals	None
Facilities	See above
Accommodation	None
Food	None
Booking	Contact center
Fees	$2 donation for the church
Expected Behavior	Etiquette strict
How to Get There	Call center

Blue Ridge Zen Group (Zen)
Mailing: 4460 Advance Mills Road
Earlysville, VA 22936
Tel: (804) 973-5435

Nonresidential ten-cushion zendo in two rooms in residential area and rural twelve-cushion rustic zendo for retreats in wilderness setting in Blue Ridge Mountains. Between fifteen and twenty-two members, including two monks. Began early 1970s and founded under present name 1975. "Small temple in the wilderness with emphasis on work and extended walking meditation on mountain trails. Members of our group have studied with various teachers giving an eclectic spirit, although the style is Renzai Zen."

Daily zazen with chanting and walking meditation Sundays. Introductory instruction for beginners. Periodic weekend zazen/walking/work retreats.

Founder/Guru	Teido Bill Stephens
Teachers	Gentei Sandy Stewart visits
Opening Times	Ask for details
Residents	None
Festivals	None
Facilities	Zendo, library
Accommodation	None
Food	Vegetarian at retreats
Booking	2 months in advance for retreats
Fees	$50 or equivalent service for weekend retreat
Expected Behavior	Be quiet, blend in
How to Get There	Call for details

Ekoji Buddhist Temple (Jodo Shinshu)
Affiliation: Buddhist Churches of America

10301 Burke Lake Road
Fairfax Station, VA 22039
Tel: (703) 569 2311
E-mail: tsuji@uno.com

New structure added to existing home on three acres in suburban town. Architecture shows Japanese influence. Space for services, Dharma study, walking meditation, and social gatherings. Membership around fifty. Founded 1981, part of the groups of Eko centers supported by the Bukkyo Dendo Kyokai. Moved to new building and grounds 1997. "Our goal is to promote Buddhism generally, Jodo Shinshu especially, in the national capital area. We are a very down-to-earth group—no mysteries. Come as you are—you are welcome."

Weekly meditation Sunday 10:00 am; traditional BCA service Sunday 11:00 am; Japanese Language Service monthly. Annual seminar (October) with invited guest speaker(s) on themes pertinent to Shin in America. Ongoing calligraphy and Taiko; occasional Kendo-Aikido. Dharma school biweekly Saturday evenings through high school age. Occasional study groups on Tannisho, Three Pure Land Sutras, etc. Publish monthly newsletter, *Kalavinka*.

Founder/Guru	Shinran Shonin (1173–1262)
Teachers	Resident: Rev. K. T. Tsuji
Opening Times	Contact center
Residents	None
Festivals	Bon
Facilities	Amida hall, social hall, library, recreation space, and see above
Accommodation	None
Food	None
Booking	Not necessary
Fees	Contact center
Expected Behavior	Common courtesy and goodwill
How to Get There	Just off the Fairfax County Parkway—Springfield bypass. Easy access from Highways 395-95, 495 southwest of Washington, DC

Guhyasamaja Center (Tibetan–Gelug)
Affiliation: Foundation for the Preservation of the Mahayana Tradition
7821 Fallstaff Road
McLean Hamlet
McLean, VA 22102
Tel: (703) 821–1887

Contact center for details.

Venerable Yohaku Arakawa (Nichiren Shu)
Affiliate: Nichiren Propagation Center
7503 Havelock Street
Springfield, VA 22150
Tel: (703) 644–0885

See **Nichiren Propagation Center,** Oregon.

Wat Yarna Rangsee (Theravada)
22147 Cedar Green Road
Sterling, VA 20164
Tel: (703) 406–8290
Fax: (703) 406–4705
E-mail: klom@erols.com

Suburban house on about three acres, with three or four resident monks. Thirty visitors or more a week. "Serious Dhamma practice in Theravada tradition."

Meditation Tuesday evenings, Vipassana, and Dhamma. Occasional Vipassana retreats. Celebrate Thai religious festivals, Vesak, and Katina.

> *If you look for the truth outside yourself,*
> *it gets farther and farther away.*
> *Today, walking alone,*
> *I meet him everywhere I step.*
> *He is the same as me,*
> *yet I am not him.*
> *Only if you understand it in this way*
> *will you merge with the way things are.*
>
> Tung-Shan quoted in *Muddy Water,* newsletter of the Zen Center of Hawaii, Hawaii

WASHINGTON STATE

Bellingham Dharma Study Group (Tibetan–Kagyu/Nyingma)
Affiliation: Shambhala International
Bellingham, WA 98225
Tel: (360) 647–5413
E-mail: pjwar@telcomplus.com

See International headquarters, **Shambhala Center,** Halifax, Nova Scotia, Canada.

Cloud Mountain Retreat Center (Nonsectarian)
Affiliation: Northwest Dharma Association
373 Agren Road
Castle Rock, WA 98611
Tel: (360) 274–4859 or Northwest Dharma Association (206) 789–5456
Fax: (360) 274–9119
E-mail: cloudmtn@teleport.com or nwdharma@accessone.com
Web site: http://www.teleport.com/~cloudmtn

Complex of several buildings near Castle Rock on five acres of wooded land with views of Mt. Rainier and Mt. St. Helens. Two meditation halls, two sleeping buildings (private rooms and dormitories), offices and library, cottage for guest teachers, shower house, sauna, small lake, organic garden, cats, and chickens. Rural retreat center conceived and built to provide all Buddhist organizations and practitioners with environment conducive to meditation and quiet contemplation or study. Accommodates up to thirty-four retreatants. Founded 1984.

Retreats scheduled regularly and led by monks, nuns, and lay teachers from Tibetan, Zen, Theravada, and Vipassana traditions range from weekend to sixteen days in length. All suitable for newcomers unless marked in schedule (contact center or see *Northwest Dharma News*).

For individuals and groups wishing to schedule a retreat, detailed information available.

Northwest Dharma Association published bimonthly newsletter, *Northwest Dharma News*. Call (206) 789–5446 for further information.

Founder/Guru	Anna Delacroix and David Branscomb
Teachers	Many from all main Buddhist traditions
Opening Times	See schedule
Residents	5 full-time staff
Festivals	Spring and fall work retreats, Founder's Day
Facilities	See above

Accommodation	Single, double, or dormitory-style.
Food	Vegetarian—accommodation made for dietary restrictions. Price included in retreat fee
Booking	Depends on popularity of retreat—see schedule
Fees	Retreats sponsored by Northwest Dharma Association $40/day; others may be higher
Expected Behavior	5 precepts; no smoking indoors; otherwise, according to demands of each retreat
How to Get There	$2^{1}/_{2}$ hours south of Seattle and $1^{1}/_{2}$ hours north of Portland, just off I-5. Detailed directions will be given.

Northwest Vipassana Center, Dhamma Kunja (Vipassana)
Affiliation: Vipassana Meditation Centers in the Tradition of S. N. Goenka
P O Box 345
Ethel, WA 98542-0345
Tel & Fax: (360) 978–5434
E-mail: DhKunja@aol.com

Retreat facility on forty acres of agricultural land a hundred miles southeast of Seattle in the foothills of the Cascade Mountains range; capacity forty-two students. Established 1991.

For further description see **Vipassana Meditation Center,** Massachussetts.

Seattle Ling Shen Ching Tze Temple (Chinese–True Buddha School)
17102 NE 49th Ct
Redmond, WA 98052
Tel: (206) 882–0916
Fax: (206) 883–7630

Large temple in Seattle facing the Cascade Mountains, overlooking Lake Sammamish. Main shrine in the temple is decorated in Tibetan Tantrayana style and consists of seven seven-feet-high Buddha statues, eight major deities, and many Dharmapala statutes. Established 1985.

Classes include Four Preliminary Practices, Guru Yoga, and Deity Yoga. True Buddha Tantric Dharma Saturdays 8:00 pm. Retreats held.

Founder/Guru	Living Buddha Lian Shen (Sheng Yen Lu)
Teachers	Resident: Sheng Yen Lu
Opening Times	9:00 am–6:00 pm daily
Residents	Over 20 monastics and 10 laity

Festivals	Blessing Ceremony, Soul Deliverance Ceremony, almost all Buddha's and Bodhisattvas' Birthdays
Facilities	Shrine, Ancestral Shrine, Light Offering, Annual Guardian Offering, Dragon Deity Hall, library, study room, meditation room
Accommodation	None
Food	Yes, no charge
Booking	Not applicable
Fees	Not applicable
Expected Behavior	No smoking, must be student of True Buddha school
How to Get There	Contact center

Richland Buddhist Center (Friends of the Western Buddhist Order)
Affiliation: Northwest Chapter of the Western Buddhist Order
Richland, WA
Tel: (509) 375–1840, (509) 967–2331, (509) 628–2055
Fax: (509) 628–2151
E-mail: cheeb54250@aol.com, ratnottara@aol.com
Web site: http://home1.get.net/swarner/index.htm

Has between five and ten active attendees. Started 1994.

Weekly meetings held Mondays 7:00 pm in Shrine Room of Emerald of Siam restaurant. Classes in Buddhism and meditation offered through Richland Community Schools and held in fall, winter, and spring sessions. Local 1-day retreats and transportation to FWBO retreats held in the Northwest—at least 3 retreats per year. *The Golden Light* published twice yearly.

Founder/Guru	Ven. Sangharakshita
Teachers	Resident Dharmachari: Anagarka Ratnottara and senior Dharmacharis visit
Opening Times	Contact center
Residents	1 Dharmachari and 4 Mitras
Festivals	Wesak, Parinirvana Day, Sangha Day, and other festivals celebrated with large Northwest centers in Seattle, Washington, and Missoula, Montana
Facilities	See above
Accommodation	None
Food	None
Booking	Contact center
Fees	Contact center
Expected Behavior	Contact center
How to Get There	Contact center

Amrita (Tibetan–Nyingma)
Affiliation: Chagdud Gonpa Foundation
2223 NE 137th Street
Seattle, WA 98125
Tel: (206) 367–7377

Contact center for details.

Dharma Sound Zen Center (Zen)
Affiliation: Kwan Um School of Zen
P O Box 31003
Seattle, WA 98103-1003
Tel: (206) 783–8484
Fax: (206) 463–5808
E-mail: barry108@aol.com

Fifty members with three locations in Puget Sound region: Seattle is residential center in a house; Redmond is a small building on private property; in Tacoma, practice at Seu Mi Sah, a traditional Korean Zen temple. Founded 1980, one of oldest Zen centers in Pacific Northwest.

Offer Zen meditation several times a week (morning and evening), six Introduction to Zen workshops each year, six-session lecture series annually on such topics as the Six Paramitas or Five Precepts. Six retreats per year of three to fourteen days. Between six and ten one-day retreats annually. All activities suitable for newcomers. Newsletter, *Dharma Sound*, three times a year.

Founder/Guru	Zen Master Seung Sahn
Teachers	Guiding: Robert Moore, Ji Do Poep Sa Nim
Opening Times	Contact center
Residents	1 monk, 3 laity
Festivals	Buddha's Birthday, Buddha's Enlightenment Day
Facilities	See above
Accommodation	None
Food	Vegetarian
Booking	Register for retreats 2 weeks in advance
Fees	Retreats $40/day non-members, $30/day members
Expected Behavior	No smoking or alcohol, 5 precepts, and temple rules
How to Get There	Seattle: 1147 NW 57th Street. Redmond: 4503 229th Avenue NE. Tacoma: 215 S 72nd Street.

Dohn-O Zen & Taoist Center (Zen and Tao)
10303 Densmore Avenue N

Seattle, WA 98133-9434
Tel: (206) 526 1274

Residential house converted to center in city; big yard with garden and fruit trees. Community of about twelve. "Sunim does energy analysis with diet recommendation from the center in Berkeley. He is also a Chinese herbalist. His analyses are personal and very accurate, and he has helped over four thousand people with many different types of health challenges."

Zen sitting Tuesday–Sunday 6:00–6:40 am and Tuesday–Friday 6:50–7:30 pm. Teach Taoist breathing meditation, called Sun-do, daily which helps to heal, energize, balance, and ground one's energies. Zen taught through Dharma talks when Sunim visits and through taped talks otherwise. Three-day Zen and Taoist healing retreat once a year in the summer.

Founder/Guru	Ven. Hyunoong Sunim
Teachers	Founder visits 3 times annually
Opening Times	As program of events
Residents	3 or 4 laity
Festivals	None
Facilities	Large practice space
Accommodation	Simple sleeping arrangement (mattress on floor)
Food	Vegetarian, wholefood included in daily price
Booking	Call before arriving—usually quite flexible
Fees	$30/day for accommodation, break and lunch, practice and instruction; monthly Sun-do and Zen $80, $70 concession, Zen only $25; 1-day workshops $60; 3-day retreats $150 (including room and board); Dharma talks by donation
Expected Behavior	No smoking; respectful of self and others
How to Get There	I-5 to exit 173, Northgate Way. West to Meridian, then south 3 blocks to 103rd. West or right off Meridian to Densmore. Cross Densmore, first on your right.

Drikung Kyoba Choling Meditation Center (Tibetan–Drikung Kagyu)
6307 California Avenue SW 1-B
Seattle, WA 98136
Tel: (206) 937–5356 or (206) 933–8075
E-mail: jbeach@slip.net (Jeff Beach)

Contact center for details.

Gold Summit Monastery (Pure Land and Ch'an)
Affiliation: Dharma Realm Buddhist Association
233 1st Avenue W
Seattle, WA 98119
Tel: (206) 217–9320

All Dharma Realm Buddhist Association branch monasteries are open to the public and have morning, afternoon, and evening ceremonies and sutra lectures every day as well as their own special programs. All activities are led by fully ordained monks or nuns.

Kagyu Shenpen Osel Choling (Tibetan–Kagyu)
4322 Burke Avenue North
Seattle, WA 98103
Tel & Fax: (206) 632–1439

Small house in Wallingford district of Seattle. Around forty students. Started 1993.
　　Meditation sessions. Classes are continuous throughout the week and by request. Beginners' courses started as needed. Retreats organized at other sites. Quarterly newsletter.

Founder/Guru	Lama Tashi Namgyal
Teachers	Resident: Lama Tashi Namgyal. Past visiting teachers have included Tai Situ Rinpoche, Thrangu Rinpoche, Kyabje Kalu Rinpoche
Opening Times	Contact center
Residents	None
Festivals	None
Facilities	Shrine room, meditation room, study
Accommodation	None
Food	None
Booking	Not applicable
Fees	Not applicable
Expected Behavior	"The usual"
How to Get There	From south, take left onto 45th for 8–10 blocks, then left on to Burke. From north, take right off I-5 onto 45th for 8–10 blocks, then left on to Burke.

Northwest Dharma Association (Nonsectarian)
1910 24th Avenue S
Seattle, WA 98144
Tel: (206) 324–5373

Fax: (206) 324–4261
E-mail: nwdharma@accessone.com

"Nonprofit, nonsectarian Buddhist organization that sponsors various activities and teachers for the purpose of supporting the growth, practice, and understanding of Buddhism and meditation in the West." Sponsor **Cloud Mountain Retreat Center,** Washington (see separate entry).

"Retreats, classes, and workshops are regularly scheduled and led by monks and lay teachers representing Tibetan, Zen, and Theravada/Vipassana traditions." Contact center for schedule of events.

Publish bimonthly newsletter, *Northwest Dharma News*, which also publicizes activities of other Buddhist organizations in the Northwest.

Rigpa (Tibetan–Nyingma)
Affiliation: Rigpa Fellowship
Seattle, WA
Tel: (206) 522–2615

Contact: The Kintons. See **Rigpa National Office,** California, for details.

Sakya Monastery of Tibetan Buddhism (Tibetan–Sakya and Rime)
108 NW 83rd Street
Seattle, WA 98117
Tel: (206) 789–2573
Fax: (206) 789–3994

Monastery with a hundred and fifty practitioners. Large building which has been extensively renovated and is now being transformed into a traditional Tibetan temple for which artists will be brought from India. Has double-life-size statues of Sachen Kunga Nyingpo and Sakya Pandita, founders of Sakya sect, and triple-life-size statue of the Buddha. Library is the Pacific Northwest branch of the Library of Tibetan Works and Archives.

Chenrezig Sundays 10:00 am and Thursdays 8:00 pm and Green Tara practice. Annual Nyen Nye retreat. Publish meditation practice books—contact center for book list.

Founder/Guru	H.H. Jigdal Dagchen Sakya and H.E. Dezhung II
Teachers	H.H. Jigdal Dagchen Sakya and H.H. Trinly Sakyapa
Opening Times	Call for an appointment
Residents	1 monastic, 4 laity
Festivals	Tibetan New Year Bazaar, traditional Buddhist holy days
Facilities	Gompa, library, small guest room, Tibetan Cultural Center

Accommodation	Small guest room $20/night at monastery or Tibetan Cultural Center
Food	None
Booking	2 weeks in advance; payment in full
Fees	Contact center
Expected Behavior	No smoking, alcohol, music, or shorts. Monastery rules.
How to Get There	I-5, take 85th Street exit, westbound to 1st Avenue NW, then left. Monastery at 83rd and 1st Avenue NW.

Seattle Buddhist Center (Friends of the Western Buddhist Order)
2765 South Washington Street
Seattle, WA 98144
Tel: (206) 726–0051
E-mail: aryadaka@aol.com

Turn-of-the-century wooden-frame building with three stories used as rooming house and nursing home in city residential area close to Lake Washington and large park with many trails. Public activities held on main floor consisting of two meditation rooms, reception area, and bookstore/library. Around forty-five visitors a week. Founded 1986 in private home. New premises purchased 1995.

Mindfulness of Breathing daily. Practice nights Tuesdays and Sundays. Metta Bhavana puja Sunday evenings. Meditation Saturday mornings. Men's and women's Dharma study groups. Weekly beginners classes. Weekly Dharma courses on various topics, e.g., Wheel of Life, Eightfold Path. Week-long wilderness retreat July/August. Satipatanna Sutra weekend retreats three times a year. Day retreats and monthly celebrations. Bimonthly newsletter, *Dharma Friends*.

Founder/Guru	Sangharakshita
Teachers	Resident: Aryadaka, Shantinayaka, and Amitaratna and various members of the Western Buddhist Order visit
Opening Times	7:15 am daily
Residents	4 men in a community
Festivals	Wesak, Padmasambhava Day, Sangha Day, Dharma Day, Buddha Day, and FWBO Day
Facilities	See above
Accommodation	For men only at center $15/night. Women can stay with friends of the center
Food	Vegetarian
Booking	1 month in advance
Fees	$10 per evening; $40–80 per course; concessions to anyone who asks
Expected Behavior	5 precepts
How to Get There	Just off Martin Luther King Way, south between Yesler and Jackson

Seattle Karma Thegsum Choling (Tibetan–Karma Kagyu)
Affiliation: Karma Triyana Dharmachakra, New York
2118 N 143 Street
Seattle, WA 98133
Tel: (206) 367–6998

Group focusing primarily on Shamata, Chenrezig and Ngondro practice.

Seattle Nichiren Buddhist Church (Nichiren Shu)
Affiliate: Nichiren Propagation Center
1042 South Weller Street
Seattle, WA 98104
Tel: (206) 323–2252
Fax: (206) 329–9059

Resident priest—Rev. Kanshin Mochida. See **Nichiren Propagation Center,** Oregon.

> *This is the quintessence of wisdom: not to kill anything.*
>
> *Sutra Kritanga*

Seattle Shambhala Center (Tibetan–Kagyu/Nyingma)
Affiliation: Shambhala International
919 E Pike Street
Seattle, WA 98122
Tel: (206) 860–4060
E-mail: Dan Peterson: peterhana@aol.com

See International headquarters, **Shambhala Center,** Halifax, Nova Scotia, Canada.

Soka Gakkai International (SGI-USA) (Nichiren)
Washington Area Regional Center
3438 South 148th Street
Seattle, WA 98168-4319
Tel: (206) 244–0268
Fax: (206) 241–8843

See **Soka Gakkai International** National Offices & Center, Santa Monica, California, for more details.

Three Treasures Sangha (Zen–Rinzai and Soto)
Affiliation: Diamond Sangha
1910 24th Avenue South
Seattle, WA 98144
Mailing address: P O Box 12542
Seattle, WA 98111
Tel: (206) 322–2447

Second-floor dojo in three-story home in Capitol Hill neighborhood. Forty-member sangha.
Zazen Monday–Friday 6:00–7:30 pm and Tuesday 7:30–8:30 pm. Seven-day sesshins January and June. Monthly one-, two-, and three-day zazenkais. Publish *Dharma Currents* newsletter four times a year.

Founder/Guru	Robert Aitken Roshi
Teachers	Jack Duffy
Opening Times	See zazen times
Residents	None
Festivals	None
Facilities	Dojo, library
Accommodation	None
Food	Vegetarian for sesshins included in price
Booking	$25 deposit 2 weeks in advance
Fees	Sesshin $225 non-members; $10/day zazenkai
Expected Behavior	Dark, unpatterned clothing; no rude noises during meditation or meals; clothes must be worn at all times; sense of humor mandatory
How to Get There	Call for directions

Vajralama Buddhist Center (Tibetan–Gelug)
Affiliation: New Kadampa Tradition
P O Box 23327
Seattle, WA 98102-0627
Tel: (206) 526-9565
E-mail: vajlama@ix.netcom.com
Web site: http://www.cnw.com/~vajlama

Residential community of eight, general teachings for the public attract sixty to eighty people per week. Founded 1994 in University of Seattle, looking for more permanent and larger premises 1996.
Daily meditation, weekly Tara and Je Tsongkhapa pujas. Introductory classes on Buddhist psychology and philosophy Monday evenings. Day courses every two months. Retreats for beginners three times a year; more in-depth retreats throughout the year. Empowerments occasionally. Foundation program in Mahayana Buddhism has classes

twice per week. Courses on Buddhist psychology, Training the Mind, and Stages of the Path to Enlightenment. Publish occasional newsletter.

Founder/Guru	Ven. Geshe Kelsang Gyatso Rinpoche
Teachers	Gen Kelsang Jangsem
Opening Times	Afternoons 2:00–6:00 pm
Residents	1 monk, 7 laity
Festivals	Contact center
Facilities	Shrine room for 30 people, library
Accommodation	Limited, $20/night
Food	Contact center
Booking	Contact center
Fees	Contact center
Expected Behavior	Contact center
How to Get There	Contact center

Padma Ling—Tibetan Meditation Center (Tibetan–Nyingma)
Affiliation: Chagdud Gonpa Foundation
West 1014 Seventh Avenue
Spokane, WA 99204
Tel: (509) 624–8715
Fax: (509) 624–8715
E-mail: gonpo@worldnet.att.net or vip@ior.com
Web site: http://www.ior.com/~vip/viphp.htm/padma_ling.htm

Two old houses, one three-story and one two-story within walking distance of downtown. High desert to the west and mountains to the east. Community of fifteen; forty visitors a week. Founded 1984. Lama Tarchin was resident lama for first 18 months. In 1987 American/German Lama Inge Sandvoss sent and joined a year later by her American husband, Lama Yontan Gonpo.

Sitting meditation weekday mornings 6:00 am and weekend mornings 7:00 am. Traditional diety practice twice daily. Variety of Tsog according to lunar calendar. Dharma teachings Thursday evenings, topic around needs of students. Study courses on Tara, Guru Rinpoche, Throma, Vajrakilaya, Vajrasattva, and others. Teach practice techniques such as Nogondro, Chod, Phowa, Dream Yoga, and beginning and advanced meditation. Annual Throma retreat over Christmas and New Year and other retreats as needed. Publish quarterly newsletter, *The Dragon's Song,* and monthly calendar.

Founder/Guru	Ghagdud Rinpoche
Teachers	Resident: see above; Tibetan and Western Lamas visit
Opening Times	6:00 am–10:00 pm weekdays; 7:00 am–9:00 pm weekends

Residents	15 laity
Festivals	Losar
Facilities	Shrine room, library, and office
Accommodation	Limited
Food	"We meet the needs of those visiting us."
Booking	Contact center
Fees	Mostly by donation with some exceptions
Expected Behavior	No smoking or drugs; 5 precepts.
How to Get There	Exit I-90 east bound at Monroe St.; west bound at Lincoln St.; go south on Lincoln to 7th Ave., turn right and it is the second house on the right.

Columbia Gorge Retreat Center (Zen–Rinzai)
MP 2.53R Berge Road
Stevenson, WA 98648
Tel: (509) 427–5009

Contact center for details.

WEST VIRGINIA

Spencer Buddhist Meditation Group
Rte. 2, Box 99
Harmony, WV 25243
Tel: (304) 927–1505
Fax: (304) 927–5171

Community of ten to twelve who meet in a local Presbyterian Church. Founded by Ken Lewis and Greg Woods.

Meet second Wednesday of every month from 6:00–8:00 pm. Monthly meditation practice, films, and discussion groups. Spencer Presbyterian Church is just north of Spencer on Route 14, on right side of road.

Bhavana Society (Theravada)
Rte. 1 Box 218-3
High View, WV 26808
Tel: (304) 856–3241
Fax: (304) 856–2111
E-mail: bhavanasoc@aol.com

Forest monastery and meditation center on thirty-two forested acres. New meditation hall (2,000 square feet), main building with women's dorm, men's guest house, single huts for individual retreats in the forest. Founded 1983; land purchased for current site and construction begun 1985; official opening 1988.

Offer daily Vipassana meditation 5:30 am and 7:00 pm. Daily puja in Pali (mornings) and English (evenings). Dhamma discussion after evening puja. Vipassana meditation retreats, annually: five weekend, five ten-day, youth retreat, family/work retreat, and year-ending retreat (two weeks unstructured for experienced meditators only).

Bhavana Society Newsletter four issues a year.

Founder/Guru	Bhante Henepola Gunaratana
Teachers	Resident: Bhante Henepola Gunaratana and Bhante Yogavacara Rahula
Opening Times	5:30 am–9:30 pm daily; please don't visit during silent group retreats
Residents	3 monks, 2 nuns, 2 laity
Festivals	Vesak, Kathina
Facilities	Separate meditation hall, library/study room will be provided
Accommodation	Single-room cabins without water and electricity (kutis); shared rooms in women's dorm and men's guest house; all gender-separated. Everything offered on donation basis.
Food	Vegetarian; donations of food or money welcome
Booking	Please register at least 2 weeks in advance for group retreats
Fees	Donations welcome
Expected Behavior	No smoking, alcohol, or drugs. 8 precepts. Noble silence during group retreats
How to Get There	$2^1/_2$ hours from Washington DC: I-66 to I-81 north toward Winchester. Highway 37 toward Romney and Berkeley Springs. Highway 50 west toward Romney and BS. Left turn soon after post office at Gore. To Route 704 and stay on this road until the Bhavana Society sign on the left

WISCONSIN

Milwaukee Sangha (Tibetan–Drikung Kagyu)
Affiliation: Tibetan Meditation Center, Frederick, Maryland
c/o Trinlay Khadro
P O Box 24708

Brown Deer, WI 53224-0708
Tel: (414) 357–8103 (Trinlay Khadro) or (414) 332–9370 (Tom Kopka)
E-mail: sari@glaci.com
Web site: http://www.churchward.com/drikung

Use Bookstore near UWM for weekly practice. Core group of eight. "Small friendly group, several newcomers, a few 'old timers' varying ages (nine to late sixties) and varying professions."

Chenrezig 7:00 pm Fridays. Occasional lama visits. Publish quarterly newsletter.

Founder/Guru	Konchog Gyaltsen Rinpoche
Teachers	Visiting teachers, one on a regular basis
Opening Times	7:00 pm Fridays
Residents	None
Festivals	None
Facilities	Not applicable
Accommodation	None
Food	None
Booking	None
Fees	None
Expected Behavior	Essentially "behave like you'd expect people to in any other sangha."
How to Get There	Contact center

Eau Claire Dharma Study Group (Tibetan–Kagyu/Nyingma)
Affiliation: Shambhala International
Rita Gross, Coordinator
126 Gilbert Avenue
Eau Claire, WI 54701
Tel: (715) 834–9612

See International headquarters, **Shambhala Center,** Halifax, Nova Scotia, Canada.

Kinzan, Ganto and Seppo were doing Zazen when Tozan came in with the tea.
Kinzan shut his eyes. Tozan asked, "Where are you going?" Kinzan replied,
"I am entering dhyana." Tozan said, "Dhyana has no gate;
how can you enter into it?"

Zen Sutra from The Solitary Bird, Cuckoo of the Forest

Drikung Kagyu Dharma Center of Madison (Tibetan–Drikung Kagyu)
6505 Olympic Drive
Madison, WI 53705
Tel: (608) 829–3541
E-mail: rdburian@students.wisc.edu

Dharma study group of five or six meets regularly in individuals' homes and arranges visits from teachers. Weekly group practices, usually Chenrezig, which is suitable for beginners. Inspiration is Ven. Khenpo Konchog Gyaltsen Rinpoche; visiting teachers include Ven. Lama Gyursam Acharya. Call for information or to be put on the mailing list.

Madison Dharma Study Group (Tibetan–Kagyu/Nyingma)
Affiliation: Shambhala International
Lora Wiggins, Coordinator
109 Acadia Drive
Madison, WI 53717
Tel: (608) 833–1767

See International headquarters, **Shambhala Center,** Halifax, Nova Scotia, Canada.

Madison Zen Center (Zen)
Affiliation: Rochester Zen Center
1820 Jefferson Street
Madison, WI 53711
Tel: (608) 255–4488

Members may become students of Bodhin Sensei and are automatically members of the Rochester Zen Center. Founded 1974; house purchased 1975.

Formal sittings six days a week. Sunday sitting includes taped teisho. Extended sittings one Saturday per month. Introduction to practice 6:30 pm first Monday of every month. Short retreats; longer retreats held at Rochester Zen Center and elsewhere.

Milwaukee Zen Center (Zen–Soto)
2825 North Stowell Avenue
Milwaukee, WI 53211-3775
Tel: (414) 963–0526

Urban lay center with daily program in three-story frame building on East Side, near University of Wisconsin–Milwaulkee. Began as small group 1970s. Rev. Akiyama (trained at training temple, Daieji, in Japan) resident head since 1985. Current building purchased 1986.

Zazen Monday–Saturday 6:00–7:30 am and Monday–Friday 6:30–8:00 pm. Morning service Monday–Saturday 7:30 am. Oryoki breakfast 7:40 am Saturdays. Weekly study class Saturdays 9:00 am. Monthly introductory course 6:30 pm first Wednesday of each month. All-day zazen third Saturday of each month. Two-day sittings twice a year in March and October. *Milwaukee Zen Center* published bimonthly. Sell incense and a few significant books on Zen and zazen by mail and at center.

Founder/Guru	Not applicable
Teachers	Resident: Rev. Tozen Akiyama
Opening Times	See daily practice times above and by appointment
Residents	1 priest
Festivals	Not applicable
Facilities	Zendo, study/dining room, kitchen, guest rooms, and teacher's quarters
Accommodation	2 guest rooms for short stays by practitioners on a donation basis
Food	Vegetarian in formal zendo meals for no fee
Booking	Write or call ahead if wanting to stay overnight
Fees	No set fees—make donation or join as a member
Expected Behavior	Follow zendo forms and keep the schedule. No smoking
How to Get There	From west or south, I-94 to Milwaukee and exit onto Hwy. 43N. From north, 43 S Exit from 43 at Locust. Go east on Locust to Stowell, and right on Stowell to # 2825, just north of Newberry.

Shambhala Center of Milwaulkee (Tibetan–Kagyu/Nyingma)
Affiliation: Shambhala International
2344 North Oakland Avenue
Milwaukee, WI 53211
Tel: (414) 277–8020
Fax: (414) 224–8818
E-mail: rKornman@csd.uwm.edu

Building in the city serving a community of fifty.
Shamatha/Vipassana Tuesdays, Wednesdays, Fridays 7:00 pm and weekends 9:00 am. Other activities via Shambhala International.

Founder/Guru	Chogyam Trunpa Rinpoche
Teachers	Many visit
Opening Times	Contact center
Residents	None
Festivals	Not applicable
Facilities	Shrine room, library, study room, and meditation room
Accommodation	None

Food	None
Booking	None
Fees	Contact center
Expected Behavior	Contact center
How to Get There	Call ahead

The Deer Park (Tibetan–Gelug)
4548 Schneider Drive
Oregon, WI 53575
Tel: (608) 835–5572
Fax: (608) 835–2964

Thirteen-acre site in countryside near Madison. Large house with living quarters, offices, and library. Annex building provides living quarters for monastic community and visitors, classrooms, and additional library space. Library, The Deer Park Collection, includes many original Tibetan texts in traditional woodblock prints and modern formats, books on Tibet and Buddhism in English and other European languages, and a complete set of audiotapes of teachings given at Deer Park. Temple originally built 1981 for first Kalachakra ceremony by H.H. Dalai Lama to be performed outside of Asia and is in traditional Tibetan style with many beautiful paintings and tapestries depicting the life of the Buddha and other religious figures. Stupa dedicated 1989 by H.H. Dalai Lama. Special connection to Sera Chay Monastic University in Lhasa and south India. Founded 1979. Welcomes all interested persons, regardless of religious affiliation or other distinctions. "We have sought to operate in a spirit of friendliness and openness to all."

Religious teachings by Geshe Sopa Sundays 10:00 am, with Jorcho puja once a month. Weekly teachings on Lamrim and Tantra for senior students. Lama chopa puja on tenth day of Tibetan month at 7:30 pm. Vajra Yogini puja on twenty-fifth day of Tibetan month. Special intensive courses and retreats at regular intervals.

Sponsor Tibetan educational and cultural programs, such as Tibetan dance, dramatic and musical performances, and the multimedia tour of the Sera Chay monks. Separate but affiliated organization works to advance the goal of Tibetan independence and human rights.

Founder/Guru	Director and founder: Geshe Lhundrup Sopa
Teachers	Resident monks and eminent visiting teachers
Opening Times	Contact center
Festivals	Wesak, H.H. the Dalai Lama's Birthday, anniversary of the death of Tsongkhapa, etc.

Wausau Zen Group (Zen)
Affiliation: Kwan Um School of Zen

5107 River Bend Road
Schofield, WI 54476
Tel: (715) 355–7050

Dharma room in a house. Group with about five visitors a week. Started 1991.
Weekly sitting meditation including chanting, sitting, and Dharma talk. Introduction to Zen meditation workshops. Monthly half-day practice. Full-day retreats bi-yearly. Annual two-day intensive retreat. Publish monthly newsletter.

Founder/Guru	Zen Master Seung Sahn
Teachers	Various facilitators and teachers visit
Opening Times	Tuesday evening 7:00–8:30 pm
Residents	Not applicable
Festivals	No applicable
Facilities	Meditation room
Accommodation	Not applicable
Food	Vegetarian during retreats
Booking	Week in advance for retreats
Fees	2-day retreat $75, 1-day retreat $20
Expected Behavior	Temple rules
How to Get There	Northbound Hwy. 51 to Hwy. 29

The well-informed holy disciples do not take delight in the senses and their objects, are not impressed by them, are not attached to them, and in consequence their craving ceases; the cessation of craving leads successively to that of grasping, of becoming, of birth, of old age and death, of grief, lamentation, pain, sadness, and despair—that is to say to the cessation of all this mass of ill. It is thus that cessation is Nirvana.

Questions of King Milina, translated by Edward Conze

Buddhist Centers in Canada

Alberta

Avatamsaka Monastery (Pure Land and Ch'an)
Affiliation: Dharma Realm Buddhist Association
1009 4th Avenue SW
Calgary, Alberta T2P 0K8
Tel & Fax: (403) 234-0644
Web site: http://www.cadvision.com/avatamsaka

All Dharma Realm Buddhist Association branch monasteries are open to the public and have morning, afternoon, and evening ceremonies and sutra lectures every day as well as their own special programs. Three- to seven-day Pure Land retreats four or five times a year. All activities are led by fully ordained monks or nuns. Irregular newsletter.

Founder/Guru	Ven. Master Hsuan Hua
Teachers	Resident: Master Heng Hing; Master Heng Tso visits
Opening Times	Contact center
Residents	2 monks
Festivals	Wesak
Facilities	Buddha hall, classrooms, library, meditation room
Accommodation	Only upon referral
Food	Strict vegetarian
Booking	Contact center
Fees	Contact center
Expected Behavior	5 precepts, no smoking
How to Get There	Call first

Buddhist Group Calgary (Tibetan–Karma Kagyu)
Affiliation: Diamond Way Buddhism under the guidance of Lama Ole Nydahl and the 17th Karmapa, Thaye Dorje

226-25 Avenue SW
Calgary, Alberta T2S 0L1
Tel: (403) 229–9081 and (403) 229–4818
Fax: (403) 262–3623
E-mail: nickj@supernet.ab.ca

Sangha of about ten meet in a member's residence. Established 1995 out of the Edmonton center. "Very young, fresh, and energetic sangha!"

Weekly group meditation, Three Lights Meditation, as taught by 16th Karmapa. Open discussion and guidance on preliminary teachings.

Founder/Guru	Lama Ole Nydahl
Teachers	Self-directed group—contact persons Nicholas Jones and Carl White. Lama Ole Nydahl and Jesper Jorgensen sometimes visit.
Opening Times	Tuesday group meditation at 8:00 pm
Residents	None
Festivals	None
Facilities	Simple meditation room for up to 15 people
Accommodation	By invitation, at residences of Sangha only
Food	None
Booking	None
Fees	None
Expected Behavior	None
How to Get There	Just south of downtown Calgary, near the Elbow River, east of 4th St. at 25th Avenue SW

Pai Yuin Tang Buddhist Congregation (Chinese–True Buddha School)
1809 Center Street N
Calgary, Alberta T2E 2S5
Tel: (403) 230–7427
Fax: (403) 230–2558

Approximately eighty members in Calgary. True Buddha School has been in Calgary since 1986, and this temple built 1994.

Founder/Guru	Master Sheng-yen Lu
Teachers	Contact center
Opening Times	Noon–5:00 pm Monday–Friday; noon–10:00 pm Saturday; noon–5:00 pm Sunday
Residents	2 nuns
Festivals	Contact center
Facilities	Contact center

Accommodation	None
Food	Vegetarian and wholefood
Booking	Contact center
Fees	By donation
Expected Behavior	Be respectful
How to Get There	Contact center

Buddhist Center Edmonton Kamtsang Choling (Tibetan–Karma Kagyu)
Affiliation: Karma Kagyu centers worldwide
c/o Roy Beebe
11115–35a Avenue
Edmonton, Alberta T6J 0A4
Tel: (403) 444–0892 (Paul Pype and Janice Dewhurst)
E-mail: INTERNET: ppype@connect.ab.ca (Paul Pype); 104123.271@compuserve.com
(Annik Foreman) or kclsf@diamondway.org for more information about Karma Kagyu
centers worldwide

House belonging to members. Polish practitioner met Lama Ole Nydahl 1987 and
moved to Canada 1991, inviting him for a visit 1993.

Meditation weekly with Three Lights Meditation, sometimes Chenrezig or Tara
practice. Organize retreats every month or two, usually on Ngondro, at different locations.
Starting up a T-shirt business 1996.

Founder/Guru	Lama Ole Nydahl
Teachers	Lamas visit
Opening Times	Not applicable
Residents	2 lay
Festivals	None
Facilities	Shrine and meditation room, small library
Accommodation	May be arranged in members' houses
Food	Vegetarian or with meat, about $10/day
Booking	2 weeks in advance, no deposit required
Fees	Weekend retreat about $100
Expected Behavior	No drugs, prefer no smoking, but people who do may smoke outside building
How to Get There	Contact center

Edmonton Shambhala Center (Tibetan–Kagyu/Nyingma)
Affiliation: Shambhala International
10110 124th Street, #207
Edmonton, Alberta T5N 1P6
Tel: (403) 482–7378

E-mail: dveastsun@ccinet.ab.ca

See International headquarters, **Shambhala Center,** Halifax, Nova Scotia.

Gaden Samten Ling Tibetan Buddhist Meditation Society (Tibetan)
9006 115 Avenue
Edmonton, Alberta T5B 0L9
Tel: (403) 477–2782 (Carol Tomlinson, secretary of group)
Fax: (403) 422–3631
E-mail: tomlic@mail.health.gov.ab.ca

Around sixty-three members and many visitors. "The aim of GSL is to provide interested students with instruction in Tibetan Mahayana Buddhism.... We are a very active group and enjoy organizing cultural events and bringing speakers and entertainers to Edmonton, such as Chaksampa's Tibetan Opera Company and anthropologist Peter Gold's sacred mask and Sacred Hootenanny workshops and lectures." Established 1986.

Twice-weekly practice, meditation and teachings—Sundays 2:00–4:00 pm and Tuesdays 8:00–10:00 pm. Lamrim study. Initiations and retreats by visiting teachers. Retreats such as Medicine Buddha, White Tara, Chenrezig, Heruka, Zhambala, Vajrasattva, and Vajrayogini. Newsletter published several times a year. Sell Dharma books, cards, malas, prayerbook covers, and other items.

Founder/Guru	Geshe Ngawang Kaldan
Teachers	Resident: Geshe Ngawang Kaldan; visiting teachers include Zasap Tulku Rinpoche and Lati Rinpoche.
Facilities	Meet at Geshe-la's home but looking for new premises. Large library.

BRITISH COLUMBIA

Partzandi Buddhist Centre (Tibetan–Gelug)
Affiliation: New Kadampa Tradition
2329 A Rosewall Crescent
Coutenay, BC V9N 8R9
Tel: (604) 334–4065

Teachers: Gwen Francis, Mark Tegtmeyer

Thubten Choling (Tibetan)
5810 Wilson Avenue
Duncan, BC V9L 1K4
Tel & Fax: (250) 746–8110
E-mail: jhampas@island.net
Web site: http://www.mala.bc.ca/~shanemanj/wwwhome.htm

One acre of treed property with a sixteen-foot stupa (the only one yet on Vancouver Island). Half acre grass and ponds around the principal residence. Cowichan River ten minutes walk away. Long-term rental suite and a smaller suite for short-term retreats and visits.

Sunday night classes on Mahayana Buddhism, Wednesday night open session of meditation. Special initiations and Vajrayana teachings periodically. Courses on dream work, meditation, and visualization through the local Malaspina College. Publish quarterly newsletter.

Daka's Buddhist Astrology (address and web site as above) offers astrological readings.

Founder/Guru	H.H. the Dalai Lama
Teachers	Resident: Kyabje Ling Rinpoche; Jhampa Shaneman, Maria Shaneman; Zasep Tulku and Lingtrul Rinpoche visit
Opening Times	Classes 8:00 pm summer, 7:30 pm winter
Residents	4
Festivals	According to Buddhist calendar
Facilities	Shrine room, library, rental suite, grounds for walking, stupa
Accommodation	Meditation hall for single nights by donation. Rental suite for longer duration $20 daily
Food	Vegetarian (Suite arranges their own diet)
Booking	Call for availability
Fees	Donation
Expected Behavior	No smoking in premises
How to Get There	Transcanada highway to Dunan, follow the Hospital signs to Gibbons Road, Wilson Ave. is on the left as you approach the Hospital entrance

Hollyhock (Vipassana and Tibetan)
Box 127
Manson's Landing, BC V0P 1K0
Tel: (250) 935–6576
Fax: (250) 935–6424
E-mail: hollyhock@oberon.ark.com
Web site: http://www.go-interface.com/hollyhock

Organizes retreats and seminars in the practical, creative, and healing arts. Wooden buildings, organic gardens, and forest trails set in coastal wilderness. Started 1982.

Meditation sittings and yoga daily April to September. Metta and Vipassana retreats spring and fall; Tibetan Buddhist retreats in fall. Annual catalog in January and annual newsletter in June. Center may be used for holidays without attending workshops.

Teachers	Buddhist teachers visit for particular events
Opening Times	April 1
Residents	None
Festivals	None
Facilities	Meditation sanctuary, 2 session houses, library, central lodge
Accommodation	Tenting ($375/week), dorm rooms for 3–6 people ($478/week), twin rooms ($550/week), single ($650/week). Prices include meals
Food	Vegetarian, wholefood, and seafood once a week $35/day
Booking	Advance booking required, $250 deposit
Fees	Accommodation prices include administration, meals, and 1 massage
Expected Behavior	Not applicable
How to Get There	Seaplane from Vancouver Harbor; flight from Vancouver or Seattle to Campbell River, then ferry to Cortes Island; or car and ferry.

Mountain Mind Dharma Center (Zen–Rinzai)
Box 232
Manson's Landing, BC V0P 1K0
Tel: (604) 935–6661

Operates out of residential house and some facilities and retreats at **Hollyhock** (see separate entry). Currently looking for land for own center. "Our Roshi especially enjoys teaching Westerners because of their freshness and sincere attitudes toward practice. He is trained in the Kensho school of Zen but realizes the difficult nature of this approach for most students of Zen and has developed ways of teaching Zen in a way that has less cultural bias and is geared toward Westerners."

Zazen twice a day and morning and evening chanting service. Open discussion groups/public lectures when Roshi visits. One–two sesshins per year with groups of around twenty to thirty people run at Hollyhock, which include intensive sanzen (dokusan). Plan to publish periodical.

Teachers	John Glade Wittmayer (Jion Shinko)
Opening Times	Roshi Shinzan Miyamai visits
Residents	1 priest, variable number of laity

Festivals	None
Facilities	Zendo area
Accommodation	During sesshins
Food	Vegetarian
Booking	2 weeks in advance with $100 deposit
Fees	$600 per 7-day sesshin
Expected Behavior	Mindfulness
How to Get There	Ferry from Vancouver to Vancouver Island and head north to Campbell River. Take 2 more ferries and short drive to Cortes Island

Kootenay Shambhala Center (Tibetan–Kagyu/Nyingma)
Affiliation: Shambhala International
Mail: Box 136
Nelson, BC V1L 5P7
Location: 444 Baker Street, Nelson
Tel: (250) 352–1714 (center) or (250) 352–6559 (contact)
Fax: (250) 354–1816
E-mail: trime@netidea.com or russelr@netidea.com

Downtown on third story of a commercial building. Also have retreat cabin on land nearby and are developing a summer-use group retreat facility for twenty practitioners and around thirty members. Began 1970s and center established 1979 at present location.

Monday night open house talks on introductory Buddhist/Shambhala topics. Further classes for advanced students on demand. Personal meditation instruction available on request. Retreats most summers with Shamatha and Vajrayana practices for qualified students. Shambhala training three–four times a year. Publish quarterly newsletter.

Founder/Guru	Chogyam Trungpa Rinpoche
Teachers	Sakyong Mipham Rinpoche visits
Opening Times	Mondays 7:00–9:00 pm, Thursdays 7:00–8:00 pm, Sundays 9:00 am–noon
Residents	None
Festivals	None
Facilities	2 shrine rooms (public and Vajrayana)
Accommodation	None
Food	None
Booking	None
Fees	Open house free; Shambhala training weekend $100 approximately
Expected Behavior	Contact center
How to Get There	Contact center

Chagdud Gonpa Canada (Tibetan–Nyingma)
Affiliation: Chagdud Gonpa Foundation
2036 Stephens Street
Vancouver, BC V6K 3W1
Tel: (604) 733–5583

Contact center for details.

Gold Buddha Monastery (Pure Land and Ch'an)
Affiliation: Dharma Realm Buddhist Association
301 East Hastings Street
Vancouver, BC V6A 1P3
Tel: (604) 684–3754

All Dharma Realm Buddhist Association branch monasteries are open to the public
and have morning, afternoon, and evening ceremonies and Sutra lectures every day as
well as their own special programs. All activities are led by fully ordained monks or
nuns.

Kamtsang Choling Vancouver Buddhist Society (Tibetan–Kagyu)
1230 E 8th Avenue, #201
Vancouver, BC V5T 1V2
Tel: (604) 876–3875
Fax: (604) 876–9697

Located in an apartment. Established 1992 by Lama Ole Nydahl. "Our center in
Vancouver is still in growing stages, but it is strong by being well connected to the
many centers around the world that work together in many ways. We are a part of an
ever growing global family bound by the common good and vision."

Weekly meditation, information and support to practitioners at any time. Weekly
Three Lights Kamapas meditation. Dorje Sempa, Clear Light, and other meditation as
requested. Support for Ngondro as requested. Refuge meditation once a month. Lama Ole
Nydahl visits (frequency depending on needs of practitioners), and teachings may include
courses on Ngondro, Mahamudra, lectures on Death and Dying, or Phowa practice.

Founder/Guru	Lama Ole Nydahl
Teachers	Lama Ole Nydahl and Ven. Lopon Tseschu Rinpoche visit
Opening Times	Any time
Residents	1
Festivals	Contact center
Facilities	Gompa, study, library, meditation space
Accommodation	Up to 4 out of town visitors at a time—donation

Food	Kitchen facility, provided food vegetarian for donation
Booking	2 weeks notice minimum
Fees	Fees vary
Expected Behavior	Contact center
How to Get There	Vancouver East—Broadway and Clark.

Lions Gate Buddhist Priory (Zen–Soto)
Affiliation: Serene Reflection Meditation Tradition
1745 West 16th Avenue
Vancouver, BC V6J 2L9
Tel: (604) 738–4453

Meditation and Ceremony 9:00 am Sundays; Meditation, Vespers, and Class 7:30 pm Tuesdays; Evening Service with meditation and Vespers 7:30 pm Thursdays. Meditation instruction 7:30 pm Thursdays or by appointment. Monthly one-day retreats. Celebration of Buddhist festivals. Bi-monthly *Lions Gate Buddhist Priory Newsletter*.

Affiliated meditation groups in Edmonton, Alberta, and Victoria, British Columbia. For further information, contact: Ian Patton, 7632 88 Ave., Edmonton, AB T6C 1K8, e-mail: ipatton@ccinet.ab.ca; tel: (403) 466–1340; or Bayne Dean, 2087 Byron Street, Victoria, BC V8R 1L8, tel: (604) 595–3252.

PTT Buddhist Society (Chinese)
514 Keefer Street
Vancouver, BC V6A 1Y3
Tel: (604) 255–3811
Fax: (604) 255–8894

Contact center for details.

Rigpa (Tibetan–Nyingma)
Affiliation: Rigpa Fellowship
Vancouver, BC
Tel: (604) 263–8842

Contact: Suyin Lee. See **Rigpa National Office,** California, for details.

SGI-Canada Vancouver Culture Center (Nichiren)
Affiliate: Soka Gakkai International Association of Canada
8401 Cambie Street

Vancouver, BC V6P 3J9
Tel: (604) 322–0492
Fax: (604) 322–0491

Contact center for more details.

Tilopa Buddhist Center (Tibetan–Gelug)
Affiliation: New Kadampa Tradition
Vancouver, BC
Tel: (604) 312–2520
E-mail: c/o vajlama@ix.netcom.com
Web site: http://www.cnw.com/~vajlama

No fixed premises. Started fall 1996 under the auspices of **Vajralama Center,**
Washington (see separate entry).
   Meet Thursday evenings for classes on Buddhist psychology and philosophy for
the general public. Occasional day courses and retreats. Spiritual guide: Ven. Geshe
Kelsang Gyatso Rinpoche. Resident teacher: Gen Kelsang Jangsem.

Vancouver Buddhist Center (Friends of the Western Buddhist Order)
456 West King Edward Avenue
Vancouver , BC V5Y 2JN
Tel: (604) 877–0269

House in city center with community of five Buddhist women living in same building.
Opened 1996. "Traditional Buddhism drawn from Theravada, Mahayana, Vajrayana, in
a Western context."
   Metta Bhavana, pujas, and chanting practices. Ongoing classes in Buddhist med-
itation, talks, Mitra study group, and general study groups. Introduction to Buddhism.
Monthly day retreats on-site and longer retreats regionally.
   Bookshop which also sells gifts.

Founder/Guru	Ven. Sangharakshita
Teachers	Various order members
Opening Times	Varies
Residents	Women order members
Festivals	Buddha Day, Parinirvana Day, Buddha's Birthday, Dharma Day, Padmasambhava Day, Sangha Day, WBO Day, and FWBO Day
Facilities	Shrine room, library, bookshop
Accommodation	For 2–3 visitors
Food	Vegetarian

Booking	Please call
Fees	Day retreats $20 or dana
Expected Behavior	5 precepts
How to Get There	Central Vancouver

Vancouver Shambhala Center(Tibetan–Kagyu/Nyingma)
Affiliation: Shambhala International
3275 Heather Street
Vancouver, BC V5Z 3K4
Tel: (604) 874–8420
E-mail: mmcclen@direct.ca

See International headquarters, **Shambhala Center,** Halifax, Nova Scotia.

Zen Center of Vancouver (Zen)
Affiliation: Rinzai-Ji, Los Angeles, California
4269 Brant Street
Vancouver, BC V5N 5B5
Tel: (604) 879 0229
E-mail: zcv@vcn.bc.ca

City Zen center in house and gardens, mountain, and island retreat facilities. Incorporated 1970 after visit by founder.

Daily zazen, daily services, and chanting, Buddhist ceremonial days. Monthly one-day sesshins on Cypress Mountain; seasonal five-day sesshins on Galiano Island. First-timers are asked to call to arrange instruction prior to the sit. Occasional newsletter.

Associated local Zen center: **Victoria Zen Society** (see separate entry).

Founder/Guru	Joshu Sasaki Roshi
Teachers	Resident: Eshin John Godfrey
Opening Times	Phone first please
Residents	Priest and 5 laity
Festivals	None
Facilities	Zendo and meeting room
Accommodation	None
Food	Vegetarian
Booking	None
Fees	None
Expected Behavior	Contact center
How to Get There	East side of Vancouver by Nanaimo Skytrain station

Shambhala Meditation Center–Victoria (Tibetan–Kagyu/Nyingma)
Affiliation: Shambhala International
1785 Carrick Street
Victoria , BC V8R 2M1
Tel: (250) 595–1952
Fax: (250) 370–1788
E-mail: kerry@pacificcoast.net
Web site: http://www.pacificcoast.net/~kerry

Heritage building in center of Victoria. Beautiful and quiet—also hosts Tai Chi and yoga classes and other Buddhist groups. Community of fifty.

Wednesdays 7:00 pm Buddhist open house; Thursdays 7:00 pm Shambhala training open house; meditation instruction provided both nights. Gateway weekend program every few months for Buddhist path and Shambhala training.

Founder/Guru	Chogyam Trungpa Rinpoche
Teachers	Visiting: Mipham Rinpoche, Khandro Rinpoche, Dzongsar Khyentse Rinpoche
Opening Times	Contact center
Residents	None
Festivals	Contact center
Facilities	Large shrine room
Accommodation	Visitors can be billeted
Food	None
Booking	Contact center
Fees	Contact center
Expected Behavior	Contact center
How to Get There	Contact center

Victoria Buddhist Dharma Society
Sakya Thubten Kunga Choling (Tibetan–Sakya)
1149 Leonard Street
Victoria, BC V8V 2S3
Tel & Fax: (250) 385–4828

House with shrine room with capacity for forty-five people, close to park and ocean with a hundred and twenty visitors a week. Founded 1974.

Schedule of different meditations, pujas, teachings, etc. each day of the week. Weekly beginners' and advanced classes in Tibetan. Courses in Basic Meditation; Meditation; View, Meditation, Action; Hearing, Contemplation, Meditation; The Three Visions; The Kadampa Mind Trainings; Mind Purification; Dealing with Anger; Impermanence; Emptiness; Death, the Intermediate State and Rebirth; Basic

Buddhism for Beginners; Foundation Practices; etc. Foundations of Buddhism, Chenrezig, Green Tara, and Vajrayogini retreats three times a year.

Prison ministry—Sister Margaret is Buddhist prison chaplain for William Head Institute, Matsqui Institute, and Wilkinson Road Institute and keeps a large correspondence with prisoners from other prisons. Sister Margaret is also the Buddhist chaplain for the University of Victoria Chaplains Service. Have produced fourteen booklets.

Founder/Guru	Geshe Tashi Namgyal
Teachers	Resident teacher is founder; eminent teachers visit
Opening Times	As per schedule
Residents	1 Geshe, 1 nun, and 2 laypeople
Festivals	4 Buddhist days
Facilities	Shrine room, small library, study room
Accommodation	1 room available
Food	Contact center
Booking	Contact center
Fees	Retreat $30/day (3 meals included)
Expected Behavior	No smoking or drugs, 5 precepts
How to Get There	No. 5 Bus to Cook and May, 1 block down Cook to Ocean.

Victoria Zen Center Society (Zen–Rinzai)
c/o Les Desfosses
4956 Cordova Bay Road
Victoria, BC V8Y 2K1
Tel: (250) 658–5033 and (250) 478–6377
Fax: (250) 658–4194
E-mail: lesdes@horizon.bc.ca and mohenly@amtsgi.bc.ca
Web site: http://www.islandnet.com/~mohenly/vzc/homepage/html

Has various locations. Thirty-five members, some dozen regularly attend. Began meeting late 1970s, incorporated as society 1980.

Zazen Mondays 7:30 pm in an interfaith chapel in the Memorial Pavilion of the Royal Jubilee Hospital at 1900 Fort Street, Victoria. Zazenkais once a month at the Queen Alexandra Hospital, 2400 Arbutus Road, Victoria. Five-day sesshins two or three times a year in a rural setting on Galiano Island.

Founder/Guru	Student of Sasaki Roshi
Teachers	Eshin Godfrey of Vancouver Zen Center visits
Opening Times	Not applicable
Residents	None
Festivals	None
Facilities	See above
Accommodation	May be possible to arrange a brief billet

Food	During Zazenkais and sesshins, price included
Booking	Only necessary for sesshins, a few days in advance
Fees	$5 donation per evening; $20 per zazenkai; $30 per day sesshins
Expected Behavior	Silence and usual Zen monastery practices
How to Get There	Contact one of the phone numbers above for details

Vipassana Foundation (Vipassana)
Affiliation: Vipassana Meditation Centers in the Tradition of S. N. Goenka
80 High Street
Victoria, BC V8Z 5C7
Tel: (604) 479–6641 Victoria or (604) 264–7637 Vancouver

Organizes ten-day courses at rental sites in British Columbia and Alberta several times a year; sponsors regular introductory evenings for the public and regular weekly group meditations and periodic one-day self-courses for experienced students in six cities; at time of writing (1996) researching sites for permanent facility. Established 1982.

For further description see **Vipassana Meditation Center,** Massachussetts.

Sea to Sky Retreat Center (Tibetan)
Affiliation: Siddhartha's Intent, P O Box 1114, Strawberry Hills, NSW 2012, Australia
East Side Daisy Lake
Whistler, BC V0N 1B1
Tel: (604) 932–1677
Fax: (604) 873–8262
E-mail: ssrc@cyberstore.ca
Web site: http://ourworld.compuserve.com/homepages/SiddsWish

Five dwellings suitable for solitary retreat and a variety of small group functions (retreats, workshops, reunions, seminars, etc.) set on forty acres of wilderness. Facilities include meeting space/shrine room; sitting room with library, fireplace, and great view of lake and mountain ranges; meditation path; and Bhutanese hot tub. Land purchased 1992; phase one completed 1995 and Khyentse Rinpoche led six-month retreat; now available to public as well as Buddhists; fire puja pavilion planned for 1997.

Regular program of events—contact center by mail, fax, e-mail, or web site. Publish *Gentle Voice* from Australian office up to four times a year.

Founder/Guru	Dzongsar Jamyang Khyentse Rinpoche
Teachers	As founder; many Lamas visit
Opening Times	By appointment/booking only
Residents	1–2 monastic, 2–3 laity

Festivals	Losar
Facilities	See above
Accommodation	Main Lodge for 14 in shared accommodation may be privately rented (Buddhist and non-Buddhist) when not used for individual retreat; rooms for stricter solitary retreats; retreat hut in forest
Food	Various possibilities; vegetarian on request
Booking	Advance booking, deposit required
Fees	Individual retreat $40/night room and board; group Buddhist event $40/person/night accommodation; others vary. Weekend program $200–300.
Expected Behavior	Contact center
How to Get There	100 km north of Vancouver (3 kms off Hwy. 99) and 23 km south of Whistler Resort. Bus stops nearby. Pickup in daylight hours by arrangement for $5.

QUEBEC

Dai Tong Lam Tam Bao Son Monastery (Vietnamese)
690 Chemin de la Rivière Rouge
Canton d'Harrington, Quebec J0T 1A0
Tel & Fax: (819) 687–2183

Main temple in traditional Chinese style. Recreation of four holy places of the history of the Buddha and other gayas: Lumbini garden, Bodhi Gaya, Deer Park, Matreiyagaya, and Avalokitesvasagaya on 337 acres. Land bought 1988 to build temple.

   Sitting and walking meditations. Retreats once a week. Tam Bao Son Institute of Buddhist Teaching for rigorous ten-year training of novice monks and nuns.

Founder/Guru	Abbot: Ven. Thich Thien Nghi
Teachers	Resident: Rev. Thich Pho Tinh
Opening Times	Weekends 10:00 am–7:00 pm; closed in the winter
Residents	15 monks and nuns
Festivals	Buddha's Birthday, Buddha's Enlightenment, and Amidha Buddha
Facilities	Library with 5,000 books in 4 languages: English, French, Vietnamese, and Chinese, meditation room
Accommodation	Contact center
Food	Vegetarian at weekends, $3 per person
Booking	For retreats, 3 months in advance
Fees	Retreat $300 per week

Expected Behavior   Contact center
How to Get There   15 north, exit 60, autoroute 364 west, then Chemin de la
Rivière Rouge

Dharma Group Montreal (Tibetan–Karma Kagyu)
Affiliation: Karma Kagyu worldwide network
c/o Lara Braitstein
P O Box 385
Hudson Heights, Quebec J0P 1J0
Tel: (514) 458–4640
Fax: (514) 458–0978
E-mail: dmarc@ego.psych.mcgill.ca

Core group of five. Started 1993 on Lama Ole Nydahl's first visit to Montreal. Also
under the spiritual guidance of H.H. the 17th Gyalwa Karmapa, Thaye Dorje and H.E.
Shamar Rinpoche. "It is our intention to provide a place where people interested in
Buddhism can meet in an open and friendly atmosphere to practice the powerful and
transformative methods of the Diamond Way."

Main practice, Three Lights Meditation, guided in English. Meditation twice
weekly—contact center for meeting place and time.

Association Zen de Montréal (Zen–Soto)
Affiliation: Association Zen Internationale (AZI)
982 Gilford East
Montreal, Quebec H2J 1P4
Tel: (514) 523–1534

Ground floor of a triplex in a peaceful and quiet neighborhood and sixty active members.
Zazen practice 7:00 am Tuesdays and Thursdays, 9:00 am Saturdays and Sundays,
7:00 pm Mondays, Wednesdays, and Fridays. Occasional informal group discussions on
specific topics. Introduction to Zen workshop over three Thursday evenings. Two-and-
a-half-day sesshins three times a year. Monthly day of zazen. Seven-day sesshin summer
camp. All activities suitable for newcomers.

Founder/Guru   Master Taisen Deshimaru
Teachers   Contact center
Opening Times   See daily zazen times above
Residents   None
Festivals   None
Facilities   Dojo
Accommodation   Members of AZI may sleep in dojo $10
Food   Generally vegetarian

Booking	Preferable to book in advance
Fees	Zen day $10, sesshins $150–175, Introduction workshop $30. Concessions available
Expected Behavior	It is important for each participant to harmonize him/herself with the group
How to Get There	Phone for details

Fondation Vipassana Foundation (Vipassana)
Affiliation: Vipassana Meditation Centers in the Tradition of S. N. Goenka
CP 32083
Les Atriums
Montreal, Quebec H2L 4Y5
Tel: (514) 481–3504
Fax: (514) 879 8302

Organizes bilingual ten-day courses at rental sites; sponsors introductory talks; holds weekly group meditations for old students; at time of writing (1996) researching sites for permanent facility. Established 1981.

For further description see **Vipassana Meditation Center,** Massachusetts.

International Buddhist Meditation Center of Canada (Theravada)
6926 St-Vallier
Montreal, Quebec H2S 2P9
Tel: (514) 948–3950
Fax: (514) 879–8329
E-mail: ibmcc@panorama.net

Based in an apartment and started 1995 by a group of various nationality mostly Buddhist-born supporters and now joined by some Canadians. "No rites or ritual, no chanting, no shrine. All emphasis is given to practice. Meditation taken very seriously. Only serious students accepted."

Private and group classes and courses of varying length. Ten-day, week-long, and month-long retreats on such topics as how to observe the mind, how impurities are formed, how to be free, how to concentrate, what is mind, and the parts of the mind. All activities suitable for newcomers.

Founder/Guru	Banthe Dharma-Ratika
Teachers	As founder
Opening Times	By appointment
Residents	1 monk and 1 laity
Festivals	None
Facilities	Meditation room

Accommodation	2 rooms available
Food	Whatever is offered
Booking	None
Fees	None
Expected Behavior	No smoking, 5 precepts, and no children
How to Get There	Metro Jean-Talon, near St. Denis and Jean Talon. Buses 95, 93, 92, 99, or 95.

Montreal Buddhist Church (Jodo Shinshu–Hongwanji-Ha)
5250 St. Urbain Street
Montreal , Quebec H2T 2W9
Tel: (514) 273–7921

Two-story house modified 1960. Community of sixty-five. Formed 1947.

Religious services twice a month mostly without minister in English and Japanese. Ministers invited from other churches four times a year. Teacher available to give monthly courses on Buddhism at Tam Bao Temple or at other institutions in English or French. Children's classes in Vietnamese language and Buddhism. Newsletter once a month to members.

Founder/Guru	Shinran Shonin
Teachers	Minister responsible for MBC is Rev. Izumi of Toronto Buddhist Church
Opening Times	Contact center for program details
Residents	None
Festivals	Hoonko, Wesak, Gotane, Obon
Facilities	Main hall which seats 60
Accommodation	None
Food	None
Booking	None
Fees	None
Expected Behavior	None
How to Get There	Contact center

Montreal Dharmadhatu (Tibetan–Kagyu/Nyingma)
Affiliation: Shambhala International
c/o Francesca Dalio
6743 Iberville
Montreal, Quebec H2G 2C9
E-mail: cguest@aei.ca

See International headquarters, **Shambhala Center,** Halifax, Nova Scotia.

Montreal Zen Center/Centre de Zen de Montréal (Zen–Soto and Rinzai)
824 Park Stanley
Montreal, Quebec H2C 1A2
Tel & Fax: (514) 388–4518
E-mail: zenlow@aei.ca

Large residential house in own grounds, with zendo and conference room in separate building. By park on the banks of the Rivière des Prairies at north end of Montreal island. Around a hundred visitors per week. Lay community only. Completely bilingual French and English. Incorporated 1975 as an affiliate of Rochester Zen Center. Moved to present address 1979. Autonomous since 1986, when present director was given transmission by Philip Kapleau.

Meditation Mondays, Tuesdays, and Thursdays 7:30–9:30 pm—individual instruction given. Morning meditation Monday to Friday 6:30–7:30 am. Workshop for beginners seven times a year. Sesshins (for members only) four per year of one-week duration, two per year of four-day duration, four per year of three-day duration and two per year of two-day duration. *Zen Gong* journal four times a year.

Founder/Guru	Philip Kapleau
Teachers	Resident: Albert Low
Opening Times	See daily session times above
Residents	None
Festivals	New Year's Eve Celebration
Facilities	Meditation room
Accommodation	By arrangement only for donation
Food	Vegetarian
Booking	At least 1 month in advance
Fees	Workshop $50; beginners' course $40; Retreats $20 per day; Monthly fees $25; out-of-town members $12.50
Expected Behavior	No smoking or drinking alcohol on the premises
How to Get There	Contact center

Pagode Tam Bao, Société Bouddhique Chanh Phap (Vietnamese–Pure Land)
4450 Van Horne Avenue
Montreal, Quebec H3S 1S1
Tel: (514) 733–3841
Fax: (514) 733–5860

Accomodates a hundred and fifty practitioners visit each week.

Breathing and sitting meditation plus chanting, "Namo Amidha Buddha." Regular service 10:00 am Sundays. Classes 2:30 pm Sundays in basic Buddhism. Public services such as funerals and weddings.

Founder/Guru	Ven. Thich Thien Nghi
Teachers	Not given
Opening Times	Saturdays 2:00–5:00 pm, Sundays 8:00 am–6:00 pm
Residents	12 monks/nuns
Festivals	Buddha's Birthday, Ulambana, New Year, Amida Buddha, Avalokitesvara Bodhisattva
Facilities	Contact center
Accommodation	None
Food	Free vegetarian meal Sundays 11:30 am
Booking	Not applicable
Fees	By donation
Expected Behavior	No smoking
How to Get There	Metro Plamondon then walk. Metro Rosemont then bus 161. Corner Lavoie and Van Horne Ave, near Côtes des Neiges

Pratique du Zen "Metro Frontenac Montreal" (Zen–Soto)
Affiliation: Association Zen Internationale (AZI)—Sutton Zen Center
1850 Percy
Montreal, Quebec
Tel: Contact Sutton Zen Center

Downtown dojo close to subway for up to a hundred people. Zazen one evening a week. See **Sutton Zen Center** for more details.

Rigpa (Tibetan–Nyingma)
Affiliation: Rigpa Fellowship
Montreal, Quebec
Tel: (514) 484–5662

Contact: Arlette Georges. See **Rigpa National Office,** California, for details.

> *When the deluded in a mirror look*
> *They see a face, not a reflection.*
> *So the mind that has truth denied*
> *Relies on that which is not true.*
>
> The Royal Song of Saraha

Rigpe Dorje Center (Tibetan–Karma Kagyu)
Affiliation: Karma Triyana Dharmachakra, New York
5413 St. Laurent, Suite 203
Montreal, Quebec H2T 1S5
Tel: (514) 278–9793
E-mail: rigpemtl@citenet.net

Founded by H.E. Jamgon Kontrul Rinpoche.
Regular weekly schedule of meditation practice and classes on Buddhism.
Sponsor seminars and practice weekends. Meditation instruction available. Books,
incense and other practice materials available.

SGI-Canada Montreal Culture Center (Nichiren)
Affiliate: Soka Gakkai International Association of Canada
5025 Buchan Street
Montreal, Quebec H4P 1S4
Tel: (514) 733–6633
Fax: (514) 733–7887

Contact center for more details.

Société Bouddhique Quan Am Buddhist Society (Vietnamese)
3781 De Courtrai
Montreal, Quebec H3S 1B8
Tel: (514) 735–9425
Fax: (514) 735–4022

Run by Vietnamese mostly for Vietnamese community.

Vulture Peak Meditation Center (Vietnamese)
6015 Rue Hochelaga
Montreal, Quebec H1N 1X5
Tel & Fax: (514) 899–8042 (Call first if sending fax)
E-mail: bmai@po-box.mcgill.ca

Three-story building with meditation hall seating up to forty. Established 1995, official
opening 1996.
Sitting, walking, Zen tea with Dharma talk and Q&A period (English and
French)—Tuesdays and Wednesdays 7:00–9:30 pm. Meditation, chanting, Dharma
talk, and vegetarian meal (Vietnamese only)—Sundays 11:00 am–1:30 pm. Monthly
one-day retreats. Repenting ceremony with 108 prostrations twice a month. *Tiếng*

Chuong Thién (*The Sound of Zen Gong*) published every four months in Vietnamese, English, and French.

Founder/Guru	Founder: Rev. Thich Quang Due; Gurus: Ven. Thich Hyuen Vi, Ven. Thich Nhat Hanh
Teachers	As founder
Opening Times	8:00 am–7:00 pm daily
Residents	1 monk, 3 nuns, 1 lay
Festivals	Vesak, Vulan (summer retreat ending Mother's Day), and Têt (Vietnamese New Year)
Facilities	Meditation hall and library
Accommodation	None
Food	None
Booking	Contact center
Fees	Contact center
Expected Behavior	Contact center
How to Get There	Bus: Métro Cadillac, Bus 32 south on Cadillac 4 blocks, getting off at Ultrama Gaz Station; Métro Frontenac, Joliette, Bus 85 east on Hochelaga; Métro Honoré Beauground, Bus 85 west on Hochelaga.

Centre Bouddhiste Kankala (Tibetan–Gelug)
Affiliation: New Kadampa Tradition
c/o 245 Sanford
Saint-Lambert, Quebec J4P 2X7
Tel: (514) 671–8213
Fax: (514) 843–5331

Teachers: Gen Kelsang Zangmo & Christine Ares Ferry. Contact center for more details.

Sutton Zen Center (Centre Zen de Sutton) (Zen–Soto)
Affiliation: Association Zen Internationale (AZI)
372 French Horn Road
Sutton, Quebec J0E 2K0
Tel: (514) 538–1790

On a family organic vegetable and goat farm surrounded with woods. Camping in log cabins, countryside restaurant. Up to fifty people for retreats. Founded 1994 by a disciple of T. Deshimaru.

Zazen four times a week. Seventy-minute meditation once or twice a month. Conferences and lectures once a week on Zen Buddhism, specializing in Dogen philosophy, physiology, and psychology of Zen practice, inter-religious links, sutra study usually in French, but can be translated into English. One- or two-day sesshins regularly. Possible to stay on farm outside of retreat times. Countryside restaurant also on the premises which is open to the public.

Also AZI centers at: **Quebec Zen Dojo** Tel: (418) 529–6081; **Rimouski Zen Dojo** Tel: (418) 725–4487; **St-Benoit Zen Dojo** Tel: (514) 258–3480.

Founder/Guru	Philippe Duchesne
Teachers	Resident: Philippe Duchesne, other disciples of Deshimaru visit
Opening Times	Full time
Residents	1 monk, 1 nun, and 1 Bodhisattva
Festivals	Music and theater at least once a month
Facilities	Dojo, hermitage
Accommodation	Log cabin for 1–5 visitors. $30/night plus $2 for each extra visitor
Food	Vegetarian and wholefood. Price included in retreat fee, or $12 for the menu
Booking	As early as possible, deposit needed for events over $30
Fees	$30 per day for retreats
Expected Behavior	Respecting silence when necessary; smoking in designated areas only; no sex or drugs during retreats; respectful behavior
How to Get There	Contact center

MANITOBA

Winnipeg Dharma Study Group (Tibetan–Kagyu/Nyingma)
Affiliation: Shambhala International
Dawn Rogers, Coordinator
847 Westminster Avenue
Winnipeg, Manitoba R3G 1A7
Tel: (204) 772–5808

See International headquarters, **Shambhala Center,** Halifax, Nova Scotia.

NEW BRUNSWICK

Fredericton Shambhala Study Group (Tibetan–Kagyu/Nyingma)
Affiliation: Shambhala International
Veit Weber, Coordinator

Nortondale, RR #1
Millville, New Brunswick E0H 1M0
Tel: (506) 463–2758

See International headquarters, **Shambhala Center,** Halifax, Nova Scotia.

NEWFOUNDLAND

St John's Shambhala Study Group (Tibetan–Kagyu/Nyingma)
Affiliation: Shambhala International
Mike Munro, Coordinator
21 Monchy Street
St John's, Newfoundland A1C 5A7
Tel: (709) 722–8056
E-mail: dimitri@morgan.ucs.mun.ca

See International headquarters, **Shambhala Center,** Halifax, Nova Scotia.

NOVA SCOTIA

Gampo Abbey (Tibetan–Kagyu/Nyingma)
Affiliation: Shambhala International
Pleasant Bay
Cape Breton, Nova Scotia B0E 2P0
Tel: (902) 224–2752
Fax: (902) 224–1521
E-mail: gampo@shambhala.org

Monastery in the Kagyu lineage of Tibetan Buddhism on the northeastern coast of Cape Breton Island. Surrounded by meadows and wooded hills above the Gulf of St. Lawrence. Founded 1983 as monastery for Shambhala International.

Offer temporary monastic ordination for both women and men for six months or a year, as well as full ordination to bikshu or bikshuni. "The Abbey is a place where you can live the life of a monk or nun. You come here because you wish to be a monk or a nun or because you wish to experience the support of the monastic environment. In any case, it's a place where you can't get away from yourself."

Individual retreats either in main house or in solitary retreat cabin. Varying length group retreats up to full three-year retreats.

Founder/Guru   Chogyam Trungpa Rinpoche

Teachers	Abbot: Ven. Khenchen Thrangu Rinpoche; Resident teacher: Pema Chodron. Others visit regularly.
Opening Times	Office hours: 1:00–5:30 pm Monday to Friday
Residents	At least 30
Festivals	Contact center
Facilities	Library, shrine room, retreat center
Accommodation	Private rooms or dormitories
Food	Primarily vegetarian with dairy products and locally caught fish
Booking	By telephone, fax, or mail with deposit
Fees	Cabin retreats and in-house retreats $25/day not including food. Scholarships available for staff positions.
Expected Behavior	5 precepts
How to Get There	Buses from Halifax to Whycocomagh and from Sydney to Cheticamp. Pick up from bus can be arranged for fee. Carpooling sometimes possible.

Annapolis Dharma Study Group (Tibetan–Kagyu/Nyingma)
Affiliation: Shambhala International
c/o Sloan
RR2, Box 2047A
Granville Ferry, Nova Scotia B0S 1K0
Tel: (902) 532–7189

Small group meets in members' houses. Shamata/vipashyana meditation, introduction to meditation, Shambhala Training.

Founder/Guru	Chogyam Trungpa Rinpoche
Teachers	4 residents
Opening Times	Not applicable
Residents	4
Festivals	None
Facilities	None
Accommodation	Billet in their homes
Food	None
Booking	None
Fees	None
Expected Behavior	None
How to Get There	In and around Annapolis Royal

Shambhala Center (Tibetan–Kagyu/Nyingma)
International Headquarters of Shambhala International
1084 Tower Road
Halifax, Nova Scotia B3H 2Y5
Tel: (902) 420–1118
Fax: (902) 423–2750
E-mail: shambint@ra.1515net.com

Older house in residential area. Formerly Karma Dzong.

Classes and courses on Buddhism, meditation, and Shambhala teachings. Meditation sessions all day Sunday and additional evening sessions during the week.

Shambhala International was created in 1993 by Sakyong Mipham Rinpoche to coordinate the varied ideas arising from Chogyam Trungpa's vision and energy. It is comprised of "Three Gates," each gate being a way of entering the world of enlightened mind and are Dharmadhatu, Shambhala Training, and Nalanda. Dharmadhatu, the Buddhist Gate, is for the study and practice of Buddhism as inspired by the Kagyu and Nyingma traditions. Shambhala Training is a nonsectarian, nonreligious spiritual path based on the teachings of Chogyam Trungpa in *Shambhala: The Sacred Path of the Warrior*. The Nalanda Gate is a variety of disciplines that explore Shambhala culture with a contemplative approach: the arts, health, psychology, social issues, family, relationships, business, and education. Courses within this gate may include kyudo (archery), ikebana (flower arranging), Buddhist psychology, wealth and livelihood, and family programs. Monthly community publication, *The Banner*.

Founder/Guru	Chogyam Trungpa Rinpoche
Teachers	Resident: Sakyong Mipham Rinpoche
Opening Times	Monday to Friday 10:00 am–6:00 pm
Residents	None
Festivals	Children's Day, Vaishaka Day, Shambhala Day, and Midsummer's Day
Facilities	Shrine room, meditation rooms, library, and offices
Accommodation	None
Food	None
Booking	None
Fees	Contact center
Expected Behavior	None
How to Get There	Contact center

St. Margaret's Bay Shambhala Cultural Center (Tibetan–Kagyu/Nyingma)
Affiliation: Shambhala International
1345 Peggys Cove Road

Tantallon, Nova Scotia B0J 3J0
Tel: (902) 826–2182

See International headquarters, **Shambhala Center,** Halifax, Nova Scotia.

Dorje Denma Ling(Tibetan–Kagyu/Nyingma)
Affiliation: Shambhala International
2280 Balmoral Road
The Falls, Nova Scotia B0K 11V0
Tel: (902) 657–9085 (Bob Rader)

See International headquarters, **Shambhala Center,** Halifax, Nova Scotia.

Wolfville Zazenkai (Zen)
Hakukaze (Hakufu) stream in the tradition of Yasuda Joshu Dainen daiosho
Affiliation: White Wind Community
P O Box 96
Wolfville, Nova Scotia B0P 1X0
Tel: (902) 542–2217
Fax: (613) 241–5731
E-mail: 70670.1514@compuserve.com or
    White_Wind_Zen_Community@compuserve.com

Small rural zendo on Knowlan Mountain just outside town. Branch of **White Wind Zen Community** (see separate entry) for information on history, publications, etc. "Except in the winter, the sound of a nearby stream rolls through the windows. In the winter, there is just snow. Snow." Call White Wind Zen Community for up-to-date information on program.

Founder/Guru	Ven. Anzan Hoshin Sensei
Teachers	As for Zen Center of Ottawa
Opening Times	Thursdays 8:00–10:00 pm, Sundays 8:00–10:00 am
Residents	Contact center
Festivals	As for Zen Center of Ottawa
Facilities	Zendo, library of teisho tapes and Dharma books, practice interview room
Accommodation	Contact center
Food	Vegetarian
Booking	Deposit required
Fees	Call for current fee schedule
Expected Behavior	Smoking in specific areas, 5 precepts, basic sanity
How to Get There	$1^1/_2$ hour's drive from Halifax—phone for details

ONTARIO

Alliston Dharma Study Group (Tibetan–Kagyu/Nyingma)
Affiliation: Shambhala International
Myra Colby, Coordinator
Tel: (705) 435–9647
E-mail: jimcolby@bconnex.net

See International headquarters, **Shambhala Center,** Halifax, Nova Scotia.

Pho-Hien Buddhist Community Temple (Vietnamese–Pure Land and Zen)
722 The Queenway
Etobicoke, Ontario M8Y 1L3
Tel: (416) 252–1761
Contact person: Pham, Tom Thuan Ngua, Secretary General
Tel: (416) 362–1375; (416) 594–1306 evenings
Fax: (416) 362–4881

Brick building which was originally a bank accommodates around two hundred visitors a week. Hue-Lam Bhikkhuni Buddhist Community Temple formed 1994 and changed to current name as members from any gender accepted. For "preserving, protecting, reviving, and developing Vietnamese Buddhist heritage, tradition, and culture in order to adapt with advanced technological civilization, multicultural, and multiracial society of Canada and North America."

Zen meditation (Saturday nights), Tai Chi, Buddhist teachings on various subjects (usually Sundays). Monthly 24-hour eight-precepts retreat. Ceremonial services for members and non-members. Educational facility for Buddhist youths. Magazine and newsletter produced quarterly.

Founder/Guru	Group of Vietnamese Buddhists
Teachers	Resident: Ven. Thich, Chan Toan; Dr. Pham Huu Dieu visits
Opening Times	Daily—first-time visitors should call before arriving
Residents	1 monk and 5 laity
Festivals	Lunar new year, Buddha's Birthday, Ulambama Day
Facilities	Shrine room, open hall for worshipping, activity room
Accommodation	Visitors welcome to stay in temple for no charge, 3 guests maximum
Food	Vegetarian Sunday lunches
Booking	In writing 1 month in advance
Fees	By donation

Expected Behavior	No smoking, 5 precepts
How to Get There	From downtown Toronto: subway westbound to Royal York; bus 76 or 15 south to The Queensway; temple 3-minute walk

Dharma Center of Canada (All schools)
RR 1, Galway Road
Kinmount, Ontario K0M 2A0
Tel: (705) 488–2704
Fax: (705) 488–2215
E-mail: Dharma@halhinet.on.ca

Main house, bathhouse, main hall, hermitage (with twelve meditation rooms), and seven retreat cabins on four hundred acres, mostly forested, with a river, two lakes, and walking trails. Accommodates about forty-five. Founded 1966 by students of Ven. Namgyal Rinpoche; incorporated 1970 and one of oldest meditation centers in North America. "The exploration of all schools of Buddhism takes place here, from Theravadan to Tibetan.... We support all types of spiritual practice. Also the land itself is exceptionally supportive to meditation due to its beauty and peaceful ambiance."

Offers support to individuals on long retreats. Various types of meditation retreat throughout the year. Programs generally available to all interested. Publishes newsletter every two months. Affiliated with **Bodhi Publishing,** which produces books written on Namgyal Rinpoche's teachings.

Founder/Guru	See above
Teachers	Various from various traditions—call for details
Opening Times	Open year-round
Residents	Contact center
Festivals	Contact center
Facilities	See above
Accommodation	Contact center for details
Food	Primarily vegetarian; can accommodate most diets with at least 1 week's notice
Booking	Contact center
Fees	At 1996: rent $25/day non-members; food $12/day; weekly rate including food and rent $225
Expected Behavior	5 precepts
How to Get There	10 km east of Hwy. 121 on Galway Rd., which is 5 km south of Kinmount and 28 km north of Fenelon Falls.

Insight Retreats (Vipassana)
128 Durham Street W

Lindsay, Ontario K9V 2R5
Tel: (705) 799–6992

Meet in members' homes. Began 1990.
Weekly meditation and discussion open to all Thursday evenings. Instruction on Insight Meditation. Discourses and discussions on the application and relevance of meditation in daily life, sutras, and themes of interest to participants. Organize Insight Meditation retreats in rented facility in rural, residential setting for up to seventy-five participants two–three times a year.

Founder/Guru	Norman Feldman
Teachers	Resident: Norman Feldman, various teachers invited
Opening Times	Not applicable
Residents	None
Festivals	None
Facilities	Members' homes and rented facilities
Accommodation	None
Food	Vegetarian on retreats
Booking	Contact center
Fees	$150 3-day retreats
Expected Behavior	5 precepts, silence on retreats
How to Get There	$1^1/_2$ hour drive northeast of Toronto

Buddhist Philosophy Association, UWO (General)
University of Western Ontario
London, Ontario
Tel & Fax: (519) 474–3380
E-mail: buddhist@julian.uwo.ca
Web site: http://www.lonet.ca/res/nwong/bpa1.htm

Club in the university. Founded 1993 by small group of Buddhists. "1. Very good for young people; 2. Very good for beginner and non-Buddhist; 3. Casual environment; 4. Library; 5. Free of charge."
Meetings usually held at university and other places for special occasions. Basic meditation and basic Buddhism each every two weeks.

Founder/Guru	Lawrance Leung
Teachers	Many from abroad
Opening Times	Call anytime
Residents	None
Festivals	None
Facilities	Library, video and audio tapes
Accommodation	None

Food	None
Booking	None
Fees	Donations welcome
Expected Behavior	Human
How to Get There	Contact center

Orgyan Osal Cho Dzong (Tibetan–Nyingma)
RR3, Box 68
1755 Lingham Lake Road
Madoc, Ontario K0K 2K0
Tel: (613) 967–7432

Large retreat center consisting of Vajrayana temple, lama house, and fifteen-room retreat house. Situated on two hundred acres of secluded forest on the slope, hills, and valley of Mount Moriah. Founded 1984. Blessed by H.H. Padma Norbu Rinpoche, and Longchen Nyingthig bestowed 1988.

Tranquillity meditation and various puja weekends. Meditation instruction on request. Dzogchen on weekends and retreats. Resident lama teaches on a wide range of Buddhist subjects, with an emphasis of Dzogchen two weekends a month. Retreats open to senior students only. Annual *Orgyan Dzong News* newsletter/journal.

Founder/Guru	Ven. Lama Jampa Rabjam Rinpoche
Teachers	Founder is resident, and Ven. Lama Jigme Pawo
Opening Times	Not applicable
Residents	Varies
Festivals	Losar, Buddha's Birth, Enlightenment, and Parinirvana, anniversaries of various teachers
Facilities	Large temple/meditation hall, 15 private retreat rooms, common kitchen
Accommodation	$10 per day, not including food and bedding
Food	Contact center
Booking	2 weeks' advance notice, 50% deposit
Fees	Teachings free of charge, formal catered retreats $22/day
Expected Behavior	No smoking or pets, 5 precepts, minimal talking
How to Get There	Hwy. 101 to Belleville. Hwy. 62 north to Bannockburn, right on Bannockburn Road to Cooper, continue through Cooper onto Lingham Lake Road, 7 km from Cooper to Retreat center.

Toronto Fo Kuang Shan Monastery (Chinese–Buddha's Light International
    Association)
6525 Millcreek Drive

Mississauga, Ontario L5N 7K6
Tel: (416) 730–1666 or (416) 560–2118
Fax: (416) 512–8800

Temple of approximately fifty thousand square feet on two acres of land designed to incorporate elements of Eastern and Western culture. Serves the Buddhist community and promote understanding of Chinese cultural heritage. Groundbreaking ceremony 1994, completion scheduled for end 1996.

Chinese meditation, chanting, prostration, pilgrimage. Dharma functions include Avalokitesvara, Bhaisajyaguru and Amitabha, Wesak, and Great Compassion repentance. Weekly Buddhism classes for different levels of understanding. Weekly meditation class. Traditional arts weekly: vegetarian cooking, flower arrangement, Chinese knot macramé, calligraphy, chorus. Eight Precepts retreat twice per year, Buddha-seven retreat once a year. All events suitable for newcomers. Monthly magazine, *Universal Gate*, published by headquarters.

Founder/Guru	Ven. Master Hsing Yun
Teachers	Resident: Ven. Yi Hung
Opening Times	10:00 am–6:00 pm Monday to Friday; 10:00 am–8:00 pm weekends
Residents	6 monastics
Festivals	Peaceful Lantern Festival
Facilities	Shrine room, library, meditation room, conference room, audio-visual room, study room
Accommodation	None
Food	Vegetarian for contribution only
Booking	None
Fees	None
Expected Behavior	5 precepts, no smoking
How to Get There	Near intersection of Highway 401 and Erin Mill Parkway

Crystal Staff (Nonsectarian)
Mailing: c/o Susan Rejall
300 Cooper Street, Apt. 35
Ottawa, Ontario K2P 0G7
Tel: (613) 238–6511 (Susan Rejall)

"Our brand of discovery, although heavily Buddhist-based, moves into the future adapting and looking toward what will communicate best to the beings of our time. In that sense, it will always be Buddhist, but may never be called that again." Current resident teacher: Qapel (Doug Duncan).

Ottawa Shambhala Center (Tibetan–Kagyu/Nyingma)
Affiliation: Shambhala International
982 Wellington Street
Ottawa, Ontario K1Y 2X8
Tel: (613) 725–9321

Second-story in commercial building in the city. Twenty-eight-member center started late 1970s.

Meditation Tuesdays and Thursdays 7:30–9:30 pm and fourth Sunday of every month. Classes and courses in Buddhism, Shambhala Training (meditation program based on principles of warriorship) and Nalanda (contemplative arts and education). Some suitable for newcomers. Weekend programs periodically. Quarterly one-page newsletter/calendar.

Founder/Guru	Chogyam Trungpa Rinpoche
Teachers	Several local students
Opening Times	Tuesdays and Thursdays 7:30–9:30 pm
Residents	None
Festivals	Contact center
Facilities	2 shrine rooms, small library
Accommodation	None
Food	None
Booking	Contact center
Fees	Vary. Membership $40/month full members; $20/month supporting members
Expected Behavior	Contact center
How to Get There	West end of the city. Call for details.

White Wind Zen Community (Zen–Soto)
Hakukaze (Hakufu) stream in the tradition of Yasuda Joshu Dainen daiosho
P O Box 203, Station A
Ottawa, Ontario K1N 8V2
or
240 Daly Avenue
Ottawa, Ontario K1N 6G2
Tel: (613) 562–1568
Fax: (613) 241–5731
E-mail: 70670.1514@compuserve.com or
        White_Wind_Zen_Community@compuserve.com

Overarching organization of centers and students practicing under the direction of Zen Master Anzan Hoshin—**Zen Center of Ottawa (Dainen-ji)** (see separate entry) is main practice center; branches include **Wolfville Zazenkai,** Nova Scotia (see separate entry). Administrative offices at Zen Center of Ottawa. Work with "total tradition of Buddhadharma through translations made from Pali, Sanskrit, Chinese, Japanese, and Tibetan sources by our teacher and senior students. Monastics and lay students have the opportunity to study directly with an extraordinary and utterly available Zen master and scholar of Buddhadharma. General, associate, and branch members study and practice with advisors who can guide them to apply Anzan Sensei's teachings in a manner appropriate to their moment-by-moment experience."

Founded 1985; first center established 1987; branch centers established by senior students; expanded into two extra buildings 1994 and moved to current location 1996.

For activities, etc., see individual centers. Quarterly newsletter, *Absolute Zero.* Own publishing house, **Great Matter Publications,** offers books by Ven. Anzan Hoshin Sensei and translations produced by **Buddhavacana Translation Groups** of classical texts from Pali, Sanskrit, Chinese, Japanese, and Tibetan languages into English. Contact center for free catalog.

Zen Center of Ottawa Dainen-ji (Zen)
Hakukaze (Hakufu) stream of tradition of Yasuda Joshu Dainen daiosho
Affiliation: White Wind Zen Community
240 Daly Avenue
Ottawa, Ontario K1N 6G2
Tel: (613) 562–1568
Fax: (613) 241–5731
E-mail: 70670.1514@compuserve.com or
        White_Wind_Zen_Community@compuserve.com
Web site: http://www.wwzc.org

Thirty-four-room, 9,700-square-foot building on three lots. Built 1875 and preserved as heritage home, with many original features preserved, renovated with Japanese and other design elements. Two main practice halls—first-floor zendo and second-floor Hatto. Main monastery of White Wind Zen Community. For history and other general information, see **White Wind Zen Community.**

Zazen Mondays to Thursday 6:00–8:00 am; Mondays, Tuesdays, and Thursdays 7:30–9:15 pm; Saturdays 6:00–8:00 am and 9:30–11:55 am; Sundays 7:00–10:30 am. Full curriculum of training for monastics and laypeople. Introductory workshops, classes in daruma-kata aiki, Shojin Ryori Zen cooking, Zen arts such as Gongfu-cha. Four- to seven-day sesshins February, May, October, and December; two-day sesshins held all other months. Individual retreats of between one and thirty days.

For publications, see **White Wind Zen Community.**

Founder/Guru Zen Master Anzan Hoshin
Teachers Resident: Ven. Anzan Hoshin sensei and 5 trained
         practice advisors, authorized to give instruction in
         beginning stages of practice

Opening Times	See zazen times above
Residents	6 monastics, 2 laity
Festivals	"Festivals and celebrations for us consist of acknowledgment of what has been transmitted to us and so the only response that we can make is to intensify our practice."
Facilities	Hatto (Dharma hall), zendo, Kaisando, Shuryo, Gongfu-cha room (tea room)
Accommodation	Guest room $35/night; in zendo $30/night
Food	Vegetarian—Shojin Ryori
Booking	At least 2 weeks in advance; deposit required
Fees	Call for current schedule
Expected Behavior	Smoking in specific areas, 5 precepts, basic sanity
How to Get There	Please call for precise instructions

Karma Kagyu Buddhist Meditatation Center of Niagara (Tibetan–Karma Kagyu)
Affiliation: Karma Kagyu Society of Canada
4 Clayburn Avenue
St. Catherines, Ontario L2P 2S2
Tel: (905) 685–9132 (Center and information); (905) 563–8971 (Center and
    information)
Fax: Call center number to arrange fax reception
E-mail: kdixon@freenet.npiec.on.ca

Shrine room in private home downtown. Members visit Toronto Center frequently.
Established 1982—founder resident here until 1985.
    Chenrezig puja Monday evenings. Those wanting instruction in Shamata can
receive it on request. All regular meetings open to visitors. Classes on basic Dharma
topics over three or four weeks offered annually. Visiting Lamas offer teachings, initiations, and pujas once or twice a year. Founder visits every other month for pujas and to
give interviews. Nyngnay retreat once every year or two.

Founder/Guru	Lama Namse Rinpoche
Teachers	Various Lamas of the Kagyu tradition visit, including founder
Opening Times	Monday 7:00–9:00 pm or by appointment
Residents	None
Festivals	None observed regularly
Facilities	Shrine room for up to 15, small library of books, tapes, and videos
Accommodation	During retreats only
Food	For some events
Booking	Not necessary

Fees	Membership $30/month. Donations welcome from visitors
Expected Behavior	No smoking. No alcohol (except for ritual purposes). Some fasting pujas have dietary restrictions. Shrine room etiquette instructions given to visitors.
How to Get There	Contact center

Ling Shen Ching Tze Temple (Jing Sim Branch) (Chinese–True Buddha School)
21 Milliken Boulevard, Unit C3
Scarborough, Ontario M1V 1V3
Tel & Fax: (416) 298–1069

Contact center for details.

Toronto Mahavihara Buddhist Center (Theravada)
4698 Kingston Road
Scarborough, Ontario M1E 2P9
Tel & Fax: (416) 208–9276

Flat house with semi-basement close to Lake Ontario with facilities for up to fifty participants. First Theravada Buddhist center established in Canada. Monks speak English and Sinhala. Open door policy.

Vipassana meditation Sunday mornings. Dhamma classes for children Sunday afternoons. Poojah and chanting 8:00 pm daily. Classes in Sutta study and Abhidhamma at the request of interested groups usually one evening per week. Uposatha Days—eight-precept practice on the Sunday closest to the Poya Day. Publish bi-annual journal.

Founder/Guru	Toronto Mahavihara Society
Teachers	Resident: Bhante Ven. A Ratanasiri and Bhante Ven. R Dhammapala; others visit
Opening Times	8:00–11:00 am and 2:00–9:00 pm
Residents	3 monks
Festivals	Vesak and Kathina
Facilities	Shrine/meditation room, library, and meeting room. New Dhamma hall and facilities are planned.
Accommodation	For visiting monks only. Possible to arrange for accommodation in homes of members of the lay community
Food	Monthly vegetarian potluck lunches to raise funds
Booking	None
Fees	Donations welcome

Expected Behavior	No smoking on premises, 5 precepts on Uposatha days
How to Get There	East end of Toronto by subway or road

Buddha Sasana Yeiktha (Ontario) (Theravada)
RR 1, Severn Bridge, Ontario P0E 1N0
Tel & Fax: (705) 689–5642

Forest-style wooden bungalow as main building with shared cabins and trailers on ten acres of wooded land. Residential meditation center with up to twenty yogis (meditators) at once. No winter facilities as yet (1996).

Vipassana meditation retreats in the style of Ven. Mahasi Sayadaw for beginners and advanced meditators. Open individual or group retreats with a week's notice at most (even a day or two may be enough) so that people can go on retreat at their own convenience. Formal organized and structured retreats by invited well-known senior meditation masters (ordained Theravada monks). One-day city retreats and special organized retreats over holidays such as Thanksgiving, New Year, etc.

Founder/Guru	Sister Khemanandi (was Upasika Daw Khin Hla Hla) and family. Spiritual Advisor Ven. Sayadaw U. Pandita
Teachers	Visiting teachers
Opening Times	Open year-round, except for severe winter months
Residents	1 nun and 1 laity
Festivals	None
Facilities	Shrine room/meditation hall
Accommodation	See above—for meditators only
Food	Vegetarian, 2 meals a day for retreatants
Booking	Open individual/group retreat, 1 week in advance, no deposits. Formal organized and structured retreats, special booking dates and deposit required
Fees	Suggested donations to cover food and part of lodging only. Participants may contribute whatever they are able or deem worthwhile.
Expected Behavior	No smoking, at least 5 precepts while at center and 8 precepts while in formal structured retreat
How to Get There	By car: Hwy. 400 North to Barrie, Hwy. 11 North past Orillia to Severn Bridge, where exit at 13 Southwood Road; follow to underpass and sign Muskoka 13, a few km on, the sign for Sasana Yeiktha is at the entrance to the driveway. By bus: from Bay St. (at Dundas), Metro Toronto Coach Terminal almost every hour to Orillia, where you can be met by prior arrangement.

Arrow River Community Center (Theravada–Thai Forest Tradition)
RR7, Box 2, Site 7
Thunder Bay, Ontario P7C 5V5
Tel: (807) 933–4434
E-mail: stu_muirhead@msn.com
Web site: http://www.hotstar.net/~gdecr/arcc/arcci.htm

Five kutis, one summer sala, workshop. Founded in 1975 as lay meditation center, became monastery 1996.

Main meditation is Anapansati. Retreats by arrangement. Monastic lifestyle. Newsletter very occasionally.

Founder/Guru	Kema Ananda
Teachers	Resident: Punnadhammo Bhikku; Sona visits
Opening Times	Not applicable
Residents	3 monks and 1 laity
Festivals	Not emphasized
Facilities	Sala, small library
Accommodation	5 kutis, in summer others in tents or sala
Food	Whatever offered
Booking	Phone ahead
Fees	By donation
Expected Behavior	5 precepts minimum, 8 preferred
How to Get There	Halfway up Highway 593, south of Thunder Bay

Buddhist Association of Canada
1330 Bloor Street
W Toronto, Ontario M6H 1P2
Tel: (416) 537–1342
Fax: (416) 537–1342

Four-story house in Chinese style with large library of ten thousand books. Started 1971. Open to the public. "Especially we welcome those students who study in university."

Conferences, Buddhism classes, meetings, etc. Annual Buddhist arts exhibition. Courses in Buddhist theory, Midway, and Hwa-yen Thought. Zen retreats weekly. Seven-day retreats. Publish *Prajna* magazine quarterly and newsletter quarterly.

Founder/Guru	Rev. Shan-Hon
Teachers	Contact center
Opening Times	Contact center
Residents	2 monastics and 1 laity

Festivals	Buddha's Birthday and other Buddhist Festivals
Facilities	Library, study room, meditation workshop center
Accommodation	None
Food	Vegetarian only
Booking	Contact center
Fees	Free—accept donations
Expected Behavior	Contact center
How to Get There	Subway to Lansedowne station, then a short walk

Chandrakirti Mahayana Buddhist Center (Tibetan–Gelug)
Affiliation: New Kadampa Tradition
1055 Yonge Street, Suite 207
Toronto, Ontario M4W 2L2
Tel & Fax: (416) 929–0734
E-mail: chandra@pathcom.com

Commercial space in Toronto visited by two hundred students a week. Founded 1993.

Pujas three times a week. General Program (introduction to Buddhism course) classes daily, Foundation Program (systematic study of five basic texts of Mahayana Buddhism) Sundays and Wednesdays. Retreats several weekends per month, some in Toronto, some in country, range from introductory teachings to advanced silent meditation. Newsletter of Kadampa Buddhism in Canada, *The New Moon*, two–three times a week. Branches in Hamilton, Oakville, Kingston, and Ottawa. Call this center for details.

Founder/Guru	Ven. Geshe Kelsang Gyatso Rinpoche
Teachers	Principal Resident: Gen Kelsang Tharchin; teachers at each branch center
Opening Times	Monday to Friday 2:00–5:00 pm
Residents	3 monks, 2 nuns live nearby
Festivals	Contact center
Facilities	Large and small gompas, Dharma shop, library/reading room
Accommodation	None
Food	Vegetarian during country retreats only
Booking	1 week in advance for weekend retreats
Fees	$7 suggested donation per class; $50–100 weekend retreats
Expected Behavior	Contact center
How to Get There	One block north of Rosedale Subway station

Jodo Shinshu Buddhist Teahouse (Jodo Shinshu)

8 Dacotah Avenue
Toronto Island
Toronto, Ontario M5J 2E5
Tel: (416) 203–3163

Rev. Doreen Hamilton, a Buddhist priest, has a small cottage filled with Buddhist art. After retiring from her post as Buddhist chaplain at the University of Toronto, she has created a space where she is available for spiritual counseling and personalized meditation instruction. Her special focus is family Buddhism, spiritual marriage, spiritual sexuality, and the spiritual education of children. She is also interested in Buddhist ecology. "I welcome any sincere seeker of wisdom and Truth, for one-to-one discussion of how to apply Buddhism to everyday life." Offers private instruction in Nembutsu meditation.

Founder/Guru	Rev. Doreen Hamilton
Teachers	As founder
Opening Times	Year-round
Residents	Teacher
Festivals	Birth of Buddha on April 8
Facilities	Teahouse
Accommodation	None
Food	Whole grains vegetarian
Booking	Please call for an appointment
Fees	Donation only
Expected Behavior	Normal
How to Get There	Ferry from foot of Bay Street at Toronto lakefront to Ward's Island. Walk 10 minutes to Algonguin Island.

Karma Kagyu Center of Toronto (Tibetan–Karma Kagyu)
39 Triller Avenue
Toronto, Ontario M6K 3B7
Tel: (416) 588–4528
Fax: (416) 778–5981

Urban center in large house with small core group of between ten and two hundred visitors depending on event. Established 1976 as a result of requests to the 16th Karmapa. "Choje Lama Namse Rinpoche is the 17th Karmapa's representative in Canada. Our center is the seat for His Holiness in Canada. We always have need for translators— lack of whom limits the amount of teaching available. Any help in this department would be appreciated. . . ."

Full range of Tibetan Buddhist teachings can be requested from Choje Lama Namse Rinpoche. Ongoing schedule of Chenrezig—Amitabha, Green Tara, Mahakala pujas daily or weekly. Also Tsoks. Special days in the Tibetan calendar.

Introductory and more advanced programs mainly by request and dependent on translator available. Specific retreats also by request, e.g., Sojong, Ngondro, Powa, White Tara. Ongoing introductory class, Meditation in Action, given by senior student. Organize visits of Lamas which are open to the public in parts and to committed practitioners for other parts. Bimonthly mailing of listing of upcoming events to centers and sanghas on their list. Are developing a newsletter. Store selling books, artifacts and practice materials.

Founder/Guru	16th Gyalwa Karmapa
Teachers	Choje Lama Namse Rinpoche
Opening Times	5:00–7:00 pm daily, 10:00–12:00 am weekends
Residents	1 lama and 3 students
Festivals	According to Tibetan calendar
Facilities	Shrine room
Accommodation	Shrine floor $15/night—very limited
Food	"Potluck generally!"
Booking	Contact center
Fees	$5 regular practice sessions, $20–25 per $1/_2$ day of special sessions
Expected Behavior	Residents and visitors respect the lama's presence and act accordingly. Smoking off premises
How to Get There	1 block east of Roncesvalle & Queen St. W. By car, Jamieson exit from Gardiner Expressway to north Queen, east to Triller, turn left. Dundas West subway station.

Maha Dhammika Temple (Theravada)
Affiliation: Burma Buddhist Association
435 Hopewell Avenue
Toronto, Ontario M6E 2S4
Tel: (416) 785-7497

Three-bedroom house in city, has about thirty visitors a week. Burma Burmese Buddhist Association organized 1985 and temple bought 1989. Caters mainly to Canadians of Burmese origin; those of Thai and Lao origin also participate.

Eight precepts given on Sundays, when participants are invited to take lunch before noon and Dharma discourse delivered. Vipassana meditation retreats once a year. Traditional Burmese celebrations observed—Katina celebrated on a large scale. Burmese, Thai, or Lao traditional events such as weddings, birthdays, funeral services available free of charge—donations accepted.

Founder/Guru	Burma Buddhist Association
Teachers	Resident: Ven. U Nanda Vumsa, Ven. U Nanda Siri; other monks visit

Opening Times	6:00 am–11:00 pm
Residents	2/3 monks
Festivals	Burmese Water Festival (April), Wesak (May), Waso (July), Lighting Festival (October), Katina (November), New Year (Chinese—January–February)
Facilities	2 shrine rooms, 1 used as meditation room
Accommodation	None
Food	Wholefood served to visitors for no cost
Booking	Not applicable
Fees	By donation
Expected Behavior	No smoking, music, or shoes in the main shrine room and upstairs areas; no food served to monks after noon apart from light beverages
How to Get There	Closest intersection: Eglington Ave. and Dufferin St.; Subway station at Eglinton east of Dufferin; buses to Duffering and/or Eglinton; short walk (7 minutes) from bus/subway stop

Mountain Moon Sangha (Zen)
Sanbo Kyodan lineage
941 Avenue Road, Apt. 6
Toronto, Ontario M5P 2K7
Fax: (416) 485–6490
E-mail: roselyn.stone@utoronto.ca

Apartment of Sei'un An Roselyn Stone, Authorized Zen Master, who spends July to early December in Australia each year and the rest of the year in Toronto. Seven members meet weekly.

Weekly zazen and dokusan, zenkais (one-day sittings) and weekend sittings, both with teisho and dokusan, and orientation program.

Founder/Guru	Sei'un An Roselyn Stone
Teachers	As founder
Opening Times	Not applicable
Residents	None
Festivals	Tetsuya (all-night) sitting in honor of Shakamuni's Enlightenment
Facilities	Zendo, dokusan room
Accommodation	None
Food	None
Booking	Only by direct application to teacher
Fees	None
Expected Behavior	Silence, follow the program, no smoking

How to Get There   "Frankly, unexpected drop-ins are not welcome. Please write or e-mail first."

SGI-Canada Culture Center (Nichiren)
Affiliate: Soka Gakkai International Association of Canada
2050 Dufferin Street
Toronto, Ontario M6E 3R6
Tel: (416) 654–3211
Fax: (416) 654–3539

Contact center for more details.

Toronto Nichiren Buddhist Church (Nichiren Shu)
Affiliate: Nichiren Propagation Center
20 Caithness Avenue
Toronto, Ontario M4J 3X7
Tel & Fax: (416) 463–9783

Resident priest—Rev. Kanto Tsukamoto. See **Nichiren Propagation Center,** Oregon.

Toronto Shambhala Center (Tibetan–Kagyu/Nyingma)
Affiliation: Shambhala International
670 Bloor Street W, # 300
Toronto, Ontario M6G 1L2
Tel: (416) 588–6465
E-mail: bs884@torfree.net

Study and practice center with about seventy members. Established early 1970s.
Offers introductory courses in Buddhism. Introduction to meditation weekly. Weekend meditation programs in Buddhism and Shambhala Training. Weekly public talks. Contemplative arts classes. Small bookstore open to visitors on Monday and Wednesday evenings.

Founder/Guru	Chogyam Trungpa Rinpoche
Teachers	Not applicable
Opening Times	Mondays and Wednesdays 7:30–9:00 pm
Residents	None
Festivals	Not applicable
Facilities	3 shrine rooms, community room
Accommodation	None
Food	None

Booking	None
Fees	Most introductory courses free or small donation;
	weekend program $100
Expected Behavior	None
How to Get There	East of Christie subway at Manning Avenue

Toronto Zen Center (Zen)
Harada–Yasutani-Kapleau tradition
33 High Park Gardens
Toronto, Ontario M6R 1S8
Tel: (416) 766–3400
Fax: (416) 769–4880

Residential-type center with some residential, some practice areas, near High Park. Membership of around seventy. Founded 1968; present location since 1985.

Zazen Tuesdays and Thursdays 7:00–9:00 pm; Mondays, Wednesdays, and Fridays 5:45–7:00 am; and Saturdays 8:00–10:00 am. Chanting at least four times weekly; special ceremonies periodically. Bimonthly all-day workshops on Zen practice for those new to the center, after which may attend all activities except sesshins, which require some experience. Weekly talks by teacher and senior practitioners on various aspects of Zen practice. Biannual 103-month student programs with intensive training activities. Periodic study/discussion groups. Two- to seven-day sesshins.

Sell some non cushions and benches and books.

Founder/Guru	Roshi Philip Kapleau
Teachers	Sensei Sunyana Graef
Opening Times	See zazen times above
Residents	2–5 laity
Festivals	New Year, Buddha's Parinirvana, Vesak, Bodhidharma
	Day, Jukai, and Buddha's Enlightenment Day
Facilities	Zendo, Buddha hall, library
Accommodation	None
Food	Vegetarian at functions
Booking	For introductory workshops at least 1 day in advance
Fees	Introductory workshops $60; membership $40 suggested;
	Sesshins $30/day
Expected Behavior	No smoking, alcohol consumption, recreational drugs,
	meat, poultry, or fish
How to Get There	Second house on east of Parkside Drive (Keele St.)
	on High Park Gdns. (intersection of Howard Park
	and Parkside Drive). Subway station—Keele;
	streetcar—last stop at west end of College Street
	line.

Zen Buddhist Temple (Zen–Korean)
Affiliation: Buddhist Society for Compassionate Wisdom
86 Vaughan Road
Toronto, Ontario M6C 2M1
Tel: (416) 658–0137
Fax: (416) 658–5855

Buddhist temple with a hundred and thirty-five members. Based in a former synagogue in a residential area and established 1975. Has three functions: offers service and meditation instruction; a community for fellowship and support; and a monastery for cultivation and training.

Public meditation services Sundays 9:30 am and 5:00 pm. Members' sittings Wednesdays 6:30–9:30 pm and Sundays 6:00–8:00 am. Introductory meditation courses in either a five-Thursday evenings or Friday evenings through Saturday afternoon format. Saturday morning Meditation Workshop for those wishing to meditate in chairs. These last three run five–six times through the year. Annual spring and fall lecture series on three–five consecutive Saturday afternoons on such subjects as Buddhism in Everyday Life. Concurrently, Thursday evening lecture series on Buddhist sutras and doctrine. One and two silent meditation retreats and three- to five-day Yongmaeng Chongjin (intensive meditation retreats) throughout the year. Two-month summer retreats for those interested in staying in the temple for training. Organizes annual fall art exhibition for Buddhist art.

Urban Meditation Retreat Center is a year-round center for individual retreats with its own meditation hall, individual rooms, and kitchen separate from the rest of the temple. Maitreya Buddhist Seminary is a three-year seminary program designed to train Buddhist priests and Dharma teachers and is open to all people who sincerely desire to undertake the training of discipleship for the spread of the Way of Buddha in the West. Publishes *Spring Wind—Buddhist Cultural Forum* biannually. Buddhist bookstore stocks a wide range of books and other Buddhist articles.

Founder/Guru	Ven. Samu Sunim
Teachers	Resident teacher as founder plus others
Opening Times	To the public during Sunday services, other times by appointment
Residents	Samso Sylvia McCormick (resident teacher and contact person)
Festivals	Year End and New Year's Day Services. Buddha's Enlightenment Day all-night sitting and Buddha's Birthday celebrations
Facilities	Meditation/Buddha hall, bookstore, social/dining room, dormitory
Accommodation	Day, week, and month rates from $30/day to $450/month
Food	Vegetarian. All meals included in accommodation

Booking	1 month's notice and 25% deposit
Fees	Courses from $60–$140; retreats $50–$60 per day
Expected Behavior	Keep silence, concentrate your mind, be grateful and happy in this moment of your life
How to Get There	From Highway 401 from Alan Road south and turn left onto Eglington to Bathurst. South on Bathurst to St. Clair, turn right, and go 2 blocks to Vaughan Rd. and turn right. Temple couple of doors down on left-hand side.

Friends of the Heart House (All traditions)
P O Box 58521
197 Sheppard Avenue East
Willowdale, Ontario M2N 6R7
Tel: (416) 410–7109

Workshops held at private residence with ten–fifteen visitors a week. Founded 1992 around the teachings of Catherine Rathbun. "Our classes, retreats, and workshops are a dynamic mixture of Eastern and Western systems for training the mind and raising aspiration for clarity and compassion in everyday living. Our teachers use meditation, creative movement, scholastic study, and artwork in order to actively engage the whole student on the inward path."

White Tara Puja Mondays 1:30 pm; meditation for beginners first Tuesday every month; Chenrezig puja Wednesdays 6:00 pm; meditation class Thursday 7:30 pm; Guru Rinpoche puja Fridays 8:30 am and Star Group Meditation on Sundays. Classes in Western and Buddhist meditations every Thursday. Class for beginners every first Tuesday of the month. No classes held in summer. Courses in Western meditations such as Tarot, Tibetan healing practices, etc.

Newsletter, *Heartbeat*, produced three times annually.

Founder/Guru	Catherine Rathbun
Teachers	Resident: Catherine Rathbun; various visit including Ven. Lama Karma Thinley Rinpoche and Geshe Ngawang Kalden
Opening Times	Not applicable
Residents	3 laity
Festivals	None
Facilities	Shrine room, Western mystery meditation space, meditation retreat room
Accommodation	For 1 person on retreat only—$10/day
Food	Self-catering
Booking	1 week in advance
Fees	Classes $20

Expected Behavior	5 precepts and no smoking
How to Get There	South of Eglinton Avenue, 10 houses east off Yonge

YUKON

Vajra North—Rigdrol Dechen Ling (Tibetan–Nyingma)
Affiliation: Chagdud Gonpa Foundation, California
379 Valleyview Drive
Whitehorse, Yukon Y1A 3C9
Tel: (403) 667–2340

Red Tara meditation practice Wednesday evenings. Dudgon Tersar Ngondro Sunday mornings. Sponsors visits of guest teachers. Retreats. Established 1984.

Founder/Guru	H.E. Chagdud Tulku Rinpoche
Teachers	Chagdud Gonpa Lama's visit
Opening Times	Program times
Residents	1 laity
Festivals	Contact center
Facilities	Shrine room in private residence
Accommodation	None
Food	None
Booking	Contact center
Fees	Contact center
Expected Behavior	Contact center
How to Get There	Contact center

Other Buddhist Resources

Umbrella Organizations

For a particular school or lineage, see under *Schools* for its headquarters, which often has lists of affiliates. There are also a few umbrella organizations in North America which cover all denominations for a particular region. Those included in this directory are:

The Buddhist Council of New York can provide a list of Buddhist groups in the greater New York area. See entry in New York for details.

Buddhist Association of the United States is in regular contact with around 180 centers around North America. See entry in New York.

Northwest Dharma Association for Tibetan, Zen, and Theravada/Vipassana events and organizations in Washington, Oregon, and British Columbia, Canada. See entry in Washington State.

Buddhist Council of the Midwest, for centers in the Midwest—see entry in Illinois.

Buddhist Centers near Washington, DC, via Tom Childers at childers@erols.com.

Bodhi Line: A free Buddhist information line. Went on-line 1993 "providing the general public with a means to find out about New York–area Buddhist centers. The taped messages include New York City–area centers' locations, schedules of classes and meditation sessions, the events of the month, and a list of bookstores and other shops. Also excerpts of taped Dharma teachings can be listened to. All by pressing the buttons on a Touch-Tone phone." All this information plus a streaming audio of Dharma teachings and an in-depth study of karma is also available on their web page at http://www.infinite.org/bodhiline.

The Internet

There is an absolute wealth of information on Buddhism on the Internet. A good place to start is DharmaNet International on http://www.dharmanet.org, a site run by volunteer help. One of the things you'll find are directories of Buddhist centers, which are only as current as the last information given and may be out-of-date.

PUBLISHERS

Many schools of Buddhism publish books, often specific to their own school, and these are listed under the relevant center/headquarters. However, the following are the largest of those that publish more generally on Buddhism.

Aro Books—Publishing company for the Tibetan Nyingma Aro gTér school.
Affiliated with **Aro Gar**
P O Box 247
Chelsea Station
New York City, NY 10113-0247
Tel: (212) 439–4780; California (510) 865–1394

Asian Classics Input Project—Collects, preserves, and digitally propagates ancient, endangered texts. It focuses on important classical Asian literature (preliminary goal of preserving the Kangyur and Tengyur collections, which were preeminent in Asian philosophical thought from 500 BCE onward). The material is published and distributed in digital form—available on the Internet, more than 10,000 diskettes and CD-ROMS, which have been sent to scholars, individuals, and institutions in 50 countries worldwide free of charge.
Contact: **The Asian Classics Institute**
P O Box 20373
New York, NY 10009
Tel: (212) 475–7752

Bodhi Publishing—Produces books on Namgyal Rinpoche's teachings.
Afiliated with **Dharma Center of Canada**
RR 1, Galway Road
Kinmount, Ontario K0M 2A0
Tel: (705) 488–2704
Fax: (705) 488–2215
E-mail: Dharma@halhinet.on.ca

Clear Light Publishers—Affiliated with the Ganden Foundation, which has a catalog available.
Contact: **Ganden Foundation**
823 Don Diego
Santa Fe, NM 87501
Tel: (505) 989–9590
Fax: (505) 989–1519
E-mail: clpublish@aol.com or books@clearlight.com

Dhamma Book Service—Distributes Dhamma literature. Donations for shipping and postage thankfully accepted.

Contact: **American-Sir Lanka Buddhist Association Inc.**
84-32 124th Street
Kew Gardens
New York, NY 11415
Tel & Fax: (718) 849–2637

Dhamma Dana—Book series established to present Buddhism in simple English (over 20 titles). Send out free books on request and supply books to prisoners.
Contact: **California Buddhist Vihara Society**
2717 Haste Street
Berkeley, CA 94704
Tel: (510) 845–4843 or (510) 452–3351
Fax: (510) 644–9739
E-mail: abs@slip.net

Dharma Publishing Publishes books mainly on Tibetan, Vajrayana, and Dzogchen Buddhism.
Contact: **Nyingma Institute**
2910 Pablo Avenue
Berkeley, CA 94702
Tel: (800) 873–4276, (510) 548–5407 or (510) 873–4276

Great Matter Publications—Publishing house of the White Wind Zen Community, offers books by Ven. Anzan Hoshin Sensei and translations produced by **Buddhavacana Translation Groups** of classical texts from Pali, Sanskrit, Chinese, Japanese, and Tibetan languages into English.
Contact center for free catalog: **White Wind Zen Community**
P O Box 203, Station A
Ottawa, Ontario K1N 8V2
or 240 Daly Avenue, Ottawa, Ontario K1N 6G2
Tel: (613) 562–1568
Fax: (613) 241–5731
E-mail: 70670.1514@compuserve.com or
         White_Wind_Zen_Community@compuserve.com

Padma Publishing—Translates and prints practice texts and commentaries from Tibetan texts and books based on oral teachings of H.E. Chagdud Tulku Rinpoche.
Contact: **Chagdud Gonpa Rigdzin Ling**
P O Box 279
Junction City, CA 96048
Tel: (916) 623–2714
Fax: (916) 623–6709
E-mail: chagdud@snowcrest.net
Web site: http://www.snowcrest.net/chagdud

Parallax Press—Produces books and tapes, most by Thich Nhat Hanh and friends.
P O Box 7355
Berkeley, CA 94707
Tel: (510) 525–1010
Fax: (510) 525–7129
Web site: http://www.parallax.org/

Primary Point Press—Small list of Dharma books by Seung Sahn and others.
99 Pound Road
Cumberland, RI 02864
Tel: (401) 658–1476
Fax: (401) 658–1188
E-mail: kwanumzen@aol.com

Purple Lotus Publishing—Publishes *Purple Lotus Journal* and books for the True
Buddha School.
627 San Mateo Avenue
San Bruno, CA 94066
Tel: (415) 952–9513
Fax: (415) 952–9567
Web site for True Buddha School: http://www.ee.ucla.edu/~yang/truebuddha.html

Rigpa Publications—Publishes and makes available a wide variety of books, tapes,
videos, and study materials, including **Rigpalink,** a monthly tape-subscription service.
Contact: **Rigpa National Office**
P O Box 607
Santa Cruz, CA 95061-0607
Tel: (408) 454–9242, orders: (800) 256–5262

Shambhala Publications—Catalog of Buddhist and other Eastern religion/philosophy/
practice books.
Horticultural Hall
300 Massachusetts Avenue
Boston, MA 02115
Tel: (617) 424–0228
Fax: (617) 236–1563

Snow Lion Publications—"Snow Lion Publications was established in 1980 to promote and protect Tibet's extraordinary religious, philosophical, and cultural traditions.
Although threatened within the borders of Tibet itself, the relevance of Tibetan culture is being recognized around the world by an ever-increasing number and diversity
of people. Our goal is to publish handsome, relevant, and informative books for the
general reader as well as scholarly works representing the entire spectrum of Tibetan
Buddhism." (Quoted from their newsletter.)

P O Box 6483
Ithaca, NY 14851
Tel: Orders and catalog requests (800) 950–0313 or (607) 273–8519
Fax: (607) 273–8508
E-mail: 75061.1026@compuserve.com
Web site: http://www.well.com/user/snowlion

Tricyle: The Buddhist Review—Published quarterly as nonprofit magazine with an educational charter to spread the Dharma.
92 Vandam Street
New York, NY 10013
Tel: (212) 645–1143
Fax: (212) 645–1493
E-mail: tricycle@mail.well.com
Web site: http://www.tricycle.com/

Tuttle Publishing
153 Milk Street, 5th Floor
Boston, MA 02109
Tel: (617) 951–4080, customer service (800) 526–2778
Fax: (617) 951–4045
Web site: http://www.tutbooks.com

Vipassana Research Publications of America (VRPA)—North American locus for publications (books and cassettes) of the Vipassana Meditation Centers in the Tradition of S. N. Goenka, allowing their centers and course sites to be free of any commercialism. **Vipassana Research Institute (VRI)** publishes books on Vipassana and the Buddha's teachings in several Indian languages and English. All VRI publications and other related books and videocassettes are available from VRPA and its affiliate, **Pariyatti Book Service.**
Contact: VRPA
P O Box 15926
Seattle, WA 98115
Tel: (800) 829–2748
Fax: (206) 522–8295
E-mail: info@vrpa.com
Web site: http://www.vrpa.com

Windhorse Publications—Handles book sales to individuals and education institutions for **Windhorse Publications,** the Friends of the Western Buddhist Order (FWBO) publishing house.
Contact: **Aryaloka Buddhist Retreat Center**
14 Heartwood Circle
Newmarket NH 03857

Tel & Fax: (603) 659–5456
E-mail: aryaloka@aol.com, vajramati@aol.com, aryadaka@aol.com
Web site: http://www.fwbo.org/ or http://bluelotus.com/sfbc/sfbc.htm (San Francisco)
or http://web.mit.edu/benbr/www/FWBOHOME.HTM or http://www.ciens.ula.ve/~toro
(in Spanish)

Wisdom Publications—Publishes books on all schools of Buddhism.
361 Newbury Street
Boston, MA 02115
Tel: (617) 536–3358; sales (800) 272–4050
Fax: (617) 536–1897

BOOKSTORES, MEDITATION AIDS, AND OTHER BUDDHIST BUSINESSES

Amitabha Enterprises—Buddhist gift and statue shop for Purple Lotus Society (Chinese True Buddha School).
629 San Mateo Avenue
San Bruno, CA 94066
Tel: (415) 952–9513
Fax: (415) 952–9567
Web site for True Buddha School: http://www.ee.ucla.edu/~yang/truebuddha.html

Buddhist Bookstore—Large stock of books on all Buddhist traditions, specializing in Shin/Pure Land traditions.
1710 Octavia Street
San Francisco, CA 94109
Tel: (415) 776–7877

Daka's Buddhist Astrology—Offers Buddhist astrological readings.
Contact: **Thubten Choling**
5810 Wilson Avenue
Duncan, BC V9L 1K4
Tel & Fax: (250) 746–8110
E-mail: jhampas@island.net

If there is joy in meditation upon the mountain,
the fruit-trees are the magic creation of the mountain;
make thyself like the mountain itself.

The Message of Milarepa

Web site: http://www.mala.bc.ca/~shanemanj/wwwhome.htm

Dharma Communications—Educational not-for-profit corporation of the Zen Mountain Monastery dedicated to making the Dharma, particularly Zen, available to everyone. Publish quarterly *The Zen Mountain Record, The Practitioner's Journal,* and *The Dharma Communications Catalog,* which offers video- and audiotapes, books, art practice sets, Buddha figures, sitting and altar supplies. Extensive on-line services: *Cybermonk* (available at e-mail address below) is an on-line senior student who answers questions on Zen practice; and World Wide Web page.
P O Box 156
Mount Tremper, NY 12457
Tel: (914) 688–7993
Fax: (914) 688–7995.
E-mail: dharmacom@mhv.net
Web site: http://www1.mhv.net/~dharmacom

Dharmacrafts—Mail order business with a huge selection of books, zafus, incense, malas, tapes, bells, statues, etc.
212 Marret Road
Lexington, MA
Mailing address: 405 Waltham Street
Suite 234
Lexington, MA 02173
Tel: (617) 862–9211

Kanzeon Jade Thread—Stitchery.
Contact: **Kanzeon Zen Center Utah**
International Headquarters of Kanzeon Sangha
1274 East South Temple
Salt Lake City, UT 84102
Tel: (801) 328–8414
E-mail: kanzeon@aol.com

Ladyworks—Manufacturers of patented hair care products.
PO Box 605
Poolesville, MD 20837
Tel: (301) 916–3500 or (800) 428–9877
Fax: (301) 916–3029
E-mail: kpc@tara.org
Web site: http://www.tara.org

New Orleans Zen Temple Store—Zen practice materials and artwork.
Contact: **New Orleans Zen Temple**
American Zen Association Building

748 Camp Street
New Orleans, LA 70130-3702
Tel: (504) 523–1213
Fax: (504) 523–7024
E-mail: aza@gnofn.org

Noble Truth Bookstore—On center grounds of **Karma Shenpen Kunchab Tibetan Buddhist Center**. Opening hours: Monday–Friday Noon–6 pm; weekends 10 am–6 pm.
751 Airport Road
Santa Fe, NM 87505
Tel: (505) 471–5336
Fax: (505) 471–5336
E-mail: janet@rt66.com or cooper@lanl.gov

Radiant Heart—Prayer flag and Dharma banners.
P O Box 1272
Redway, CA 95560
Tel for questions and information: (707) 923–3891
Tel & Fax for orders: (800) 853–2010
E-mail: radiantheart@asis.com
On-line catalog: http://www.asis.com/~radiantheart

Samadhi Cushions—Produces meditation cushions on-site at **Karme Choling** and also sells books, practice materials, and gifts.
Contact: **Karme Choling**
RR 1, Box 3
Barnet, VT 05821
Free catalog: (800) 331–7751

Shaolin Communications—Produces music and audiobooks and publishes books and the newsletter *Shaolin Zen*. Other products include herbs and weaponry. **Shaolin Music** is a music publishing company. **Shaolin Film & Records** produces videos, cassettes, CDs, and artwork. **Tai Chi Youth** is a nonprofit corporation for youths at risk.
Contact: **Shaolin Chi Mantis**
P O Box 58547
Salt Lake City, UT 84158
Tel: (801) 595–1123

Shasta Abbey Buddhist Supplies—Operate mail-order service providing extensive range of Buddhist meditation supplies. For catalog, send $3 (refundable with first purchase).
3724 Summit Drive
Mount Shasta, CA 96067-9102
Tel & Fax: (916) 926–6682

Web site: http://www.OBCON.org

Student's Bookstore—Associated with **California Buddhist University** (Shaolin Zen). Books on China, especially Chinese culture and Chinese Zen. Store specially built in Chinese style in Chinatown.
933 1/4 Chung King Road
Los Angeles, CA 90012
Tel: (213) 628–3449

Tara Enterprises—Produces Buddhist images and fine artistic collectibles.
c/o **Kunzang Palyul Choling**
Poolesville, MD 20837
Tel: (800) 775–TARA
E-mail: kpc@tara.org
Web site: http://www.tara.org

Temple Treasures Bookstore—Also supplies meditation aids.
Contact: **Cleveland Buddhist Temple**
1573 East 214 Street
Euclid, OH 44117
Tel: (216) 692–1509
Fax: (216) 692–2012

Theravadanet—e-mail sangha. Reading, practice instruction and guidance, and detailed questions. Consists of about thirty members and a Theravada teacher.
Web site: http:/www.sover.net/~asbarker/sangha.html

Three Jewels Buddhist Bookstore—Sells books, gifts, and teas. Run by **Mahayana Sutra and Tantra Center (MSTC)**
211 East 5th Street
New York, NY 10003
Tel: (212) 475–6650

Tibetan Treasures—Sells Dharma-related gifts and supplies and books by Padma Publishing. Associated with Chagdud Gonpa Foundation.
P O Box 279
Junction City, CA 96048.
Tel: (916) 623–2714
Fax: (916) 623–6709
E-mail: chagdud@snowcrest.net
Web site: http://www.snowcrest.net/chagdud

Zen Home Stitchery—Manufactures meditation cushions, clothes, and supplies.
Contact: **Newport Mesa Zen Center**

711 West 17th Street, A-8
Costa Mesa, CA 92663
Tel: (714) 631–5389
Fax: (714) 631–8891

RESTAURANTS

Aryaloka Buddhist Retreat Center—Hope to open vegetarian restaurant 1997/98.
14 Heartwood Circle
Newmarket, NH 03857
Tel & Fax: (603) 659–5456
E-mail: aryaloka@aol.com, vajramati@aol.com, aryadaka@aol.com
Web site: http://www.fwbo.org/ or http://bluelotus.com/sfbc/sfbc.htm (San Francisco)
or http://web.mit.edu/benbr/www/FWBOHOME.HTM or http://www.ciens.ula.ve/~toro
(in Spanish)

Bo Kong—Buddhist Chinese cuisine
3068 Main Street (near 14th and Main)
Vancouver, BC
Tel: (604) 876–3088

Bo Kong—Buddhist Chinese cuisine
80-8100 Ackroyd Road
Richmond, BC
Tel: (604) 278–1992

Bodai Vegetarian Restaurant—Buddhist Chinese cuisine
337 E Hastings
Vancouver, BC
Tel: (604) 682–2666

Bodhi Tree Inn—B&B run on-site by **Karuna Tendai Dharma Center**
1525 Route 295
East Chatham, NY 12060
Tel & Fax: (518) 392–7963
E-mail: tendai1@aol.com

Bo-Jik—Variety of Buddhist dishes
820 W Broadway
Vancouver, BC
Tel: (604) 872–5556

Buddha's Vegetarian Foods—Buddhist Chinese cuisine
666 Dundas Street West
Toronto, Ontario
Tel: (416) 867–1020

Buddhist Vegetarian Kitchen—Buddhist Chinese cuisine
3290 Midland
Scarborough, Ontario
Tel: (416) 292–7095

Buddhist Vegetarian Restaurant
100N Beretania, Suite 109
Hawaii
Tel: (808) 532–8218

Greens
Fort Mason, Building A
San Francisco, CA 94123
Tel: (415) 771–6222

Kowloon—Buddhist Chinese cuisine
909 Grant (Chinatown)
San Francisco, CA
Tel: (415) 362–9888

Le Veggie—Buddhist Chinese cuisine
1096 Denman Street
Vancouver, BC
Tel: (604) 682–3885

Lotus Garden—Buddhist Chinese cuisine
532 Grant (Chinatown)
San Francisco, CA
Tel: (415) 397–0707 or (415) 397–0130

Lucky Garden—Buddhist Chinese cuisine
37 East 29th Street
New York, NY
Tel: (212) 686–9692

Miu Jay Garden—Buddhist Chinese cuisine
363 East Hastings Street
Vancouver, BC
Tel: (604) 687–5231

Sutton Zen Center—Run a countryside restaurant on the premises which is open to the public.
372 French Horn Road
Sutton, Quebec J0E 2K0
Tel: (514) 538–1790

The Angry Monk—Tibetan restaurant
96 Second Avenue
New York, NY 10003
Tel: (212) 979–9202

The Vegetable Garden—"Chinese Buddhist cuisine using no animal products, no onions, and no garlic. Vegetarian, organic, and macrobiotic."
11618 Rockville Pike
Rockville, MD 20852
Tel: (301) 468–9301
Fax: (301) 468–1518

Tibet Shambhala—Tibetan restaurant
488 Amsterdam Avenue
New York, NY 10024
Tel: (212) 721–1270

Tibetan Kitchen—Tibetan restaurant
444 Third Avenue
New York, NY 10016
Tel: (212) 679–6296

Uncle Chen Seafood & Vegetarian Restaurant—Uncle Chen is serious about Buddhist vegetarian values. Fish and vegetarian food are cooked in separate woks and cut with separate knives.
2209 El Camino Real
Palo Alto, CA
Tel: (415) 327–2888

The Way is perfect like a vast space
Where nothing is lacking and nothing is in excess.
Indeed, it is due to our choosing to accept or reject
that we do not see the true nature of things.

Seng-ts'an *Hsin Hsin Ming*

MAJOR CENTERS IN THE UK AND EUROPE

The following list of centers is designed to represent as many schools of Buddhism as possible and so may list only the main center in the whole of Europe for a particular school or subschool. For example, Friends of the Western Buddhist Order have centers all across Europe, but their principal center is in the UK and this is therefore the only one listed.

European Buddhist Union

An umbrella organization of Buddhist organizations, centers, and groups in Europe. For lack of a permanent secretariat, the following addresses can be used:

Ven. Lama Denys Teundroup, President
Congrégation Dachang Rimé
Institut Karma Ling
Hameau de Saint Hugon
73100 Arvillard
France
Tel: Institut +33 4 79 25 78 00
Fax: +33 4 79 25 78 08

Aad Verboom, Vice-President
EBU c/o SJBN
P O Box 1519
3500 BM Utrecht
The Netherlands
Tel: +31 30 2888 655
Fax: +31 30 2898 294
E-mail: averboom@knoware.nl

The European Buddhist Directory Project:
EBU c/o BUN
P O Box 17286
1001 JG Amsterdam
The Netherlands

Network of Engaged Buddhists
Ken Jones
Plas Plwca
Cwmrheidol
Aberystwyth, Dyfed SY23 3NB
Wales, the UK
Tel & Fax: +44 1970 84603

AUSTRIA

Österreichische Buddhistische Religionsgesellschaft
Fleischmarkt 16
1010 Vienna, Austria
Tel & Fax: +43 1 512 3719
Umbrella organization for all Buddhist activities in Austria.

BELGIUM

Institut Yeunten Ling (Tibetan–Kagyu)
Château de Fond L'Evêque
St. Jean l'Agneau 4
4500 Huy, Belgium
Tel: +32 85 21 48 20
Fax: +32 85 23 66 58

Nichiren Shu Hokkeji (Nichiren Shu)
Knaagreepstraat 8a
8890 Moorslede, Belgium
Tel: +32 51 779434
Fax: +32 51 701346

Bouddha Dhamma (Theravada)
Bruggestwg 82
8755 Ruiselede, Belgium
Tel & Fax: +32 51 689 582

Centrum voor Shin-Boeddhisme (Pure
    Land–Jodo Shinshu)
Jikoji—Temple of the Light of Compassion
Pretoriastraat 68
2600 Berchem-Antwerpen, Belgium
Tel: +32 3 218 7363
Fax: +32 3 281 6333

Association Zen de Belgique
(Zen–Soto–Association Zen
Internationale)
11 Rue Cattoir
1050 Bruxelles, Belgium
Tel & Fax: +32 2 648 64 08
Contact this center for addresses of other
AZI dojos in Belgium.

DENMARK

Buddhistisk Forum
Sekretariat
c/o Lisbeth Lundbye
Tjørnegade 5, st. th.
2200 Kbn. N.
Denmark
For information on all main Buddhist
traditions in Denmark.

Tarab Institute—Denmark
(Tibetan–Tarab Ladrung Institute)
Stor Søhøj
Hørsholm Kongevej 40
2970 Hørsholm, Denmark
Tel/fax: +45 45 76 00 44 and +45 42 86
20 27

There are Tarab Ladrung Institutes in
Copenhagen, Paris, Brussels, Budapest,
and Vienna.

Thai Buddhist Temple (Theravada)
H. P. Hansensvej 3
3660 Stenløse, Denmark
Tel: +45 42 17 11 80

FRANCE

**Foundation for the Preservation of the
Mahayana Tradition**
European Regional Office
Reynies, route de Castres
81500 Lavaur, France
Tel: +33 5 63 58 66 31
Fax: +33 5 63 58 66 98
E-mail: 100647,3553@compuserve.com
Contact for other FPMT centers in Europe.

Association Zen Internationale
17 rue Keller
75011 Paris, France
Tel: +33 4 18 05 47 43
Headquarters for Association Zen
Internationale.

Sakya Tsechen Ling (Tibetan–Sakya)
5 Rond-Point du Vignoble
67520 Kuttolsheim, France
Tel: +33 3 88 87 73 80 or Secretary +33 3
88 60 74 52
Fax: +33 3 88 60 74 52
Headquarters of the Sakya school in
Europe.

Urgyen Samye Chöling
(Tibetan–Nyingma)
Laugeral
St. Léon sur Vézère, France
Tel: +33 5 53 50 75 29
Fax: +33 5 53 50 56 85
Affiliated centers in Spain, England,
Switzerland, and the USA. Contact this
center for details.

Plum Village—Village des Pruniers
(Zen–Vietnamese)
Meyrace
47120 Loubes-Bernac, France
Tel: +33 16 53 96 75 40 and +33 16 53 58 48 58
Fax: +33 16 53 94 75 90
E-mail: parapress@aol.com
Main center of the Order of Interbeing—
Thich Nhat Hanh's base.

Centre d'Etudes de Chanteloube
(Tibetan–Rime)
La Bicanderie
24290 St Léon sur Vézère, France
Tel: +33 4 53 50 75 24
Fax: +33 4 53 51 02 44
Affiliated groups around France, England, Holland, Switzerland, and the USA.

Institut Karma Ling (Tibetan–Kagyu)
Hameau de Saint Hugon
73110 Arvillard, France
Tel: +33 4 79 25 78 00
Fax: +33 4 79 25 78 08
Ask for list of affiliated centers in Europe.

Kagyu Ling (Temple of a Thousand Buddhas) (Tibetan–Kagyu)
Plaige
71320 La Boulaye, France
Tel: +33 4 85 79 43 41
Fax: +33 4 85 79 43 09
Has affiliates and list of Karma Kagyu centers worldwide.

Dhagpo Kagyu Ling (Tibetan–Kagyu)
24290 St. Léon sur Vézère, France
Tel: +33 4 53 50 70 75
Fax: +33 4 53 50 80 54

GERMANY

Deutsche Buddhistische Union
Amalienstr 71
80799 München, Germany

Tel: +49 89 28 01 04
Fax: +49 89 28 10 53
Umbrella organization of 37 Buddhist associations of all main traditions.

Zen Kreis Bremen (Zen–Rinzai)
Ji-Kai-Zen-Kutsu
Atrium Hof
Vor dem Steintor 34
28203 Bremen, Germany
Tel: +49 421 381985 or 2182771
Contact for other meditation groups around Germany.

Shambhala
(Tibetan–Kagyu/Nyingma–Shambhala)
Wilhelmstrasse 20
35037 Marburg, Germany
Tel: +49 6421 17020
Fax: +49 6421 170222
European center for Shambhala International

Vien Giac (Zen–Pure Land Vietnamese)
Karlsruher Str 6
30519 Hannover, Germany
Tel: +49 511 879 630
Fax: +49 511 879 0963
Largest Buddhist monastery in Germany as well as the largest Vietnamese Buddhist monastery outside Vietnam.

EKO—Haus der Japanischen Kultur
(Pure Land–Jodo Shinshu)
Brüggener Weg 6
40547 Düsseldorf, Germany
Tel: +49 211 574071
Fax: +49 211 573546

Zen Institut Deutschland
(Zen–Rinzai–International Zen Institute of America)
Striehweg 32
72820 Sonnenbühl, Germany
Tel: +49 49 7128 784
Organizes events at different locations in Germany, the Netherlands, Spain, and the USA.

Zen Zentrum Mumon-Kai (Zen–Rinzai)
Frohnauer Str. 148
13465 Berlin, Germany
Tel: +49 30 401 30 69
Has affiliates.

Jodo Shinshu Germany (Pure
    Land–Jodo Shinshu)
c/o Rev. Jotoku Thomas Moser
Edelweißstr 5
83435 Bad Reichenhall, Germany
Fax: +49 8651 65114

Buddha-Haus (Theravada)
Uttenbühl 5
87466 Oy-Mittelberg 3, Germany
Tel: +49 83 76 502
Fax: +49 83 76 592
Meditation groups throughout Germany
and in Austria, Switzerland, the
Netherlands, and England.

Chodzong Buddhistisches Zentrum
(Tibetan–Gelug)
Hauptstr 19
91474 Langenfeld, Germany
Tel: +49 9164 320
Fax: +49 9164 1494
Headquarters for associated centers and
groups in Germany.

HUNGARY

Buddhista Misszió
H-1221 Budapest
Alkotmány u. 83, Hungary
Tel: +36 1 226 10 10
Has list of Buddhist centers in Hungary.

ITALY

Centro D'Informazione Buddhista
(nonsectarian)
Via Pio Rolla 71
10094 Giaveno (Torino), Italy

Tel: +39 11 93 78 331
Buddhist information center.

Kunpen Lama Gancen (Tibetan–Gelug)
Via Marco Polo 13
20124 Milan, Italy
Tel: +39 2 290 10263
Fax: +39 2 290 10271
E-mail: ganchen@micronet.it
Headquarters of Lama Gangchen's activi-
ties worldwide as well as a Dharma center.

Soto Zen Monastery Shobozan Fudenji
(Zen–Soto)
Bargone 113
43039 Salsomaggiore (PR), Italy
Tel: +39 524 565667

**Merigar, Associazione Culturale
Comunità Dzogchen** (Tibetan–Dzogchen)
58031 Arcidosso
Grosseto, Italy
Tel: +39 564 966837
Fax: +39 564 968110
Headquarters of Dzogchen community.

NETHERLANDS

Boeddhistische Unie Nederland (BUN)
P O Box 17286
1001 JG Amsterdam
The Netherlands
Umbrella organization for Buddhist centers
in the Netherlands.

Ehipassiko Maha Vihara
(Theravada–Myanmar and Sri Lankan)
Veneburen 23
8423 VH Makkinga, The Netherlands
Tel: +31 516 441848
Fax: +31 516 441823
Affiliates throughout Europe.

Kanzeon Zen Centre Amsterdam
(Zen–Soto/Rinzai synthesis–Kanzeon
    Sangha)

Krayenhoffstraat 151
1018 RG Amsterdam, The Netherlands
Tel: +31 20 6276493 and 6187922

Buddhavihara Temple (Theravada–Thai)
Den Ilp 38
1127 PC Den Ilp, The Netherlands
Tel: +31 20 4826512 or +31 20 4826883
Fax: +31 20 4826883

SPAIN

Jiko An Zen Centre (Zen–Soto)
El Alamillo
18460 Yegen (Granada), Spain
Tel & Fax: +34 (9)58 343185

O Sel Ling Centro de Retiras
(Tibetan–Gelug–Foundation for the
  Preservation of the Mahayana Tradition)
Apartado 99
18400 Orgiva (Granada), Spain
Tel & Fax: +34 (9)58 343134

SWEDEN

Stockholm Zen Center (Zen–Integral
Zen)
Östgötagatan 49
116 25 Stockholm, Sweden
Tel: +46 8 641 6382
Fax: +46 8 641 6382

Karma Shedrup Dargye Ling
(Tibetan–Kagyu)

Hökarvägen 2
129 41 Hägersten, Sweden
Tel & Fax: +46 8 886950

Stockholm Buddhist Vihara
(Theravada–Sri Lanka)
Sångvägen 9
17536 Järfälla, Sweden
Tel & Fax: +46 8 58031323

SWITZERLAND

**Schweizerische Buddhistische Union /
Union Suisse des Bouddhistes**
Wiedingstrasse 18
8055 Zürich, Switzerland
Produces list of Buddhist monasteries,
centers, and groups of all schools in
Switzerland.

Sayagyi U Ba Khin Gesellschaft
(Theravada–Myanmar)
Kehrgasse 59
3018 Bern, Switzerland
Tel & Fax: +41 31 992 11 62
E-mail: 100256.3576@compuserve.com

Rabten Choeling (Tibetan–Gelug)
Centre des Hautes Études Tibétaines
1801Le Mont-Pèlerin, Switzerland
Tel: +41 21 921 36 00 Secretary,
+41 21 921 7253 Ven. Gonsar Tulku
  Rinpoche
Fax: +41 21 921 7881
Runs courses and groups across
Switzerland.

---

*In Buddhism there is no place for using effort. Just be ordinary and nothing
special. Eat your food, move your bowels, pass water, and when you're tired
go and lie down. The ignorant will laugh at me, but the wise will understand.*

Lin-chi

Dhammapala Buddhist Monastery
(Theravada–Thai)
Am Waldrand
3718 Kandersteg, Switzerland
Tel: +41 33 75 21 00
Fax: +41 33 75 22 41

Wat Srinagarindravararam
(Theravada–Thai)
Buddhistisches Zentrum
Im Grund 7
5014 Gretzenbach, Switzerland
Tel: +41 62 858 60 30
Fax: +41 62 858 60 35

Karma Yeshe Gyaltsen Ling
(Tibetan–Karma Kagyu)
Hammerstr 9
8008 Zürich, Switzerland
Tel: +41 1 382 08 75
Fax: +41 1 382 08 75 or +22 1 380 10 44
E-mail: 100553.3425@compuserve.com
Other associated Karma Kagyu centers in
Switzerland

Zentrum für Buddhismus (Zen–Rinzai)
Bodhibaum Zendo
Friedheimstr 24
8057 Zürich, Switzerland
Tel: +41 1 312 1062
Fax: +41 1 312 1062
E-mail: 100116.3443@compuserve.com

UNITED KINGDOM

London Buddhist Centre (LBC)
(Friends of the Western Buddhist Order)
51 Roman Road
London E2 0HU, The UK
Tel: +44 181 981 1225
Fax: +44 181 980 1960
E-mail: lbc@alanlbc.demon.co.uk
Principal center of Friends of the Western
Buddhist Order.

Rigpa Fellowship

(Tibetan–Nyingma–Rigpa)
330 Caledonian Road
London N1 1 BB, The UK
Tel: +44 171 700 0185

The Buddhist Society (Main Buddhist
traditions)
58 Eccleston Square
London SW1V 1PH, The UK
Tel: +44 0171 834 5858

The Buddhapadipa Temple
(Theravada–Thai)
14 Calonne Road
Wimbledon
London SW19 5HJ, The UK
Tel: +44 181 946 1357
Fax: +44 181 944 5788
Lay Buddhist Association: 0181 337 2173

London Fo Kuang Temple (Chinese
Buddhism–Pure Land and Zen)
84 Margaret Street
London W1N 7HD, The UK
Tel: +44 171 636 8394
Fax: +44 171 580 6220
Part of Buddha's Light International
Association (BLIA).

The London Buddhist Vihara
(Theravada–Sri Lankan)
Dharmapala Building
The Avenue
Chiswick
London W4 1UD, The UK
Tel: +44 181 995 9493
Fax: +44 181 994 8130

Sakya Thinley Rinchen Ling
(Tibetan–Sakya)
121 Somerville Road
St. Andrews
Bristol BS6 5BX, The UK
Tel: +44 117 924 4424
Member of the Dechen community of
Buddhist centers in Europe. Contact this
center for other addresses.

Western Ch'an Fellowship (Ch'an/Zen)
c/o Dr. John Crook
Winterhead Hill Farm
Shipham
North Somerset BS25 1RS, The UK
Tel & Fax: +44 1934 842 231
Please contact address for retreat program
at the Maenllyd Centre, Wales, and
regional groups.

Soka Gakkai International (Nichiren
    Shoshu)
Taplow Court
Taplow
Near Maidenhead
Berkshire SL6 0ER, The UK
Tel: +44 1628 773 163
Fax: +44 1628 773 055

Manjushri Buddhist Centre
(Tibetan–Gelug–New Kadampa Tradition)
Conishead Priory
Ulverston
Cumbria LA12 9QQ, The UK
Tel: +44 1229 584029
Principal center of the New Kadampa
Tradition and home of Geshe Kelsang
Gyatso Rinpoche.

**Cittaviveka, Chithurst Buddhist
Monastery** (Theravada–Thai)
Chithurst
Near Petersfield
Hants GU31 5EU, The UK
Tel: +44 1730 814 986
Fax: +44 1730 817 334

Reiyukai Centre (Nichiren–Reiyukai)
Unit 24
Saint Mary's Works
Duke Street
Norwich NR3 1QA, The UK
Tel: +44 1603 630 857
Fax: +44 1603 760 749

Kongoryuji Temple (Shingon–British
    Shingon Association)

London Road
East Dereham NR 19 1AS, The UK
Fax: +44 1362 698 962

Throssel Hole Priory (Soto Zen–Serene
Reflection Meditation Tradition)
Carrshield
Hexham
Northumberland NE47 8AL, The UK
Tel: +44 1434 345 204
Fax: +44 1434 345 216

Pure Land Buddhist Fellowship (Pure
Land)
Contact address: c/o Jim Pym
3 Field Road
Kingham
Oxfordshire OX7 6YR, The UK
Tel: +44 1608 658 425

The Longchen Foundation (Tibetan)
30 Beechey Avenue
Old Marston
Oxford OX3 0JU, The UK
Tel & Fax: +44 1865 725 569
E-mail: lcf@compuserve.com

Wat Pah Santidhamma
(Theravada–Thai)
The Forest Hermitage
Lower Fulbrook
Near Sherbourne
Warwick CV35 8AS, The UK
Tel & Fax: +44 1926 624 385

**The Birmingham Buddhist Vihara
Trust** (Theravada–Myanmar)
47 Carlyle Road
Edgbaston
Birmingham B16 9BH, The UK
Tel & Fax: +44 121 454 6597

The International Meditation Centre
(Theravada–Myanmar–International
    Meditation Centre)
Splatts House
Heddington

Calne
Wilts SN11 0PE, The UK
Tel: +44 1380 850 238
Fax: +44 1380 850 833
E-mail: 100330.3304@compuserve.com

Lam Rim Buddhist Centre
(Tibetan–Gelug)
Pentwyn Manor
Penrhos
Raglan
Gwent NP5 2LE, The UK
Tel: +44 1600 780 383

Samatha Trust (Theravada–Thai)
Greenstreete
Llangunllo
Near Knighton
Powys LD7 1SP, The UK
Classes and groups across the country.

Samye Ling Tibetan Centre
(Tibetan–Kagyu)
Eskdalemuir
Langholm
Dumfriesshire DG13 0QL, The UK
Tel: +44 13873 73232
Fax: +44 13873 73223
E-mail: samye@rokpa.u=net.org
Web site: http://www.samye.org
Branch centers in Glasgow, Edinburgh,
Norfolk, Holy Island of Arran, Ireland,
Belgium, Spain, South Africa, Russia,
and Poland.

MAJOR CENTERS IN ASIA

INDIA

Tibetan–Sakya

Sakya Centre
187 Rajpur Road

248 009 Rajpur
Dehra Dun
UP, India

Tibetan–Gelug

Drepung Monastic University
Lama Camp No. 2
Tibetan Colony 581411
Mundgod
Distt. N. Kanara
Karnataka State, India

Office of H.H. the Dalai Lama of Tibet
Thekchen Choeling
McLeod Ganj
Dharamsala
Distt. Kangra
Himachal Pradesh, India

Library of Tibetan Works and Archives
Ganchen Kyishong
Dharamsala 176215
Disst. Kangra
Himachal Pradesh, India

Tibetan–Rime

Rigpa House
RA46
Inderpuri
PO Pusa
New Delhi 12, India

Tibetan–Karma Kagyu

Drikung Kagyu Institute (Jangchub Ling)
P O Box 48
Sahastradhara
Dhera Dun
Uttar Pradesh, India 248001

JAPAN

Nichiren
Nichiren-Shu Shumin

Administrative Headquarters
1-32-15 Ikegami
Ota-ku
Tokyo 146, Japan
Tel: +81 3 3751 7181
Fax: +81 3 3754 5855

Rissho Kosei-kai Headquarters
2-11-1 Wada
Suginami-ku
Tokyo 166, Japan
Tel: +81 3 3383 1111

Zen–Soto

Soto Zen Headquarters
2-5-2 Shiba
Minato-ku
Tokyo 105, Japan
Tel: +81 3 454 5411

Eiheiji Tokyo Betsuin (Rinzai)
2-21-14 Nishi Abazu
Minato-ku
Tokyo 106, Japan
Tel: +81 3 400 5232

Zen–Rinzai

Daitokuji
53 Daitokujicho
Marasakino
Kita-ku
Kyoto 603, Japan
Tel: +81 75 491 0543

Ryutakuji
Mishima-shi
Shizuoka-ken 411, Japan
Tel: +81 559 86 2206

Pure Land

Hongwanji International Center
Higashi-nakasuji
Rokujo Sagaru
Shimogyo-ku

Kyoto 600, Japan

KOREA

Zen–Korean

Songgwang-Sa
Songgwangmyon
Seungjukun
Cholla Namdo Province
South Korea

Seoul International Zen Center
Head Temple in Asia of Kwan Um School
of Zen
Hwa Gye Sa
487, Suyu 1 Dong
Kang Buk Gu
142-071 Seoul, Korea
Tel: +82 2 900 4326
Fax: +82 2 995 5770
E-mail: SIZC@BORA.DACOM.CO.KR

MALAYSIA

Vipassana

Malaysian Buddhist Meditation Centre
355 Jalan Mesjid Negeri
11600 Penang, Malaysia

MYANMAR

Vipassana

Mahasi Centre (Mahasi Sayadaw)
16 Thathana Yeiktha Road
Yangon (Rangoon) 11201, Myanmar

Chanmyay Yeiktha (Ven. Sayadaw U
Janakabhivamsa)
55-A Kaba Aye Pagod Road
Kaba Aye p.o.
Yangon (Rangoon), Myanmar

Tel: +95 01 61479
Vipassana Meditation Centre Panditarama
(Ven. Sayadaw U Panditabhavamsa)
80-A Thanlwin Road, Golden Hill Avenue
Bahan
Yangon (Rangoon), Myanmar

SRI LANKA

Theravada

Island Hermitage
Dodanduwa, Sri Lanka

Vipassana

Vipassana meditation centre Kandubodha
Delgoda, Sri Lanka

TAIWAN

Fo Kuang Shan
Headquarters of Buddha's Light
International Association
Ta Shu, Kaohsiung
84010 Taiwan
Republic of China

THAILAND

Theravada

Wat Pa Nanachat
Bahn Bung Wai

Amper Warin
Ubon 34310, Thailand

Vipassana

Ven. Bodhipalo
c/o Section 1, Wat Mahadhatu
3 Maharaj Road
Bangkok 10200, Thailand

Vipassana Meditation Centre Sorn Vivek
Asom
Soi Prachanakul 7
Tanon Bahnbung
Amper Muang
Chonburi 20000, Thailand
Tel: +66 38 283766

Vipassana Meditation Centre Sorn Thawee
Sametnua
Bangkla
Cha Choengsao Province, Thailand

**International Network of Engaged
Buddhists**
303-7 Soi Santipap
Nares Road
Bangkok 10500, Thailand
Tel: +66 233 2382 and +66 233 2792

TIBET

To find out which monasteries and temples
are still open, contact your nearest Chinese
embassy.

The way is not in the sky.
The way is in the heart.

from The Dhammapada, translated by Thomas Byron and quoted
in a flyer from Bodhi Tree Dhamma Center, Florida

APPENDIX: PRECEPTS

Some centers may ask you to conform to the five, eight, ten, or sixteen precepts.

The **five precepts** are
1. To refrain from killing living beings;
2. To refrain from taking what is not given;
3. To abstain from sexual misconduct;
4. To refrain from telling lies and using abusive or cruel speech;
5. To refrain from self-intoxication with alcohol or drugs.

These are all based on behavior which will not harm others in any way and translate positively into loving-kindness, generosity, contentment, truthfulness, and awareness. These are considered to be the minimal ethical requirements of Buddhism, and practicing Buddhists are expected to make efforts to work toward them. Interpretation of them may vary, especially refraining from sexual misconduct, which may range from celibacy in some places to the avoidance of adultery in others.

Theravadan centers sometimes ask visitors to comply with the **eight precepts.** These comprise the five precepts and *also* ask you to refrain from:
1. Taking food at unseasonable times, i.e., not after midday;
2. Dancing, music, singing, and unseemly shows;
3. The use of garlands and perfumes, unguents, and things that beautify and adorn the person;
4. From using high and luxurious seats and beds.

These are also expected of lay Theravadan devotees on auspicious occasions including full and new moon days.

When more deeply involved in Buddhist training, some centers ask participants to comply with the **ten essential or grave precepts**, which are:
1. Not to kill but to cultivate and encourage life;
2. Not to take what is not given, but to cultivate and encourage generosity;

3.   Not to misuse sexuality, but to cultivate and encourage open and honest relationships;
4.   Not to lie, but to cultivate and encourage truthful communication;
5.   Not to intoxicate self and others, to cultivate and encourage clarity;
6.   Not to slander others, but to cultivate and encourage respectful speech;
7.   Not to praise self at the expense of others, but to cultivate and encourage self and other to abide in their awakened nature;
8.   Not to be possessive, but to cultivate and encourage mutual support;
9.   Not to harbor ill will, but to cultivate and encourage loving-kindness and understanding;
10.   Not to abuse the Three Treasures (Buddha, Dharma, and Sangha), but to cultivate and encourage awakening, the path and teaching of awakening, and the community that takes refuge in awakening.

The **sixteen Bodhisattva precepts** are sometimes taken by Dharma teachers. These are a combination of: the three refuges (taking refuge in Buddha, Dharma, and Sangha); the three pure precepts (to do no evil, to do good, and to save all beings) and the ten essential or grave precepts.

GLOSSARY

5, 8, 10, or 16 precepts see *Precepts*.

Abhidharma (Sanskrit; *Abhidhamma*, Pali)   Lit: higher teaching. Third division of the Theravadan scriptures, which is largely a commentary and analysis of the Sermons. The Myanmar sangha specializes in its study.

Aikido (Japanese)   Japanese martial arts teaching techniques to turn opponent's momentum against him/herself.

Ajahn (Thai)   Thai form of the Sanskrit Acharya (teacher). Meditation master.

Amida Buddha (Japanese)   Buddha of Infinite Light and Life, which includes Infinite Wisdom and Compassion. In Pure Land Buddhism, the intermediary between Supreme Reality and mankind.

Amitabha (Sanskrit)   One of the deities of the Tantric pantheon. The Buddha of Infinite Light, the perfected state of our faculty of perception/discrimination.

Anagarika   Lit: homeless one. Someone who has adopted a homeless life without formally ordaining as a monk.

Anapana Sati (Pali)   Meditation on mindful breathing.

Anatta (Pali; *Anatman*, Sanskrit)   One of the Three Marks of Existence which are part of the basic teachings of Buddhism. Doctrine of nonseparateness of all forms of life; applied to people, there is no immortal ego or self, the unchanging and immortal being the possession of no one human being.

Ango (Japanese)   Longer intensive practice period.

Anila (Tibetan)   Respectful form of address for a nun.

Atisha (982–1054)   Indian scholar; in Tibet from 1038 till his death. Entirely reformed the prevailing Buddhism. Founded the Kadampa school of Tibetan Buddhism.

Avalokitesvara (Sanskrit)   Bodhisattva of Compassion.

Bardos (Tibetan)   The state between two other states of being, especially the intermediate state between one life and the next.

Bhavana (Sanskrit, Pali)   Self-development by any means, especially meditation, mind development, and concentration; meditative practices.

Bhikshu (Sanskrit; *Bhikkhu*, Pali)   Those living from alms or offerings given by lay Buddhists. Often translated as "monk."

Bhikshuni (Sanskrit; *Bhikkhuni*, Pali)   The feminine of the above. Often translated as "nun."

Bodhicaryavatara (Sanskrit)   A text of Shantideva (Indian seventh-century Bodhisattva).

Bodhichitta (Sanskrit; *Boddhicitta*, Pali)   Compassionate wish to gain Enlightenment for the benefit of all sentient beings.

Bodhidharma Indian Buddhist who went to Chinese court in 520 CE; founder of Zen Buddhism.

Bodhisattva (Sanskrit) A being pledged to become a Buddha so as to be able to help all other beings to escape suffering by becoming Enlightened.

Bon (Tibetan) see *Schools*

Brahmaviharas (Sanskrit, Pali) The four sublime states or virtues which elevate man. These are loving kindness, compassion, sympathetic joy, and equanimity.

Buddha (Sanskrit and Pali)   "Awakened One." One who has attained Enlightenment. Particularly applies to Siddhartha Gautama, also known as Shakyamuni, the founder of Buddhism. The Buddha principle which manifests in various forms. For Theradavans, only one Buddha is accepted in each age; for Mahayanans, there are countless transcendent Buddhas which represent embodiments of various aspects of the Buddha principle.

Buddhadharma (Pali) The Buddha's teachings.

Buddharupa Statue or image of the Buddha.

Chado (Japanese) Tea ceremony used as a meditative practice in some Zen traditions.

Chenrezig (Tibetan) Tibetan equivalent of Avalokiteshvara, embodiment of the compassion of all the Buddhas and supreme protector and patron deity of Tibet.

Chogyal (Tibetan) Title. Lit: Dharma Raja or Religious King or Protector of the Buddhist Religion.

Dana (Sanskrit, Pali) One of the basic Buddhist virtues, it is the opposite of greed and translates as "generosity" or "giving."

Daruma-kata aiki (Japanese) Movement forms designed to harmonize body, breath, speech, and mind. Esoteric Zen practice traditionally reputed to have been taught by Bodhidharma.

Dathun Month-long meditation retreat.

Dharma (Sanskrit; *Dhamma*, Pali) Has numerous meanings. Among other things it can mean truth or reality. Also stands for those teachings and methods which are conducive to gaining Enlightenment and thereby seeing things as they truly are, refers particularly to the teachings of the Buddha.

Dharmacarya Lay Dharma teacher.

Dharmasala Rest house for pilgrims.

Dharmata (Sanskrit) Ground of being, the essence of everything; unifying spiritual reality; the absolute from which all proceeds.

Dogen (1200–1253) Japanese founder of Soto Zen; studied in China for four years before taking it to Japan; founded Eiheiji Monastery.

Learned Audience, when you hear me talk about the Void, do not at once fall into the idea of vacuity, (Because this involves the heresy of the doctrine of annihilation.) It is of the utmost importance that we should not fall into this idea, because when a man sits quietly and keeps his mind blank he will abide in a state of 'Voidness of Indifference'.

The Sutra of Wei Lang (or Hui Neng), translated from the Chinese by Wong Mou-Lam

Dojo (Japanese) Zen training hall.

Dokusan (Japanese) In Zen, a question-and-answer session with the Master or Roshi duirng which progress is tested.

Empowerment Ritual performed by eminent Tibetan Lamas; an essential prerequisite for the practice of Tantra.

Enlightenment An individual's awakening to the mind's true nature. A state of perfect wisdom and limitless compassion. The achievement of a Buddha.

Gampopa (1079–1153) Tibetan scholar, disciple of Milarepa and Marpa, whom he succeeded; one of the founders of the Kagyu school of Tibetan Buddhism.

Gen-Mai (Japanese) Traditional rice soup; sometimes offered after practice sessions at some Japanese Zen centers.

Geshe (Tibetan) Gelugpa title equivalent to Doctor of Divinity.

Gestalt therapy (non-Buddhist term) A psychological school founded on the principle that the mind tends to perceive events and situations as a pattern, or whole, rather than as a collection of separate and independent elements.

Gompa (Tibetan) Teaching and practice hall; isolated place or monastic site.

Green Tara see *Tara*.

Guru (Sanskrit) Teacher, particularly a spiritual master.

Hannya Shingyo (Japanese) Diamond Sutra—main Buddhist sutra chanted by Zen practitioners.

Hatha Yoga (Sanskrit) Form of yoga involving physical exercises and breath control.

Hatto (Japanese) Dharma hall.

Hevajra (Sanskrit) One of the Tantric texts of Tibetan Buddhism.

Hitsuzendo (Japanese) Calligraphy used as a meditative practice in some Zen traditions.

Hondo (Japanese) Sanctuary.

Hoza (Japanese) Form of group counseling used by Rissho Kosei-kai school.

Ikebana (Japanese) Flower-arranging used as a meditative practice in some Zen traditions.

Jewels, Three The Buddha, the Dharma, and the Sangha—the three highest values of Buddhism.

Jukai (Japanese) Precepts-taking ceremony.

Kaisando (Japanese) In Zen, founder's hall and dokusan room.

Kanna-Zen (Japanese) Form of Rinzai Zen founded in the twelfth century.

Kannon (Japanese) see *Kuan Yin*.

Karma (Sanskrit) Lit: action. Cause and effect; our willed actions (including mental and vocal) will have consequences for us in the future.

Karmapa (Tibetan) Title of the head of the Karma Kagyu school; alternative name for the school itself.

Kesa (Japanese) Zen monk garment.

Khenpo (Tibetan) Title usually of an Abbot; indicates high scholarship in Nyingma, Sakya, and Kagyu schools.

Khyentse (Tibetan) Lit: one in whom wisdom and compassion are prefectly combined, name of a number of exceptional Nyingma Lamas during past two hundred years.

Kinhin (Japanese) Formal marching during periods of rest from zazen to loosen stiff joints and exercise the body.

Koan (Japanese) Formalized riddle, used in Rinzai Zen as a device to throw the student against the ultimate question of his or her own nature.

Kum Nye (Tibetan) Gentle Tibetan yoga system.

Kusen (Japanese) Oral teachings.

Kuti Accommodation for individual meditation.

Kuan Yin (Chinese; Japanese, *Kannon*; Tibetan, *Avalokiteshvara*) Bodhisattva of infinite compassion and mercy.

Kwan Yin see *Kuan Yin*.

Kyudo (Japanese) Art of archery used as a meditative practice in some Zen traditions.

Lama (Tibetan) Spiritual teacher who may or may not be a celibate monk venerated as an authentic embodiment of the Buddhist teachings. For the Tibetan, he is particularly important because he not only teaches rituals but conducts them. May be head of one or more monasteries and possess political influence. Today, often used as a polite form of address for any Tibetan monk regardless of his spiritual development.

Lamrim (Tibetan) Lit: Graduated Path. System of teaching founded by Atisha (eleventh-century Indian Master) in which all the stages of the path to enlightenment are laid out in a very clear and sytematic manner. All four main schools of Tibetan Buddhism have produced Lamrim texts.

Lodjong (Tibetan) Lit: mind training. Based on Lamrim teachings—explains how to train the mind in daily life for the development of Bodhicitta.

Longchen (1308–1363) Greatest scholar of the Nyingma tradition of Tibetan Buddhism.

Mahamudra (Sanskrit) Has several meanings; as a practice it is popular in Kagyu and Gelug schools of Tibetan Buddhism; as a path it is a sequence of systematic advanced meditations on emptiness and pure appearance.

Mahathera Title for Bhikkhu of twenty years' standing, usually called *Theras*.

Mahayana see *Schools*.

Maitreya (Sanskrit) Embodiment of loving-kindness of all the Buddhas; historical figure—a Bodhisattva disciple of Buddha Shakyamuni; the coming Buddha, fifth in the line of the thousand Buddhas who will descend to this world. Currently said to reside in Tushita—a Buddhist heaven.

Mandala (Sanskrit) In the context of Tantra, a symmetrical design used as an object of meditation.

Mantra (Sanskrit) String of sound symbols recited to concentrate and protect the mind.

Mara (Sanskrit) Lit: death. Evil influences that impede one's spiritual transformation. Personified as a "tempter" whose baits are the sensory pleasures.

Marpa (1012–1097) Tibetan founder of the Kagyu school of Tibetan Buddhism; most famous pupil was Milarepa.

Metta Bhavana (Pali) Meditation on loving-kindness.

Milarepa (1038–1122) Tibetan poet-saint; one of the founders and greatest figure in the Kagyu school of Tibetan Buddhism.

Mudra (Sanskrit) Lit: seal, sign. Bodily posture or symbolic gesture imbued with symbolic significance which may be used in ritual. In Tantra, may refer to a female consort.

Naropa (eleventh century) Indian master and accomplished scholar; teacher of Marpa and Milarepa; particularly famous for his Six Yogas of Naropa.

Nembutsu (Japanese) Recitation of The Name of Amida Buddha, which in Japanese form that most Shin Buddhists use is *Namu Amida Butsu* or *Namuamidabu*, which literally means "I take refuge in Amida Buddha." Principal practice of Pure Land Buddhism.

Ngondro (Tibetan) Preliminary practices normally undertaken by a meditator prior to engaging in Tantric practice.

Nirvana (Sanskrit) Ultimate goal of Buddhist endeavor—permanent cessation of all suffering.

Noble silence During retreats, when students should not talk among themselves, but may speak to teachers and managers.

Nyinthun (Tibetan) Meditation practice for a whole day.

Nyung-Neh (Tibetan) Fasting ritual normally led by a monk or nun.

Oryoki (Japanese) In Zen, formal meal.

Osho (Japanese) Zen priest.

Padmasambhava (eighth century) Indian Buddhist who visited Tibet at the invitation of the king and taught various Buddhist principles; credited with founding the Nyingma school of Tibetan Buddhism.

Panna (Pali) Wisdom.

Paramitas (Sanskrit) The Ten Perfections cultivated by a Bodhisattva. They are generosity, morality, renunciation, wisdom, energy, patience, truthfulness, determination, loving-kindness, and equanimity.

Phowa (Tibetan) Ejection of consciousness at the moment of death. Transmission of consciousness.

Precepts 5, 8, 10, or 16 guides to behavior. Centers sometimes ask that visitors behave according to one of these sets of precepts. For a full description see *Appendix: Precepts*.

Puja (Sanskrit) Sacramental offering which may be associated with body, speech, and mind.

Qi Gong (non-Buddhist term) Chinese martial art or physical meditation practice.

Rain retreat months see *Festivals*.

Rakusu (Japanese) Zen monk garment.

Retreat Intensive periods of meditation which may be long- or short-term.

Right livelihood Fifth stage of the Noble Eightfold Path. Earning a living in accordance with Buddhist ethics.

Rinpoche (Tibetan) Lit: precious one. Honorific of a high lama, denotes reincarnation of a realized master.

Roshi (Japanese) Lit: old venerable master. Title of a Zen master who can be either monk or lay, man or woman.

Sadhana (Sanskrit) In Tantra, a type of text and the meditation practices presented in it which relate to deities to be experienced as spiritual realities.

Sakyamuni Sage of the Sakyas—a title applied to the Buddha.

Samadhi (Sanskrit) Lit: union. Profound meditative state; focus on a single object through calming of mental activity; one-pointedness of mind.

> *When the deluded in a mirror look*
> *They see a face, not a reflection.*
> *So the mind that has truth denied*
> *Relies on that which is not true.*
>
> The Royal Song of Saraha

Samsara (Sanskrit, Pali) World of rebirth and death; the succession of rebirths until liberation is attained; cyclic existence.

Samu (Japanese) Manual work used as part of meditative practice in Zen schools.

Sangha The Buddhist community as a whole, sometimes referring to the community of Buddhist monks, nuns, and novices.

Sangye Menla (Tibetan) Prayer ritual for sick people.

Sanzen see *dokusan*.

Satipatthana (Pali) System of mind development by the analysis of consciousness.

Sayadaw (Myanmar) Equivalent of Mahathera or Bhikku of twenty years' standing; title given to highly respected Bhikkhus.

Sensei (Japanese) Teacher.

Sera (Tibetan) Large monastic college in Lhasa, Tibet. One of the three main monasteries in Tibet, with Ganden and Drepung.

Sesshin (Japanese) Lit: to search the heart. Intensive Zen retreat.

Shamatha (Sanskrit; *Samatha*, Pali) Basic meditation practice common to most schools of Buddhism, whose aim is to tame and sharpen the mind as a springboard for insight (*Vipashyana*; *Vipassana*).

Shantideva (7th century) Indian compiler and writer of important Buddhist works.

Shiatsu (non-Buddhist term) Japanese healing massage technique using acupressure points.

Shikantaza (Japanese) A form of zazen consisting of just sitting with no supportive techniques such as counting the breath.

Shine Meditation for developing calmness.

Shuryo (Japanese) Study hall.

Silas (Pali) Lit: obligations, precepts. Morality or virtue.

Six Yogas of Naropa System of advanced Tantric meditation originating from the Indian Master Naropa and used by the Kagyu and Gelug schools of Tibetan Buddhism.

Soji (Japanese) Temple-cleaning after a practice session.

Stupa (Sanskrit) Originally a structure built to commemorate a Buddha or other highly developed person, often containing relics; became a symbol for the mind of a Buddha.

Sutra (Sanskrit, *Sutta*, Pali) The sermons of Gautama Buddha; any collection of teachings.

Tai Chi or *Tai Chi Chuan* (non-Buddhist term) Chinese exercise system and gentle martial art.

Tantra (Sanskrit) Form of Buddhism using yogic practices of visualization, mantra, mudra, and mandalas, as well as symbolic ritual and meditations which work with subtle psychophysical energies; the texts or teachings in which these are described.

Tara (Sanskrit) An emanation from the Bodhisattva Avolokiteshvara. Embodies the feminine aspect of compassion, seen in both peaceful and wrathful depictions and in various colors, the Green Tara and the White Tara being the forms most frequently seen.

Teisho (Japanese) Presentation by Zen Master addressing students directly in the moment.

Thangka (Tibetan) Tibetan religious painting.

Thera (Pali) Lit: elder. Bhikkhu of ten years' standing.

Three Jewels see *Jewels, Three*.

Transmission Passing on of oral teachings and scriptures with related commentary in an uninterrupted lineage or succession form person to person from ancient times.

Tsechu (Tibetan) Offering ceremony.

Tsog (Tibetan) Feast offerings.

Tsongkhapa (1355–1417) Tibetan reformer of Buddhism. Founded Ganden Monastery and founded the Gelug school of Tibetan Buddhism.

Tulku (Tibetan) Voluntary reincarnation of a religious figure of some distinction.

Upasaka (Sanskrit, Pali) Buddhist lay member who takes refuge in the Buddha, the Dharma, and the Sangha and who vows to observe the five precepts.

Upasika (Sanskrit, Pali) Female *upasaka*.

Vajrasattava (Sanskrit) One of the meditational deities of Tantric Buddhism.

Vajrayana (Sanskrit) Lit: The Diamond Vehicle. Buddhist Tantra of India and the Himalayan region. Sometimes used as an alternative term for Tibetan Buddhism. Arose in first millennium in northern India from Mahayana and spread to Tibet, China, and Japan. Characterized by a psychological method based on highly developed ritual practices.

Vajrayogini (Sanskrit) One of the female meditational deities of Tantric Buddhism.

Vihara Buddhist temple or monastery.

Vinaya (Sanskrit, Pali) Lit: discipline. Third part of the Tripitaka containing the rules and regulations for running and living in a monastery or nunnery, especially the ethical codes involved.

Vipashyana (Sanskrit; *Vipassana*, Pali) Insight, clear seeing. With *Shamatha* (*Samatha*), one of the factors essential for the attainment of enlightenment.

Wat (Thai) Temple or monastery.

Yana (Sanskrit, Pali) Vehicle or means of progress to salvation from the wheel of Samsara as in Mahayana.

Yidam (Tibetan) In Tantra, a personal meditational deity embodying an aspect of Enlightenment whose nature corresponds to the psychological make up of the practitioner.

Yoga Lit: union. A method of meditation or physical exercise designed to bring about spritual development.

Zabuton (Japanese) Thick rectangular mat used under the zafu in Zen meditation.

Zafu (Japanese) Round cushion used in Zen meditation

Zagu (Japanese) Zen monk's garment.

Zazen (Japanese) Sitting meditation used in Zen schools.

Zazenkai (Zen–Soto) All-day sitting retreat.

Zen (Japanese) see *Schools*.

Zendo (Japanese) Zen training hall.

FURTHER READING

General

The World of Buddhism (1984) H. Bechert and R. Gombrich. London: Thames and
   Hudson
The Buddhist Handbook (1991) John Snelling. Rochester: Inner Traditions
   International
The Elements of Buddhism (1990) John Snelling. London: Element Books
What the Buddha Taught (1974) W. Rahula. New York: Grove Press
A Short History of Buddhism (1980) Edward Conze. London: Allen and Unwin
Buddhist Scriptures (1959) Edward Conze. Harmondsworth: Penguin
Entering the Stream (1993) Samuel Bercholz & Sherab Chodzin Kohn. Boston:
   Shambhala Publications
Introducing Buddhism (1990) C. Pauling. Glasgow: Windhorse
The Dhammapada (1976) Thomas Byrom, trans. New York: Vintage

Life of the Buddha

Life of the Buddha (1971) Bhikkhu Nanamoli. Kandy: Buddhist Publication Society
The Buddha (1973) Trevor Ling. Harmondsworth: Penguin
Old Path White Clouds (1987) Thich Nhat Hanh. Berkeley: Parallax Press

Meditation

The Heart of Buddhist Meditation (1983) Nyanaponika Maha Thera. London: Rider Books
Meditation in Action (1991) Chogyam Trungpa. Boston and London: Shambhala
Meditation (1992) Kamalashila. Glasgow: Windhorse
Being Peace (1987) Thich Nhat Hahn. Berkeley: Parallax Press
Path to Bliss: A Practical Guide to Stages of Meditation (1991) Dalai Lama. New York:
   Snow Lion Publications

Theravada

Theravada Buddhism (1988) R. Gombrich. London: Routledge & Kegan Paul

Mahayana

Mahayana Buddhism (1989) Paul Williams. London: Kegan Paul

Tibetan

The Jewel in the Lotus (1987) ed. S. Batchelor. London: Wisdom Publications
Foundations of Tibetan Mysticism (1987) Lama Anagarika Govinda. London: Century
Introduction to Tantra (1987) Lama Thubten Yeshe. London: Wisdom
A Guide to Dakiniland (1991) Geshe Kelsang Gyatso. London: Tharpa
Tibetan Book of Living and Dying (1994) Sogyal Rinpoche. London: Rider
Magic and Mystery in Tibet (1965) Alexandra David-Neel. London: Unwin

Nichiren

Nichiren Shoshu Buddhism (1988) R. Causton. London: Century
The Flower of Chinese Buddhism (1986) Daisaku Ikeda. New York: Weatherhill

Pure Land

Shinran's Gospel of Pure Grace (1981) Alfred Bloom. Tucson, Arizona: University of
   Arizona

Zen

The Zen Teaching of Huang Po (1975) John Blofield, trans. New York: Grove Press
The Three Pillars of Zen (1989) Philip Kapleau. New York: Anchor
Zen Flesh, Zen Bones: A Collection of Zen and pre-Zen Writings (1989) Paul Reps.
   Rutland, Vermont: Charles E. Tuttle
Zen Mind, Beginner's Mind (1970) Shunryu Suzuki. New York: Weatherhill

Western Buddhism

New Currents in Western Buddhism (1990) Sangharakshita. Glasgow: Windhorse
   Publications
Buddhism for Today and Tomorrow (1996) Sangharakshita. Glasgow: Windhorse
   Publications
A Path with Heart (1993) Jack Kornfield. New York: Bantam
How the Swans Came to the Lake (1992) Rick Fields. Boston: Shambhala Publications

INDEX OF CENTERS
BY SCHOOL

CH'AN

CHINESE

Nichiren

Nichiren Shoshu

Nichiren Shu

PURE LAND

JODO SHU

JODO SHINSHU

REIYUKAI

RISSHO KOSEI-KAI

TENDAI

THERAVADA

> Fortunately we live in a time when all over the world many people are becoming familiar with meditation. It is being increasingly accepted as a practice that cuts through and soars above cultural and religious barriers, and enables those who pursue it to establish a direct contact with the truth of their being. It is a practice that at once transcends the dogma of religions and is the essence of religions.
>
> Sogyal Rinpoche The Tibetan Book of Living and Dying

THERAVADA THAI FOREST TRADITION

TIBETAN

BON

DRIKUNG KAGYU

> *Whether a man remains deluded or gains Illumination depends upon himself,*
> *not upon differences or similarity of doctrine.*
>
> The Zen Teachings of Hui Hai

DZOGCHEN

GELUG

KAGYU

KAGYU/NYINGMA–SHAMBHALA INTERNATIONAL

NYINGMA

SAKYA

VIETNAMESE

VIPASSANA

WON BUDDHISM

ZEN

> *I had lost a head and gained a world .... it felt like a sudden waking from the sleep of ordinary life, an end to dreaming .... It was the revelation, at long last, of the perfectly obvious.*
>
> Douglas Harding On Having No Head

KOREAN ZEN

RINZAI ZEN

SHAOLIN ZEN

SOTO ZEN

VIETNAMESE ZEN

WESTERN BUDDHISM

MIXED TRADITIONS

NONDENOMINATIONAL/ALL MAIN BUDDHIST TRADITIONS

OTHER